Christine El Mahdy is a widely renowned Egyptologist whose interest in the subject started as a child (she taught herself to read hieroglyphs at the age of nine). She has worked in the Egyptian departments of Bolton Museum, Lancashire and Liverpool University Museum and, in 1988, she founded the Egyptian Society which she now runs. She has previously written two internationally bestselling books on ancient Egypt: *Exploring the World of the Pharaohs* and *Mummies, Myth and Magic*.

Also by Christine El Mahdy

Mummies, Myth and Magic
Exploring the World of the Pharaohs

Tutankhamen

THE LIFE AND DEATH OF A BOY KING

Christine El Mahdy

HEADLINE

First published in 1999
by HEADLINE BOOK PUBLISHING

First published in paperback in 2000
by HEADLINE BOOK PUBLISHING

10 9 8 7 6 5 4

ISBN 0 7472 6000 1

Printed and bound in Great Britain by
Mackays of Chatham plc, Chatham, Kent

HEADLINE BOOK PUBLISHING
A division of the Hodder Headline Group
338 Euston Road
London NW1 3BH

www.headline.co.uk
www.hodderheadline.com

This book is dedicated to my beautiful daughters,
Nadine and Yasmine.

Contents

—

Foreword   1

Part One – The Archaeological Tutankhamen

Introduction   11
The Early Evidence for Tutankhamen   33
Discovering the Tomb   48
The Accepted Story   78
Evidence from the Objects in Tutankhamen's Tomb   92

Part Two – The Historical Tutankhamen

Introduction   129
Amenhotep III and Queen Tiye   148
Akhenaten and the Religion of the Aten   177
Evidence from Tell el Amarna   212
Akhenaten and Nefertiti   237
The Elusive Smenkhkare   253

Part Three – The Real Tutankhamen

The Life of Tutankhamen   277
The Death of Tutankhamen   298

Appendices

Family Tree   315
The Restoration Stela   317
The Scarabs of Amenhotep III   320
The Dream Stela   323
The Great Hymn to the Aten   326

Suggested Reading   330
Index   332

Foreword

—

Archaeology has two distinct faces. Its public face is exciting, a dazzling roll-call of excavations, unveiling treasures of gold, of which the discovery of Tutankhamen's tomb in 1922 is one of the most extraordinary examples. Its private face is the time-consuming, meticulous examination of often tiny and seemingly meaningless fragments of dusty materials in the forgotten back rooms of small museums – a much less glamorous pursuit. Yet it is in those back rooms that the most exciting discoveries are often made. After all, what does the discovery of a gold-filled tomb indicate? That the owner of the tomb was rich and royal? We know that already. The thorough examination of small finds after the initial excitement, on the other hand, can tell us hitherto unknown details about the person who was entombed. The forensic detective work involved in archaeology can tell us things about the dead that they themselves might have scarcely realised were there when alive.

I have always been fascinated by archaeology's private face. My interest began by chance when I was seven years old living in Bolton, in the north of England. Thrust for the first time into an adult library, I picked up by chance a book about ancient Egypt. I entered what seemed to me a more magical world than that of fairytales, because this world was exotic, yet filled with real people. I examined the reproductions of their paintings and their sculptures, and the world of ancient Egypt became a place of enchantment for me. The following day I persuaded my father to take me to the local museum. Here, I could see a mural through the fanlight of a door, but I could not get into the gallery as it was not finished. Over the following months I devoured everything I could on the subject, even teaching myself the meanings of the basic Egyptian hieroglyphs so that I could read their words for myself. By the age of nine, I knew what I wanted to be – an Egyptologist, though no one I knew seemed to have heard of it!

Among the first stories about Egypt that I had read when I was seven was that of Tutankhamen, the 'boy-King' of the Eighteenth Dynasty. The discovery of the tomb and its astounding treasures had long aroused wonder among the public at large. But I found the private face of Tutankhamen far more intriguing than the alluring glitter of the gold he was buried with. It was a story of a young boy, of about my own age at that time, who had become the most powerful person in the world – the equivalent, today, of a child elected President of the United States. Yet the story was also steeped in mystery. The tomb told us he was a king, and a very wealthy one. But *who* was he? Who were his parents? What sort of childhood had he had? What must he have felt like, knowing that he could have everything he wanted, that everyone around him would do exactly what he wanted? And how could such a young boy have died so unexpectedly? I read all the books available, trying to find out the truth – if there is ever any truth in history. But the things I wanted to know were just not there. No one seemed to know who Tutankhamen really was. The stories that the books told about him just did not seem to make sense.

I was determined to find out more. I became a detective searching through time itself, and it has taken me almost a lifetime to put what I have found together. Sometimes, for months or even years, I came across areas of Tutankhamen's life that were shrouded in impenetrable darkness; and then, suddenly, unexpectedly, and often from completely unsuspected places, another tiny bit of information would emerge, and cast a little more light on these mysteries.

My search for the real Tutankhamen has been somewhat akin to the search for a murderer in a TV detective 'soap'. The detectives in these programmes are given blatant 'clues' that invariably lead to the wrong answer; the wrong people have accusing fingers pointed at them; then along comes another, more painstaking, detective looking at the apparently insignificant bits of evidence and starting to ask questions about things that do not fit; and another story starts to emerge – people start to ask themselves, 'Why didn't I see that? It seems so obvious!' It seemed to me, even at seven, that people were too quick to jump to conclusions. After all, an almost intact tomb had been found – so the answers *had* to be there somewhere if the science of forensics was valid. A group of people living 3500 years ago had deliberately chosen and assembled the objects that they thought were most important to Tutankhamen, and somewhere in those pieces must be the information we needed.

Almost twenty years and several degrees after I had first started my studies of ancient Egypt, a twist of fate brought me back to Bolton Museum where I had begun, but now as a student of Egyptology working as a volunteer to gain first-hand experience of identifying pieces. Of course, there was nothing from Tutankhamen's tomb for me to examine in Bolton. But like any good detective, I worked slowly around the edges of the 'crime'. If I was to find out who Tutankhamen was, I needed to know more about the people around him.

As he had come to the throne when he was about six or seven years old, he must have been born in the middle of the reign of Akhenaten, the monarch called by many scholars 'the heretic King'. Akhenaten is one of the most charismatic, elusive and fascinating individuals in history. He broke away from centuries of conformity in Egypt to 'do his own thing'. Like an ancient Egyptian hippy, he left home, found his own place to live with his supporters around him, changed every aspect of life he could and lived thenceforward in splendid isolation at the site we call today Tell el Amarna, halfway between Cairo and Luxor. Unfortunately for Egypt and for history, Akhenaten was born to be king. If he had been an ordinary man, a religious leader perhaps, posterity would have regarded him more kindly. But as King of Egypt, he had responsibilities towards his country and his people, responsibilities that he clearly shirked. Whether he did this deliberately is open to question. But after his reign, Egypt was never the same again. And Tutankhamen, his successor, was thus born in the middle of a state crisis.

The site of Tell el Amarna is, archaeologically speaking, a time capsule. Founded in the fourth year of Akhenaten's reign, it was occupied until he died thirteen years later, and inscriptions there show that Tutankhamen probably lived there for a short time afterwards before the city was completely abandoned. In all probability, Tutankhamen was born and spent his childhood here before he was made King within the city. It was in these streets that he had once played. What evidence could I find of him there? My intellectual search for his roots led me to deepen my researches into Tell el Amarna.

The site of Tell el Amarna today, although currently almost inaccessible to tourists because of political problems caused by the recent upsurge of Islamic fundamentalism in Egypt, is an abandoned, empty desert plain. After the death of Tutankhamen, perhaps a decade later, the implacable enemy of the old royal family, the Commander-in-Chief of the Egyptian army General Horemheb, seized the throne in what was apparently a military coup and systematically started to erase all memories of the whole family of the mid-Eighteenth Dynasty. Horemheb and his friend and successor Pramesse, later Ramesses I of the Nineteenth Dynasty, referred to Akhenaten henceforward as 'the Great Criminal'. For the ancient Egyptians, immortality came through the remembrance of your name. If someone should refer to you by name in 3000 years' time, then to all intents and purposes you have achieved immortality; destroy that name, and your very existence is obliterated. The Ramesside rulers of the Nineteenth Dynasty tried to destroy all evidence of Akhenaten and his successors. They smashed statues, dismantled buildings and erased names. Only Tutankhamen has survived to us, by an accident of fate, through his tomb.

To find Tutankhamen, I began a meticulous study of the fragments of Tell el Amarna. The summer of 1976 found me sitting at a desk in the recesses of Bolton Museum, rank-smelling dust rising from the pile of broken material in front of me. Many unenlightened people would have thought of these bits and pieces of stone and pottery as having been scavenged from some rubbish tip. The scene was worlds away from the well-publicised golden image of Egypt that had first fascinated me, and I considered, not for the first time, what a strange world it was that I had entered. I picked up yet another small terracotta mould with the impress of a bunch of grapes on it. This had been used 3500 years ago, in a much hotter climate than that of Lancashire, to make a glazed wall tile. The resulting tile, fixed perhaps on some painted palace wall, had probably been stunning. But the mould itself was similar to a hundred others I had already examined. My job was to measure, study and describe every piece precisely, so that in future years others sitting at the same desk would be able to distinguish exactly which piece I had catalogued. There were, I reflected wryly, only just so many words, even in the rich English language!

Almost mechanically I picked up the next piece. I stared at it: this one was different. It was a piece of quartzite, a purplish stone that was one of the hardest used in Egypt. It had come from the bottom of a packing case that had been shipped from Tell el Amarna to Bolton almost fifty years earlier. Provincial museums are generally under-staffed and underfunded, and over the intervening half-century, no one had had the opportunity even to open the case before me. The fragment was part of a smashed wall, perhaps, for on one face it had a hieroglyphic inscription. I noticed at once that the inscription had been carved over another, earlier one, that had been deliberately erased. It was what we in archaeology call a palimpsest. Here, at last, I reflected, was something a bit more interesting. There were no labels on the piece to show where it had been found, or when. It was just the first one of a pile of similar pieces that now awaited my attention. As usual, I turned to the records from the dig to see if I could find out more about them.

The excavation reports from Tell el Amarna covering the years 1921 to 1935 are not as complete as many people might think. It has been said, justifiably, that all that separates a tomb robber from an archaeologist is the archaeologist's publication of finds. On an archaeological site work is often hectic, especially in the treasure-laden sands of Egypt. Egyptologists would first have recorded the location of every piece found on site cards, and then passed the piece on to others to be recorded. Some important pieces may have been photographed; but in the 1920s and 1930s it was more usual for them to be hand-copied by helpers, many of whom were less qualified in the field. (Hand-copying is drawing the object as accurately as possible by eye.) If any errors were made at this point, then, in theory, they would be corrected soon after. The pieces, marked and recorded, would be passed to the site headquarters – in this case, London – where they would be shared out between subscribing museums and collectors. A distribution list would be made, and the cases containing the pieces would then be sent to the museum where, again in theory, a smiling and relaxed expert would at once unpack them, study them again and correct any errors that had been made on site.

In practice, of course, this seldom happens. It was much more likely that the boxes would arrive at a place where the keeper was busy on some exhibition or some other area of urgent work. The boxes would then be listed routinely in the day book as 'miscellaneous pieces', labelled with the site name, and stored until their turn for examination finally arrived. Sometimes, as in this case, this would take some time! If problems arose with the piece, the site cards would be studied by the archaeologists and prepared for publication in the excavation reports. There is, however, a limited market for these specialised reports, and publication costs are high: so often only the location of major pieces would be recorded. The rest would be tucked away, hidden within generalised references such as: 'House 12, rooms A–F, miscellaneous fragments including . . .' Back in the museum, the expert examining the pieces would study the reports to see if the fragments that the museum had been given matched anything in them. If it did, it could be 'accessed' – given a new museum number, studied if needed, and then added to the collection for future research. In the case of small pieces, unlisted in the report, new numbers would be given until the time could be made to look at the site cards themselves in the hope of finding the exact provenance of the pieces. It was a lengthy business, and could take years before the work was complete.

In the case of the quartzite fragments I was lucky. Because they had included palimpsest inscriptions they had received quite a lot of attention. I found they had been discovered in 1923, in the south of the plain of Tell el Amarna at a palace site known as the Maruaten. They had come from buildings that the archaeologists at the time called 'Sunshades'. The fragments had been hand-copied on site, and included references to the original inscriptions which had once lain underneath what was immediately visible today. It was obvious that the pieces were of considerable importance.

But there was something else, something extraordinary about these bits of stone, as I found when I turned to the distribution list. At once I was electrified – these pieces were not supposed to be here at all! According to the list, they had been allocated to Boston in the United States, in 1923! This was not the first time that something like this had happened, and we knew all the signs. The pieces would have been shared out, the distribution list typed out and then someone had typed an address label for the packing case, putting an 'l' instead of an 's' – and the case had ended up in Bolton, not Boston.

The implications of this were huge. It meant that for fifty years, if anyone had wanted to study these important pieces, they would have contacted Boston, which, of course, would have been unable to trace them. By a twist of fate, the pieces had apparently vanished completely into thin air. Who could have guessed they were hiding in the bottom of a box in the basement of a small local museum in Lancashire.

I now felt excited, almost as Howard Carter must once have felt as he first chipped into the closed door of the tomb of Tutankhamen in 1922. Would what I saw be vital – or simply routine? This was the gripping private face of archaeology. As I read the inscriptions under the oblique rays of a strong lamp, a thrill ran through me as it must once have shot through Carter. The fragments had been misread and mispublished: the inscriptions were not what the excavation reports said they were. By an extraordinary chance, pieces of the jigsaw I had been putting together slipped neatly into place, and for the first time I began to see the outlines of the real Tutankhamen take shape.

That afternoon I did not walk home: I floated on air. I felt as if my discovery were somehow written on my face, as if people would see and come up to congratulate me. Of course, it was not so; to passers-by I was just another anonymous figure. I rejoiced inwardly, for all my childhood dreams had come true. For me, the private face of archae-ology had proved itself unquestionably more exciting than the public one, and at that moment I would not have changed places with Howard Carter for a single instant.

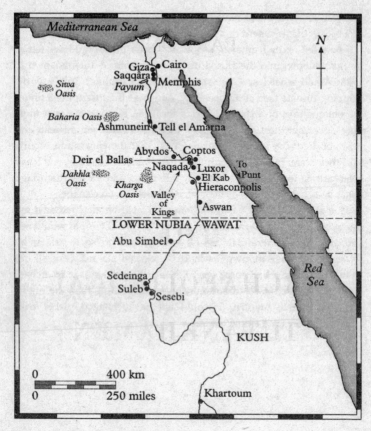

Egypt and Nubia in the Eighteenth Dynasty.

PART ONE

THE
ARCHAEOLOGICAL
TUTANKHAMEN

Introduction

The land of ancient Egypt is a distant one – not just geograph-
ically, but in time. But the time that has elapsed since the demise
of the dynasties does not seem to have touched what remains. The
monuments left behind by its people, the brilliantly coloured tombs
and honey-gold temples, lure visitors into this ancient world daily as
if into a world that is still alive. The archaeological remains in other
countries are often fragmentary, and most of it may be available only
to the specialist, but in Egypt, the warm dry climate has preserved
everything more or less intact. The linen still lies in folds where
someone placed it 3000 years ago; dried-out dishes of pigeon cas-
serole still fill bowls that some chef served 4500 years ago; and the
paint on the ancient tomb walls seems so fresh that, if you touched it,
you feel sure that it would smudge. Leaving Cairo behind, that
bustling, overpopulated, noisy and polluted capital city, you step
back in time to a land where centuries disappear in the blinking of an
eye. You may even see the faces of the great pharaohs in today's
Egyptians. A replica of Ramesses II may shine your shoes; Seti I may
serve you coffee. It has happened to me! Egypt is a world where
ancient and modern meet, and jostle equally for attention. Somehow,
the magic that this country exerts makes you forget how very long
ago it all happened.

In this book, I want to lead you not just to the land of ancient
Egypt, but to a specific time and place. The time is the fourteenth
century BC; the place is Luxor. In these sun-scorched streets, along
the stone-lined processional routes of the temples, there once walked
a young boy. Born Tutankhaten, he inherited the throne of Egypt and

received the crown in the temple of Karnak. Nine years later, having changed his birth-name to Tutankhamen, he died suddenly, under mysterious circumstances. In late March, around 1325 BC, a burial was held within the silent walls of the Valley of the Kings on the west bank of the Nile in Luxor. Songs were sung, dances completed; then the tomb was sealed and forgotten. Not until AD 1922 was that lost world rediscovered.

The forces that shaped both that lost world and that long-ago boy were complex. Let us take a look at them.

Life in ancient Egypt: philosophy and belief

Egypt, as a politically united country, had come into existence some 1500 years before the time of Tutankhamen. During this period Egypt was in a state of cultural stasis: it seemed unchangeable. In many areas of Egyptian culture – art, medicine, architecture – once a satisfactory method was found, it was never altered. Egyptians regarded the physical world in its entirety as perfect order, which emerged from primeval chaos, with Egypt standing at the very heart of creation, the first mound of land to emerge from the oceans. They called this moment of creation the 'First Occasion'.

In the Egyptian creation myth, on the First Occasion, when man had been brought into existence, everything was perfect, in harmony and complete balance. This state they personified as a goddess called Maat. Later, things began to get out of balance. The Egyptians believed that to maintain any order at all in the world, the harmony of the First Occasion needed to be recalled, using ceremonies and special words carried out by people with knowledge. There was thus a constant, ongoing struggle to return to the time of perfection. They considered that there could be only one solution to any given problem: if that solution was applied, order would be restored. So why consider another solution?

This philosophy of life was applied to all areas of knowledge and science along the banks of the Nile. A person was sick; set remedies were applied. The person lived, the remedy was recorded and in all future cases, the same remedy was then applied. There was no experimentation: research and development were frowned upon. If you developed a new method and it failed, you were directly culpable, because you had broken the link with Maat.

Life was tranquil; everyone knew their place. Egyptian society was rigidly hierarchical, and can be seen schematically as forming a pyramid. At the peak was the king; below him, a small group of close, trusted advisers; below them, the courtiers, the governors of provinces; below them, the mayors and skilled craftsmen; below them, the foremen and overseers; and at the bottom, the largest group – the workers who raised the crops and cut and moved stone for building works, to provide the wealth on which those at the top of the pyramid could grow rich and fat. Yet this bottom stratum seemed to have felt little resentment. After all, fate provided your status in life and there was nothing to stop you rising up through the pyramid – even to the very pinnacle itself.

There were rules that showed people how to act towards the other groups in society. From time to time, people such as Ptahhotep, Hordjedef, Ani and Amenemope recorded their thoughts for posterity in what we today call 'wisdom literature'. Through all these texts, which are instructions from elders to the younger generation on appropriate behaviour in every aspect of life, shines the awareness of others' needs. This was a philosophy based not on revenge but on understanding the needs of other people. Those philosophers said, you are rich; tomorrow those riches may be removed from you. It is your duty to look after those less fortunate than yourself and without gloating about it; tomorrow you may need that help, and you would not want anyone gloating over you.

Everyone, according to this ideal, should be benevolent and caring. Every high official in the court, according to the inscription of the appointing of a vizier (the king's right-hand man) in the tomb of the courtier Rekhmire, on the west bank of Luxor, would have his words and actions judged by others. They were accountable not only to those above, to the king, but also those below – every poor man in the land. Every person was born to fulfil a preordained destiny, and this brought not only rights but also responsibilities. It was not for a man to be jealous of his neighbour. Every man, no matter how poor, may have food on the table or a child under his roof that would make him rich in another man's eyes. Thus he should not brag about his position, but rather needed to work to maintain the responsibility that had been given to him. This applied to every individual, no matter what his status. Chief among all men on the social pyramid was the king; and his was the greatest responsibility of all.

The duties of a king

To understand a king's role in ancient Egypt, we need to look more closely at how life itself was seen by Egyptian society. Order was prized above all. Every day the sun shone; every night the stars appeared; every year the Nile rose in its bed and flooded its banks, bringing life-giving water to the land; every year crops would grow. The ideal Universe was one of perfect balance, when everything came at its due time and gave according to requirements. This was the essential nature of Maat. The goddess Maat was a young girl with an ostrich feather in her headdress, or sometimes simply the feather itself. Some writers have characterised Maat as representing truth, but she was far more than that. Maat represented the events of the First Occasion, that ideal time when everything was naturally in balance. For equilibrium to exist, good as well as bad was needed; if everything was entirely good, then balance would not be achieved and Isfet, the twin of Maat, representing imbalance or chaos, would return.

The king of Egypt was not the most blessed and lucky individual according to these beliefs, but instead was the ultimate servant. The highest social rights brought with it the highest responsibility. His was the essential preservation of Maat, first within Egypt, and then the rest of the world and the cosmos. Exactly *how* he was expected to do this is open to debate, and seems to have changed subtly over the years, according to the concept of kingship evidenced at any one time. About 2500 BC, during the time of the Old Kingdom, when the great pyramids were built, texts make it clear that the king was considered to be a living god. Coming into his presence was felt as terrifying. At the end of the Old Kingdom, however, as officials left their home towns to gain promotion at the feet of Pharaoh, work in the local regions became unorganised, and often stopped altogether. When the floodwaters of the Nile subsided, for example, the first priority of local officials was to order and organise the cutting of drainage ditches to enable the land to be drained speedily so that crops would grow. This was not done, and in the flooded fields the crops rotted. People starved. In the provinces, officials left autobiographical texts in their tombs that spoke of cannibalism in some areas as people tried to survive.

The king who emerged from this chaos and ruled during the time of the Middle Kingdom was not so much deemed a living god as seen as the propitiator of the god Amun. His duty was to ask the gods for their cooperation in the maintenance of Maat. How precisely this was done is uncertain. It is clear that the king 'requested' aid daily from the chief national god of his time. To do this he entered the temple alone, and went into the sanctuary, a hidden, dark and secret place where 'lived' the statue of the god. Here the king undertook secret ceremonies that ensured the continuation of Maat, the growth of crops, the regularity of the inundation, the circulation of the sun – in short, by carrying out these ceremonies correctly, the people of Egypt could give their entire consideration to their own responsibilities, whatever these might be, to ensure that their contribution to Maat was successful. If these ceremonies were abandoned or carried out incorrectly, it was feared that the uncontrolled chaos of Isfet would return, and Maat would be driven out. If this ever happened, succeeding kings would have their work cut out to satisfy the forces of the cosmos in order that Maat might be restored.

It was in the middle of the Eighteenth Dynasty, about 1350 BC, that these fears suddenly and unexpectedly became justified. A king, Akhenaten, came to the throne and did not carry out the continuity of service, broke with the old ways, turned his back on the First Occasion and tried instead to introduce a new order. It was not so much his new ideas that seemed to be frightening Egypt; it was the abandonment of Maat.

We now need to take a look at the world-within-a-world that Akhenaten so shook up – the royal families of Egypt.

The Egyptian royal family

At the start of the Eighteenth Dynasty there had been no inkling of what was to come. By 1550 BC, Egypt, having been occupied for a short period by foreign rulers (see page 82), fought its way back to independence. The family from Luxor who formed the Eighteenth Dynasty was made up in part of fighting men proud of their strength and military prowess. While they were away in battle, their women, back home in

Upper Egypt, held the reins. Queens Tetisheri, Ahhotep and Ahmose-Nefertari in succession took political control and ruled, as well as raising troops and sending supplies northwards for their husbands.

The example of these three great women at the start of the dynasty seems to have made a profound impression on the royal family. Yet there had been no dearth of powerful women in the early years of Egypt's history, when they had played an important part in ruling the country. In those times, there seems to have been no discernable difference between the roles that could be played by male and female. For the following five centuries after the unification of Egypt, during the Old Kingdom period, women encouraged and supported their menfolk, were depicted in art as equal in size, had independent status and, often, tombs and estates of their own, and were often given ranks and titles of great status. At the end of the Old Kingdom, this attitude, seems to have changed profoundly, as did the whole nature of king-ship. The women of the Middle Kingdom suddenly became relatively insignificant, powerless and historically characterless.

At the start of the New Kingdom Tetisheri, Ahhotep and Ahmose-Nefertari changed all that. But it should not be thought that they were a feminist force determined deliberately to change the status of women; rather, they reacted to circumstances. After generations in which women had been anonymous and powerless, they might have been condemned for their forwardness, but they were greatly admired. The tomb of Queen Ahhotep, discovered by Auguste Mariette in 1859, contained three huge flies, the size of an open hand, cast in gold. These were referred to in a military inscription as a royal award for military valour. Since these were awarded only by the Pharaoh and usually to men who had fought bravely on the battlefield, they must have been given to her either by her husband Seqenenre Tao II or by her son King Amosis. The question of whether she received them for actually lead-ing men into battle, or for providing troops and supplies for them, is currently open to debate.

The honouring of these remarkable women is emphasised by an inscription of a stela or commemorative stone found in Abydos and now in the Cairo Museum. It tells how King Amosis wanted to remember his grandmother, Queen Tetisheri, by building a pyramid, a memorial chapel and a garden on the sacred land of Abydos, the place where Egypt's first kings had been buried 2000 years earlier.

This inscription was written in pictures that we call hieroglyphs. Whatever their meaning, the pictures themselves are extremely informative. In the back of Sir Alan Gardiner's *Middle Egyptian Grammar*, first published in the 1940s and still the principal grammar in English, there is a comprehensive list of symbols. Included in this are fifty-eight symbols showing men and their occupations. These are as varied as might be expected, and include some highly unlikely ones, such as 'man hiding behind a wall' and 'man standing on his head'! In contrast, there are only five pictures of women, showing them either as a queen, a 'mistress of the house' – an honourable position that demanded they be waited on hand and foot and so showed them with their hands tucked inside an all-enveloping cloak – or as pregnant, giving birth or suckling a child. This limited list would seem to imply that women were subjected to total discrimination by men. Yet nothing could be further from the truth. Women were respected, treasured and given an equal place in society, even under the law, although they were seldom expected to work outside the home. Because of this past, royal women in ancient Egypt often held posts that were merely honorific.

Apropos of this last point, the titles of 'Queen' and 'Princess' are non-existent in the ancient Egyptian language, even though you will find those words in even the most respectable translations. Where they are used, they are mistranslations of the titles 'King's Wife' and 'King's Daughter'. There may not seem to be much difference at first sight. But 'Queen' is a title held by a woman in her own right, while 'King's Wife' only gives her status by virtue of marriage to a royal husband. Although these titles, together with 'King's Sister' and 'King's Mother', were the highest any ancient Egyptian women could hope to acquire, they too were purely honorific. They did not entitle her to any income or loyalty from the court except what was given to her by the king himself.

But in those extraordinary early years of the Eighteenth Dynasty there appeared a new female title, 'God's Wife' or sometimes 'God's Wife of Amen'. This title is much debated today. It was given to a very limited number of royal ladies, was often inherited by their daughters, and seems to have been an actual office of state rather than a simple honour. When a woman acquired this title, she would use it in preference to all the other titles that she held from the king. This would imply that it was an office of her own, rather than one gained from her proximity to the king. It brought with it status, high income and the service of high-ranking courtiers.

The start of the Eighteenth Dynasty also saw the rise of another title for royal women, 'Great Royal Wife'. The woman who took this title seems usually to have been given it on the day of the king's coronation, whether they had been 'married' before or not. At the moment there is no suggestion that she was actually crowned alongside him, although one suspects that some ceremonial would have been needed in order to elevate her to this lofty rank. Many books assume that the title merely belonged either to the first wife that the king took, or to the mother of the king's first child – in other words, that the title was automatically given. This is not the case. This title belongs to a significant royal head of state, a lady whose royal rank equalled that of her husband. As the king was considered to be of divine nature, so was she. As he acted as god's chief representative within the temple and on state ceremonies, so she acted similarly towards the goddess. She was publicly at his side, as goddess to his god. As the king represented the male element in creation, so she represented the female.

All this meant that she was not necessarily wife first and foremost, but was rather official state consort. To illustrate what I mean in British terms, this might be compared to the offices of mayor and mayoress. The latter has her own defined duties. The two people holding office may be man and wife; but they may not be related at all. The mayor might well be married to a wife who does not want the official position and thus hands it to another woman. By so doing, she does not also hand over her role as wife, nor does the mayoress become his wife just because she holds the office. On some occasions the mayor may even be a woman, but a mayoress will still be appointed. And of course this does not in any way mean that there is any sexual relationship between the two. Exactly the same relationship existed between a king and his 'Great Royal Wife' – she may have been his actual wife, but then again, she may not have.

Because of this vital role that she played in the maintenance of Maat, the choice of Great Royal Wife was one of the most important decisions a new king had to make at the start of his reign. It was vital that she 'knew the ropes' – was aware of the public role demanded of her. She would often be very closely related to the king, frequently his full or half sister. This emphasised her divine status. Although it is generally believed that the ancient Egyptian ruling class always married their sisters, brother–sister marriages were, in fact, the practice only within the central royal family. But in the Egyptian creation myth, brother and sister deities married in order first to create and then to maintain the stability of the cosmos. So the marriage between a king and his sister showed them as being no longer of humankind, but rather as veritable gods on earth, with similar responsibility for maintaining Egypt. These brother–sister marriages were seldom consummated.

There was nothing to stop the king, however, from marrying the woman of his own choice and elevating her to the position of Great Royal Wife; and then, of course, the marriage was a full one, and her son could indeed succeed his father. If a king ruled for many years, his Great Royal Wife died and he had no living sister to replace her, he sometimes elevated one of his daughters to the title. The great king of the Nineteenth Dynasty Ramesses II, for example, ruled Egypt for sixty-seven years. This relationship was then similarly one of state and not an incestuous one.

Official queens were not the whole story, however. Kings usually also had other wives, seldom seen in public and having no state role. These wives lived together in their own apartments, often badly translated as 'the Harem', and bore the king children. Chief among these ladies was the so-called Senior Royal Wife. It was very often her children who succeeded to the throne.

Life, then, was a complex business for Egypt's royals. No less complex were the arrangements, ceremonies and beliefs associated with their deaths.

Royal burial in the Eighteenth Dynasty

For around a thousand years the kings of Egypt were buried within pyramids. While arguments may rage about the purpose of pyramids, the fact remains that there are, today, ninety pyramids known in Egypt. Every one is a different size and height, and every one has differently angled sides, and is often of different construction. But many of the pyramids still have sarcophagi within them.

All the pyramids stand in the midst of a field of smaller tombs in which their officials and family members were buried. Even if most of the pyramids are uninscribed, there are enough inscriptions within the tombs around them to tell us virtually all we need to know about the person entombed within the pyramid. And, no matter how people may argue over the reason pyramids were built, since they contain burial places it would seem foolish to suggest that they were not used.

By 1550 BC, however, every one of the pyramids had been disturbed, and the burial places of the earlier Egyptian kings had been interrupted. It was Tuthmosis I, the Vizier and brother-in-law of the last direct member of the preceding royal family, Amenhotep III, who ordered his architect Ineni, according to an inscription, to look for somewhere else that kings might be buried. With his instructions, usually translated as 'no one seeing, no one hearing', Ineni went to the west bank of Luxor and investigated the great range of limestone hills that fringed the fertile plain there. A thousand years before, in the time of the building of pyramids as burial places for the kings of Egypt, every pyramid had had a small chapel against one face where people might bring offerings of food and drink for the soul of the dead king. This was deemed necessary for the continued existence of the king's soul. This ceremony brought people into close contact with the very building that they needed to keep secret, to prevent tomb robberies. Ineni decided to separate these two elements of burial. Behind the hills that fronted the Nile, Ineni and his men came across a hidden set of valleys, at the head of which stood a natural pyramid of limestone. The locals called this peak Meretseger, which translates as 'She who loves peace and quiet'. The place was certainly quiet and isolated. The cliffs there were riven with natural crevices caused by the occasional flash floods that would turn the valleys into torrential rivers. The limestone was soft and easy to work. It was an ideal place. From now on, kings would be buried in the secret valley, while offering places, the mortuary temples, were built on the other side of the hills facing the Nile, dividing the two basic sites for security.

To build the tombs of the kings, the finest workmen in Egypt were assembled and housed in a village on the west bank of the Nile, opposite the modern city of Luxor, not far from the royal valley. The site today is called Deir el Medina. Here, for the next 500 years, craftsmen would live and raise their families. Unlike most sites in Egypt, where artisans had cottage gardens in which to grow food to supplement their basic diet, the workmen's village is in the desert, with no greenery even for shade. All their basic needs – even water for drinking and washing – had to be supplied from outside. In the ten-day week, the workers would walk to the Valley of the Kings on the first day, receiving their equipment from the village janitor before they set off. The paths they trod on the rocky hills are visible to this day. Arriving at their place of work, they would split into two gangs – that of the right side and that of the left side. They would live in small, crude overnight settlements built next to the tomb they were working on, while their food would be brought up to them by messengers from the village below. From the cutting of the stone, the plastering of the walls to the final applications of paint, they would carry out every task needed. One inscription from the Valley of the Queens lists the time taken for the decoration of a large tomb as around two years.

The Valley of the Kings, as we call it today, is misleadingly named. It is, in fact, several valleys running off each other, all cut with tombs. The paths from the Nile Valley to the Valley of the Kings were patrolled day and night by Medjai. These security guards seem originally to have been a Nubian regiment, but were later composed of Egyptian soldiers. Because of the tight security they offered, nothing and no one could pass them; and thus the royal tombs, as they were cut, were seldom hidden, but simply shut behind mud-brick doors. The notion that the workmen who cut the royal tombs were killed after they completed their job so as to hide the location of the tombs is a figment of Hollywood's imagination. In charge of them was the Overseer of the Place of Eternity who, in Tutankhamen's Egypt, was Maya.

In the past, the kings' bodies had usually been secreted within burial chambers in the heart of the pyramid, sealed tight from the outside so that no one could disturb their eternal rest. With the tight security in force on the hills surrounding the Valley of the Kings, it was decided for the first time to leave the body above the ground within a burial chamber, the whole tomb now acting as an extended burial vault. Pyramids were abandoned: it seems as if the natural peak above the Valley, Meretseger, served duty as a pyramid for all the dead kings buried in the valleys below. Passages, painted with the inscriptions and pictures the kings would need in order for them to achieve their afterlife with the gods, led deep down into the bedrock. Chambers cut at intervals along the passages, each given names – such as the Hall of Chariots – were seemingly filled with objects at the time of burial. Deep in the heart of the tomb, towards its foot, was the burial chamber itself.

After death, the king's body would be taken to be prepared for burial. It would first enter the Per-Wabet, or Place of Purification, where the evisceration and the dessication would be carried out. This unpleasant, malodorous procedure seems to have often taken place in a mobile building that could be moved to a place where it would be uninterrupted by casual visitors – perhaps a tent. The body would then be laid in a bed of natron (a salt obtained from the northwestern delta) to dry. After a period, it was transferred to the Per-Nefret, the Place of Beautification, where perfumes, oils and resins were applied along with complex layers of bandages, interleaved lavishly with prescribed amulets and jewellery. Finally, over the king's head would be placed a mask of gold, and the whole reverently lowered into a coffin, also very often of gold. Over the body would be poured perfumes, oils and resins. The inner coffin would be placed in a continuing series of further coffins. At length, it would be moved into the Valley as part of an enormous funeral procession. From inscriptions and pictures, we know that dancers, musicians and mourning women, shrieking and crying, would be mixed with men pulling sledges laden with the goods that were going to be packed into the tombs – furniture, clothing, all the things the king had become accustomed to in life and would thus need during death.

In the Valley, a ceremony known as the final Opening of the Mouth would take place (see page 97). This would be carried out by the king's heir. Although the details of the ceremony are unknown, we do know that the heir would use a ceremonial carpenter's adze, in theory made of iron, to symbolically restore the senses of the body to the king and transform his body, ready for its journey into the afterlife. According to the story of Osiris as told by Plutarch, the goddess Isis wrapped the dead body of Osiris in cloths, thus making the first mummy, after which their son, Horus, performed the ritual in order to become the next king. By custom and example, then, the man who carried out the rite would be crowned the next king. The body would be slid into place down a sloping ramp, dragged into the bottom chamber where a sarcophagus, a huge rectangular stone container, awaited it. The encoffined body would be lifted carefully into the sarcophagus, and the lid put into place. The lid of Ramesses III, today in the Fitzwilliam Museum at Cambridge, is one of the few royal lids to have survived. Standing over twelve feet tall, it has the recumbent figure of the king as the mummified and wrapped Osiris carved in relief on the top. It is truly a masterpiece of the sculptor's art.

In many of the royal tombs, the sarcophagus stood within a lowered pit in the floor of the burial chamber. This would enable the heavy coffins and lid to be slid, rather than lifted, into position. When the body was within the sarcophagus, a nest of 'houses', or gilded shrines, would be assembled on the top. These wooden panels, covered heavily in gold, would have images of the dead king carved over them. Each finished shrine had a door at one end, and all the doors were constructed to face the same direction. With everything completed, the shrine doors would finally be closed, and each in turn would be sealed with a rope knot and fixed with a mud-seal impressed with the king's seal. In most of the tombs, with the shrines in place over the sarcophagus, the pit in the floor of the burial chamber would have been filled level with the floor of the tomb. The mourners would then withdraw, allowing the treasures to be packed inside. Finally the outer door would be sealed. On the outside of the door, the dead king's seals would be imprinted for the very last time.

The death of a king threw Egypt into a time of public sorrow. Although we have few details, we know from pictures and inscriptions that the funerals of the nobility would be accompanied by large processions of the bereaved, professional mourners, musicians and funerary dancers, together with people carrying grave goods, while the route to the tomb would be lined with those who knew the dead person. We can expect nothing less for a king. Indeed, a state funeral would have affected everyone living in the area. The routes leading towards the Valley would have been crammed with people wanting a glimpse of the things as they passed by. Only the Valley of the Kings would have been silent and empty as the coffins and the shrines, together with the rest of the funerary objects, were secretly crammed inside.

And only when the tomb was filled and the door was finally sealed could the next king be crowned.

The choice of a king

It has frequently been said that the right to the throne of Egypt passed through the females. Much of the reason for this was the knowledge that Tutankhamen married the last surviving daughter of the previous king, Akhenaten. Since he had no right to the throne, but she did, reason suggests that he took the throne only because he married her. In fact, this theory has little basis in reality. We know that women and men had equal rights under the law in ancient Egypt, except that when a man died, his son inherited his goods. If he had never had a son, the goods would pass to his brother or nearest male relative. This led one man in the New Kingdom to draw up an official document adopting his childless wife as his 'son' so that she could inherit his estate. This being the case, it is hard to say with any authority that the highest estate in the land, that of the office of kingship, should be passed through the female line if the lower estates could not without legal alteration.

For the throne to pass through the female line, it should follow that every king of Egypt should be the son of the previous heiress, but this was very seldom the case. In many instances, the king took as his principal wife an absolute commoner. This indicates that the line of inheritance, with the throne as with all things in ancient Egypt, passed from father to son.

Yet the inheriting of the throne was by no means a foregone conclusion. The kings of Egypt, as we have seen, had many wives and children. By 1998, the excavation of the tomb of the children of Ramesses II had revealed 115 chambers with passages still stretching off in all directions into the distance. So it was all well and good for a dying king to leave his throne to a particular son, but the time that elapsed between the deaths and the final application of his seals on the tomb door might be several months. Much might change within these months.

The interval between the death of one king and the coronation of the next was, for Egyptians, the time when Isfet showed her greatest power. Egypt was then like a ship without a rudder, and the gods drew their breath and paused, waiting to see if the customary services would begin again soon. Within the royal households, it was a time for jostling of position. Chief among the contenders were not only the sons of the king, but also the widows. One of the highest positions any woman could hope to achieve was that of king's mother. A king, after all, might have hundreds of wives, but only one mother. Most important burials of royal women were carried out not by their husbands, but by their sons. The mothers of the princes, therefore, had all to fight for and little to lose when their spouse died.

History reveals that the greatest infighting took place, unsurprisingly, within the harems, or women's palaces, while the mummification of the husband was in process. In some instances, even the coronation of one king did not ensure that another contender would not push them to one side. This happened, for instance, after Radjedef inherited the throne in the Fourth Dynasty, after the death of Cheops or Khnum-Khufu, and was deposed by Chephren. Another case was that of Hatshepsut and Tuthmosis III in the New Kingdom period. Sometimes avaricious women may not even have waited for their noble lord to die of natural causes. It seems highly probable, in fact, that both Amenemhet I of the Twelfth Dynasty and Ramesses III of the Twentieth Dynasty were actually murdered by their wives.

When the old king was finally sealed within his tomb, the coronation of the next could take place. In previous times, this had always taken place in Memphis, the ancient capital of Egypt, in the temple of Ptah. In the Eighteenth Dynasty, as we know from names and inscriptions, many of the kings were crowned instead in the temple of Karnak in Luxor, the city from which their ancestors had come.

An essential aspect of the coronation was the recitation of the king's names, which we'll look at next.

The names

Every king of Egypt was given a total of five names, recited for the first time at his coronation. Three of these names would be used only on the most official of his monuments, but the other two would be used regularly. One of these, the ⟨𓅭𓇳⟩, was the name he had received at birth. Traditionally the first son would be given the name of his grandfather at birth; the second son, the name of the father. In the Eighteenth Dynasty, the most common king's names were Tuthmosis and Amenhotep. If the first son of the king inherited the throne, then the names would alternate. If, on the other hand, the older son died and the younger inherited the throne, succeeding kings would have the same name, so that Amenhotep III would be followed by Amenhotep IV.

But these names were dropped, forgotten, when the king was crowned. At his coronation he would be given a new name, unique to him in all history. It was this by which the Egyptians knew their kings. So we may write of Amenhotep III, but strictly speaking this is wrong. The kings of Egypt never attached numbers to their names as we do. At his coronation Amenhotep III was given the new name of Nebmaatre, by which he would have been known publicly forever afterwards. Unfortunately, we have grown accustomed to calling the kings of Egypt by their birth names. This has resulted in some great mistakes.

Some confusion always arises over the writing of the names of ancient Egyptian kings, and within scholarly circles there are many different approaches to the subject. The reason for this lies in a gap in our understanding of how ancient Egyptian words and names were pronounced. The ancient Egyptian language, being written in hieroglyphs, lacks many of the vowel 'separators' within words. Where a strong vowel sound existed, such as in 'up' or 'in', a character would be assigned to it. Where there was only a weak vowel sound, as in 'pen' or 'pan', the central sound has long been lost to us. As a result, we have no idea how the names of the ancient Egyptian kings actually sounded. When the Greeks settled in Egypt from the fifth century BC onwards, they wrote stories of the Egyptian kings, but wrote their names in Greek instead. Taking the name of one of the kings of the Eighteenth Dynasty, Amenhotep, a transliteration of the way the Egyptians wrote it is 'Imn–htp'. Although we do not know how it was pronounced, the first part, the name of the god, is now written either as Amen or Amun; and the second part, 'htp', either as 'hetep' or as 'hotep'. Thus the name may be written in books as Amenhotep, Amunhotep, Amenhetep, or Amunhetep. To complicate things further, some writers adopt the Greek version of the name, Amenophis.

Every Egyptologist adopts their own preference when it comes to the names of kings. My custom is to use the form closest to the Egyptian wherever possible, but if the Greek form is more recognisable to readers, to use that instead. Since the kings were not called by these names in any case, but by their throne name, and since we do not know how any of the names were pronounced, this seems an academic irrelevance.

Daily life in ancient Egypt: cities and society

It is strange that, among all the monuments from Egypt to survive, we do not have a palace to show us exactly how a king lived in the Eighteenth Dynasty. The principal city in ancient Egypt was Memphis. Today situated some fifteen miles south of Cairo, all that remains of this once great metropolis are small and insignificant ruins lying among palm trees and fields outside the modern village of Mit Rahina. In ancient times, it was home to many thousands of people. The original name of the settlement meant 'white walls', no doubt a description of the first king's palace to have been built there, which was presumably surrounded by white-painted walls. Once standing on the banks of the Nile, over the years it lost this distinction as the river moved eastwards. Probably at the end of the Old Kingdom or at the start of the Middle Kingdom, the increase in foreign trade required the building of great new dockyards, and the buildings around them took the name Men-nefer from one of the pyramids in the area. The Greeks heard this name as 'Memphis'.

Memphis was home of the Egyptian government, civil service, the judiciary and the inland revenue. The largest temple in the city was that of 'Ptah-south-of-his-wall', presumably so named because it lay outside the original white walls. Excavations have revealed the layout of the royal palace of Merenptah, son and successor of Ramesses II of the Nineteenth Dynasty. It seems to have followed very much the layout of a standard temple.

As we've seen, the family of the Eighteenth Dynasty came from Luxor, about 400 miles south of Memphis. Remains of royal residences are few and far between, but enough paint survives on the walls and ceilings of temples on both east and west banks to show that the use of colour must have been riotous here. Walls would have been painted with white backgrounds, and over the top would have been laid images in a mass of juxtaposed primary colours, especially the much-loved bright reds and blues. Luxor was known, it seems, from texts and from the Old Testament as 'No', from the ancient word *niwt*, which means simply 'town' or 'city'. Even today, in many cultures, people speak of visiting the capital as 'going to town'. Like Memphis Luxor would have had thriving docks into which ships sailed carrying luxury goods. The people within the town, bearing in mind its connection with the king, grew rich and powerful. Many officials chose to be buried here rather than in Saqqara, near Memphis, in the hills near the royal tombs. The relatively small chambers are painted with autobiographical pictures that show a little of the dizzy life of parties that would have taken place within the royal court.

Of royal palaces in the area, however, there is no sign. We know that Amenhotep III built a palace-city for himself on the west bank, directly opposite the temple of Luxor. Before his time, we have no indication at all of where the kings lived.

During the Eighteenth Dynasty, Egypt controlled most of the Middle East. The early kings, especially Tuthmosis III, had taken control by military means but still allowed the countries they conquered some autocracy. At the start of the dynasty, the Egyptian army had been made up principally of either mercenary regiments, or infantry regiments made up of conscripted Egyptians. Neither force was satisfactory if the Egyptians wanted to post permanent garrisons of troops through their new empire to maintain control on behalf of the king. They began to recruit professional soldiers; and from the middle of the dynasty, tomb inscriptions in both Luxor and Saqqara record the pride that many Egyptians started to show in their military titles.

Officers were recruited from educated boys. Boys from all social classes could be sent away from home to school. Education was available to anyone who could 'afford' it. This meant that a family not only had to be able to spare the very valuable work that a healthy son might provide, together with the income that he might earn, but they would also have to support all his needs while he was living away from home – his food, clothes and tools of the trade. Once trained, the boy would be able to climb quickly up the social ladder and earn many times what an uneducated boy might earn. But first the family had to spare him – and it has been suggested that no more than 1 to 2 per cent ever learned to write. Many boys were lucky just to attend school. Having received four or five years of training in how to write in hieratic, a cursive script of ancient Egyptian, they would simply return home. The more able children progressed into careers, receiving higher education at the same time as being trained for a specific job. Careers open to them had usually included draughtsmanship; astronomy/ astrology; engineering; mathematics and accountancy; and now the army was added to the list. Many boys rose to high ranks within the army. Yuya, for example, took charge of the king's horse. His daughter became Great Royal Wife to Amenhotep III, while his son Ay, having inherited the military title, went on to become Pharaoh after Tutankhamen died. Two more commanders-in-chief, posted in Memphis, rose from the ranks of farmers to take the highest ranks within the army. One of them, Horemheb, seized control when Ay died and put Egypt under military rule; his friend, Ramesses, became the founder of the great Nineteenth Dynasty.

Thus boys came into the army from all walks of life. They would have learned how to handle weapons, how to drive chariots, and – one of the most important tasks for the army of the Eighteenth Dynasty – how to manage and control horses. The horse was the single most important element in the army in this era. It gave the Egyptians swiftness in attack, and the ability to move quickly over rough terrain. Horses only arrived in Egypt around 1650 BC, but a century later the Egyptians' skill at breeding the animals meant that the country had one of the finest cavalry forces in the Middle East. Not only this: Egyptians also found themselves in the position of being able to trade back their animals from the very people from whom they had taken them in the first place.

By 1360 BC Egypt was thus in a position to plan attacks and carry them out professionally, and then to have sufficient manpower to deploy small numbers of troops wherever they were needed. The country was now in control of most of what we today call Syria, Lebanon, Israel and Jordan, although all maintained some independence. Egypt had, during its period of conquest, removed the sons of princes from the places they had conquered; and these youths, educated in Egypt and then sent back home when old enough, also kept up loyalty to Egypt.

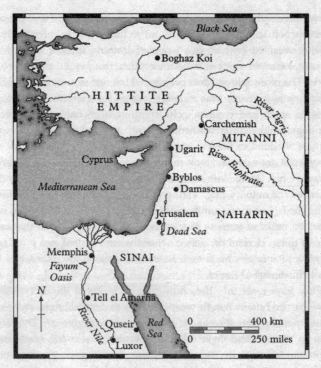

Egypt and neighbouring countries in the Eighteenth Dynasty.

The big division in Egypt's control in the north was the river Euphrates. To the west of the river up to the sea, Egyptian control was tight; but to the east Egypt had little hold. Realising this, Tuthmosis III took his troops on a campaign to Lebanon, where he ordered ships to be made, mounted on ox-drawn carts and towed across the mountains in order to allow the Egyptian army to sail across the Euphrates to try to conquer the east bank. Although in his inscriptions he claimed success, in reality Tuthmosis III was repulsed. Across the river lay the land of Mitanni; to the west, the land of Naharin. These are now, roughly, Syria and part of Iraq. In the time of Amenhotep III, the two countries seem to have operated as one. To the north of them lay the land of the Hittites. In the early Eighteenth Dynasty, they posed no challenge to Egypt's domination. During the early reign of Amenhotep

III, however, they regrouped and started to attack Egyptian-held territory. Naharin and Mitanni found themselves torn between two superpowers. During his reign Tuthmosis IV, the father of Amenhotep III, sent many deputations to Naharin/Mitanni to request the hand of one of their daughters in marriage, in order to seal an alliance. Although the marriage was arranged, relations between the two countries remained uneasy. Amenhotep III followed his father's example in also requesting to marry a princess from these lands – with what success, we shall see later.

Recent excavations in Egypt from the Eighteenth Dynasty are revealing enormous artistic influence in Egypt at this time from Crete. The Minoan civilisation was at its height, and many objects of Minoan origin have been found in Egypt. Until recently, most of this had been credited to Egyptian trade, but we now know that many houses and palaces in Egypt from the period were decorated in Minoan style. It is possible, of course, simply to say that the art from Crete was fashionable at the time, but Egypt, over the centuries, always had the tendency to pass on her art to others rather than absorbing theirs. It seems, therefore, that there was for the first time considerable movement of people around the Eastern Mediterranean, through Egyptian-held territory. There must have been many foreigners in Egypt during the Eighteenth Dynasty. Egyptian influence is also seen strongly for the first time in Cyprus, and clearly that island was absorbed into the Egyptian maritime trade cycle around the Mediterranean.

Whenever Egypt's monarchy weakened, both Nubia and Libya took the opportunity first to rebel and then to begin to enter Egypt. The strong kings at the start of the Eighteenth Dynasty had few problems. Their western borders with Libya were secure, and although settlers came into the western delta, as they always had, they were peaceful immigrants for the moment – although their power was to increase significantly during the following two dynasties. Down in Nubia, the Pharaoh appointed a King's Son of Kush, or Prince of Nubia, to rule there. The system seems to have worked well, and during the reign of Tutankhamen, the Kushite Prince Huya, buried in Luxor, is depicted as bringing lavish offerings to the young King.

By the middle of the Eighteenth Dynasty, most of the Eastern Mediterranean was thus peaceful and settled, with the exception of the Hittites, who were now waiting in the wings for the right time to act.

Into this setting, then, we can place the characters of our drama, a story, so it seems at first, of murder and royal intrigue along the banks of the Nile. Given the romance of this exotic setting, it is easy to fictionalise these 3500-year-old events. But what really happened all those centuries ago is more startling than any fiction.

CHAPTER ONE

The Early Evidence
for Tutankhamen

—

Many books on Tutankhamen begin with the discovery of the tomb in 1922. But the discovery of the tomb was merely the culmination of one man's dream. In reality, the archaeological story had begun many years earlier.

By 1906, Luxor had become a magnet for hundreds of visitors each year, from the ever larger groups of British 'Cook's tourists' on their organised tours, who moved swiftly from one site to the other, to the more leisurely journeys of the wealthy 'gentlemen-travellers', the last followers of the Grand Tour. Jostling with vessels ranging from large cruise ships to *dahebeyehs*, the wooden boats hired by smaller private parties, the Nile was becoming a busy thoroughfare.

Back in Europe, the publication of Charles Darwin's revolutionary theories on the origins of humankind had fired a need to understand our roots, and so inspired a more methodical and focused approach to delving into the past: in short, archaeology was born. Because of the poor state of preservation of sites and artefacts in the cool, wet countries of the north, antiquarians, as the early archaeologists were known, had had to develop slow and careful methods, scientifically devised by specialists in their field who measured and recorded everything meticulously. But in Egypt, where the age of archaeology had scarcely dawned, there were unimaginable riches preserved by the hot, dry climate. The sands were liberally littered, as far as the eye could see, with objects many thousands of years old. Here, you did not have to mark out a site in yard-squares and scrape away slowly at levels in the wet soil. Here you simply bent down and picked the things up.

Luxor had been noted already in several archaeological publications as a rich site, with its temples of Karnak and Luxor on the east bank and its wide temple-encircled plain on the west bank. The temples all dated to the New Kingdom – the time encompassing the Eighteenth to the Twentieth Dynasties, when ancient Egypt's wealth and influence were greatest. The hills on the west bank that fringed the fertile plain concealed a huge number of tombs that together could contain a mine of unimaginable riches.

It was a finding twenty-five years before that fuelled speculation about treasures in the hill tombs. In 1881, in a hidden cliff-tomb at Deir el Bahri on the west bank, archaeologists had found fifty-three royal mummies in a great secret cache hidden there some 3000 years before. The mummies had been some of the New Kingdom's greatest pharaohs, moved to safety here after the tombs in the Valley of the Kings had been smashed by a marauding Nubian army. Now, in 1906, the mummies were on view to the public, laid out naked in glass cases for the prurient casual tourist to gaze upon in the Egyptian Museum in Cairo's Tahrir Square. The exhibition included a recent addition of sixteen more mummies, fourteen of which were also royal; and some of these were the mummies of kings missing from the original group. These sixteen mummies had been found just eight years earlier, in a second cache in the Valley of the Kings itself. But the bodies of many kings were still missing. While archaeologists privately speculated that the others had been destroyed long ago, anticipation for the tourist of 1906 was high, and many hoped that the hills and valleys of Luxor might hold yet more treasures.

Europe's fascination with Egypt had started at the beginning of the nineteenth century with the publication of the *Description de L'Égypte*, the scientific report of the work of the scholars who had come through Egypt with Napoleon. From the 1830s, tourism had increased steadily, soon having grown to such an extent that trafficking in antiquities was taken for granted. Nile travellers in those years felt themselves ill-equipped on their homeward journeys if they were not accompanied by the odd mummy, coffin, papyrus or decorated pot. The avid

Europeans would have bartered for these objects with Egyptians for what seemed, in European terms, ridiculously low prices, although to the native Egyptian they were small fortunes. By the mid-nineteenth century the trickle of tourism had turned to a flood, and Egypt's antiquities, once seemingly limitless, began to appear badly depleted by the trade. In 1857 Auguste Mariette, an Egyptologist at the Louvre Museum in Paris, had persuaded the Khedive – Egypt's ruler at the time – to set up two bodies simultaneously: the first Egyptian Museum, based in Boulaq in Cairo, where some treasure might be displayed, and the Antiquities Organisation, which was controlled by French director-generals and would issue licences, or concessions, to archaeologists.

It now seems incredible, but before 1857 there was no control over excavation in Egypt. Frequently, would-be archaeologists would literally come to blows over who would dig a particularly interesting site. The new concessions stated that when a site was identified, an inspector had to be present at its initial examination; that if a site had been robbed, the objects found had to be presented to the museum, which would have the choice of the pieces, the remainder reverting to the concession holder; but that if an intact site were found, the objects should belong to Egypt as an entire group, although it was within the prerogative of the Department of Antiquities and the Egyptian government to give the concession holder some pieces at their discretion. The system started to bring order to an otherwise chaotic situation, although the export of antiquities was still permitted under licence, and the flood of antiquities began to slow a little.

In the post-Napoleonic era of mistrust between the English and the French, the creation of the Antiquities Organisation was welcome. But there were inherent problems with the organisation – namely, the persistent appointment of French rather than British directors. However, by the start of the twentieth century, it had been agreed that two British inspector-generals would be appointed, one based in Luxor, the other in Saqqara, that huge necropolis of Memphis, the ancient capital.

In 1906, the Inspector-general of Antiquities for Upper Egypt, based in Luxor, was Arthur Weigall. Photographs show him to have been dapper and clean-shaven. His books – several of which are still in print – show that he knew the sites of Upper Egypt, south of Cairo, as no one else did. *Who's Who in Egyptology*, however, describes his life's work as 'marred by the author's eccentric approach to certain philological and historical matters, and displaying considerable arrogance towards other contemporary Egyptologists'. Weigall was responsible for supervising any excavation work going on in Luxor. His patience must have been sorely tried by the people flooding into the area in the hope of 'trying their luck' by digging in the western hills.

Weigall's immediate predecessor was Howard Carter, a young man from Norfolk, who had first arrived in Egypt as a painter employed to copy tomb paintings in Middle Egypt, between Cairo and Luxor, and in 1895 had arrived in Luxor to copy the paintings in the mortuary temple of Hatshepsut at Deir el Bahri on the west bank. Carter had trained under the great Egyptologist Flinders Petrie, and under his guidance had become an archaeologist of some repute. As was common among Englishmen of the time, Carter was given to jingoism, and was often intolerant of others, especially 'foreigners'. He was also a loner who made friends with difficulty, and often found other people irritating. As an inspector, he wrote of the amateurs digging in Luxor as people 'bored with life's mild adventures, dallying with relics in the hope of finding some thrill to stimulate their sluggard imaginations'. Like others in his field then, he dressed in Egypt as he did in England, and was usually to be found, even in the hottest weather, in heavy tweed three-piece suits complete with bow-tie, walking-stick and a smart hat.

From 1903, the concession to dig in the Valley of the Kings had been held by Theodore M. Davies, a wealthy, retired American lawyer who had invested huge amounts of his own money in trying to find the missing kings and their tombs. He had endowed an entire gallery in the Egyptian Museum for his finds and was thus highly regarded by the impecunious Antiquities Organisation. But not all shared the organisation's views. The Director of the Antiquities Organisation, Gaston Maspero, had appointed Howard Carter to supervise all activities in Luxor, even those of Davies in the Valley. And while Carter liked and respected Maspero, of whom he wrote, 'A more charming gentleman or kinder master could not be found', his relationship with Davies was more aggressive. Carter saw his job as that of the professional archaeologist offering guidance to the untrained gentleman-digger, while Davies, equally irascible, believed that as he was footing the bill for the work, he was entitled to overall control. The two men clashed. As a result, in January 1905, Carter was moved away from his beloved

Howard Carter photographed c.1925.

Luxor and sent north instead, to Saqqara. The milder-mannered Weigall replaced him.

It seems that Weigall and Davies reached a tolerable understanding. Davies was undoubtedly a difficult person to work with, being often intolerant of anyone else's ideas. The work that he did within the Valley was generally sumptuously published, although the 'excavation reports', which he wrote himself, often had little in the way of accepted archaeological detail and frequently lacked even the most basic measurements, plans and layouts. Davies would generally ignore the suggestions of archaeologists working with him. As Nicholas Reeves has written, '[Davies'] interest in careful clearance work was minimal, his employment of basic conservation methods almost non-existent, while his splendid series of publications manages to record everything but the facts.'

Carter hated his move to Saqqara, and was on edge when he arrived there. On 8 January 1905, he was involved in a public brawl in the ancient necropolis. Carter's telegram to Maspero the following day explained the incident, saying, 'Fifteen French tourists were here today in a drunken state. The cause of the affray was started by the rough handling of my Inspector and the Gaffirs [local Egyptian Inspectors] both sides being cut and knocked about.' The French claimed to have been assaulted over a demand for tickets. The affair quickly became public knowledge. Newspaper reports revealed that whatever the cause of the dispute, Carter had ordered his men to use their truncheons to break up the affray. The local press related lurid tales of French women and children running from the danger while their valiant menfolk were under attack. Whatever the truth of the matter, by February 1905 Maspero told Carter 'not to take offence', but to meet with the complainants and make some apology, for the use of the truncheons at least. Maspero emphasised that the Antiquities Organisation would shoulder some of the blame. But on the appointed day, Carter refused to turn up, insisting that the French should apologise first. Maspero did his best to pour oil on troubled waters, but at length suggested that, for the sake of peace, Carter should take three and a half months' leave from 14 March. At this suggestion Carter's temper surfaced once more, and he immediately tendered his resignation.

Now unemployed and with little money, Carter moved back to his beloved Luxor, where he set up a small shop selling watercolours and, as a profitable byline well-known at the time, selling antiquities. His role excited little attention. Alfred Lythgoe from the Metropolitan Museum of Art in New York wrote of him, 'There is no one more familiar with the Egyptian market.'

So in 1905 Carter made contact again with Theodore Davies. This time, though, the tables were turned. Carter no longer had any say in archaeological work in the area. Davies also by now had a willing helper in the Egyptologist Edward Ayrton, a biddable young man of twenty-three.

In early 1906, Davies was relaxing with Ayrton in the Valley of the Kings when he made a momentous discovery. He wrote, 'My attention was attracted to a large rock tilted to one side, and for some mysterious reason I felt interested in it; and being carefully examined and dug about by my assistant Mr Ayrton with his hands, the beautiful blue cup was found.' The 'beautiful blue cup' was a small glazed-composition, or faience, cup of the type used at funerals in ancient Egypt, bearing the name 'Nebkheprure'. This was the throne-name of Tutankhamen, and the cup was the first piece ever found in the Valley that bore his name. For the first time it seemed probable that Tutankhamen, one of Davies' missing kings, might have been buried somewhere nearby.

At this time virtually nothing was known about Tutankhamen except that he had existed. Much of this was due to peculiarities not only in royal history in ancient Egypt, but also in the recording of it. Even today establishing the order of the succession and length of reign of Egyptian kings is complicated. The Egyptians themselves had no systematic method of writing their own history. All events were dated by the current reign-year of the king at the time (for example, year 1 of Amenhotep Nebmaatre). This means that our knowledge of how long any king might have ruled depends on the highest number of years that has been found. This could be changed at any time by the discovery of another piece with a higher number. Sometimes individual kings, or even entire families, ruled in different places in Egypt at the same time. Courtiers could serve only one king, so they might list in their autobiographical texts the year of a certain king in which they achieved a certain feat, omitting to add that there was another king ruling somewhere else in Egypt at the same time. King-lists, carved on the walls of several temples in Upper Egypt, purportedly list every king of Egypt from the very beginning, from Menes through to the time of the carving. But in fact the lists omitted anyone the Ramessides did not approve of, including all female kings and all the turbulent rulers of the mid-Eighteenth Dynasty, including Tutankhamen. Since no tomb had been found for Tutankhamen, only a few pieces had been discovered belonging to his reign, and the king-lists omitted him altogether. Even trying to find out where in the order of kings he ruled was problematical, and there were no clues at all as to how long he reigned.

By 1906 much of the basic history of the early New Kingdom had been established. It was known that around 1650 BC Egypt had been occupied by a group of foreigners called the Hyksos. The Hyksos were driven out around 1550 BC by the family from Luxor who formed the Eighteenth Dynasty. The first kings of this dynasty had been great warriors, forging the world's first empire. For many decades Egypt prospered, until the reign of the notorious King Akhenaten, known by many as the heretic king. During his time, the temples were shut, and the treasury drained as countries refused or failed to send tribute; and the great empire crumbled. On Akhenaten's death, the throne had fallen first for a short period to Smenkhare, then to Tutankhamen and finally to Ay. The names of all these kings were omitted from the king-lists. As we've seen, when Ay died, the Commander-in-Chief of the Egyptian Army, Horemheb, staged a military coup and ruthlessly began to eradicate all memory of the previous royal family. He had no heir, and before he died he chose a colleague in the army, Ramesses, to become the next king and the first ruler of the Nineteenth Dynasty. Ramesses I, his son Seti I and his grandson Ramesses II carried on Horemheb's campaign to obliterate all memory of the Eighteenth Dynasty family. Everywhere they removed every trace of their names, destroyed their sites, overcarved their inscriptions and kept them off the king-lists. It was as if Akhenaten, Smenkhare, Tutankhamen and Ay had never existed. And the destruction of their remains by the Ramessides almost worked. But enough fragmentary pieces survived to show us that they had lived, although nothing else about them was known. The English Egyptologist Sir John Gardner Wilkinson had noted Tutankhamen's name on a statue as early as 1837, but Davies' find, the blue cup, was the first intimation of Tutankhamen's presence in the Valley of the Kings. From that time onward, Tutankhamen's name was added to Davies' list of names of missing kings still to be found in the Valley.

Some time in the early months of 1906 Davies contacted Carter, and asked him to work for him as a freelance draughtsman. Given the previous ill-will between the two and Carter's pride, we can speculate that Carter would have refused the offer, had it not been for the discovery, in February that year, of the intact tomb of Yuya and Thuya in the Valley of the Kings. The publication of the discovery captured the public imagination as nothing had before. Yuya and Thuya were the grandparents of Akhenaten on his mother's side, and their mummies were perhaps the finest ever found in Egypt. Carter was thus persuaded to accept the job. Yet the move hardly reconciled the two men. September found Carter writing in a letter, 'Davies has behaved like a bear to me of late.'

At exactly this time, the stage was set for the arrival of the final player. George Edward Stanhope Molyneux Herbert, Fifth Earl of Carnarvon, was then forty years old. Born into a wealthy aristocratic British family, he had made an auspicious match when he married Almina, daughter of the banker Baron de Rothschild, on his twentieth birthday, receiving from his father-in-law a marriage gift of £250,000. Carnarvon had a passion for fast cars which he liberally indulged, entering several Grand Prix races. Three years before, in 1903, he had had a motoring accident while on holiday in Germany. His companion at the time, his chauffeur (though Carnarvon was driving), said that Carnarvon's heart had stopped beating several times in the minutes after the crash, and had to be restarted.

On returning to England from Germany, Carnarvon's recovery had been slow and uncertain. Finally his doctors advised him, for his health's sake, to travel to a warmer climate for the winter. He arrived in Cairo for the first time in the winter of 1903 with his wife, his five-year-old son and heir, and his daughter Lady Evelyn, then just two years old. Carnarvon seems to have developed an instant passion for the place and its past, an enthusiasm that his wife did not share. Before he died, he recorded that the idea of digging in Egypt himself had come to him in 1889 when he was only twenty-three, the year his father had died and he had come into his inheritance. It seems that this first visit fulfilled a long-standing ambition, and that Egypt did not disappoint his imagination. He made enquiries in Cairo and finally, in late 1906, he was given permission to dig in Luxor. He recorded, 'With the idea of keeping me out of mischief as well as keeping me employed, I was allotted a site at the top of Sheikh Abd el Qurna.' As fate would have it, this village on the west bank was where Carter was building a house for himself, today called 'Castle Carter'. It is probable, therefore, that the men met socially for the first time soon after Carnarvon's arrival. Carnarvon's initial enthusiastic but amateur attempts at digging seemed to have horrified the locals, who reported him to the Antiquities Organisation. Maspero then wrote to him and suggested he should employ the services of someone properly trained in the field, specifically recommending Howard Carter. The formal introduction of the two men was an instant success, and these two aloof, rather intolerant men struck up an instant friendship based on mutual respect that was to last until Carnarvon's death in 1923.

That winter was the first that the two men dug together. The discovery of the blue cup and the tomb of Yuya and Thuya drew Carter to the Valley of the Kings. Carter told Carnarvon that he wanted the concession, but Davies had no intention of handing it over.

Suddenly, in January 1907, in the space of one week, two discoveries were made in the Valley that were vital to the story of Tutankhamen, and alerted Carter and others to the probable location of the tomb of the lost Pharaoh.

The Cache Tomb

On 3 January, a pit was found in the Valley (known technically as KV54) that contained eight large, sealed, unglazed pots in a bed of screwed-up, soiled linen and general debris. The jars bore on them the title 'Nebkheprure' – the throne name of Tutankhamen – and dates between years 6 and 8 of his reign. Davies gave the order for them to be lifted out at once and carried to his local dig-house. The jars, when opened, were each found to contain the remains of what appeared to be a meal, together with a floral broadcollar, a necklace made of papyrus with petals, leaves and berries stitched on to look like jewellery. Examination later showed that the flowers concerned were in bloom between March and April of the year Tutankhamen died. These necklaces were later subjected to brutal despoilation by Davies, who routinely offered them to dinner guests, inviting them to tear them apart to see how strong they were.

Davies was convinced that he had found Tutankhamen's tomb,

although other archaeologists warned that it was not the case. Years later, in 1912, he ignored all advice and published his 'excavation report' of the pit as 'the tomb of Harmhabi and Toutankhamanou'. This excited much opposition from scholars. H. E. Winlock, from New York's Museum of Modern Art, suggested later in an article that these were the remains of an embalming and funerary feast, and that the tomb of Tutankhamen lay elsewhere, still undiscovered.

Three days later, on 6 January 1907, Ayrton and Davies uncovered a hidden, sealed door leading to a tomb, the discovery and treatment of which still fascinates and intrigues archaeologists to this day.

Tomb 55

The tomb lay close to the public entrance to the Valley, at the junction between the Valley's walls and floor. Behind a crude stone wall, a sealed mud-brick door bore the impression of the official seal of the necropolis guard – a recumbent jackal over nine tied captives – and, Davies claimed, the seal of Nebkheprure. Weigall soon joined Ayrton and Davies. The details of the discovery, however, remain a mystery to this day. In his book *Akhenaten*, the eminent British Egyptologist Cyril Aldred writes that

> The evidence is all too clear that instead of proceeding with caution and skill, these men, two of them at least with specialised training and experience, somehow managed to carry out one of the worst pieces of excavation on record in the Valley. The word 'record' is used only loosely. The official publication is perfunctory in the extreme, no plans or dimensions are given, the descriptions are slipshod and incomplete and the various accounts that eye-witnesses subsequently gave, sometimes long after the event when the recollections were at fault, are often conflicting where they are not so vague as to be worthless.

The door had been broken down by Ayrton and Davies, and the doorway led to a sloping corridor strewn with rubble, on top of which lay what seemed at the time to be a hinged door-leaf of wood, and a wooden panel covered with gold. On it Ayrton saw and copied the image of Queen Tiye, the daughter of Yuya and Thuya and the mother of Akhenaten. Davies was entranced. Here was another of his missing

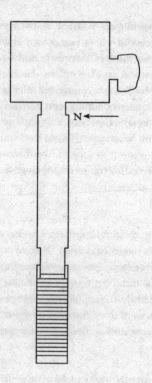

Tomb 55 (plan)

characters, and a queen at that. Harold Jones, a freelance excavator and watercolourist who often worked in the Valley, copied the pictures on the panel together with the hieroglyphs; amazingly, no attempt whatsoever was made to preserve either of these objects. A plank was laid over the panels, allowing everyone access to the tomb over it. Thereafter the panels, probably already in a fragmented state because of flooding over the centuries, quickly began to break up. An American Egyptologist, Charles Connolly, who visited the site, said that 'gold leaf seemed to be flying through the air in every direction'. A passing tourist recalled being invited in later to collect handfuls of the gold-filled dust. At any rate, the panels were totally destroyed.

The corridor led to a chamber much damaged by floodwater over the intervening centuries. The seals of Tutankhamen were observed around the chamber, while on the right, near an open niche in the wall, there stood the remains of a low bed which had once borne a coffin. This had collapsed and thrown the coffin off, jerking the lid to one side to reveal the mummy within. This mummy was immediately removed and carried outside by Davies, convinced that he had the mummy of one of his beloved queens. A passing GP was assailed and told of Davies' beliefs. The bewildered doctor agreed to look at the mummy, and the 'examination' was later transformed into a positive medical identification of Queen Tiye's body. Davies then 'examined' the mummy, later, observing in his reports that it was in poor condition, since 'the hair separated easily from the head when it was pulled'. The same test was applied to the teeth, which apparently also fell out, confirming his suspicions that the mummy was badly deteriorated. The body was then sent off to Cairo to be examined while Ayrton was ordered to clear the tomb as quickly as possible so as to move on elsewhere. The few surviving photographs of the coffin within the tomb show that at the time of discovery the face was made of gold. The head of the coffin had, however, clearly been cut from another coffin and added on. Moreover, down the front of the lid, and under the feet, the name had been carefully and deliberately cut out long ago, to hide the identity of the person interred. Later, when the coffin lid arrived in Cairo, the golden face was missing, together with a golden vulture collar. Both had apparently been cut away and probably sold locally to defray the cost of excavation.

Davies published the discovery as the tomb of Queen Tiye in 1910.

The confusion over the Cache Tomb and Tomb 55 seems to have excited little public interest at the time. Weigall's *Guide to the Antiquities of Upper Egypt*, published early in 1909, records that despite Davies' conviction that the Cache Tomb was indeed the tomb of Tutankhamen, 'the tomb of Tutankhamen has not yet been found'. In the same book he lists 'nos. 49–54 Uninscribed tombs. These tombs have been discovered during the past few years but they were mostly empty. They are of no interest to the tourist.' Interestingly, he also records 'Tomb 55. The tomb of Queen Tiye', although he notes that 'her body was removed from it to make room for that of the "heretic" King Akhenaten which had been brought back to Thebes from Tell el Amarna, probably by Tutankhamen. The latter's body was found in the tomb when it was opened in 1907.' Weigall's comment is the first tentative identification of the body as that of Tutankhamen, but it seems to have aroused little interest at that time – or this.

From Weigall's text, it appears that the confusion over the identity of the mummy in Tomb 55 was an open secret long before Davies published his controversial findings, in which he clearly ignored contradictory medical evidence. In fact, it was in 1907 that the pathologist Elliot Smith wrote in a letter to Arthur Weigall, 'Are you sure that the bones you sent me are those which were found in the tomb? Instead of the bones of an old woman, you have sent me those of a young man. Surely there is some mistake?'

The letter is fascinating. Whose remains were these if not Queen Tiye's? At first, the mummy was believed to be that of Akhenaten himself, until the postmortem showed it to be the remains of a person in their early twenties. Since Akhenaten reigned for seventeen years and was a father at the start of his reign, this ruled him out. Perhaps the identity of the mummy might have been written on its wrappings, since Elliot Smith says some inscriptions in hieratic were found on some of the bandages. These bandages disappeared, however, before they could be studied, having been purportedly stolen by a young laboratory assistant. The examination of the body seems to have resulted in the removal of all flesh, since all that is left today is the skull and sundry other disconnected bones. The whereabouts of the mummified tissue is unrecorded. Bearing in mind the destructive nature of Davies' 'examination' however, coupled with Smith's saying he had not received 'the bones of an old woman', it could suggest that little but bones were left of the body in any case by the time it arrived in Cairo. The problem of the tomb and the identity of its occupant will be examined in greater depth in Chapter 9, but for the moment, the suggestion is that what should have been a highly significant discovery in the story of Tutankhamen was a travesty.

While Davies was discovering such potentially exciting finds in the Valley – and making a mess of both the excavation and the publications – Carter and Carnarvon were digging outside, frustrated at their inability to get hold of the one concession that they really wanted. The two men found a sympathetic ear in members of the excavation team from the Metropolitan Museum of Art, who were also working outside the Valley, and the excavation leader H. E. Winlock became good friends with Carter. Carter became convinced, however, that the sites of Davies' three finds – the cup and the tombs – when triangulated, would show where the tomb of Tutankhamen lay – somewhere in the centre. The three points focused on an unexplored patch of ground in front of the tomb of Ramesses VI, which was heaped high with debris from the clearing of the tomb. Just as today, this tomb was then one of the most visited tombs in the Valley. For the moment, all the two men could do was sit and wait patiently until Davies finally gave up the concession and allowed them the opportunity to follow up Carter's theories.

The year 1907 had started with no one knowing anything about Tutankhamen but his name, and that he ruled in the Eighteenth Dynasty after the controversial King Akhenaten. By the end of the same year, it was known, from dates on the jars in the pit tomb, that he had ruled for at least eight years; that he had been mummified in the Valley of the Kings and must presumably have been buried close by; and that he had participated in the burial of a curious unnamed individual (Tomb 55) who may or may not have been related to him. For Davies, the search for Tutankhamen was over. For Carter, the mystery was only just beginning.

CHAPTER TWO

Discovering the Tomb

O ne of the few things clearly understood about the middle years of the Eighteenth Dynasty was that Tutankhamen came to the throne soon after Akhenaten. Perhaps more has been written about Akhenaten than about any other character in ancient Egypt. Pictures, reliefs and statues show Akhenaten as grotesquely distorted in shape – some would say deformed. One archaeologist termed him 'frankly hideous'. Certainly it is difficult to overlook him; in any case, we shall see the truth of this matter in later chapters.

In 1907, as a few facts were beginning to emerge about Tutankhamen himself, the picture of Akhenaten was starting to become a little clearer too. Since Tutankhamen had inherited the throne from him, his reign concerns us in our search for who Tutankhamen really was.

What was known about Akhenaten already was that he was a great heretic, that he had abandoned Luxor early in his reign and had gone with his wife, the beautiful Nefertiti, and their daughters, to live in a brand new city he had ordered to be built on a desolate plain on the east bank of the Nile in Middle Egypt. He dedicated his city to his new god, the Aten, calling it Akhetaten; today the site is known as Tell el Amarna.

Akhenaten was the son of Amenhotep III and Queen Tiye. Called Amenhotep at birth, when he moved into his new city he had changed his name to the one we know him by and devoted the rest of his life to serving the Aten, visualised as the disc of the sun. Cutting himself off from civilisation, he lived a life of apparently obsessive degradation until he died, having ruled Egypt for seventeen years. Akhenaten was succeeded for a short time by a young man called Smenkhkare, of whom even less is known than Tutankhamen, and the throne was taken at Smenkhkare's death by Tutankhaten, who later changed his name to Tutankhamen.

It seemed, however, as though the trail in Luxor had gone cold. Although most people believed that Davies was wrong, and that the pit, or Cache Tomb, was not the tomb of Tutankhamen, most scholars believed that the objects he had found there had originally come from Tutankhamen's tomb, and thus that the tomb, if it was ever found, would be totally empty. Weigall's belief that the body in Tomb 55 belonged to Tutankhamen was not his idea alone: it was coming into general discussion at the time. The evidence all added up to the usual story – that the tomb of Tutankhamen had been robbed in antiquity, although some odd bits had been pushed aside in various places. If we wanted to know more about Tutankhamen, then perhaps the answers lay not in the Valley of the Kings, but in Tell el Amarna. In this city, Tutankhamen had certainly lived as a child. In all probability he had been born there. Perhaps the evidence concerning him would come from there.

Excavation in Tell el Amarna

The site of Akhenaten's city lies about halfway between Cairo and Aswan in Middle Egypt. The modern name 'Tell el Amarna' is actually misleading. In the Middle East, the word 'tell' is applied to city-mounds. When a city begins to fall down or is damaged or destroyed by attack, the inhabitants knock down some of the walls, level the rubble and build afresh. Thus the level on which the city rests rises. Centuries pass and repeated rebuilding goes on until the floor of the city stands on a pronounced mound made up of the remains of previous buildings. Visitors expecting to see such a thing in Tell el Amarna will be disappointed. There is no mound, just a bare desert plain surrounded by limestone cliffs. To the casual observer, even the remains of the city walls are undetectable.

'Tell el Amarna' is, in fact, a name concocted by persons unknown, at the turn of the century. The first visitors to the site found modern villages with the names of Hawateh, Et Till and El Amrah. They took the names of the last two villages and from them invented the name

Tell el Amarna. Today, the title 'Amarna' is applied not just to the city's site, but to the whole period of the reign of Akhenaten and the early reign of Tutankhamen. We thus refer to Amarna kings, Amarna art, Amarna pottery, and so on.

The remains of the city buildings and the tombs lie on the east bank, almost opposite the site of Ashmunein, an ancient city dedicated to Thoth, and its associated necropolis, Tuna el Gebel. In 1798, when Napoleon's army of soldiers and scholars marched southwards through the area, the first Westerners in Egypt for many centuries, they seemed not to have noted the site at all, although some Pharaonic ruins scattered in Ashmunein were published by Napoleon's scholars in the *Description de L'Égypte*. The site seems first to have been visited and cursorily excavated in 1843 by Karl Richard Lepsius of the Prussian Expedition, the first truly archaeological expedition to Egypt.

Some forty years later Urbain Bourriant, a man who had studied under the great Maspero in Paris, visited the site and in 1884 published a book entitled *Deux jours de fouillées à Tell el Amarna* (*Two Days' Excavations in Tell el Amarna*). That this should appear to be an excavation report is astonishing: the British Egyptologist Flinders Petrie was later to declare the site impossible to excavate systematically, being roughly the size of Brighton. Petrie first assessed how the site should be excavated in 1886, using Lepsius' plans and maps for guidance, and noted several areas of unevenness as being worthy of future attention.

The arrival of a series of archaeologists in such a remote area in such a short time seems to have excited local interest. It became known that these foreigners were willing to pay good money for old things. The year after Petrie had visited the site, a local villager presented bewildered archaeologists with baskets of baked mud-clay tablets that they had found. When examined, they were found to have been written in Akkadian, the language of the Syrian city-state of Akkad. When the messages on them were translated, the tablets were found to be letters to and from other countries written during the life-span of Tell el Amarna. Ostensibly they were the foreign office records of ancient Egypt. From the letters emerged a picture of the chaos that Akhenaten had wrought upon the Egyptian empire during his reign – an unprecedented eye-witness view of diplomacy at the highest level. The precise whereabouts of the villager's find has never been established to this day, and it is still unclear whether all the tablets were retrieved and handed over.

Shortly afterwards, rumours abounded of the discovery of golden objects in a 'royal tomb', said to be located at the back of the plain up a dried-up river bed, or *wadi*. Although the tomb was found, it contained no gold, and the fragmentary pictures and litter within it excited little interest at the start. When visiting the site shortly before this time, the British archaeologist A. H. Sayce recorded that, one night, he saw a torchlit procession of villagers going up the *wadi*, and returning carrying objects which they then burned. So if the tomb and some of the objects had indeed escaped pillage in ancient times, it is possible that the local people themselves destroyed them later to save them from being exhibited in museums. This practice was understandably felt to be dehumanising and disrespectful to the dead, as well as to Egyptian custom.

In late 1891, Petrie returned and pinpointed the exact area he thought worthy of excavation, where the royal palace may have stood.

In December 1891 Howard Carter, then only seventeen years old, arrived in Egypt for the first time. As we've seen, he came as a copyist of wall paintings. Working under the Egyptologist Percy Newberry and the Archaeological Survey, Carter's first task was to copy wall paintings in the Middle Kingdom tombs of Beni Hasan and Deir El Bersheh, but at Christmas he and Newberry made a visit to Petrie's excavations a little further south at Tell el Amarna, where Carter met but failed to impress the great Petrie. Carter returned to Beni Hasan, but stayed there for only a short time. When an argument within the Archaeological Survey group caused Newberry to return unexpectedly to England, Carter moved to Tell el Amarna where, aged only eighteen, he began to work as an excavator under Petrie, concentrating on the temple in the middle of the main city. This experience probably awakened his interest in the Amarna era, a most complex period of Egyptian history. The following year, Petrie was given the first ever Chair in Egyptology in London, at University College, with the result that he did not return to Amarna, and Carter had to return to Beni Hasan.

One single season's excavation took place under Ludwig van Borchardt from 1913 to the start of 1914, with the Deutches Orientgesellschaft, the German Oriental Society, before the First World War intervened. At the end of this war, a British team began systematically to excavate the site from 1921 until 1935. Finally, between 1979 and 1986, the Egypt Exploration Society, a British body, carried out work in the town and in the tombs.

Discoveries at Tell el Amarna

The picture that emerged from the years of excavation was a disturbing one. The site is clearly marked by a series of fourteen boundary stelae cut into the faces of the cliffs on both east and west banks. These huge carvings on the cliff faces, which marked the limits of the new city, had been made in the first year Akhenaten had visited and chosen the site, and clearly showed that he and his family had moved in only twelve months later. Although most of the walls had been razed to the ground, it was found that the plaster foundations of the buildings had been hastily laid on sand, rather than on bedrock. Much more information came from the tombs of the nobles, cut into the cliffs at the back of the eastern plain. Carved reliefs on their walls, though badly damaged, showed exactly how the city had looked in its heyday. Many fragmentary objects from the city had inscriptions showing the names of the royal family, as had been expected. Most common were the names of the king, who as we've seen changed his name from Amenhotep IV to Akhenaten. It is instructive to realise, though that it was his birth name that he changed and for most of his reign he was called by his throne name, Neferkheprure Waenre. The foreign office records – baked clay tablets found within the city – showed that this, the name Egyptians would have known him by, was pronounced Niphuria. Names of his Great Royal Wife, Nefertiti, also appeared in many inscriptions. When her husband changed his name, she changed hers, to Nefernefruaten Mery Waenre, this being the name by which she was actually known within the city. It could also now be established that they had had six daughters, Meritaten, Meketaten, Ankhesenpaaten, Nefernefruaten, Nefernefrure and Setepenre, all referred to in inscriptions as 'his beloved, of his own body'. Stones from buildings in the city were eventually found. They had been used as rubble foundations and wall infill within the buildings of Horemheb, on the site of the city of Ashmunein, opposite. On these the six girls were seen everywhere accompanying their parents, yet of a son there was no sign. Could Tutankhamen, Akhenaten's successor, have been his child?

During the 1913–14 German excavation, the workshop of the sculptor Tuthmosis, who carved statues for the royal family in the city, had been found. It seemed to have been simply abandoned at some point; the artist had apparently just walked out, leaving behind several masterpieces, including two fine busts. These, although unnamed, were identified as Nefertiti on the grounds of the distinctive tall, flat-topped crown she habitually wore. The public who saw them were astounded by the great beauty of this queen. She was even compared with Helen of Troy. At the same time comparisons were made with her husband, who was consistently depicted as deformed, with elongated skull, long chin, fleshy lips, a pendulous belly, fat thighs and spindly limbs. Scholars and public alike speculated what power it was that had drawn together such a beautiful woman and such an ugly spouse, even though he was King of Egypt.

More disturbing evidence of Smenkhkare also started to emerge. This young man's name turned up regularly in the later years of Akhenaten's reign. The discovery of a group of inscriptions proved that in Akhenaten's year 12, Nefertiti disappeared from central Tell el Amarna. The disappearance of the Queen was horrifying even to the scholars excavating the site. In the years before her disappearance, never had a queen occupied such a prominent place on the state scene as Nefertiti did. Pictures from tombs in Tell el Amarna show the young royal couple in frank and open embraces, even cuddling openly in the streets, unlike their stiff and formalised ancestors who were so terrifying that even courtiers summoned into their presence used to tremble from the experience. Inscriptions suggested that Nefertiti had not simply left but had been thrown out of the palace. As her name was found in the Northern Palace (see map on page 194), it was inferred that she fled there and died from a broken heart. In the meantime, there appeared everywhere the insidious image of Smenkhkare. Images were found of a couple in close embrace after the disappearance of Nefertiti in year 12. A disquieting picture began to emerge, implying that Akhenaten had rejected Nefertiti in favour of a male lover – none other than Smenkhkare. Since Tutankhamen was not included among the children of Akhenaten and Nefertiti, it was a simple step to link Smenkhkare and Tutankhamen. With no positive evidence to support the idea, it was suggested that they were brothers.

Further excavation work in the royal tomb at Tell el Amarna showed it comprised two main corridors, one leading off the other. Side rooms and chambers bore carved reliefs, many of which had been deliberately hacked out. One scene showed a disturbing and harrowing event. Dated around the year 12 of Akhenaten's reign it showed a bier holding the body of the second royal daughter, Meketaten, and her utterly grief-stricken parents clinging together while they wept over their loss. The courtiers shown alongside were no less shocked, with arms flung around each other. Never before had such a private scene been depicted in Egypt.

Meanwhile, the search for evidence for Tutankhamen proved increasingly successful. Fragments were found bearing the name Neb-kheprure or Tutankhaten, his first name, together with dates from the first two years of his reign. But after that date, there was nothing. With the disappearance of Tutankhamen around his second year, the city seemed simply to have died.

Evidence was now beginning to pile up, and even in the minds of scholarly Egyptologists sinister events seemed to be indicated. The trial and imprisonment of Oscar Wilde in 1895 had brought homosexuality some way into the public consciousness. So some of the emerging details seemed less puzzling and a tale of dark passion on the banks of the Nile began to unfold, spiced with hints of murder triggered by homosexuality and madness – a tale with young Tutankhaten right at its centre.

More evidence from Luxor

In the temple of Karnak, alongside the third pylon, which was the great gateway to the temples and was built by Amenhotep III, a broken stela relates the sad and sorry tale of Egypt at the time of Tutankhamen's coronation. Called today the Restoration Stela, this stone stands almost unseen in a corner of the Cairo Museum. On it, Tutankhamen's name has been overcarved by Horemheb after the latter's accession at the end of the Eighteenth Dynasty. It reads:

> His Majesty was crowned King, the temples of the deities from Elephant-
> ine down to the marshes in the Delta had fallen into decay, their
> sanctuaries were deserted and had become ruins, overgrown with weeds.
> Their chapels were as if they had never been while their processional

routes served as footpaths. The land was turned upside down and the gods had turned their backs on the entire land ... If one prostrated oneself before a god to ask a favour, god did not respond ... But after many days My Majesty arose upon the throne of his father and ruled over the territory of Horus, both the Black Land and the Red Land being under his control.

The stela says openly that it was Tutankhamen who had restored the old gods after the chaos of the Amarna period. Inscriptions in the temple at Luxor confirmed this. Lightly carved reliefs on the walls of the tall colonnade depict Tutankhamen's revival of the Opet festival.

This festival was beloved in Luxor, and centred around the gods Amun and Mut. In the north of the town, deep in the temple of Karnak, dwelt the statue of Amun, the local god of Luxor. About half a mile south from the outer walls of Karnak there stood a second temple, the home of Amun's wife and divine consort, the goddess Mut. Here she stood most of the year in the silence and darkness, which were interrupted only by the daily ministrations of the servants of her cult. The divine couple had a child, the godling Khons. But how, reasoned the logical minds of the ancient Egyptians, could Khons exist at all if the parents never met? So once a year, to great ceremony and accompanied by free food and drink issued by Karnak temple over a period of several days, the two statues of the divinities, enclosed within the cabins of boat-shaped shrines, were carried south to Luxor temple for their *opet*, or honeymoon. After some days spent together in the privacy of the sanctuary, they would be removed and carried 'home' again. Nine months later, the statue of Mut would once more emerge, to be carried into her nearby birthing house, or *mammisi*, there to give symbolic birth to Khons.

The Opet festival was the highlight of the year for the people of Luxor. The loss of it during the Amarna period must have been sorely felt by the local people. The renewal of the ceremony by the young Tutankhaten must have been warmly welcomed and thought to signify a full return to the old religion of Amen, and the demise of worship of the Aten.

Years had passed, and, by 1922, putting together all the bits of evidence was yielding more data about Tutankhamen. But who exactly was he? Why was he never pictured in his youth? The interest in this king increased, although it was actually Akhenaten who began to take centre stage. More than anyone, Howard Carter became increasingly convinced that the tomb of Tutankhamen might still be found and would certainly, even if robbed, add to the fund of information. But nothing significant could be expected. After all, intact tombs were not supposed to exist.

Carter's teamwork with Carnarvon since 1907 had been a success archaeologically, but had hardly glamorised them in the eyes of the public. In 1912, the two published an account of their work together so far, in *Five Years' Exploration at Thebes*. In August of that year, the two men holidayed together in Europe, and on their return were offered a concession to dig in the Nile Delta. They visited the proposed site but did not find it to their liking. Carter's hopes were still centred on the Valley of the Kings. On their return home, Carter seems to have persuaded Carnarvon to apply again for the concession to dig in the Valley. But it was to no avail. In 1913 Davies managed to renew his concession. Then, suddenly and quite unexpectedly a few weeks later, Davies changed his mind and gave up the concession, saying that there was, in his opinion, nothing left to find in the Valley.

Carter, as we know, was convinced Davies was wrong. Even though others tried to persuade Carnarvon that the work would be a waste of his money, Carter persisted. In late 1913, the two men heard that they had at last been given the licence they had chased for so long. Carter immediately started work – and almost as immediately, Britain declared war. Carnarvon rushed home to Highclere Castle, which his wife had turned into a convalescent home for wounded officers. It seemed that his partnership with Carter was doomed. Carter was at least financially secure, however, largely thanks to his trade in antiquities, and he had little intention of returning to Britain. Instead he volunteered for war works in North Africa. To this day, it is unclear what part he played in the war effort. To those who asked he claimed that he was 'King Messenger', an official servant of the War Department entrusted with the most secret messages. However, he certainly never officially belonged to this élite corps of men. It is probable that he was used for a short time to convey messages, especially given his knowledge of the people, terrain and language, but once again his irascible temper intervened and he was dismissed from war service of any kind in 1915.

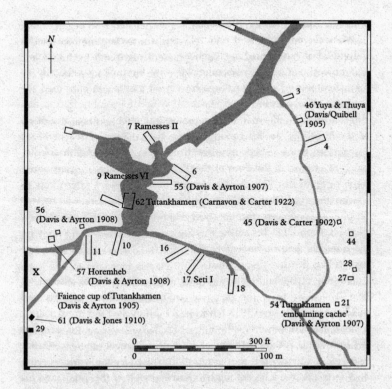

The Valley of the Kings.

Over the following season, Carter returned to dig in the Valley. He made several discoveries which promised to be exciting but then petered out. While most of the world was embroiled in war, and with no tourists in Luxor, tomb robberies started to increase and Carter was again involved in local brawls over sites. On one occasion he intervened in a fight between two rival groups of tomb robbers. Carter was taken by one of the groups to the top of the Valley of the Kings, where he was shown a new tomb. He took control of digging and sent in gangs of men to explore further, but they were overcome so often by the lack of air towards the lower levels that the bottom of the tomb had to be left unexplored. It was probably the tomb of Hatshepsut, although a lower chamber contained the sarcophagi of both her and her father Tuthmosis I.

Whatever might be said about Carter, it is certain that he was an individual of exceptional intelligence – some might say even genius – and powerful intuitive reasoning. He saw Egyptology primarily as forensic detective work, and was convinced that if you examined the evidence closely and applied reason, it would inexorably lead to one single answer. In this manner, through examination of maps and plans of the Valley of the Kings, and noting the position of the previous discoveries, he came back time and time again to that small triangular patch of ground in the floor of the Valley of the Kings in front of the tomb of Ramesses VI (see plan above). In early 1913, Carter wrote to Carnarvon suggesting that they explore this patch, saying that he was absolutely convinced that this was where the tomb of Tutankhamen might be found. His reasoning was logical, sound and based purely on his research. And in November 1917, Carter at last got his wish and moved into the unexplored area.

Nothing in the entire story of Tutankhamen is quite as it seems at first. The clearing of the patch of ground took many months and yielded very little until 1919 when, as the pit in the floor grew deeper, a small cache of jars from the Ramesside period was found. Then, at the foot of the pit, the remains of a small settlement emerged. Carter was able to identify this as a group of huts used by the workmen who had decorated the adjacent tomb of Ramesses VI. At this point, and for quite inexplicable reasons, Carter changed his mind and decided to close up the site and move elsewhere. Various writers have attributed this sudden change of heart to Carter's disappointment at finding so little, or perhaps to Carnarvon's insistence that they should try elsewhere. In a diary, Carter himself said, 'I was still hopeful, but we decided to leave this particular area until, by making an early start in the autumn, we could accomplish it without inconvenience to visitors.' He was to use this reason also to others, suggesting that the work was interfering with the passage of visitors into the tomb of Ramesses VI, although the Antiquities Organisation has always strongly denied that they asked Carter to leave the spot. In fact, Carter had interfered little with the passage of tourists to the tomb and, far from backfilling the hole, continued to work at the site. Photographs of the site taken in 1920 show that a retaining wall about twelve feet high, which held up the sand at the entrance to the tomb of Ramesses

VI, was in the process of being constructed. It was probably finished by 1921.

The matter of the wall is intriguing (see photo overleaf). Carter knew there was little apparent chance of success anywhere in the Valley, but digging the pit had proved two things. The Ramesside cache of pots found there proved that the spot had not been touched by any other excavator in modern times, and presumably since Pharaonic times. Secondly, it showed that the ground *below* the workmen's huts could not have been touched since the Twentieth Dynasty – about two centuries after Tutankhamen. If there was anything there to do with Tutankhamen, it had to lie *under* the huts. Carter was an outstanding excavator. It is hard to believe that he would have given up an excellent chance of finding something simply to move elsewhere unless he had been ordered to leave – and there is no suggestion that that had happened. The logical thing to have done would have been to investigate underneath the huts. He never gave any indication that he had: but there are strong clues to suggest that that is precisely what happened.

Did Carter take a look underneath the huts, realise that there *was* something there and deliberately cover it up and move away? It is intriguing to note the position of that wall. It was built before the tomb's existence was even suspected, to hold back the sand so that visitors entering the tomb of Ramesses VI could do so safely. News film and photographs, however, show that when the famous tomb was discovered, in 1922, the retaining wall had been built precisely against two sides of the tomb entrance and the staircase that lead down into the tomb. The mathematical odds of constructing a wall that happened, by chance, to fall in exactly the right place must be astronomical. But that is what seems to have happened. The adjacent supporting wall was not built yards to one side of the tomb's entrance, nor yet over the top of it, but exactly in the right place for the tomb to be entered, two years later.

So perhaps Carter did dig down below the workmen's huts, and realised that there was something there. If that is the case, why then abandon the site? By 1919, the relationship between Carter and Carnarvon's family was not running as smoothly as might have been expected. Lady Evelyn, the daughter of Lord Carnarvon who had accompanied him on his first trip to Egypt, was now a beautiful

The entrance to Tutankhamen's tomb, photographed straight after the discovery in 1922, shows clearly the supporting walls built in earlier years by Carter to hold back sand from the entrance to the tomb of Ramesses VI. Could they really have been built in this position by accident?

eighteen-year-old as passionately fond of Egypt as her father was. She would regularly accompany her father on trips, and it is clear that Carter had a soft spot for the girl, as she certainly had for this seemingly exciting older man. On many occasions Carter would encourage her to dig out objects that he located 'with her own hands'. But her family could never risk the relationship between them developing into something more. Lady Evelyn was one of Britain's foremost debutantes, and as such was assured of a wealthy and influential match. The constant companionship of her father and Carter meant that Evelyn was often herself in Carter's company, an occurrence she clearly relished. The family would have preferred to keep them further apart. At the same time, work in Egypt was costing the Carnarvon family huge sums of money. It was not, as many books have implied, that their money was running out. It was rather that the situation as a whole was giving everyone involved headaches. Carter could see this clearly, and as a man of intelligence could foresee the day when his partner would decide to withdraw his patronage. Perhaps if he had something positive to offer when that time came . . .

If, as the evidence suggests, Carter knew that something lay beneath the workmen's huts, this would logically account for what followed. In October 1922 Carter was called to Highclere, where Carnarvon told him, reluctantly, that finance was to end forthwith. J. H. Breasted, the first Professor of Egyptology in Chicago and a friend of Carter's, recalled that Carter told him what had happened at the meeting with Carnarvon. Breasted said that Carter had begged Carnarvon to continue for just one last season. So sure was Carter of finding something that he would do it at his own expense, provided that Carnarvon would maintain the concession just a little longer. If, at the end of the season, Carter had found nothing, he would, he said, agree to the concession being handed back. If Carter found something, Carnarvon would reimburse Carter's expenditure to that point. Carnarvon agreed to continue the funding for one more season. But however did Carter persuade the worried Earl that, after all this time, something worthwhile would be found?

Carter returned to Egypt in late October 1922, and at the beginning of November had the workmen digging at the exact spot that he had abandoned three years earlier. Despite his comments that he was leaving the area because of the 'inconvenience to visitors', nothing significant had changed in that respect. But now the time was right for him. And only two days after digging started, on Saturday 3 November, the sound of singing and the clatter of shovels suddenly stopped, and a foreman rushed over to Carter to tell him that a step had been found in the sand just below the level of the workmen's huts.

The story that follows has already enchanted millions of readers for more than seventy years, but it loses nothing in being told again. There is still an electric tingling down the spine as you wait for the next part. Carter had indeed found a tomb. The first step in the sand led to fifteen more, and a door beyond.

But what are the chances of finding a tomb just like that – two days after work commences, and just as all hope of finding anything at all had been virtually abandoned, and after Davies had given up his concession because he believed that the Valley of the Kings was empty of treasure? Just – luck? The hard truth is that archaeology does not yield up her secrets easily, nor just for the asking, but requires years of long and painful devotion. Despite what the story may imply, you cannot simply pick up a spade in Egypt and two days later find a tomb. There was far more to it than that. Indeed, in the years of lecture tours that followed, Carter's own version of what really happened varied from time to time. It is probable that the truth will never be known.

The discovery of any tomb could be Carter's assurance of continuing financial support. The final proof that he knew of the tomb's existence already is in what happened next. Carter ordered the first step to be cleared and found a second below it. Two days later, he had cleared to the twelfth step out of sixteen, and uncovered the top of a mud-brick sealed door. The top left-hand corner of the door had been broken open and resealed at some point in the past. The signs were bad. Carter, as every Egyptologist would immediately recognise, had found a robbed tomb. The fact that it had been resealed meant nothing. Beyond the door he could only expect chaos and few material finds. The situation was similar to many other discoveries in the area over the years. But strangely, Carter did not give orders to his men to clear the final steps and the lower part of the door. He was usually a careful worker, and this apparent slovenliness must have been deliberate. The seals on the bottom part of the door gave the name of the owner. It all suggests that he did not *want* either to know whose the tomb was, nor to see if the bottom of the door had also been broken into. All he wanted was a tomb – and he wanted Carnarvon there when he uncovered the entrance in order to re-enthuse him and ensure continued patronage. Again, rather curiously, he ordered the staircase backfilled and sent his famous encoded telegram off to Carnarvon; 'AT LAST HAVE MADE WONDERFUL DISCOVERY IN VALLEY – A MAGNIFICENT TOMB WITH SEALS INTACT; RECOVERED SAME FOR YOUR ARRIVAL. CONGRATULATIONS, CARTER.'

The words show exactly what Carter's intentions were. Carter surely knew full well, from the broken and resealed door, that it was not a 'magnificent' tomb at all; but the clear implication of the telegram was that he had found an undisturbed royal tomb. Carter knew that the tomb had been entered at some time. And, since he did not know who the owner was, it may not even have been royal. Yet what was more likely to excite the renewed interest of a jaded partner than the possibility of a 'magnificent discovery'? Even if the tomb had proved later to be empty of all but a few paltry and broken objects, even if it proved not to be royal – the drama of the arrival and reading of the telegram at Highclere; the panic packing of Lord Carnarvon and Lady Evelyn's belongings; the excited, sleepless nights spent discussing what the tomb might possibly hold on the long journey to Egypt – none of this would ever be forgotten. And the intelligent Carter could assure himself of continued backing for many years to come. If nothing else, he was playing a well-calculated hand.

Lord Carnarvon and his daughter arrived at Luxor station on 23 November 1922, and were met with great ceremony by Carter and the Governor of the Province of Qena. Carter had ordered a lot of equipment to be made and delivered in the meantime, ready for use in clearing the tomb when the Carnarvons arrived, even though at that point he had no idea if anything at all might be found. It all, however, contributed to the tense atmosphere of anticipation.

After leaving their luggage at Carter's house on the west bank, the group made its way quickly to the Valley and digging began again, this time in earnest. By early the following day, the lower part of the first door was uncovered and now, for the first time, the royal seal with the name Nebkheprure could be seen. Remember that Tomb 55 had also been found with Tutankhamen's seal on the door, so the seal on this door was still no proof that this was the King's tomb, but simply showed a link between the entombed person and the

Lord Carnarvon and Lady Evelyn Herbert were driven from Luxor railway station to meet Carter in an Egyptian government automobile in 1922, after arriving in Egypt, summoned by Carter's dramatic telegram announcing the discovery of the royal tomb.

boy-King. Finally, the outside mud-brick door was broken down. Beyond it, a rubble-filled passage was seen, although behind the ancient repair to the door a narrow entry, large enough for a person to crawl through, could clearly be seen. The robbers, then, had evidently penetrated the tomb itself. At once, in the rubble, sherds of broken material containing the names of many kings of the period were discovered, from Tuthmosis III down to Smenkhkare and Tutankhamen himself. Once more, all the signs pointed to this being yet another pillaged tomb. Carter revealed little of his feelings or expectations, except that from 24 November he slept at the tomb for the following few nights to ensure that no one crawled through the robbers' hole. This itself implies that, despite everything, he was pinning his hopes on finding something important.

By midday on Sunday 26 November, the sloping, rubble-filled passage had been swept clear and a second mud-brick plastered doorway revealed. Since the dimensions of the outside door had been taken, a metal security door had been ordered: this would fit into place once the second door was broken down. Late in the afternoon, although the time is not precisely recorded, the moment finally came. Carter slowly and carefully knocked a hole in the door and lifted up a candle to the hole. At first it guttered and provided no light as the air within rushed out. Even then, it was hard to see much. 'Lord Carnarvon said to me, "Can you see anything?" I replied to him, "Yes! It's wonderful!"' (The first words vary, depending on the account you read.) From the official records it seems that only Carter, Carnarvon and Lady Evelyn saw the tomb, although other sources suggest there were others there with them at the time. Later in the day Carter recorded, 'He advised the Chief Inspector of the Antiquities Department who was with us at the commencement of the opening of the first doorway and asked him to come as soon as possible ... for careful inspection of the extraordinary and pleasing discovery.'

As the hole was gradually widened, the light of the candle was thrown back at them in myriad sparks. 'Details of the room emerged slowly from the mist. Strange animals, statues, and gold – everywhere the glint of gold.' The small group found themselves standing in what was later called the antechamber (see plan on page 101), which was packed from floor to ceiling with objects no mortal man could ever have expected to see in his wildest dreams. Here were chariots in pieces, furniture hitherto only seen in paintings on tomb walls – and everywhere, ominous signs of chaos and disorder. The dusty floor itself maintained eerie footprints of the last people to breathe that very air 3500 years earlier. As Carter later recorded,

As you note the signs of recent life around you – the half-filled bowl of mortar for the door, the blackened lamp, the finger-marks on the freshly painted surface, the farewell garland dropped upon the threshold – you feel it might have been put there yesterday. Time is annihilated by such intimate details as these, and you feel an intruder.

This solemn moment must have seemed to the three to last an age: time itself seemed to stand still, then rock a little on its foundations. But reality has a way of forcing itself upon you, and with the setting sun and the oncoming night, the dazed and bedazzled group must have asked themselves, 'Now what?'

Official accounts of what followed show a cover-up that is now an open secret. The official version shows the three fitting the new door, returning to their rooms and waiting until the following day for the arrival of the inspector before they looked around, as the concession demanded. Yet there was a factor that militated powerfully against such a scenario. They were assured by the evidence of the robbers' hole and the chaos within the chamber that what they were witnessing was a robbed tomb – one only briefly robbed, probably very soon after the burial, then tidied a bit and sealed up again – but still, for all that, a robbed tomb. And under the terms of the concession, while duplicate objects would be handed to the Cairo Museum for them to choose, the bulk of the objects would belong to the tomb's discoverers.

Thus the official version seems unbelievable. These three had, after all, searched for something for a decade, found it, and seen what few had ever seen. Having witnessed these astounding treasures, would it be possible to sleep at all? And indeed, events proved otherwise. Carter, Carnarvon and Lady Evelyn returned to the tomb secretly that night and explored it more fully, even breaking down the foot of the plaster wall between two guardian statues that stood on the right as you entered the antechamber, and dropping down into the burial chamber beyond. As they went, they collected a few items that they could carry with them. Why not? Later, others recalled seeing the objects openly on display in Carter's house. Knowing the relationship between them, no doubt Lady Evelyn was allowed special favour in this secret foray. It has been suggested that she was the first to slide into the burial chamber – and granted that she was slim and lithe, this seems perfectly possible. Within the chamber, the three drew back the bolts on the outer door of the first gilded shrine that protected the dead King's body, and observed that the ancient seals within were unbroken. Thus Carnarvon, for all that has been said, undoubtedly knew that he had found the King secure at last, and even if he never saw the King face to face, at least he could be assured that he had stood within inches of him that first night.

It was only later that the events of that night mattered. At the time there was no guilt involved, no feeling of duplicity or of covering up for something that they had done wrong. So far as the concession was concerned, perhaps they should have waited for the inspector; but that was only a minor thing caused by understandable human frailty.

Moreover, the things that they removed were but the smallest fraction of what remained within. It was only later, after the law had been changed, that the objects they had removed became important.

The following morning, mayhem erupted within hours of the announcement as the news stormed across the world. The first article, written by Carter, appeared in the London *Times* on 30 November 1922 and filled two pages with news of 'the most sensational discovery of this century'. Faced with invasion by the world's media, Carter shut the tomb for a few days and went north to Cairo to buy more equipment. It was during this period that he contacted his friend H. E. Winlock of the Metropolitan Museum of Art and asked for the museum's help – and the loan of it's photographer, Harry Burton. Help was readily agreed.

It has always been a point of some concern that Carter's request was made to an American museum and not to the British Museum. It is still

The royal tomb of Seti II in the Valley of the Kings was used by Carter and Carnarvon (to centre and left) to examine and then pack the objects removed from Tutankhamen's tomb in order to transfer them to Cairo Museum.

unclear why this happened. The Egyptologist Thomas Hoving, in *Tutankhamen – The Untold Story*, his controversial account of the subject, suggested some deal had been made between the excavators and the New York museum. Through this deal, the museum would become the eventual home of the bulk of the treasures. This does seem highly likely, but was scarcely the 'underhand' deal that Hoving implies. After all, the treasures would eventually need a permanent home. The cost of conservation, storage and exhibition would be astronomical. It could be foreseen that the public would be strongly against the pieces 'disappearing' into the hands of a private collector, but would demand access to these unique items. The Carnarvon family would hardly approve of turning Highclere Castle into a public exhibition hall on a huge scale. A large institution, well-endowed and well-equipped with the expertise that would be needed, such as the Metropolitan Museum, would seem an excellent choice.

As a result of the agreement between the museum and the concession holders, the services of outstanding men – from conservators, pathologists and analytic scientists to packagers and removal men – were thus made freely available to Carnarvon and Carter. In the meantime, other Egyptologists worldwide were quick to offer their congratulations and their assistance, including leading British scholars of their day. Despite Hoving's assertions, there was no basis at all to his idea of British ire over the fact that American, rather than British, aid was sought. In all probability, given the scale of the problem now facing Carter, it was a very sensible decision.

Those people who know little of the quiet academic life of archaeologists in general and Egyptologists in particular might imagine that Carter now lived in an aura of joy and delight at his secured immortality. It might be imagined that the discovery of such huge amounts of gold would dominate his thoughts, assuring him of a materially comfortable future. The sale of even one or two items from the Tutankhamen cache would, after all, have enabled him to retire. This idea is far from the truth. Carter found himself in a nightmarish situation. In a letter he wrote:

> The seasonal volume of mail at the Luxor post office was doubled and trebled. The telegraph office was completely buried under a deluge of newspaper dispatches. Tourist shops quickly sold out their stocks of

cameras and films and of books on the history of Egypt. The two leading hotels in Luxor set up tents in their gardens where many guests were fortunate to be accommodated for a single night on army cots.

Under the strain, tempers started to fray.

Imagine finding an object 3500 years old – a linen robe, for instance, or a piece of furniture. Imagine first the joy – and then the trepidation that would quickly follow. Imagine that the piece is going to be given into your charge by the Egyptian government. It is not a gift but a massive responsibility. Is it strong enough to allow you to touch it in the first place? Does the technology exist for it to be preserved? Where should it go for that treatment? How should it be taken there? What materials are needed to save it forever? And, much more to the point, who will pay for it all? The conservation of a single piece of such great age requires hours of skill from highly trained conservators, and such work does not come cheap. A thousand problems spring to mind. Now multiply them – if you can – by several thousand, and you can begin to imagine Carter's problem. The discovery itself had taken but a few minutes; the job in front of him was almost too much for a lifetime, while the cost of looking after it would be incalculable. And all of this had to be carried out in the heat of Egypt and with the full glare of the world's media upon him. The Pathé news of the time, played everywhere in cinemas, showed the people who flocked down to be near the tomb. It was, it recorded, 'like Derby day' with Charleston tunes playing from portable record players while ladies paraded under parasols in the heat. Hundreds of these tourists sent messages down into the tomb to the bedevilled Carter, begging him, cajoling him,

A colourful marquee erected in the Valley of the Kings gives shelter to official visitors during the excavation of Tutankhamen's tomb.

bribing him, pleading with him to be allowed just one little glance within.

It was, in short, anathema to the quiet and careful work of an archaeologist. Today, public relations is a field of expertise of its own. In the 1990s a professional media team would have been put in place within hours to arrange everything – someone would have been brought in to manage materials and staff, others to bring refreshments, sell pictures and souvenirs and, most importantly, to organise media coverage – press releases that could be broadcast simultaneously around the world. Such back-up would have brought Carter some peace and put Egypt at the centre of the world's stage, attracting tourism and money on an unprecedented scale. But in 1922 public relations scarcely existed. Moreover, the Egyptian people were on the brink of revolution against the occupying force – the British, whom Carter represented. Far from being seen as a triumph for Egypt, Carter's find seemed yet another instance of British exploitation. The local people were in no mood to help Carnarvon and Carter. Egyptian public opinion was in favour of taking control of the tomb entirely. In the month after the discovery of the tomb, large numbers of people had rioted openly in the streets, and military control had been imposed.

Now was definitely not the right time to fight for British rights in the matter. What was needed was a soft, diplomatic approach. But sadly this was lacking, and confrontation seemed increasingly inevitable. Pursued relentlessly by the world's press, Carnarvon signed an agreement with the London *Times* in January 1923, giving them exclusive press rights to the Tutankhamen story. Probably the Earl did not fully realise what he had done, although it certainly took a great weight off the shoulders of Carnarvon and Carter at first. Henceforth, they needed only to write material for one single journal which could then be circulated to the others. In reality, the exclusivity of the contract meant that if an Egyptian newspaper in Cairo wanted to find out and publish what was happening in their own land, they had to go through London to do it. It was a totally unsatisfactory situation.

Within two weeks of the agreement, resentment flared up in Egypt as rumours spread like wildfire that when the body of Tutankhamen was found, it would be taken to England and put on public display in Highclere Castle. Carnarvon's effort to deny the rumour in an article in

El Ahram, the leading Egyptian newspaper, only made matters worse. When he said in a letter that 'he had arranged' for the body to remain in Egypt, it only made matters worse – who was Carnarvon to arrange anything with regard to the ultimate destination of an Egyptian king? The relationship between Carter and Carnarvon suffered as a result of all this stress. Colleagues related tales of bitter rows between the two, interspersed with icy hostility. Rows also erupted with the Egyptian government, which now seemed to be following public opinion by insisting that the tomb was as good as intact, and by the spirit, if not the word, of the agreement, everything should remain in Egypt. Some colleagues urged Carnarvon and Carter to give up quietly and sign over the objects voluntarily before feelings got out of control. Many saw this as an argument the two men could never win – but they disagreed, and the arguments continued and increased.

At the start of March 1923, after a massive row, Carter ordered Carnarvon out of his house and told him never to return. Those close to them believed that the argument concerned Lady Evelyn's feelings for Carter. In any event, the following day, having moved into the Winter Palace Hotel on the east bank of Luxor, Carnarvon was bitten on the cheek by a mosquito. He accidentally cut off the top of the bite while shaving shortly afterwards. Infection immediately set in. Carnarvon had never been a well man since his motor accident, and had come to Egypt a convalescent. The problems and rows of this time had left him at a low physical ebb, and the infection spread rapidly. Soon he was diagnosed as having pneumonia.

Hearing of Carnarvon's condition, Carter visited him and the two settled their differences. Carnarvon was now very ill indeed. The rest of his family were called over from England while he transferred, with his daughter, to the Continental Hotel in Cairo. This was before the age of antibiotics, and he sank quickly. At 2 am, on the morning of 5 April 1923, Lord Carnarvon died peacefully with his wife, son and daughter at his bedside.

The following morning rumours abounded of mysterious 'signs' said to have attended the death of the Earl. At the time of his death there was a power cut in Cairo, which Weigall, always prone to explanations redolent of mysticism and spiritualism, exaggerated as 'inexplicable'. For those who know Cairo, even today, over seventy-five years on, power cuts hardly come as a surprise. Neither was there any truth in the rumour that a similar bite was found upon the face of Tutankhamen, when it was eventually revealed.

The problems Carter had had before Carnarvon's death were nothing to what he now faced. It was discovered that Carnarvon's will made no mention of the concession. Since the concession had been granted to Carnarvon and Carter was only his employee, then, on the face of it, the concession reverted to the Egyptian government on Carnarvon's death. This meant that Carter could be regarded as summarily unemployed and apparently had no right whatever to fight the case. While Lady Carnarvon, the major inheritor of her husband's estate, assured Carter that she intended to continue to maintain the concession, it could be by no means assured. Not only would the Antiquities Organisation have to approve the change of name on the concession; the antagonism between Carter and the family, because of Lady Evelyn, had also to be taken into account. What happened next was, naturally, a private family matter, but Lady Evelyn left Egypt for good after her father's death. Soon after arriving home from Egypt she was married to Sir Edward Brogrove, a prominent Member of Parliament, and with her reputation intact and secure, in later years she and her husband often welcomed Carter to their home as a guest.

Carter resumed work later in 1923, but by then the Egyptian government was restricting access to the tomb, sending Carter lists of who must and must not be permitted entry. Carter's always short temper became almost impossible, although those who knew him admired the way he forged on, despite the problems he faced on every side. In February 1924, Egyptian officials demanded that their instructions be followed to the letter, no matter how tiresome they might seem.

In the tomb, Carter had already officially broken down the wall to the burial chamber. He had, of course, secretly been into the chamber before, so he knew that it contained a massive wooden shrine, like a huge rectangular box, heavily plated with gold and covered with a blue linen pall studded with gold rosettes. It had two doors at one end, bolted and with mud seals. He organised the lighting at the official opening to give the most dramatic effect and was gratified by the stunned gasps of awe that went up as the wall of gold within became visible to the audience for the first time. In the days that followed, the blue linen sheet was pulled back and work commenced on dismantling the shrine, which now turned out to be the outermost of four, one within the other.

The rope ties which were bound around the entrance doors to the second, third and fourth shrines, with mud seals attached, were also intact. It was now certain that Tutankhamen's body lay undisturbed. Within the fourth and smallest gilded shrine there lay a granite sarcophagus, the rectangular stone chest that invariably contained the anthropoid coffin and, within that, the body of the King himself. Finally, on 12 February 1924, the lid of the sarcophagus was lifted to reveal a gilded coffin within. All those who witnessed the event testified to the breath-stopping feelings that the moment aroused in them. The lid of the coffin was removed and it could now be seen that there was a second coffin inside. This was covered by a blackened linen shroud overlaid with wreaths of flowers, almost as fresh as the day on which they had been placed on the coffin thousands of years previously. This second inner coffin fitted tightly within the outer coffin – so tightly that not even a fingertip could be inserted between them. The coffins were very deep. Carter took the decision to separate the two by lowering the outer one while raising and suspending the inner one. Although he had little choice in the matter, since the two coffins were such a good fit, it must have been a moment of near-terror as he screwed a series of ringed bolts into the wood of the second coffin, threaded ropes through them, slung them over a pulley suspended above the sarcophagus and pulled on the ropes. Would the ancient wood into which the bolts were screwed hold – or would they rip out, destroying part of this unique find? Luckily the bolts held, despite the excessively heavy weight they were asked to support. As the second coffin rose above the outer one, planks of wood were slipped between them and the inner coffin, now part suspended and part maintained on the ancient wood of the outer coffin, hung ready to be opened and examined. As this was the very first time that such a royal burial had been found, no one knew how many more coffins might be found within the second coffin.

The following day, newspaper reporters, editors and their wives had been invited by Carter to enter the tomb to witness the now uncovered coffins. But on the morning of the event, Carter received a letter forbidding access to all women and the families of the visitors. It was a reasonable request for the Egyptian authorities to make. Under Islamic law, it is forbidden for a woman or child to enter into the actual burial place of any man. In Egypt to this very day, although there are many family tombs still in use, it is customary always for men and women to be buried in separate vaults; and at the time of burial, when the body is being placed in the vault, only adults of the same sex may enter the burial chamber. So as far as Egyptian officials were concerned, this was a gentle reminder of what was to them a well-understood practice. But for Carter it was the final straw. His anger finally burst and within hours of receiving the letter, he posted a notice outside the tomb announcing that he was shutting it down until further notice, with immediate effect. He sent a telegram to *The Times* requesting them to 'strongly attack Egyptian authorities'.

Carter then made his way to Cairo, where he started legal proceedings to get full ownership of the tomb and the objects in it established once and for all. Colleagues advised him to drop the case, but it was to no avail. On 22 February the Egyptian authorities arrived at the tomb, read out in public Carter's letter saying that he had ceased all work on the tomb, cut off his locks and replaced them with their own. The Egyptian government now officially took over the tomb. At this point they considered that Carter had given up all right to work there in the future, and tried to appoint other Egyptologists to take up the work. But to a man they refused, not so much to back Carter, but because the work would tie up a large part of their future careers, and to little end, since the tomb would always be remembered as the discovery of Carnarvon and Carter. In any event, as far as the authorities were concerned, the concession was finally at an end. If Carter were ever to return, they would have to draw up a new agreement under their own terms.

Carter did not see things in the same light. In his opinion the concession still stood; only he was now insisting that before he agreed to return to work he would have to have an undertaking from the Egyptian authorities that they would stop meddling in his affairs but would leave him in peace to get on with the work as he saw fit. As a result, he served the Egyptian government with notice to quit the tomb two days later.

The case came to court in Cairo on 24 March 1924. It was chaotic, and the judge's job was an unenviable one. Egypt's civil system was still largely controlled by the British, so to an extent it would have been easy to understand if he had found in Carter's favour. But Egyptian nationalism had taken up the case of Tutankhamen's tomb as their own, and a decision in Carter's favour would have seemed like a public blow against Egypt itself. The judge could not win whatever way the case went. He clearly decided to be as painstakingly fair as it was possible to be and went to great lengths to have every small point made very clear to everyone listening. Crowds gathered outside awaiting the verdict, seeing the case as a further attempt by the British to humiliate them and deprive them of what were their own belongings – namely, the body and material goods of one of their own kings. At a midway point in the trial, those present say that the judge seemed ready to find in Carter's favour, but suddenly pointed out the obvious flaw in his case. Had not Carter voluntarily given up his rights to the tomb when he walked out and posted the notice on the door? Carter's counsel argued this was not the case. 'Mr Carter had been forced out by the Egyptians acting like thugs and bandits.'

The statement was inexcusable. The judge found against Carter and the Carnarvon estate. In September 1924 the Carnarvon family was required to sign a document in which they gave up all automatic claim to objects from the tomb under the terms of the previous concession, although privately they hoped that mediators would eventually see fit to reconsider the situation and that they might receive some few objects as gifts in return for the expenditure they had undergone in its discovery. The Dowager Lady Carnarvon, Almina, was so disgusted by the whole affair that, after following her late husband's request to sell off his Egyptian collection to the Metropolitan Museum for a fraction of its true value, she would not even allow the word 'Egypt' ever to be spoken within the family again, and both her son and grandson were well aware of the consequences should they ever try to ask about the exploits of the Fifth Earl in front of her.

In January 1925, after much negotiation, a jaded and disillusioned Carter was finally invited to return to the tomb to finish the work of emptying it. But before his readmittance, the Egyptian government insisted that a full and thorough inspection of all the objects and Carter's record cards should be carried out by its men to make sure that everything was in order and every piece accounted for. And at first, everything seemed fine, until someone took it upon themselves to check Carter's personal possessions. To everyone's horror, a finely painted wooden head of Tutankhamen arising from a lotus flower was

The modern procession, bearing the funerary goods of the King Tutankhamen, wends its way through the Valley of the Kings towards the Nile and ships to bear them north to Cairo. The procession uncannily mirrors what must have been seen 3500 years before, as the goods were first carried into the Valley for burial.

found in an empty wine-case and no record card could be found for it. The authorities approached Carter. He apologised, saying that it was an oversight. Whatever the truth of the matter, the authorities were keen for Carter to return and finish the job, so this incident was quickly smoothed over.

On 25 January Carter once more began work in the tomb. But everything was different now. The dream had turned sour. Carter faced years of arduous work knowing that there was no reward at the end. When the last object was finally carried off to the Cairo Museum and the tomb was swept clean ahead of allowing tourists to enter, he left Egypt, never to return. To his death, Carter remained embittered, convinced that he had been somehow cheated. It was said that in his last days he swore to those who knew him that he had worked out the location of the tomb of Alexander – but that he would go to his grave without telling anyone his secret.

When Carter had started his venture in 1922, he could never have anticipated the scale of what he was going to find, nor the cost it would impose on him personally. As an Egyptologist, Carter had experienced his 'day of days' when the door to the antechamber was opened, and no one could ever take that away from him. Despite all the problems that he had faced on a personal level, the lack of knowledge about Tutankhamen before the tomb was found meant that from an intellectual and academic perspective, the experience must have all seemed very exciting. Carter must have felt that from the material in the tomb he would now be able to add much more to the known history of the period through the accounts of a royal eye-witness to the events of Akhenaten's reign. He may have hoped to find out more about the terrible state of Egypt at that time, as related on the Restoration Stela. For instance, particular gifts found in the tomb might show the people's gratitude to Tutankhamen for restoring the old religion of Amen and freeing them from the heretic Akhenaten. More importantly, it should now have been possible to find out more about the mysterious events surrounding Tutankhamen's life. Certainly there would be details about his parentage, and, from an examination of his mummy, at last it would be possible to know how he had died.

For Carter, the ultimate tragedy was not the long and bitter fight for the tomb, nor the years of tribulations he had to undergo, first with the political problems and then with emptying it. The real tragedy was that the tomb seemed to contain no answers at all. By the time the last speck of dust was swept away, there was no obvious answer to any of the questions. Tutankhamen remained a complete enigma. As Carter wrote later, 'Perhaps the most notable thing about Tutankhamen was that he died.' Seventy-five years later, the search goes on.

CHAPTER THREE

The Accepted Story

As in any science, it is vital for an archaeologist always to be as objective as possible. Such a person should in theory expect to excavate a site armed not only with knowledge, but with a mind free from expectation. The practice is harder than the theory, though. The problem with the ideal lies with human nature. Archaeologists are drawn to their work in the first place not for love of money – for there is little in the field – nor for the hope of immortality or glory, but rather from a love of romance and adventure. Today, many more people than in the past can share some of these feelings when they escape their humdrum everyday existence by entering into the world of computer games or Hollywood films. The adventures of such fictitious characters as Indiana Jones, or Lara Croft of Tomb Raider fame, enable ordinary people to be drawn into a new world of excitement, far from the grey world around them. These characters affect the public image of what an archaeologist, or an Egyptologist, actually does. Many times I have been asked by young children whom I am trying to introduce to ancient Egypt how often I have had to run to escape from rolling balls of stone in tomb corridors.

Archaeologists have to undergo years of rigorous training before they can practise competently in the field, and the training is frequently repetitive, if not boring, to many outsiders. But archaeologists are only human, and it is romance and excitement that draw us into the field. This is not the expectation of finding a chamber filled with gold. Rather, there is a quieter magic for us, of finding a fingerprint embedded in a clay pot and understanding that the last hand to touch it was of someone who has been dead for over 3000 years; or seeing a footprint in the sand on the floor of a chamber not entered for thousands of years. Imagine entering such a place and breathing the very air that had been sealed up there since long-forgotten times!

Inside all of us there is a desire to know, to find answers to the eternal questions about our origins and our destiny. Different people look for the answers in different places. Archaeologists seek to find answers in the distant past by looking at the lives of those who died many hundreds of years ago. The examples of those who came before entice us. Curiosity first drives us into the field, then leads us into the silent and lonely world of isolated study through which we enter, in our minds, another world, another time, a place where there is no stress and nothing ever changes. We start, after a time, to identify increasingly with the shades of the people we study. It is a short step from that to feeling that we actually 'know' these people, and to empathising with their very feelings. It is a dangerous position, for by this identification we lose objectivity.

To start to understand exactly what happened in a particular place long ago, we must have a mind free from preconceptions. Like a pathologist examining a cadaver, for example, we must first list exactly what we find, and then, and only then, interpret those findings. A pathologist who believes from the start that the person being studied was murdered tends, even subconsciously, to look for the proof needed; and, in looking for the proof, they will undoubtedly find it – but perhaps by 'not noticing' things that do not fit. It is not deliberate; it is just human nature to try to prove what you believe.

An archaeologist must be a pathologist of time. First the material must be found, either on a site or perhaps even in a museum collection where it already lies. Then it must be examined closely and studied in great depth. Only then should the results be published. Accurate publication is vital, for it is this that everyone else can access and study. The published report of the professional can then be added to what else is known to form new ideas and theories. Whatever the new theory presented, it is vital that the professional basis is sound. Publication is the cornerstone of archaeology, and a vital way of preserving excavated sites. Archaeology is, by definition, destructive.

When a site is excavated, the layers are removed; after examination, and once removed, they are lost forever. The excavator is distinguished from the tomb robber only by their publication of their discoveries.

The excavation site is a busy, demanding environment. Archaeologists in charge of excavating a site may be assisted by several students, all demanding guidance and trying to draw on their expertise. They may have several colleagues in the field, but their specialisms will require that work progresses differently from what they may want. Workmen will be constantly demanding the archaeologist's attention in different areas at the same time. It is not the place for immediate evaluation of material. What date is this pot? What does this inscription say? It is simply not possible for the excavator to interpret the material on the spot; that will require time and consideration. It is vital to record and photograph everything first – and record the exact location of every tiny fragment. Even a tiny potsherd, which may seem of no possible interest at the time, may take upon itself a whole new importance several years later, as knowledge progresses. And then it is vital that the student of the future should know exactly in what position and what context the fragment was found, and should have maps, plans and photographs taken at the time of excavation to tell all that he or she needs to know.

Only later, after the problems of the site have been forgotten and peace and quiet once more reign, can the calm, reasoned analysis of excavated material take place. The excavation report that starts the ball rolling only records, never analyses. But every little piece found has a story to tell. Only later will historians be able to put together all the reports to try to understand what really happened. Eye-witness accounts, or primary sources, can be heavily biased. Secondary sources, the quiet, reasoned analysis of events by someone with all the facts at his or her disposal, can be far more revealing of the truth – if, of course, such a thing ever existed in history.

The further back in time we tread, the more problematical the evidence and the more complex the analysis of it. In the case of Tutankhamen, you can buy any two books on the subject, and they will be widely contradictory. People often ask me, in complete bewilderment, which account they should believe. It is hard to explain that in the matter of history – which is, by definition, a review of factual events

– there can be wide differences in the way in which those facts are presented. It is vital, however, that all the facts are known and are correct before any discussion or interpretation can take place. The allure of Egyptology in general, and Tutankhamen's gold in particular, has led many people into the field with little knowledge of its background and an inability either to read or to understand the original material for themselves. They must often rely on the translations of others.

I regard my field as a science. On a certain day, the first stone of a pyramid was laid. On a certain day, the last one was laid. If I examine and interpret the evidence correctly, then I should be able to establish these dates; if I misinterpret the evidence, at some point I shall discover something that will prove that my lines of research are wrong – the 'facts' will not fit. As a scientist, I should then be able to reassess my entire hypothesis. This is the basis of all science. But while with other fields it would never be acceptable for unspecialised views to be taken seriously, for some inexplicable reason, in Egyptology the views of all are given equal footing. It would not be acceptable for someone, for example, to present a TV programme saying, 'I am not a neurosurgeon, but this is how I think brain surgery should be carried out.' Why, then, should it be possible for someone to say, 'I am not an Egyptologist but this is how I think mummies were made'?

The gold of Tutankhamen has overwhelmed everyone who has studied it. Many have the impossible dream of finding an intact tomb, as Carter did. But for the professional Egyptologist, the gold itself is of little interest. Most of us would exchange all Tutankhamen's gold for one simple papyrus that told us the truth of what happened during his life, and death. But the gold, and the mystery, encourage speculation. Some of this is wild. Foreign origins have been suggested for the personages of the period – some sources say Akhenaten was Moses, and Queen Tiye's father, Yuya, was Joseph from the Book of Genesis, that Queen Nefertiti was a foreigner who brought a strange religion with her from abroad that perverted those around her; that Tutankhamen's tomb was cursed with written inscriptions that the professionals have sought to 'cover up'; that Tutankhamen was in some way 'odd' to be buried with so much gold and so had some mysterious 'secret'; that his body was 'protected' by magic, radioactivity, force-fields, and so on and that Tutankhamen was mysteriously murdered.

All of this has succeeded only in obscuring the truth, rather than letting it out. Yet these theories seem, to some, more exciting than the truth. So the 'conspiracy theory' books multiply while the historical facts often lie unexamined.

The emptying of Tutankhamen's tomb took Carter more than ten years from the date of its discovery. After the seemingly endless political wrangling, he had finally re-entered the tomb in 1927, and he left it empty in 1932. As soon as the objects from the tomb were put on display, members of the public joined the specialists in asking who Tutankhamen was, what his life was like, how he died and why his tomb had been forgotten. Archaeologists tried to answer their questions as fully as they could from the little evidence that was available at the time. And quite by chance, in 1923, excavation in Tell el Amarna seemed to add the final piece of the jigsaw.

Under pressure for answers, an official story was published, and although reinterpreted as years went by, this version is still generally accepted as the truth. The story that was published is very disturbing. In Part Two I shall re-examine this story bit by bit and, using the historical evidence, I shall demonstrate what I think of the interpretation of the material in it. But first, let me tell you the story as it is generally told, complete with all its strange inconsistencies.

The familiar story

Tutankhamen became King of Egypt around 1334 BC during the high point of the Eighteenth Dynasty (see Chapter 1). His predecessor on the throne was Smenkhkare, a ruler of uncertain origins who ruled very briefly, perhaps only for a few months. Before him, the throne was occupied for seventeen years by Akhenaten, born Amenhotep, one of the strangest characters in the whole of Egyptian history. In order to understand who Tutankhamen was and how and why he acted as he did, it is necessary to examine his birth and childhood.

Akhenaten was the second son of Amenhotep III, a man who ruled Egypt when its status in the world of the eastern Mediterranean was at its highest point for centuries. His ancestors 200 years earlier had had to cope with an invading group of people known to us as the Hyksos. These powerful people arrived in Egypt and settled with apparently very little opposition from the Egyptians. It seems that the original invaders must have come from the north and the east. The word 'Hyksos', deriving from the Egyptian ⌐𝔸𝔸𝔸𝔸, means 'Princes of Foreign Lands'. Their individual names indicate that they did not originate from one single place although the name of one of their Kings, Khyan, suggests that he, at least, came from way out east, perhaps in the region of the steppes. It seems that the original marauding force had entered the Middle East mounted on light-sprung chariots with spoked wheels drawn by small, powerful horses, previously unknown in Egypt. As they travelled swiftly overland, using powerful composite bows and bronze weapons of war, they must have been a terrifying sight to the cities that stood in their way: their military technology was light years ahead of their opponents'. Some people, seeing their strength, joined them voluntarily, swelling their force. Others defied them, but ran in front of them as refugees.

It was thus a very mixed band that finally crossed Egypt's northeastern borders, not needing, according to the evidence, to use extensive force. They settled there, in an area known today as Tell el Daba. This area was not much favoured by Egyptians, as it was often troubled by cross-border skirmishing. Soon the Hyksos had built a walled city they called Khutwaret (the Greeks later called it Avaris). Most Egyptians accepted them and, when they claimed the Egyptian kingship, accepted that also. However, the group did find opposition from one single family, based in Luxor. An Upper Egyptian fighting force, headed by the redoubtable Seqenenre Tao, and after his death by his two sons Kamose and Amosis, finally made the Hyksos' stay in Egypt intolerable. While the men of Luxor attacked the Hyksos, threw down their city walls and forcibly ejected them from Egypt, back home in Luxor a succession of their womenfolk, Queens Tetisheri, Ahhotep and Ahmose-Nefertari, raised armies, maintained supply lines and held the country stable.

Once the Hyksos had been ejected, the kings from Luxor formed the powerful Eighteenth Dynasty and extended the boundaries of Egypt both northwards and southwards further than ever before, determined to ensure that no invaders could ever emulate the Hyksos' example. King Amosis, the final victor against the Hyksos, left behind a son to inherit the throne, Amenhotep I. Amenhotep, however, seems to have left no living heir; and everything suggests that on his death the throne instead passed sideways into the hands of his vizier, Tuthmosis.

Tuthmosis I, as he became, married the sister of Amenhotep I to smoothe the succession. He led his armies far into the north, even going so far on one campaign that he crossed over the Euphrates into what is now Iraq, to defeat Egypt's enemies there. When he died, he left a daughter by his Great Royal Wife, and a younger son by a lesser wife. There is no indication that, on his death, there was any conflict of interest between his two children; on the contrary, his daughter Hatshepsut became the Great Royal Wife of her half-brother, Tuthmosis II. Tuthmosis II achieved significantly less, politically speaking, than his father and does not seem to have needed to fight abroad. He was probably of indifferent health; in any case, he died after a short and relatively unexciting reign. He left behind a young son by a minor wife to inherit the throne. This son, probably when a baby, was crowned in the temple of Karnak as Menkheperre Tuthmosis III, with Hatshepsut, his stepmother and aunt, standing in as viceroy to protect the boy's interests. Her altruism lasted only for a short time. Within two years, after a visit to the temple of Karnak which affected her profoundly, she usurped the throne from the child and had herself crowned King of Egypt. According to her inscription, Hatshepsut had been told by Amen in Karnak that he, not Tuthmosis I, was her true father.

For the women of the Eighteenth Dynasty, there were unparalleled opportunities for independence and the furthering of ambitions. Beginning with the Theban wives, who had steadied Egypt's helm while their menfolk fought the Hyksos, these women showed themselves to be a tough breed. This independent nature is exhibited most clearly in the career of Hatshepsut. Unlike any other royal woman before her – and several had held the office of king before her, despite what some books may say – she had herself frequently depicted as male, wearing male clothing. Hatshepsut set a dangerous precedent to her female descendants, as we shall see.

Tuthmosis III was arguably Egypt's greatest king, even though he did not leave behind him great monuments. After finally inheriting the crown from Hatshepsut, he spent most of his years as King leading military campaigns north and south. He extended Egypt's boundaries in every direction further than any other king. He would often use a scorched-earth policy, ordering his armies to demolish cities he vanquished and laying waste to their arable land and livestock to prevent enemies regrouping against Egypt. He was a great military tactician, forming a professional corps of officers trained in warfare and the use of weaponry, and he often used surprise manoeuvres in battle that left his opponents gaping. The devastation he left in his wake is clearly traceable in excavations of Syria and Israel. While he destroyed all those who opposed him, he would still show mercy to those who prostrated themselves before him.

He also showed himself to be an able administrator. Having founded a great empire for Egypt, he held it secure not by military means, but more effectively by taking captive the sons of foreign princes. He brought them back to Egypt, placing them in ⌒⊓ or the royal school, where they were educated as Egyptians. As soon as they were old enough, they would be returned to their homes, now fundamentally loyal to Egypt and on first-name terms with both the Pharaoh and the royal princes. This perceptive and highly intelligent policy meant that Egypt had strong allies over the future decades. Not only did he secure and maintain his territory by brotherhood rather than by force; he also assured his successors of low-cost control and vast tributes or taxes.

As a result of Tuthmosis III's foreign policy, succeeding kings still had to maintain an occasional military presence abroad, but on the whole the Egyptian empire was secure and prosperous. As Egypt dominated and controlled all the trade of the Eastern Mediterranean, the royal treasure rapidly filled to bursting point. There was virtually no opposition. City-states to Egypt's north had little time or funds to rebuild, and in the meantime relied entirely upon Egypt.

First Tuthmosis III's son, Amenhotep II, and then his grandson, Tuthmosis IV, reaped the benefits Tuthmosis III had laid down with little effort on their part. By the time Tuthmosis IV's son took the throne as Amenhotep III Nebmaatre, Egypt's foreign wars were at an end, and the region bathed in the warmth of unprecedented prosperity and peace. Protestations of loyalty flooded in with treasure from every side. All of Egypt flourished. Down in Luxor, one of the places to benefit the most was the small rural temple of Amen in Karnak, which was now rebuilt to become the largest and wealthiest in the land. Successive kings in the earlier period had gone into the temple of Karnak to ask for Amen's help in battle, and when it was given, in return they poured almost unlimited gifts into the god's keeping. The priests there became wealthy beyond any dream of avarice. Since the jobs of the high priests were inherited by their sons, several families also became so powerful they were in a position to challenge the throne itself.

Then there was a shock to the system. Instead of marrying a member of his own family, and making her Great Royal Wife as was customary, Amenhotep III Nebmaatre, greatest and wealthiest ruler of the world in his time, fell in love with a commoner. So great was his passion for Tiye that he made her Great Royal Wife, bucking tradition. With his vast wealth he built on a huge scale. Temples and palaces grew up all over Egypt, but Luxor in particular swelled from being a quiet country backwater into one of the greatest, bustling, cosmopolitan cities of the ancient world. Foreigners brought in new styles in clothing and architecture, and new philosophies, deities and ideals brought swift change to Egypt. Although the capital remained in Memphis, where the government offices and the state archives were, in the time of Amenhotep III and Queen Tiye, Luxor became the place to be.

As the years went by, they had many children, boys and girls who survived the perilous years of early childhood. The eldest son, Tuthmosis, named after his illustrious ancestors, seemed destined to inherit the throne and was therefore groomed as Crown Prince. Their second son was probably a disappointment to them all. Deformed, ugly, looking more female than male, Prince Amenhotep was mentally unstable, a dreamer. Suddenly disaster struck. Prince Tuthmosis was sent north to the Temple of Re in Heliopolis – the usual destination for Crown Princes in the Eighteenth Dynasty who were seeking the wisdom they would need as king – and then suddenly disappeared from view. There is no doubt that he died prematurely, although his burial place has never been identified. This left Prince Amenhotep as the only surviving son, a totally unsuitable heir to the throne in every respect. When Amenhotep III died after ruling for thirty-nine years, his younger son was catapulted onto the throne of Egypt as Amenhotep IV Neferkheprure Waenre.

The hidden madness of the new King grew, and erupted very soon after his coronation. Despite his dreadful ugliness, he married one of the most beautiful women of the ancient world, Nefertiti, whom he made his Great Royal Wife. No doubt overcoming natural aversion, she quickly became pregnant, and in the months and years that followed she bore him a succession of six daughters. Amenhotep IV ignored all state affairs; in truth, he was probably incapable of dealing with them. Instead he pursued his dreams, and made public his total devotion to a new god that he called the Aten. While Egyptians worshipped many gods, which we know from the many statues they left behind sporting strange animal, reptilian and even insects' heads, the Aten was unprecedented in having no such image, but being visible to everyone as the sun in the sky. To the conservative Egyptians, it was totally unacceptable. In an age of paganism, this King showed himself to be a heretic. He declared that the Aten was the only god, whom he worshipped in the form of the disc of the sun, while denying the existence of all the others.

The new King's heresy terrified and alienated the people. More seriously, he angered the powerful priesthood of Amen in the temple of Karnak, threatening their livelihood. Within a short time they made his life so intolerable that they forced him out of Luxor, demanding that he find somewhere else to carry out his strange obsession. Publicly humiliated and swearing revenge on the temple, he sailed away northwards. Two hundred miles to the north, he found an ideal site – a deserted plain on the east bank of the Nile. Here he founded a city for himself and his god which he called Akheteten – today's Tell el Amarna.

The King ordered building work to start, and a year later moved in with his family. He renamed himself Akhenaten, while Queen Nefertiti took the name Nefernefruaten Mery Waenre ('the beloved of Waenre', one of the names of Akhenaten). As soon as the city was finished, Akhenaten exiled himself within it, swearing never to leave it again so long as he lived. Here all the old gods were forbidden. He then sent out teams of iconoclasts, zealous converts whom he filled with his own hatred for the pagan idols of the old religion, who went through Egypt closing temples and destroying the names of Amun and the old gods wherever they could.

Among the forbidden practices in Tell el Amarna were the old burial rites under the aegis of Osiris. The inhabitants of the new city, confused and bewildered, sent their dead home to be buried under the old ways. As Akhenaten's paranoia increased, Egypt's self-confidence was destroyed, and family fought family.

Meanwhile, outside Egypt, even the empire tottered. For many years the Hittites in Anatolia, southern Turkey, had fought among themselves for control over the throne. Taking advantage of this, the Egyptians carried vast amounts of trade-goods along the Silk Road right through the middle of their lands without challenge. Now, at just the wrong time for Egypt, the Hittites settled their differences, united behind a single king and concentrated all their efforts in throwing Egypt out of their lands. Some cities, abandoned by Egypt, went over willingly to the Hittites, while others resisted strongly. Cities loyal to Egypt now wrote to Akhenaten requesting military aid. But Akhenaten, deep in his fundamentalist zeal, did nothing. They wrote a second, a third time, their pleas becoming increasingly urgent. But still he ignored them. While Tell el Amarna basked in the drowsy heat of an Egyptian summer, Akhenaten remained inactive, and the empire slowly slipped away as the Hittite army advanced ever closer to Egypt's borders.

Akhenaten had ruled for twelve years. When it must have seemed as if things in Egypt could not get worse, total chaos erupted. The second daughter of Akhenaten and Nefertiti, Princess Meketaten, died suddenly and unexpectedly. Was it this tragedy that finally warped the King's mind? Soon after the burial of the Princess, Queen Nefertiti was thrown out of the palace and the now insane King Akhenaten announced publicly for the first time that he was homosexual. Nefertiti was publicly humiliated. She withdrew to the Northern Palace in Tell el Amarna where she languished, rejected and isolated. Finally she died of a broken heart.

In the royal palace, her place was taken immediately by the royal catamite Smenkhkare. Exactly who the young man was is uncertain except that he had a little brother, Tutankhaten. To try to settle public opposition, Akhenaten forced his lover to marry his eldest daughter, Princess Meritaten. Smenkhkare was crowned co-Regent, ensuring that after Akhenaten died, he would inherit the throne without dispute.

After seventeen years as King, Akhenaten finally died and Smenkhkare and Meritaten took the throne. They had ruled for only a very short time – perhaps a matter of a few months – when they both disappeared mysteriously at the same time.

The only possible claimants to the throne of Egypt from this unholy family was Smenkhkare's younger brother, Tutankhaten, and the third daughter of Akhenaten and Nefertiti, Princess Ankhesenpaaten.

Amenhotep III, shown here with the crocodile-headed god Sobek

A 'news scarab', used exclusively by Amenhotep III as a medium for disseminating political information around Egypt's empire

Three golden flies, the highest award for military valour in ancient Egypt, given to Queen Ahhotep, in whose tomb they were found

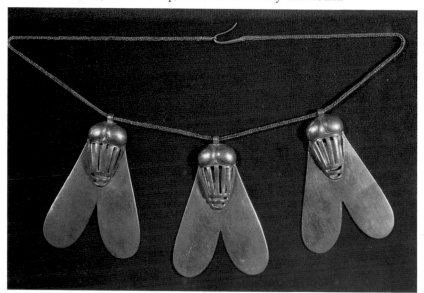

The face of this colossal statue of Akhenaten shows the 'distorted' features adopted by artists and craftsmen, probably at the King's orders, after the move to Tell el Amarna

A talatat block showing a relief carving of the King, wearing a *khat* or bag-wig, under the rays of the Aten

This finely carved stela depicts the King with his Great Royal Wife Nefertiti, with three of their daughters. The baby held over the shoulder by the Queen is the infant Ankhesenpaaten, later wife of Tutankhamen

Akhenaten, Nefertiti and their daughter Meritaten offer libations to the Aten

There are few remains visible today in Tell el Amarna. Here,
a staircase once led to a roof from the private royal quarters of the
Northern Palace, probably Nefertiti's own domain

Ay is heavily laden with gold collars, royal reward for loyalty,
given to him by his son-in-law Akhenaten

Traditionally thought to show Smenkhkare and Meritaten, the male figure here is actually Tutankhamen

Among the talat blocks recovered from pylons of Horemheb at Karnak was this finely carved relief. The figure stands below the rays of the Aten, a position usually restricted to members of the main royal family. The features suggest this is Princess Meritaten, Heir Apparent to the throne

This exquisite quartzite head, found by Borchardt in the workshop
of the sculptor Tuthmosis in Tell el Amarna, probably depicts one of
the royal princesses, though it is unnamed. Despite the stylized shape,
it is breathtakingly beautiful

Akhenaten's supporters forced the two of them to marry so that Smenkhkare's brother could become the next King of Egypt. To their dismay, within a very short time the new King totally rejected the heresy of Akhenaten, abandoned Tell el Amarna and returned with his wife to Luxor. Here he restored the worship of Amen, changing his name to Tutankhamen and that of his wife to Ankhesenamun. Finding the temple of Karnak closed and the halls filled with weeds, he forbade the worship of Aten and ordered the festival of Amen to be celebrated once more.

Tutankhamen was destined to rule only for a short time, around nine years, before he too died. The widowed Queen, Ankhesenamun, the last surviving member of the royal family, carried the right to the throne but was unable to take it herself. She was thus threatened by an old man, Lord Ay, the brother of Queen Tiye. He forced his unwanted attentions on the devastated widow, who wrote in anguish and terror to the King of the Hittites for help. She wrote that if he would send his son to Egypt she would marry him and make him the next King. The King of the Hittites, not surprisingly, did not believe her but replied voicing his doubts. She, angry and indignant, wrote a second time: 'I have no son whom I can marry and I will not marry a commoner. Send me your son and I will make him King of Egypt.'

After some discussion, the son of the Hittites' King, Prince Zannanzash, was sent. But he never arrived. His party was ambushed by an Egyptian raiding party and massacred on Egypt's northern frontier. Ankhesenamun now had no choice but to marry Ay, who thus took the throne and, according to some versions, in all probability had her murdered shortly afterwards.

Ay ruled for only four years afterwards. An old man, he died without leaving an heir. Every member of the old royal family was now dead, and the throne passed to Horemheb, Commander-in-Chief of the Egyptian army, who at once placed a confused and chaotic Egypt under tight military rule. One of his first acts was to issue an edict in which he stated the general lawlessness prevalent in the land. He prescribed punishments for many crimes, trying to restore order at the point of a sword. In order to secure his position he had, at some point earlier, married Mutnodjme, Nefertiti's sister. Despite his attempts to father a child with her, he, like Ay, died without an heir. As a result he had little choice but to hand the throne sideways to another family. In the last year of his life he chose his greatest friend from the army to be the next king. Pramesse was the son of a peasant farmer from the Delta, but like Horemheb, he had risen through the ranks of the army to reach a position of highest command. Also like Horemheb, he was already a very old man and could not be expected to rule for much longer. But this old man, later crowned as Ramesses I, had two distinct advantages – a living son, Seti, and a lively, healthy grandson, Ramesses. Certain that the throne would be secure for at least the next three generations with Ramesses as King, Horemheb, by appointing him, thus founded the next, Nineteenth Dynasty.

Horemheb now turned all his attention to eradicating all the unhappy memories of the past and to restoring Maat. He dismantled every single monument of Akhenaten's, removing the buildings of Tell el Amarna stone by stone and using them as rubble infill for his own building works. And everywhere he obliterated the name of the great heretic king who had threatened Egypt's very existence. From this time forward, he and his successors either ignored Akhenaten's existence completely or, if they had to, referred to him indirectly as 'the great criminal' or 'the great enemy'.

The plans of the Ramesside rulers of the Nineteenth Dynasty almost succeeded. By the early 1920s, we knew almost nothing about these kings. Then, against all the odds, the tomb of Tutankhamen was found almost intact. For the very first time we had the chance to find out exactly what had happened. The archaeologists of the time all knew the story of the period well, so they had lists of questions ready to be answered. Who were the parents of Smenkhkare and Tutankhamen? How had Tutankhamen felt when his brother was given power and Nefertiti was rejected? What had it been like to live in Egypt under the great heretic? Was Tutankhamen forced to marry the princess or had they married for love? How had Egypt welcomed him as a king? How had he deprived the Atenist heretics of their power? And how had he died? Had he been murdered? And what record did the power-hungry Ay and the terrified widowed Queen leave behind at his funeral? Might we find her poor body there also, murdered by the ambitious Ay?

These questions, and a thousand more that rose from the accepted story, filled the minds of those who watched the emptying of the tomb. But as I said at the start of this chapter, it is a dangerous state of affairs when archaeologists have preconceptions. In this case, as the objects were finally placed on public display and the material from the tomb was gradually published, most mysteriously there were, as Carter notes, no answers at all. Not one single piece told us anything about Tutankhamen's parents, his childhood, the meteoric rise of his brother or even his sudden religious conversion from Aten to Amun. By 1932, when the emptied tomb was finally swept clean, nothing more was known about Tutankhamen than on the day when the tomb was found. This mystery has undoubtedly fed the wild guesswork that continues to this very day.

The preconceptions that we started with are, indeed, very dangerous – particularly because they are wrong. For, as I am about to show, the whole of the accepted story that I have just related is completely untrue. There were no answers in the tomb – because they were asking the wrong questions.

To discover the right questions, we have to go back to the archaeological beginning – the tomb. Another searching look at what was found there, and we may at last be on our way.

CHAPTER FOUR

Evidence from the Objects
in Tutankhamen's Tomb

———

So what would you take with you after your death if religion allowed it?

As we saw earlier, little ever changed in most aspects of ancient Egyptian culture. Their art, their medicine, their mathematics – seldom were any new ideas applied to any of them. But their religious beliefs do seem to have changed from time to time. In fact, the ancient Egyptian religion is one of the most complex aspects of their long civilisation.

While pyramids, tombs and artefacts show us how they were made, we seldom get an insight into why they were made. An aspect of archaeology is romanticising the past, and often accrediting it with ideas that may never have been there in the first place. It is impossible to put yourself into the mind of one of your contemporaries, let alone the mind of someone on the other side of the world who lived centuries before your time.

To illustrate the point, let us imagine that in the future, 3000 years or more from today, our current civilisation has disappeared and been long forgotten. The only reminders of our time are fragmentary inscriptions and a few decorated stones from a wide variety of religious establishments, all completely contradictory. Imagine the scene: our towns have disappeared, all but footings and foundations, and the only complete texts to survive to tell about life in the twentieth century are a pile of GCSE papers by a class of students of varying ability. Now imagine, if you can, the archaeologist of the future trying to make sense of all this. To add to his information, he would excavate the field where your town had once been. In what had once been private gardens, in the central flower bed, surrounded by the remains of decaying roots of flowering plants, he finds by chance a collection of garden gnomes. At once his find will be heralded as 'major and significant', since nothing of the like has ever been seen before. But in interpreting them, the gnomes will become 'local gods'; the house behind it will become the 'local temple'; and the biggest gnome, the one with fishing rod sitting over a well, will become the 'king of the gods', given responsibility for the 'food offerings' and 'libations' that the 'faithful' once dropped into his well.

Now you may think this amusing and far-fetched. But this is precisely what archaeology often does. From ancient Egypt we have exactly the same sort of evidence that I have imagined above as having been left by our own culture to be puzzled over by future generations. You can see the problem that we face in trying to enter the world of ancient beliefs. In the past, archaeologists tended to call objects that they found 'religious, symbolic or cultic' just because they did not understand them. Today we try to be more objective, but it is often exceedingly difficult. Many of the things we find probably had practical uses, but since we cannot start to imagine the needs and the solutions that the ancient Egyptians had, the pieces are often impossible for us to recognise – and if we *could* recognise them, it would probably change our whole understanding of them. Sometimes to think of objects as 'religious' gets us out of a problem.

And so it is with ancient Egyptian remains. It is impossible, after all these elapsed centuries, to ourselves identify with the motives of ancient Egyptians, and it is all too easy for archaeologists to read meanings into objects and monuments they have left behind. But while we cannot for certain say what they believed or how they put those beliefs into practice, so much material has survived from their burials and their tombs that we can get a glimpse into what they believed might happen to them after they died.

Beliefs in a life after death are common to many cults. As far as ancient Egypt is concerned, however, this is a complex field that has often been misrepresented. Egyptology has been closely identified with the mystical and the occult since the times of the Greeks and

Romans. During the early centuries of Christianity in Egypt, there was a positive effort to portray the ancient Egyptian beliefs as the worst possible kind of paganism, with allusions being made to secret cults that even involved human sacrifice. None of these implications had any basis in reality – but they did much to persuade people to convert to Christianity.

The first group of people that we can see clearly added to the 'mystery' of ancient Egypt were the Arab settlers. When they arrived in Egypt in AD 641 they found themselves taking charge of a land where the people kept themselves to themselves. The new Arab rulers, perplexed by a lack of communication and a total lack of understanding, unable either to read the hieroglyphic texts or to understand the monuments they found, created their own stories about Egypt instead. The tales of *The Arabian Nights*, of Aladdin and Ali Baba, lost treasures, magical doors, genii and magical potions – most of these demonstrate the Arabic response to the ancient Egyptian monuments they found themselves surrounded by. From the medieval period to the present, books were written to try to explain the basic lack of knowledge about the monuments by taking the mystic route instead. To find gold in tombs, the authors of these books suggested that all you had to do was to recite the correct magical words (such as 'Open Sesame'), burn the correct substances at the right time and perform the correct actions. The gold would then appear from absolutely nowhere. These mysteries were called by the traditional ancient name of Egypt: Keme, the Black Land. The Arabic word for this was *al-Keme* or alchemy, the transmutation of metals.

In this way, together with many other misunderstandings and misinterpretations added later, much of our understanding of the ancient Egyptians' thought processes have been coloured by false explanations. To this very day the idea persists that the Egyptians were pagan polytheists, given to the actual adoration of animals, reptiles and insects while carrying out unspeakable secret rituals. In his book that examines the basic precepts of ancient Egyptian religion, Henri Frankfort summed up this idea in the very title of his work, *Before Philosophy*. Before the Greeks, he and others imply, there was no philosophy, no process of logical thought – just a morass of pagan heresies based on cause and effect.

The truth is very different. While our understanding of ancient

Egyptian philosophy is currently undergoing scholarly study, it is possible, by putting together information from their texts and the inscriptions from tombs and pyramids, to tell a great deal about their attitude to death and the life hereafter.

Unlike Western theologies, which imbue humankind with a body and soul, a philosophy that gives rise to much discussion and debate, the ancient Egyptians saw humans as a complex web of both physical and spiritual aspects. First, at the time of conception, came the making of the physical body. Several different pictures and inscriptions show that the Egyptians believed the body to have been formed on a potter's wheel by Khnum, a local 'god' from Aswan – actually more in the nature of a saint, or intercessor – often shown with a straight-horned ram's head. The body was then placed within the womb of the mother. At the very same moment, Khnum also created the *ka*. This spiritual form was a double, looking exactly like a person in every way. Planted in the body of the foetus, it would grow and develop along with it. It was the guiding force of the body, so, as the wisdom texts would explain (see page 13), on occasions your *ka* might misbehave and lead you into doing things you otherwise would never consider.

Apparently you could have more than one *ka*, if Khnum deemed fit. Hatshepsut, the female King, records in her mortuary temple on the west bank of Luxor, Deir al Bahri, that she had nine *ka*s, eight of them male. This afforded an explanation for every misdemeanour. If you ate too much, for example, or became involved in some nefarious activity, your *ka* would be blamed. In some texts it is stated that semen comes from the *ka*, so that a child, when born, is the child of the *ka* and not of the body. This explains how some Egyptians believed they were literally the child of a 'god', in that another *ka* had briefly taken over their body during the time a child was conceived. In modern terms, a transsexual would be easily understood in the light of this philosophy; they are simply people in whose bodies *ka*s of the wrong sex have been placed.

A *ka* could be freed from the body either during waking or sleeping. In the Late Period one inscription tells of a king whose *ka* travelled by night to Nubia, where it received a beating in public. The following morning the king awoke to find the scars on his back where the *ka* had brought them back. The story has a modern parallel in the out-of-body experience.

Having always been associated with the body from its conception, the *ka* experienced the moment of bodily death as terrible: at this time it would be painfully torn from the body. During a person's life their tomb was prepared as the 'home for eternity' for the *ka*, where all its needs would be met. Earthbound forever, the *ka*'s continuing existence depended entirely on the food offerings left by friends and relatives, first at the time of burial and then later through regular visits to the tomb by the bereaved. As time passed and memories of the deceased faded, the same food and drink could be given 'spiritually' by pictures and inscriptions within the tomb. The objects and pictures in a tomb were believed to be vital to provide for the immortal needs of the *ka*. While the body was buried in an undecorated sealed chamber below ground, the upper rooms would be left open for visitors, who would either provide food physically or would say the words for it to be provided spiritually.

Until such a secure place as the Valley of the Kings existed for the burial of Egypt's kings, it is highly doubtful that anything other than the basic needs of the *ka*, provided through paintings, models or relief carvings, would be placed within a tomb. As visitors were encouraged to walk openly in and out of the chapel above the burial shaft, it would be unreasonable to place great treasures out openly for anyone to pick up. And people were also encouraged to enter the tombs. As several inscriptions on tomb walls relate, they wanted travellers to 'drop in'. 'O you who are still living on the earth, as you travel north or south and come to the entrance of this tomb, enter and say, "A thousand loaves of bread, a thousand jugs of beer, a thousand jars of wine for the *ka* of . . ." ' and the person's name was then added. In this way they felt the immortality of the *ka*'s needs would be met. There was never a curse on entering a tomb (see page 129); on the contrary, entering it was needed to keep the *ka* going. Only when the burial place could be assured to be safe and secure, as in the Valley of the Kings, was it considered proper to include actual objects within the burial chambers.

The second spiritual element of a person was the *ba*, which as we shall see was a kind of kickstart mechanism. This is usually depicted as a bird with an anonymous human head. We might perhaps say this was the equivalent of the 'life-force'. Inscriptions speak of it leaving the body by the left ear at death. It is described as aimless, fluttering around the tomb after death looking for another body on which 'to perch'. It would thus attempt to enter into a new body. This is not, as many people claim, a belief in reincarnation. The Egyptians believed that the earthly existence was short, painful and troubled – in other words, not to be repeated if there was any choice. The *ba*, as it entered into another individual, carried with it no sense of identity, but merely acted, to use a modern analogy, like a spark-plug. So, after one 'engine' 'dies', the spark-plugs can be removed and transferred into another engine, which then 'comes to life'. But the spark-plug has no more memory of the engine it has left behind than does the *ba* as it enters another human body. A stillborn child was believed by the ancient Egyptians to simply be one for whom no *ba* was available at the time of birth – a somewhat comforting thought, especially at a time when infant mortality must have been commonplace.

So if the *ka* was your earthbound, tomb-residing 'ghost', and the *ba* was simply the 'breath of life', what then survived of you after death? It was certainly neither the *ka* nor the *ba*. As we've seen, at the point of burial in ancient Egypt, the body was carried to the grave or tomb where the last rites would be carried out over it – the so-called Opening of the Mouth. In this an adze, a simple carpenter's tool, was applied ritually – no one knows exactly how – to the eyes, nose, mouth, ears, hands, genitals and feet of the dead person. The coverings – whether the mat that was wrapped around the body of a poor man or the gold-embellished mummy of the King – would be symbolically 'lifted' to 'restore' full senses to the corpse. After the last touch was made to the body, texts speak of the body's transformation into an *akh*. This is described as a 'shining' or 'perfect' being. The body is thus miraculously 'transformed' into a spiritual being, best likened, in today's understanding, to an angel. In the Gospel of Matthew, Jesus is described as having undergone a similar transfiguration: 'His appearance was like lightning, and his clothes were white as snow.' The *akh* is literally the resurrected body, which is now no longer simply a broken piece of empty flesh but a revived and reinvigorated form which needed burial immediately. It was no longer a part of the earth of the living, but was destined to join similar beings in another, parallel, existence. Accompanying the setting sun over the western horizon, the *akh*, fully equipped for its journey, would travel into the realms of Osiris for judgement, acquittal and an eternity spent in paradise – a land that was an exact copy of Egypt, but without any of the problems.

The ancient Egyptian philosophy of life, afterlife and the nature of humankind is thus complex, intriguing and intellectually very sophisticated. The ancient Egyptian era certainly does not deserve to be dismissed as a time 'before philosophy'. These ideas answer many of the eternal problems that religion is now expected to answer, dealing as it does with such things as sin, forgiveness, judgement, immortality, the nature of life and death and even the nature of ghosts.

So according to Egyptian concepts, after Tutankhamen's death it would have been anticipated that the Opening of the Mouth ceremony would transform the king for his journey to the hereafter as an *akh*, while the tomb would be eternally inhabited by his *ka*. The *ka* needed all the things that it had always needed in life. So the farmer would need his tools and seeds; the painter, his pigments and brushes; the scribe, his writing materials; the king, reminders of his earthly glory in the form of jewellery, clothes and regalia. In addition, he would have needed some things reminding him of the others whose life he had shared – his family and close friends.

If these were your beliefs and you thought that you could literally take everything that you wanted with you when you were buried, what would you take? Would you have the car you had always driven painted on the walls of your tomb – or the one you always wished you had driven? Would you have yourself painted in your favourite gardening clothes or the clothes you had always wanted to wear? In most cases, most people would opt for dreams rather than for harsh reality. Because of this natural desire to represent the ideal in the hereafter, many ancient Egyptians' tomb paintings, although autobiographical, are highly idealised and thus intrinsically need to be interpreted cautiously. But the objects that accompanied you in the tomb are different. You cannot provide the actual Dior or Christian Lacroix outfit that you always wanted if you never owned it and could not afford it. In fact, it would be far more likely that anything of value you owned would be left for your relatives, while you would be given the unwanted cast-offs. The Egyptians may have been idealists and, often, dreamers – but they were not stupid. The needs of the living outranked those of the dead. Many of the things buried with you would certainly be your favourite things. Frank Sinatra, for example, has gone to his rest accompanied by the things that mattered to him – a bottle of whisky, a packet of cigarettes, his favourite lighter and a handful of ten-cent pieces for the pay telephone, so that he would never be caught without change. In the same way you might want your favourite book, or clothes, or the things you had as a child.

So in the tomb of Tutankhamen, the objects might represent his childhood (his favourite things); gifts from those who cared for him; objects he had used during his life (which may well have been things unwanted by the living); and things prepared specially to equip his *ka* for eternity. In these categories we might expect favourite toys from childhood; named gifts from mourners; furniture and clothes that he had outgrown; and food and drink for the *ka*. But it has to be remembered that Tutankhamen was special, not just any ordinary ancient Egyptian. Not only did he have personal memories; but he had also had duties to fulfil. He was, after all, a crowned King of Egypt. After his death, his *akh* would not simply progress to an afterlife to live with the souls of ordinary mortals; it would be expected that he would mingle with the spirits of other long-dead kings and heroes that the Egyptians called *netjeru*, which we translate as 'gods'. So the equipment that he would need to 'take with him' would have to reflect this status.

Tutankhamen's tomb is unique. To date, it is the only royal tomb ever to have been found virtually intact. Although several other royal tombs were found at Tanis in 1939, dating from the Twenty-first and Twenty-second Dynasties, they represented Egyptian culture at a very low point and were thus comparatively poor and ill-equipped. Despite the two robberies which had interrupted Tutankhamen's rest very soon after his burial, most of the objects that were put in his tomb were still there, even if they were not in their original places. Most of the chests had been originally sealed using pieces of rope, with wooden labels attached which listed the contents. A later comparison of these dockets with a compilation of the pieces that survived revealed exactly what was missing. To most people's surprise, the amount of gold missing from the tomb, according to these lists, was relatively small. Most of the major losses were of oils, perfumes and linen. Presumably these must have been easier for the thieves to dispose of than gold, which would have been easily traced back to them.

But because the tomb is unique, it is dangerous to make generalised statements about the nature and state of the objects within it. Many of the pieces of furniture in the tomb were too small for the King when he died, were broken or were of poorer quality than might be expected of a Pharaoh's goods. This has led some people to speculate that either some things were broken by the robberies or by the security forces who tidied up after them, or that Tutankhamen had been badly served – given shoddy goods by people who did not respect him. Neither of these statements may be true. It is possible that tombs were regularly provided with goods of lower quality. Since Tutankhamen's tomb is the only tomb so far found virtually intact, the objects in his tomb may be typical and not at all exceptional. Many tombs of officials of the Eighteenth Dynasty have been excavated in Saqqara since 1976 by a joint British–Dutch team, and they have yielded many surprises. A number of coffins found intact in shafts are of such very poor quality and inscribed with such nonsensical hieroglyphs that had they been found illegally and offered for sale either to a museum or a private buyer, they would immediately have been described as very poor fakes. Similarly, a few funerary statues or *shabtis* have also been found in the Saqqara tombs that would otherwise have been described by experts as forgeries. This should make us very cautious in future when examining pieces from Egypt. As most ancient Egyptians could not read or write, it is possible that even elementary 'inscriptions', no matter how false they might appear to our eyes, may well have satisfied their needs. In other words, in expecting new or unbroken material in a tomb, we might be accused of being more purist than the ancient Egyptian themselves were.

So we would expect two principal groups of objects. First, there should be personal pieces made for and used by Tutankhamen during his life. These things should tell us a lot about his likes and dislikes, his hobbies and his family. Secondly, we would expect objects made for his death, his burial and his afterlife. By examining these two groups a picture should emerge to tell us what he was really like. After all – these were the things either he or his family had chosen.

The objects within the tomb can be studied on two levels. First, following the archaeologist's need simply to record, they can be itemised, measured and described. Nowhere is this done better than in Nicholas Reeves' book, *The Complete Tutankhamen*, and it would be unnecessary for me to emulate his work in any way. But secondly, there is the deeper need to try to understand the significance of the pieces. To conduct a detective search for the very life and death of the Pharaoh

Tutankhamen, we need to understand not just the pieces that exist, but also what they represent. Only by examining the objects on this level can we hope to start evaluating the evidence to form positive conclusions.

The tomb

Some fourteen feet below the floor of the Valley of the Kings, in front of the entrance to the tomb of Ramesses VI, there is a series of sixteen steps cut into the bedrock leading down to a mud-brick door, broken in the upper left corner and later resealed, which was impressed with the stamps of the Valley's security force – a jackal recumbent over nine tied captives – and with the crown-name of the King, Nebkheprure. Behind it, a sloping corridor led down to the second door, which Carter opened in the presence of Carnarvon and Lady Evelyn to reveal gold packed into the chamber within. This was the transverse antechamber, with dismantled chariots to the left, funerary couches opposite and a pair of

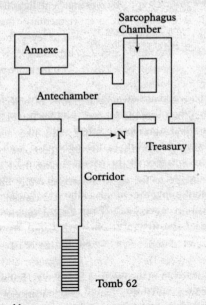

The tomb of Tutankhamen.

In a small chamber, named 'the annexe' by Carter, lay a jumble of objects used by Tutankhamen in his everyday life.

black, gilded wooden guardian statues to the right, protecting an area of filled plaster. When this plaster was ultimately broken down, the burial chamber, filled almost completely with gold-covered wooden shrines, was revealed beyond. In the right-hand wall of the burial chamber was the entrance to the treasury, guarded by a recumbent figure of the dog god Anubis, behind which lay a shrine with the Canopic chest, continuing the entrails of the embalmed body and many of the King's most precious objects. From the antechamber, a hole in the wall under one of the funerary couches led into the crammed and chaotic annexe, in which were stored the majority of the King's personal items.

Of the four chambers in the tomb, only one, the burial chamber, was decorated, its walls painted simply and somewhat hastily. The floor of the burial chamber lies some three feet lower than the antechamber and the treasury. Today, the base of the sarcophagus still stands in the centre of the burial chamber. In it, under a pane of glass, the lid of the outer gilded wooden coffin covers the King's mortal remains. Because of the difference in the floor levels, the visitor to the tomb today stands at the edge of the antechamber and looks down over railings to the sarcophagus beyond. It remains the only tomb yet found in the Valley which still contains the remains of the person for whom it was intended, and visitors are today reminded on entering that it is not a museum, but a tomb.

Objects used in life

Furniture
A total of six chairs, twelve stools, six beds for daily use and sixty-nine boxes or chests (parts of boxes) were discovered in all the chambers in the tomb.

The chairs
All the chairs and stools, which vary in size, belonged to the King during his life; and most of them were well used. While five of the six chairs are virtually identical in shape and basic style, one, the so-called 'Golden Throne', is completely different, as we shall see below. Two of the chairs were clearly made for a little child, as they are small, their seats only big enough today to hold a child around the age of five. Another, elaborately patterned with an estimated 45,000 tiny pieces of inlay, was misleadingly entitled by Madame Desroches-Noblecourt, the now retired keeper of Egyptian antiquities at the Louvre in Paris, 'the Ecclesiastical Throne', a name that has since stuck. She described it as 'the prototype of the episcopal thrones of the Christian Church', despite the fact that it was sealed in the tomb and thus unknown until 1922. The random ivory panels inlaid into its curved seat mimic the skin of a leopard, and it has crossed leg-frames in the form of ducks' heads and beaks made of dark wood, the details picked out in ivory. The chair back bears the name of the King at the time of his coronation, Tutankhaten.

The general design of all these five chairs is almost identical with *meshrabeyeh* chairs, still made in Egypt. The term covers a whole range of furniture often said to be Turkish in origin, even though the design is

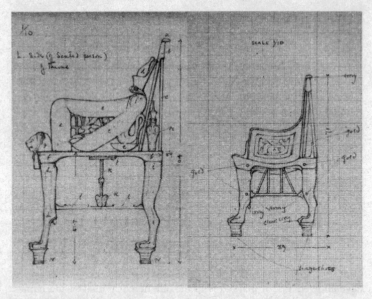

Carter's own sketches of two of Tutankhamen's chairs show his meticulous draughtsmanship. Note that the name on the arm of the so-called Golden Throne is his birthname, Tutankhaten, although elsewhere on the back panel his name was altered to Tutankhamen – just one of the curious examples of contradiction on objects found in his tomb.

a direct copy of furniture made in ancient Egypt. In ancient Egypt, such pieces often had red-gold wood framework lined with darkwood strips, with white or gold inlays within, usually as strips but sometimes in geometrical patterns or even hieroglyphic inscriptions.

The exceptional chair of the group is the 'Golden Throne'. This was found wrapped in black linen. The chair is solid, heavy and strongly cuboid in shape, with a completely flat seat, not curved like the others. The whole is heavily decorated in gold, with pictures of the King and Queen on the flat back. The arms of this chair have lions' heads at the front while the side view shows crowned hooded cobras bearing large cartouches, shapes resembling a loop of rope with a knot, inscribed within with the name 'Tutankhaten'. In the picture on the chair back, the young King rests an arm on the back of his chair while his wife, Ankhesenamun, gently holds out a protective hand towards him. She wears a diadem with twin plumes – the *atef* crown, usually associated with Amen, the god of Karnak, and, in a woman, frequently worn by the God's Wife. Between and above the figures, radiating from a central sun-disc in the top frieze, hang the life-giving rays of the Aten.

The chair poses huge problems. If, as has been suggested, Tutankhamen banished the Aten, shut all the Aten temples and restored the religion of Amen, then why does this chair depict the Aten on the back? It might be possible to suggest that the chair was made before the young King banished the heretical religion – except that on the front of the chair both his and his wife's name end in '-amen', adopted after the old religion had been re-established. If the chair had been altered, as Reeves and others have suggested, it is hard to accept that they left the clear image of the Aten intact in the centre of the back, together with the prominent names of Tutankhaten on the arms. It must surely have been possible either to cut them out or to disguise them. And if that were not possible, then one would have expected the chair to have been destroyed, as all the other buildings naming the Aten were. To have allowed a chair marked with the old, heretical images and names of the King and Queen to survive in Luxor, the epicentre of the anti-heretical movement, for nine years of the King's reign, and then to have it interred within his tomb, poses many questions.

It has often been suggested by writers that this chair was the coronation throne of the King. But this suggestion poses even more problems. Could the King who had restored Amen be crowned on a throne that bore the name and image of the Aten, and allow it to survive? It is interesting to note that this chair is considerably larger than the others in the tomb. Knowing that Tutankhamen was crowned when he was only a very little boy, it might be expected that a chair used by him at the start of his reign would have been much smaller – similar in size to the other small chairs found in the tomb. It is no use to suggest that the coronation throne was bigger because it was inherited – the images and names are those of the boy-King.

While little is known of furniture of the Eighteenth Dynasty (we do not as yet, for example, have any detailed study showing the types of wood, joints or carving which might identify any one workshop or individual craftsman), what can be said with confidence is that five of the six chairs in the tomb share a common origin, while the sixth, the Golden Throne, clearly comes from somewhere else. The five similar chairs have much in common with most of the boxes in the tomb. Boxes and chairs with identical designs can be seen in several tomb paintings on the west bank of Luxor, such as the funeral procession from the tomb of Sennefer, Mayor of Thebes, in the Theban Tomb 96. It would seem reasonable, from the evidence, that five of the chairs originated in Luxor, while the sixth did not. The Golden Throne's design elements, style and names show that it came from Tell el Amarna, where we know Tutankhamen spent some of his early life.

An almost identical situation applies to the beds found in the tomb. Once again, four of these were of similar design to each other, with the dark wood and inlaid strips that suggest a Luxor origin. All the beds were of a similar size, being around seven feet in length, with the typical Egyptian woven 'mattress' that sloped downward towards the footboard. One of the beds was a unique folding bed, comprising three panels hinged together which could thus fold up into a small neat package. The sixth bed, again, is completely different from all the others. It has a very heavy frame, is gilded all over, and is much shorter than all of the other beds. It is heavily worn and scratched from constant use, suggesting that it was a favourite of the King in life. Once again, its design, gilding and size all suggest it originated, like the 'Golden Throne', in Tell el Amarna.

Together with the beds were found eight headrests, three of which appear to be a matching set, made of plastered and gilded wood. These were probably associated with the funerary couches (see below). The other five were presumably used by the King to go with the five beds, and are remarkable in their design and manufacture, one being made of blue glass, one of deep blue glazed-composition (faience), one of alabaster and two of ivory. There has been much discussion in recent years as to the comfort of such headrests when sleeping. Ancient Egyptian beds were designed to slope downwards towards the footboard, the latter serving to stop the sleeper sliding off the end of the bed. The headrest was placed at the top of the bed, and the sleeper lay on it not, as many people think, with the back of the head, but with the cheek resting on the upward-curving top. The 'column' of the headrest was designed to match the exact height of the sleeper's shoulders, and thus were personal items, not to be used by just anybody. With the cheek supported at exactly the right height above the bed, the spine was kept straight, the head was kept elevated above the feet, and the column of the headrest allowed air to move around the neck. All in all, they were designed to be exceptionally comfortable and healthy.

Personal items

Fifteen writing palettes were found in the tomb, with one elaborate gold pencase and a papyrus smoother or burnisher, together with several cakes of pigments of black and red probably used for writing. One palette, found between the paws of Anubis in the treasury, bore the names and titles of Princess Meritaten. It has six indentations for colour and thus may have been a colourist's palette. Another ivory palette, not actually listed among Carter's finds although known to have come from the tomb, bore the name of Princess Meketaten.

Two wooden boxes, according to the labels on them, contained personal items from the King's childhood. One held clothing suitable for a little boy, while the other, a white-painted box, had a docket listing 'the equipment of His Majesty (Life Prosperity Health) when he was a child – razors, jars, linen.'

The tomb contained many pieces of clothing, ranging from tunics, shirts, sashes, kilts, triangular cloths, to caps, headdresses and gloves. Many of these await further examination. Some triangular pieces of linen were found. When two points of these were wrapped around the waist and tied, and the third point then tucked between the legs and up through the front tie, the piece of linen would have formed the distinctive triangular-fronted kilt associated with the soldiers of the New Kingdom. They seem more likely to have been kilts than the 'underclothes' suggested by Nicholas Reeves, but the pieces are so small that they would have fitted only a little child.

There were twenty-seven gloves, most of them found in pairs, of exquisite design. Each was woven to shape, including fingers and thumbs, rather than being cut from a piece of cloth and the fingers channel-stitched as might generally be done these days. One pair, resembling gauntlets, was made of woven tapestry, with ties around the wrist. It is uncertain why and when gloves were worn in ancient Egypt. Many people who do not know Egypt well think of it as constantly scorching hot, but this is untrue; in the winter months it is frequently cold and frosts are not unknown in January. It has been suggested that the gloves were 'ceremonial', but given the climate, it is more likely that they were practical, worn either in cold weather or when driving chariots.

Associated with the gauntlets and probably worn at the same time was an elaborate breastplate made of small hinged pieces of gold inlaid with coloured stones, comprising a broad collar, shoulder straps and a broad chest/waist band in a single piece. This was clearly an article designed to be worn in battle.

The King also had many weapons buried with him. These included forty-six bows, varying in length, some for shooting from the ground, others from the running board of his chariots. There were also 427 tang and barbed arrows together with two quivers to hold some of them. There were four wrist-protectors, worn during archery to stop the cord cutting the skin as it looses the arrow. There were also two curved bronze swords like scimitars, and two remarkable jewelled daggers, both in sheaths. One of the daggers had a blade of iron. This – one of the two iron objects ever found in Egypt – shows no sign at all of rust. It is suggested that it was forged from a fallen meteor. The other, of gold, has a pommel decorated in granular gold-work, not a craft native to Egypt, while the sheath, patterned with random dog and game animals in a hunting scene, once more suggests foreign origin. The King also had a total of eight shields. These objects, together with his chariots (see below), show that Tutankhamen was an athletic young man, much given to hunting and archery – the athletic equivalents of football today. It is interesting to note that these objects are all more used than his writing equipment, showing that he preferred sports to academic pursuits.

There was a substantial collection of sticks, generally termed 'walking sticks' although there is little evidence for such a thing in ancient Egypt. Tutankhamen most likely did not use them for support in walking. On the contrary, many officials and dignitaries carried staffs as a mark of their office, and still do today; and sticks were also used for sport, rather as an épée today might be used in fencing. One of the simplest of the sticks, a reed, was mounted with a gold bezel inscribed with hieroglyphs reading: 'A reed cut by His Majesty's own hand.' This, of all the objects in the tomb, is one of the most touching. Most mothers' reactions to a little boy bringing a reed-stick into the house, as boys do, would be to get them to throw it away outside. But Tutankhamen had no mother to tell him, and was, in any case, King of Egypt.

The plastered entrance to the burial chamber is flanked by a pair of guardian statues wearing the strange *shendyt* kilt. Experiment has shown that this effect could only have been obtained by boning.

One can imagine sycophantic courtiers fawning over the little boy, keen to cap his little stick in gold for him!

Some bundles of reeds were found that have never been explained, but I believe I have found the solution for these. The King, like many officials of the Eighteenth Dynasty, is frequently depicted wearing a most unlikely kilt, called, in Egyptian, a *shendyt*. These kilts, seen most clearly on the guardian statues that stood each side of the plastered entrance to the burial chamber, jut out in a pronounced manner. They slope outwards from the waist to the front of the hem; they slope out sideways; and they slope out from the underskirt worn by the wearer. The kilt forms sharp points at each lower corner, from which lines radiate outwards towards the centre. In the centre is a sash, as usual. It is generally stated that these kilts were 'pleated', with linen gathered at the bottom corners of the kilt and radiating upwards. As a keen needlewoman I have tried for many years to reproduce an example of one of these kilts without success. Pleating is not the answer – it simply doesn't work. The only way in which the kilt can be made successfully is to use boning – in other words, to use channel-stitched panels of linen with stiffening rods pushed inside them. The bundles of reeds found in the tomb are of an ideal thickness and length for them to have been used in these strange kilts.

There were two linen slings for throwing stones and a collection of thirty-four assorted throw-sticks, some curved and some angled, although none were designed to return to the thrower like boomerangs. The sticks were used to 'drop' birds – the impact would have made them fall to the ground. These throw-sticks vary in size and many of them have linen wrappings, still marked with dirty fingerprints – presumably where the King himself once held them.

In a hot climate like Egypt's, it is hardly surprising that the King's objects from life included eight fans mounted on staffs and with gilded feather mounts. When found, these all had ostrich feathers intact, shown in photographs and described as 'brown-white in colour' – in other words, undyed. The feathers soon rotted away when exposed to the air. One of the fan-mounts depicts Tutankhamen on an ostrich hunt.

To complete this picture of the great love of hunting were six chariots, all found dismantled. Four were within the antechamber (the Hall of Chariots) and two in the treasury. Two of the chariots were similar in design, with running boards mounted on a pair of light six-spoked wheels and with gilded and coloured wooden body-panels. The running boards are big enough for two people to stand on. One of the chariots, heavily decorated with gold, has depictions of the King's enemies on both sides dominated by matching pictures of a great sphinx.

Probably used with these chariots were four whips, one of which is inscribed as for 'The King's Son Tuthmosis', in all probability the older brother of Akhenaten.

For his entertainment, the King also had four games boards in his tomb, together with fifty-six game pieces and two sets of casting-sticks used as we use dice, for throwing to ascertain the number of moves to be made in turn by the players. There were also several musical instruments. Most tomb pictures of musical instruments show that they were either played by women or by professional musicians (such as the harpers). It is not surprising, therefore, that two of the instruments, trumpets, were for official use, probably to herald the King's presence. Given the association of women with musical instruments, it is much more surprising that the tomb contained a pair of ivory clappers and a pair of *sistra*. The latter, gilded wooden handles mounted with metal loops above, these threaded through from side to side by narrow rods, each bearing a series of metal discs – were carried by ladies and used at times of joy or of state or religious celebration. Scenes on the panelled wall of the small golden shrine show Queen Ankhesenamun playing such an instrument before her husband. While the *sistra* are rather .crude and uninscribed, the clappers, used like maracas, bear the intriguing inscription of 'The Great Royal Wife Tiye, given life, and the Princess Meritaten'. It would be reasonable to believe that all these instruments belonged to the Princesses and Queens and not to Tutankhamen, although the linking of the names of Tiye and her granddaughter, Meritaten, is intriguing.

Jewellery
While many pieces of jewellery on the lists attached to the various chests and boxes were missing from the tomb, removed presumably by the robbers who were interrupted in antiquity, enough survived to make this the largest corpus of jewellery ever found intact in Egypt. Some pieces had been made especially for his death and burial, some to be worn during life. Of especial interest are those made for the coronation.

Many of the pieces made for the King's coronation were found in the treasury. Among them is a selection of 'pectorals', or chest ornaments. These pieces of jewellery, generally large, rectangular and heavy, are something of a mystery. Although one or two pieces were found suspended from matching decorated bands, the majority were found loose. A 'pectoral', akin to a very large pendant on a necklace, was rarely depicted in tomb paintings, most people favouring broad-collars. Close scrutiny of these same paintings, and particularly the kilts worn by the kings during the New Kingdom, reveals that the kilts were kept in place with a heavily decorated sash. These sashes also preserved the wearer's modesty at the point where the fabric met around the front. One of these sashes, belonging to Ramesses III, survives in the Liverpool City Museum. It is an extremely long, tapering piece of woven tapestry with a multicoloured, feather-like (*rishi*) design. This tapestry-weave sash, probably made of wool, is firm and heavy and would have been extremely bulky to wear. They would have had to be folded many times around the waist, like a very elaborate and long bow-tie, and would have been particularly bulky at the front. The best depiction of such sashes are the portraits of Seti I, from his pilgrim-temple at Abydos. At the bottom of these sashes may be observed a rectangular ornament, often surmounted with a frieze of rearing hooded cobras with the sun-disc on their heads. I suggest that many of the 'pectorals' are in fact sash-ornaments or weights, worn in this way.

Among the necklaces worn by the King (definitely 'pectorals', given that they were mounted on straps) was one spectacular piece comprising, the centre, a winged scarab beetle of translucent green feldspar, standing on top of a lotus frieze and pushing above it a large gold and lapis lazuli ship containing a *wadjet*-eye (the healed and magic eye of Horus), and, at the top, a disc showing the king receiving the crown and regalia from the gods. On another piece, Tutankhamen, dressed in the diamond-chequered short cloak usually associated with jubilee festivals, receives the crown and regalia from Ptah, the tutelary god of Memphis, and his consort Sekhmet. An exquisite, tiny gold figurine depicts the King at his coronation, wearing the crown and a tiny bead necklace around his neck, and carrying the crook and flail, described below. A pair of earrings, well-worn and clearly a favourite of the King's, are matching gold loops surrounded by rings of stones with six tiny sections of beaded chains hanging down from them. In the centre of each loop stands a minuscule figure of the King at his coronation, again wearing the crown and carrying the regalia. The figures, perfect in every detail, are made of polished cornelians. Two staffs, one of gold and the other of silver, are capped by solid effigies of the King during his coronation.

In addition to these pieces, most exciting of all the finds of jewellery were real examples of the so-called 'crook and flail' emblems of regality handed to the King at his coronation. Three crooks were found with two flails, two of the crooks and two flails being matching pairs. The smaller set are inscribed with the name 'Tutankhaten'; the larger set with 'Tutankhamen'. Associated with them was a sceptre, the ⌐𝄎𝄽, made of wood, gilded and inscribed, interestingly, with the message 'The Good God, the beloved, Glittering in his face like Aten when he rises, Son of Amen, Nebkheprure'. The inclusion of the names of the two gods Amen and Aten on the same piece, and the fact that that piece was used by the King on state occasions, like the 'Golden Throne', creates problems with the view that Tutankhamen outlawed the religion of the Aten while reinstating that of Amen.

Memorabilia: Tutankhamen's Gifts

Many pieces in the tomb did not belong to Tutankhamen at all, but were reused from other burials or were perhaps pieces that had been made with no one special in mind but were used by him. Some pieces, though, were clearly either inherited by him or given to him at his funeral.

Among these, of special interest are the aforementioned writing palettes and ivory clappers, both bearing the name of Princess Meritaten, the eldest daughter of Akhenaten and Nefertiti, and the latter also bearing the name of Queen Tiye, the wife of Amenhotep III. To this group could be added the linen shawls that were wrapped around the statues, most of which have inscriptions in pen and ink showing they originated in the reign of Akhenaten, and the box, of which only a portion survives, which carried the names of Neferkheprure Waenre (Akhenaten), Nefernefruaten Nefertiti and 'the Great Royal Wife Meritaten'. Among reused pieces, many originally bore the titles of Ankh(et)kheprure, including the bands across the front of the King's body, a bow, and items of decoration of unknown use, called by Carter and then Nicholas Reeves 'sequins'.

Other pieces are even more intriguing. A series of four small coffins, one inside the other, were found in the Treasury. Inside the smallest was a lock of red-gold hair bearing the inscription of the Great Royal Wife Tiye. Among the *shabtis* (see page 118), a set of five had been presented to the King by the commander, Nakhtmin (sometimes called Minnakht). This man, probably a relative of Ay and Tiye, was clearly very close to the King. The lower part of a statue (that was probably his) in the Cairo Museum, shows him seated, with his wife and son carved in relief behind him. He is described here as, the 〈hieroglyphs〉 or 'God's Father', a title that requires further investigation (see below).

Another simple wooden statue is of the King dead, lying mummiform upon a bier, with a *ba* bird perched alongside. The figure was found within its own specially made coffin-like case, which was heavily coated with sticky black resin – perhaps residue from the resins poured over the body after mummification. The inscription at the side recorded that it was presented by the 'Overseer of Works in the Place of Eternity, Overseer of the Treasury, Maya'. The 'Place of Eternity' was the Valley of the Kings, and Maya's job was to supervise the cutting of the tombs there. A part of a jar found in the annexe was inscribed in hieratic with the name and title of Maya, together with his assistant, Tuthmosis. The same two men were later to enter into the tomb of Tuthmosis IV in the reign of Horemheb and leave their names behind on the walls. The tomb of Maya, identified originally at Saqqara by Karl Lepsius in his 1842–45 expedition, was found again in 1978 by the joint British–Dutch excavation team. This has revealed some magnificent painted reliefs showing the very high status of Maya.

Food and drink

As we've seen, every *ka* needed provision for the afterlife, and Tutankhamen was no exception. Food was found scattered throughout the tomb, probably disturbed by the robbers. The most common foodstuff, in life as in death, were pieces of bread of many different shapes and sizes. Packages containing pieces of preserved meat and poultry were found, and there were also packages of spices – garlic, fenugreek, coriander, cumin and sesame, spices still commonly used in Egyptian cooking today. Tutankhamen was also left two jars of honey, evidently a rarity, together with a selection of fruits and nuts.

Surprisingly, no jars of beer were found, although there were over thirty wine jars, sealed and dated on the shoulders, found within the burial chamber and annexe. Twenty-six jars bore the titles of the vintners and, sometimes, the category of wine. Of these, the majority (seventeen) were dated to either year 4 or 5 of Tutankhamen or, perplexingly, of the Aten, while six were dated year 9, again with the same name. One jar bore a year 10 date and another, an exception, bore year 31. The final jar was undated, but listed as the gift of Penthu, known to be a vizier of Tutankhamen's. The jars with the low dates are presumably those of Tutankhamen, although the names of the Aten on them remains a puzzle. Once again, like so many of the other pieces, it suggests that the Aten was not completely banned by Tutankhamen. The jar dated year 10 is a problem. Either it belonged to the reign of Akhenaten, thus making the jar about eighteen years old when placed in the tomb; or, alternatively, it shows that the King had just entered his tenth year on the throne when he died, a more probable explanation. The jar with the date 'year 31' can only have come from the reign of Amenhotep III.

Since all the Egyptian pottery vessels were unglazed, the liquid within slowly evaporated through their porous walls. It has been calculated that within three years of the jars being filled, nothing would remain within them except a sticky deposit in the bottom. This means that most of the wine jars of Tutankhamen were already empty when they were placed within the tomb.

Objects prepared for the King's death

Funerary couches

Some of the first things to strike the eyes of Carter, Carnarvon and Lady Evelyn as they entered the tomb of Tutankhamen were the three huge, gilded beds that faced them and stood against the wall opposite the entrance door. The beds appear to have had to have been dismantled before they were brought into the tomb and then put back together again, since Carter had to take them apart to get them out of the tomb again. Two of the beds, that of the cow Mehetweret and of the leopard Isimehtet, had been muddled up during manufacture, with the wrong heads placed on the wrong beds. Presumably the mistake was spotted, but instead of abandoning the projects, the craftsmen had carried on regardless, putting leopard-like spots all over the bed with the cow's head, and leaving the leopard bare of spots.

The three beds are clearly not designed to be used in life, since they are huge, the mattress standing over three feet above the ground, and heavily ornamented. The legs are joined together at the base into a flat-bottomed sledge. Although many sources suggest they were used for the mummification of the King, as suggested by some tomb paintings and reliefs elsewhere, this is not so. The sledge bottom indicates that the beds were made to be moved, so it is more likely that they were used to transport objects into the tomb as part of the funeral procession.

The mummified children

In a small wooden box in the treasury, two small anthropoid (human-shaped) coffins were found placed head to foot. Opened by Carter and given a cursory examination, the coffins were found to contain the tiny mummified remains of two infants. These were examined closely by the British pathologist Douglas Derry in 1932. He declared them to be the remains of newborn girls, one a five-month-old obviously miscarried foetus, and the other, a full-term stillborn child. X-rays of the mummies performed by Professor Harrison revealed that both shared common problems, including scoliosis or twisted spines, and all the signs of spina bifida. The two also shared Tutankhamen's unusual skull shape (see below).

The burial chamber

Within the burial chamber, the King's coffin was protected, as we have already seen, by a series of four huge, gilded wooden shrines, one inside the other. In the interior of the innermost shrine there was a rectangular stone sarcophagus. When the lid of the sarcophagus was raised, it revealed the outer of a series of three nestled coffins. Over the outside of the shrines was placed a huge linen sheet, studded with gold rosettes.

The shrines had been made in separate panels, and were so large that they had to be assembled within the tomb, and thus had to be dismantled there also when they were removed. Each piece had been marked by the makers with a black ink symbol indicating in which direction it was to be placed – for example, north. These guidelines had not been followed: instead, the pieces had been assembled hastily in the wrong order, banged together with such ferocity that dismantling them proved to be a nightmare for Carter and his team.

The sarcophagus within the shrines was found to have been cut from a single block of yellow quartzite, the hardest rock in Egypt. It evidently did not belong to the King – it was too small for the coffins, the outermost of which had had to have its feet cut down in order to fit inside. The lid, made from rose granite, did not match the sarcophagus, and had been cracked from side to side at some point. This lid had been painted, presumably at the time of the burial, to try to make it match the sarcophagus. Since paint had run down into the crack in the lid, it would seem that it was already broken when it was brought into the tomb and not when, as some suggest, it was being placed on the sarcophagus.

The outer two coffins were made of gilded wood. Below the lid of the outer coffin when it was first lifted, a blackened linen shroud was seen, covered with floral garlands. Among these flowers was a tiny wreath placed around the serpent on the King's headdress, called the uraeus. Although the wreath was uninscribed, Carter was later romantically to say that he found nothing more moving than this wreath in the whole tomb, imagining it as a last offering made by the widowed girl Queen Ankhesenamun to her dead husband. Although this has no basis in reality, it was a touching thought.

The innermost coffin, also covered in folds of linen, was found to be of pure gold, weighing nearly 300 pounds. Although Nicholas Reeves values this, as scrap metal, at over £1 million, I received a direct quotation from a jeweller of over £4.5 million.

The statues

Thirty gilded wooden statues were found within the tomb, some showing the King wearing his crown and regalia, or carrying out ritual hunting as Horus, the bringer of good, hunting Seth, the bearer of evil. The rest show a variety of assorted 'deities' or protective amuletic figures. Both of these sets are in some way strange. Many of the figures supposed to be Tutankhamen are unnamed, while the characters, distinctly Amarnan in type (see page 220) often do not look like the King at all. In fact, many of them, as Nicholas Reeves points out, clearly depict a woman. The statues of the 'deities' are a strange, unmatched and unfinished set, many representing curious, virtually unknown figures, while familiar figures such as Thoth are missing. Several statues supposedly of Tutankhamen were found wrapped in linen shawls which were marked in hieratic with dates in the reign of Akhenaten.

The Canopic shrine and chest

Within the treasury and dominating the room was another large gilded shrine, each side wall of it depicting, in relief, an image of a tutelary goddess. Four statues of these goddesses stand around the shrine, one at each wall, their arms outstretched. Two of these figures, Nephthys and Selkis, have been muddled up and placed on the wrong sides, so that they do not face the corresponding shrine wall.

Inside the shrine was a chest of Egyptian alabaster (actually calcite), with four human-headed stoppers covering four internal partitioned sections. Inside each of these compartments was found a small, solid gold coffinette, each containing a package of some of the King's internal organs. The faces of the stoppers bear no resemblance to Tutankhamen, and may have been either borrowed from elsewhere or used from stock. Similarly the coffinettes were not intended for him but had been reused, with the titles changed from Ankh(et)kheprure to Nebkheprure (Tutankhamen).

The shabtis

The ancient Egyptian word *wesheb* means 'to answer' or 'to respond'. One of the things hardest for Egyptians to accept during life was the heavy burden of work imposed on them, and clearly it was undesirable to face eternity knowing you would have to work hard there forever. So from the Middle Kingdom onwards, the Egyptians provided little 'worker' figures in their tombs which were intended to 'answer' when the deceased was called upon to work in the afterlife. These are today called *shabtis* or *ushabtis*.

The King had a total of 413 of these figures within the tomb. There were 365 workers (one for every day of the year, so none would be overworked); 36 overseers (one for every ten workers – that is, one foreman a week); and 12 top overseers, one for each month of the year. Most of the figures were marked with only the King's name, though others bore the inscription believed to reinvigorate them when they were called. Five were gifts from General Nakhtmin (see page 113).

The mummy

The mummy of the King was found lying within the third, innermost coffin of solid gold, with a gold mask covering his head and face. This mask was inlaid with stripes of glass on the headdress; with lapis lazuli in the beard and part of the broad-collar necklace); with quartz in the eyeballs; with turquoise in part of the snake decoration on the headdress, or uraeus; with cornelian as part of the broad-collar necklace; and with obsidian in the eye outline, eyebrows and pupils. Below the mask, the body was covered with linen that appeared blackened and sooty in consistency. The King's hands, marked with gilded pieces of wood, held the larger gold crook and flail. Around his neck was a broad-collar made up of flower petals and berries stitched onto a piece of shaped papyrus. Above this, a stone scarab beetle hung from a gold band. Below the hands, another broad gold band stretched the length of the body down to the feet, crossed in three places by narrow horizontal gold bands. None of these gold bands belonged to Tutankhamen, but had been rescued from the earlier burial of Ankh(et)kheprure. The body itself was stuck firmly into the gold coffin by large quantities (estimated at four gallons) of solidified gums and resins which had been poured over the body at the time of burial.

In November 1925 a decision was taken to examine the King's body while it still lay within the coffin. After making some frustrated attempts to preserve the outer wrappings using paraffin wax, one of the few preparations available at the time, the bandages were cut vertically and the mummy was then examined as much as was possible. Some 112 amulets and pieces of jewellery were found around the body, most pieces lying either around the neck or the arms. Because of the poor preservation of the wrappings and the difficulties encountered in getting to the mummy while it was still embedded in resins, unhappily not much of these outer wrappings have survived for further forensic examination.

The body of the King was in generally poor condition, with the little flesh that remained on the limbs brittle, carbonised and in places virtually absent. The head, however, protected by the golden mask, was much better preserved, although it still stuck obstinately to the base of the coffin. It is far from clear how the head and mask were finally extracted. Carter's official record differs from his notes. It is evident that the resins were so hard that initial attempts to free the body using chisels were useless. The official report says simply that 'hot knives' were used with success. Thomas Hoving suggested, on the basis of records he studied, that the team first used the heat of the sun, turning the coffin with the body in it upside down outside in the heat of the Valley, but that this also proved unsuccessful. He suggested that the body was finally removed by heating the coffin directly over burners. This may be closer to the truth. Hot knives would have had little effect on a great depth of rock-hard resin. To remove the mummy would have involved tediously sticking hot knives into the resins at the side; and then, somehow, trying to slide them underneath the body and the mask. If this were possible at all, which I doubt, it would have been extremely time-consuming. As one part was freed by inserting a hot knife into the resin, it would

The body of the boy-king, photographed during the first examination of the body, reveals him to have been a slim, fit young man with, oddly, a shaven head and tight-fitting skull-cap.

naturally reseal the previous section. The mask today is totally clean from all resins, although at the back of the striped headdress many pieces of inlaid glass are missing, presumably lost during the removal process. As these pieces are not stuck to the inside of the gold coffin today displayed in the Cairo Museum and have not been saved to be restored, then one can come to only one of two conclusions: either that the mask was damaged in the first place, and was thus reused despite the rather severe damage; or that the resins, at the time of the extraction, were completely melted by the general application of heat and were then spooned away, with the subsequent loss of pieces of the inlay which went unnoticed in the softened resinous matter. The last suggestion seems the most logical.

The King's body was observed to have been fully eviscerated, the internal organs being removed by a long abdominal incision in his left flank. There was no evidence of any corpulence, in folded skin and tissue, suggesting that the King must have been a fit and slender young man. The body measures 5 feet, 4.12 inches in height. In life he would have been somewhat taller, around 5 feet 6 inches. His head had been completely shaved and the only growth of hair remaining was fractional and probably postmortem. His scalp had been lightly coated with a white fatty substance and over this was placed a tight-fitting beaded cap which had the early Aten name on it. Under the cap and over the skull was a low conical pad of linen. The King's chin was shaven and, like the head, bore signs of only minimal postmortem growth. From neither of these could his hair colour be discerned. His ears had been pierced, and even after dessication the holes for earrings in the lobes were around half an inch in diameter.

On the first examination there was no opportunity to X-ray the body, and no apparent cause of death was visible. Derry, the examining pathologist, noted from the visible bones that the epiphyseal joints of the long bones had not fused, something that in most people happens between seventeen and nineteen years of age.

In 1963, the bones from Tomb 55 in the Cairo Museum were re-examined, X-rays and minute tissue samples were taken, and measurements of the bones were made (see below). In 1967 the Egyptian government, led by the Antiquities Organisation, gave approval for a full examination of the royal mummies in the Cairo Museum to be made using the latest X-ray equipment available at the time, with the caveat that the bodies had to be examined within their glass cases and with the minimum disturbance to either the bodies or the visiting public. As a result, by 1968 all the royal mummies had been examined save that of Tutankhamen. Permission was given for a final examination of the King's body to be made by a team headed by Professor R. G. Harrison from Liverpool University, the same person who had examined the human remains from Tomb 55 five years earlier. Once again, strict guidelines were laid down. The examination had to be carried out as quickly as possible within the tomb, the body was to be removed only briefly and the public were not to be kept out of the tomb while the examination took place. As a result, only mobile equipment could be used, and the X-ray plates could neither be developed nor examined until after the body was sealed back into the tomb.

Most of the X-rays were a remarkable success, with the exception of the full survey of the King's teeth. The dentist who accompanied the group, Frank Leek, devised a new method of X-raying the mouth using a slender radioactive isotope, intended to be inserted into the soft lower palate to record a panoramic survey of the teeth onto a photographic plate bound around the King's mouth. It was discovered, however, that the resins had hardened the palate to such an extent that the isotope could not be inserted at all. However, the general skull X-rays did give Leek enough evidence to publish a description of the dentition. The X-rays showed clearly that the King's vertebrae were in excellent condition. With tuberculosis prevalent in Europe in the 1950s, there had been some public speculation that this could have brought about the King's premature death, but this could now be discounted. Leek observed that the molar teeth were unerupted within the gums, a process that usually starts around the age of sixteen.

The initial estimate of the King's age at death was in the range of seventeen to nineteen, but later examination of other mummies from Egypt showed that the pathological data on which this was based, which had been taken from European bodies, needed to be readjusted as the development stages of people of North Africa and the Middle East took place somewhat earlier in life than in Europeans. For example, the fusing of the epiphyseal plates in Egyptians took place earlier than in Europeans; and this, together with the evidence of the teeth, suggests an age at death for the King of between sixteen and seventeen years.

Harrison also confirmed observations that the King's skull was unusual in shape, being wider, flatter on top and jutting out further at the back than is usual. Using Harrison's data, in 1992 an exact copy of the mummy of Tutankhamen was made under the guidance of Dr Michael Ridley for the Tutankhamen exhibition in Dorchester. Using a human skeleton of approximately the same age and dimensions that had been left for medical use, an exact facsimile was created for display. It was found that the only part of the body which needed considerable alteration was the skull, whose shape was dramatically different from the norm.

Comparing X-ray plates of Tutankhamen's skull with that of the skull in Tomb 55, it was observed that the two were identical in shape. Harrison further observed that there was a thinning of the bone of the skull behind the left ear, caused by pressure beneath the bone, probably a subdural haematoma or blood-swelling on the surface of, or within, the brain. While this was within normal parameters, it could have been, he suggested, caused by a blow to the back of the head and this, in turn, could have brought about the King's death.

X-ray plates of the skull show that the brain had been removed according to the usual Egyptian practice of the time, by breaking the ethmoid bone at the back of the nose and removing the brain tissue through the nostrils. Resins had subsequently entered into the skull. These formed two distinct levels. One level was, as might be expected, at the back of the skull, with the surface of the hard resin parallel to the face – in other words, the resin had entered the head while the body was laying flat on its back. The other level, surprisingly, was at right angles to the first, filling the top of the cranial cavity, demonstrating that at some point in the process the King's skull had been hanging upside down. Also to be observed was a small piece of bone at the back of the skull. Harrison never commented on this fragment, although it clearly did not come from behind the left ear where the bone was intact and not fractured; nor did it appear to be the broken ethmoid bone used for brain extraction. Since examining the skull, radiologists seem united in deeming the damage slight and postmortem, caused by the rough handling of the body at some point during the mummification process.

X-rays also showed unusual similarities between the bones of the arms of both Tutankhamen and the body in Tomb 55. Both had inherent 'holes' just above the joints – so-called epitrochlear foramen. It was subsequently found, when blood groupings were established by Dr Connolly of Liverpool University, that the King was of blood group A2 with the antigens M and N present, although the rhesus factor could not be fixed. This was identical to the blood group of the body in Tomb 55.

From the data, it could be established that the two bodies were very closely related indeed. Using the historical evidence available to him at the time, Harrison surmised that the body in Tomb 55 was in all probability Tutankhamen's brother, Smenkhkare. That the King died early was now proven, and the possibility suggested during the post-mortem, of a blow to the back of the head, aroused some excitement and controversy. Many books after 1968 have postulated that Tutankh-amen was either murdered or died from an accidental blow to the head, culminating in the hypothesis of Bob Brier's *The Murder of Tutankhamen*, which brings old evidence together with surmise to suggest that the assailant was Tutankhamen's successor, Ay.

The complete picture

All the evidence from the tomb shows that the burial of the King was an extremely hasty one. The sarcophagus was borrowed; the lid was found as scrap and some attempt had been made to paint it; the burial shrines were banged together in the wrong order; the paintings in the burial chamber are distorted and the painters had not cleaned up the mess they made; and much of the important funerary equipment, such as the Canopic jars for holding human viscera and the bands along the King's body, were not his. The statues, many of which belonged to a woman and not to him, display all the signs of being taken from elsewhere. They are a nonsensical and incomplete set. Most of the furniture and many of the other pieces belonged to his early childhood, things he had long since outgrown.

The King died around the age of sixteen or seventeen, a fit young man who loved going out hunting with his dog and, despite the writing palettes, most of which were unused, seemed, like most teen-agers and most of his ancestors, to have little real interest in formal education. He clearly loved the active life, with soldier's kilts and equipment being made for him from childhood. His chariots had been used, so clearly he had been taught to drive; and the breastplate made for a soldier in action suggests he may even have carried out at least one campaign. The furniture within his tomb reflected what was known about his life – that although he spent most of his short reign in Luxor, he was probably born and brought up in Tell el Amarna, where one or two pieces originated. All through the tomb, the names of Akhenaten and his daughters were found on objects that he presumably inherited from them. Several pieces, those bearing the names of Maya and his assistant Tuthmosis, and of Nakhtmin, give evidence of personal friendships beyond the call of pure loyalty to a King. The walking-stick/reed show that even as a child he was indulged and respected.

There is no evidence at all of his parents; nor of his brother Smenkhkare. On the contrary, the materials used by him at his coronation show him standing alone. There was no evidence of the civil turmoil suggested on the Restoration Stela commemorating his coronation. He may or may not have been the father of two daughters, both of whom died before the end of a full-term pregnancy.

Evidence concerning his death comes from his mummy. There is no evidence whatever of a fracture, while the thinning of the skull behind the left ear shows long-term pressure beneath the bone. If the King had been murdered then the murderer had first to hit him on the base of his skull behind his ear, neither an easy nor a natural place for a would-be murderer to strike an unexpected blow; and the King clearly survived it for some months afterwards. Not, one might surmise, the most successful murder attempt. There are, however, other possibilities. Could he, for example, have died accidentally? We know from evidence in the tomb that he was keen on hunting. A misthrown throw-stick or badly aimed arrow might have struck the King on the back of the head. And we must not discount the possibility that he might have died of purely natural causes. The shape of his skull, for example, is far from normal and could well have presaged an eventual problem that might have brought about his death.

From the tomb, taking into consideration the 'accepted story' outlined in the previous chapter, there seems at first to be no answers. The trail apparently stops here. Or does it? Perhaps we are, again, simply asking the wrong questions.

PART TWO

THE HISTORICAL
TUTANKHAMEN

Introduction

—

Public interest in Tutankhamen had deepened after the discovery of the tomb in 1922. The photographs and illustrations of Egyptian objects inspired artists worldwide, and the designs and colours entranced architects, carpenters, interior decorators, jewellers, textile manufacturers and fashion houses. Ancient Egyptian motifs were soon to be found everywhere. Everyone wanted to know more – and the media, from Hollywood to the international press, were happy to oblige.

After the initial excitement over the discovery of the tomb had died down, the reporters gathered outside the tomb in the Valley of the Kings became bored with how slowly events were moving, and started looking for new angles. In the early months of 1923 Marie Corelli, an American novelist who specialised in the 'Gothic' horror novels so much in vogue at the time, wrote a letter to the *New York Times* saying she had in her possession an old Egyptian book which contained the line, 'Death comes on wings to him who enters the tomb of a Pharaoh.' Bearing in mind the early Arab interest in the occult side of Egypt (see above, page 94) the existence of the book and the statement is reasonable, but it was based on no genuine ancient Egyptian inscription. In her letter, Corelli predicted doom, gloom and unexpected death to Carnarvon and Carter. And it was very soon after the letter appeared, in April 1923, that Carnarvon died.

Shortly afterwards, a reporter from the London *Times* was interviewing the novelist Sir Arthur Conan Doyle on a different matter. Conan

Doyle was known by his contemporaries not only as the 'biographer' of Sherlock Holmes, but also as a fervent spiritualist. He had, for example, given credibility to the infamous photograph of the Cottingley fairies taken by two small girls in Yorkshire, England. The reporter mentioned to him the death of the Fifth Earl, which had been accompanied by the sudden powercut in Cairo, and the inexplicable howling of the Earl's dog at Highclere at the exact moment of death. He referred to Corelli's letter and asked Conan Doyle if, in his opinion, there might be any truth in Corelli's prediction of a 'pharaoh's curse'. Conan Doyle appears to have agreed that the curse could well have been responsible for the death. And so the curse was publicly launched.

Within a short time, newspapers had carried word of 'Tutankhamen's Curse' around the world. They reported that the statement 'Death comes on wings' appeared on the doorway of the tomb, or on 'magical bricks' within it. It was but a short step to convincingly worded articles claiming that the tomb was 'magically protected' against intruders. Some tried to make rational explanations – that Tutankhamen had died of some infectious disease that the excavators had caught; that bats' droppings had entered their lungs and caused breathing difficulties; or, if nothing else, that Tutankhamen's spirit was defending itself against the unwelcome intruders. Nor did the belief diminish as the years went by. The scientific discovery of radioactivity naturally led to suggestions that Tutankhamen's tomb had been protected by radioactive material. The theories came thick and fast.

Egyptologists have protested long and hard that no such curse ever existed, but to no avail. It has often been pointed out that Carnarvon had been ill when he went to Egypt and was at a low ebb at the time of his death due to political circumstances; that powercuts are common in Cairo; and that many others involved in the tomb, such as Carter and Lady Evelyn, lived to a ripe old age. But nothing can ever convince the followers of the curse. Today television programmes have joined in the fun. Announcers with husky voices, accompanied by eerie music and actors dressed in unlikely linen skirts with rubberised 'bald' heads, will intone, 'Of course there is no truth in the curse – BUT . . .'

To demonstrate the sheer improbability of this delusion, fifty years after the discovery, in 1972, following diplomatic discussions between the governments of Egypt, Britain and the United States, a major collection of Tutankhamen's treasures was permitted to leave Egypt for the first time, to be mounted on display in British and American national museums. Given the nature of the turmoil around its discovery, it was little short of a miracle of generosity that such an exhibition should be considered at all, and amply demonstrated the trust felt by the Egyptian government. Millions queued up to see the treasures in both countries; I was one of them, standing in the sun for five hours just to get a glimpse of the exhibition.

The treasures, including the famous golden mask that covered the dead King's face, arrived in Britain on a special RAF flight. Several years later the *News of the World* printed front-page reports that the 'curse' was still alive. The evidence was hilarious. The flight crew had apparently been bedevilled by bad luck ever since flying the accursed treasures over. One of them, who had reputedly played cards on the case containing the mask, had kicked it, joking to a friend, 'Look, I'm kicking the most expensive thing in the world.' Some time later, he broke the same leg! And if that were not enough, another member of the same flight crew had been divorced! What more evidence could be needed?

The curse, while demonstrably totally fallacious, still has many followers today. The truth of the matter, as the objects within the tomb suggest, is that Tutankhamen's burial was in no way special or ominous. The tomb contained exactly the same chambers as any other royal tomb, although on a small scale and organised in a different way. The King whose body it had protected for so long was apparently a very minor ruler who, from the inscriptions on the wine jars associated with his name, ruled for nine years and, from one inscription, may just have celebrated his tenth anniversary on the throne at the time he died. So far as the Egyptians were concerned, he was, in the long run, of less importance than many of the other great kings of the Eighteenth Dynasty. Efforts to wipe out his very existence had almost been successful, and had it not been for the discovery of the tomb, he would be an historical nonentity to this day. One of the reasons the tomb may have survived intact at all was that it was of such little importance that people simply forgot it. There was certainly no cause to protect it. The only way in which the tomb was unique was that it survived to the present. It makes one wonder about the material goods that some of the long-living, great kings of Egypt would have 'taken with them' to their eternity. The splendours of the burial of Ramesses II, who ruled for sixty-seven years in the Nineteenth Dynasty, fought some of Egypt's most noted battles and built some of her greatest monuments, can only be imagined with awe.

These tales of mystic curses have diverted people's attention from the real problems of pinning down the historical Tutankhamen. Here, we were told, was the tomb of a young man who had become, as Pharaoh, one of the wealthiest and most powerful rulers of his time, who had no right to the throne, who was the younger brother of the homosexual lover of the previous king, who tried to reintroduce Maat into Egypt – yet there was not the slightest hint of any of this in his tomb.

The tomb contains many basic anomalies. Items such as the borrowed sarcophagus with its broken lid pose more questions than they answer. While royal officials may, out of desperation, have reused or 'borrowed' equipment from previous owners, the idea of one of the great kings of the Eighteenth Dynasty needing to do so seems almost unbelievable. Although burials at Tanis, in the northeastern delta region, from the Third Intermediate Period used borrowed burial equipment, this was a time of poverty and confusion in Egypt. The Eighteenth Dynasty, by contrast, was the very heyday of Egyptian culture. Even if Tutankhamen was not a powerful or long-living king, he still represented Egypt, the land where, as one prince wrote, 'Gold is more plentiful . . . than sand.' Is it realistic to suppose that a king who was buried in a coffin valued today at £4.5 million in scrap metal alone had no access to basic burial equipment like a sarcophagus, but had to get it from another tomb?

The painting on the walls of the burial chamber were very hastily done: the lower part of the walls, below a dado, are not only unpainted but still bear clear drips of paint that have not been wiped up. The ceiling in the burial chamber still has smoke circles left by the lamps used for light by the painters. These were not even cleaned off, let alone overpainted with the usual astrological ceiling illustrations that royal tombs often had. The figures are squat and distorted. Add to this the fact that the gilded shrines had, as we have seen, been hammered together the wrong way round, and no matter how you try to explain it, it all indicates an extremely hasty burial.

There are other major problems. If you examine the chart on page 316, you will observe that Tutankhamen ruled for nine years; Smenkhkare for perhaps two; and Akhenaten, before that, for seventeen. Among the wine-jars in the tomb of Tutankhamen, most, as we have seen, came from the reign of Tutankhamen, while a few, from the year-dates on them, came from the reign of Akhenaten. But one jar is dated year 31. It cannot have come from the reigns of Akhenaten, Smenkhkare or Tutankhamen, none of whom ruled that long. If you look at the chart, it can only have come from the reign of Amenhotep III, who ruled for thirty-nine years. This jar of wine, therefore, was eight years old when Amenhotep III died. If we add to this all the years of the reigns of Akhenaten, Smenkhkare and Tutankhamen, the wine-jar was around thirty-six years old when it was buried in Tutankhamen's tomb.

Now this fact may not, to us, arouse much surprise. After all, in our day wines may be hundreds of years old – and are more valuable for their age. A wine thirty-six years old to us is a relatively common thing. But this was not the case in ancient Egypt. Wine was made in these jars after the grapes, usually black (from the remains in the jars so far examined), had been pressed under foot. The juice was poured into the jars and allowed to ferment, probably using natural yeasts present on the skin of the grape. The jars would then be sealed and the date and place of its manufacture, together with the class of wine, was marked on its shoulders. Jars were sometimes burnished with a stone before firing, but with the exception of the fine faience vessels were completely unglazed. As we have seen, the walls of these jars were extremely porous, and after three years only a thick concentrate would have been left in the bottom of the jar. In other words, it was quite impossible for Egyptian wine to be 'racked' to mature; it had to be drunk within the first year.

What is immediately apparent from the dates on the jars in the tomb is that the majority of them would have been past their sell-by date. They would have been completely empty at the time of the burial. This perhaps should not be surprising. As we have already pointed out, it is one thing to provide a valuable substance for burial with the dead, but one needs to consider the requirements of the living first. Thus the inclusion of most of the jars, even in a royal tomb, must have been only symbolic. But is it not strange, under these circumstances, that a sealed wine-jar thirty-six years old should exist at all, let alone be placed within a royal tomb? The Egyptians were making wine at least 2000 years before Tutankhamen ruled Egypt, so it is quite unrealistic to suggest that they did not know about the evaporation of wine. That being the case, a jar so old would surely usually have been smashed, or at least reused.

The commonest dates on the wine-jars are year 4 and 5. Some of these bear the names of vineyards associated with Tutankhamen, others with the Aten. If we assume that those associated with the name of the Aten were bottled in years 4 and 5 of Akhenaten's rule and not in the reign of Tutankhamen, even these jars would be around twenty-five years old. If none of these jars contained wine at the time they were buried in the tomb, then most probably they were included as memorabilia – in other words, because Tutankhamen or his friends and relatives saw some relevance in including the name of Amenhotep III – a king who had died twelve years before Tutankhamen had been born, and whom he had never known. So why should the name have been included?

Another great problem lies in the picture on the 'Golden Throne'. On the back of it, Tutankhamen and his wife are shown sitting beneath the rays of the Aten. It has been suggested that the chair had been owned by someone else, and had depicted them, but had been repossessed and altered by Tutankhamen. This is far from clear, however. The chair originated in Tell el Amarna, whence Tutankhamen presumably took it. But according to the Restoration Stela, Tutankhamen, finding the country in chaos at the time of his coronation, restored the old religion of Amen and re-endowed the temple of Karnak. The colonnade of Luxor temple, once attributed to Amenhotep III, has been demonstrably proved to be the one major standing monument of the reign of Tutankhamen. On its inner walls are pictured scenes from the Opet festival of Tutankhamen. Inscriptions from Tell el Amarna show that the city was finally abandoned sometime around year 2 or 3 of Tutankhamen's reign. During his restoration of the old religion to please and placate the priesthood and the people, the young King even changed his name from Tutankhaten to Tutankhamen, and that of his wife from Ankhesenpaaten to Ankhesenamun. Yet the chair implies that after they restored the religion of Amen, they kept the chair with them in their palace in Luxor, a chair that showed the King and Queen participating in the very heresy that they were publicly trying to deny.

Many books have even called this chair 'the royal throne'. This not only suggests that the King publicly denied the heretical cult while sitting on a chair which actually celebrates it – but that he used it in public on state occasions! And then, even more than that, it had had to be carried along in procession in public view to the King's burial chamber for interment there. It makes no sense whatsoever. Why should this chair, showing the royal couple plainly under the rays of the Aten, the god they were publicly rejecting, have been saved for his burial – and in Luxor, home of the heresy's rejection? And why should the King's name on the chair back be 'Tutankhamen' – the 'Living Image of Amen' – while bearing the name Tutankhaten on the arms and the image of the Aten – the two images that were supposed to be 'at war' with each other?

A very similar anomaly can be seen on the sceptre (see page 112) which also clearly shows the names of both the Aten and Amen on the same piece of regalia. Even if the 'Golden Throne' had been used only in private, this was not the case with the royal sceptre. This sceptre's name means 'power', the power and authority of kingship itself. Are we to assume that the powerful and rich state of Egypt could not afford to replace it when Atenism was declared a heresy? That the heretical inscriptions could not have been erased? Imagine if Decian or Diocletian, Roman emperors who proscribed Christianity and denounced its adherents as heretical, had carried a sceptre that bore the name of Christ! There is clearly huge confusion among these pieces that needs further attention.

A little detective work

Despite the fact that no corroborating evidence for the accepted story was found within the tomb of Tutankhamen, each piece has its own story to tell.

The funeral 'couches' for example, found in the antechamber, are regularly described as having being used for the King's mummification. The couches are heavily gilded and ornate with mattresses of interwoven cord. Mummification, which involves the bloody evisceration of the body and its subsequent laying-out in natron, was a smelly and extremely messy process. Even the last stages of bandaging required the use of pints of resins and perfumes. Not only do the couches bear no sign of any staining, as they would surely have done if used for any part of the mummification process, but their mattresses stand over three feet above the ground and are very wide. Even a person of unusually great height would be unable to bend across them, over a body laid on top, to reach the middle of the bed easily. Nor would there have been any use for three couches. As mentioned above, on each, their four legs are joined by a sledge, and thus they are clearly designed to be moved by sliding. Since they were funerary in design, this would suggest that they were intended for moving something into the tomb. On the wall of the burial chamber adjacent to the treasury, the funeral procession of the King is shown with the body being dragged on one of these couches. The King's body was enclosed within three coffins; there are three couches. It seems logical that each couch carried a coffin on its journey into the tomb. They would have been used like hearses. The 'mistaken identities' of two of the three beds is still a problem. Perhaps, as was stated earlier, we are being too purist; perhaps it is simply that mistakes sometimes happened.

The jewellery within the tomb also has a clear message to tell. It has been said frequently, and is a feature of the accepted story, that Tutankhaten was the brother of Smenkhkare and thus had no claim to the throne in his own right. To establish this right he had to marry Ankhesenpaaten, the surviving daughter of Nefertiti and Akhenaten. Yet all the regalia, the crook and flail, the sceptre, the pectoral, the staff and the earrings show Tutankhaten totally alone at his coronation. He is not pictured alongside his young wife anywhere except on pieces that bear his name in a cartouche – in other words, after he was crowned. There is no evidence whatsoever that he owed his coronation to his royal wife. On the contrary, the pieces in the tomb suggest that he was crowned alone, in his own right.

It is perplexing that there is also no evidence whatever to show that Queen Ankhesenamun, as she was at the time of her husband's death, was actually present at the funeral. Although there are gifts from courtiers, there are no named gifts from her. The scene painted on the burial chambers rear wall, which shows the Opening of the Mouth ceremony and the King being welcomed into the afterlife, does not picture her, as might be expected. The tiny wreath of flowers on the second coffin of the King, interpreted by Carter as the 'last offering of the widowed Queen for her dead husband', was no such thing. It bears no inscription. The attribution is simply that of the excavator's romantic imagination. The wall adjacent to the treasury shows the funeral procession, with a group of people, including two who can be recognised as the viziers of Egypt, but not the Queen. Interestingly, there was no provision for her own burial within the tomb. If she died before her husband, she must have been buried elsewhere. Since many items were moved into Tutankhamen's tomb from other tombs, and since the mummified foetuses were included in the tomb, there is no reason why, if she had predeceased him, she could not have had her burial alongside that of her husband. Take, for example, the burial of Yuya and Thuya in the Valley of the Kings; or that of Kha and Meryt from the workmen's village Deir el Medina. Both tombs were found intact. In both tombs, the mummies of both people were found lying in the tomb. The notion that in both cases, both partners died at exactly the same time seems unreasonable. By no matter how narrow a margin, one must have died first. To be buried together one must have been 'stored' after death until the other died; or the first one must have been buried and then the tomb reopened later. Ankhesenamun was not, and was never intended to be, buried in the tomb of her husband. She must have been buried alone somewhere else – but where? Since we do not have the burials of any of the Queens of the Eighteenth Dynasty (the so-called 'Valley of the Queens' contains only the burials of ladies and children related to Ramesses II of the Nineteenth Dynasty), this suggests that there is, somewhere in Egypt, an entire missing 'Valley of the Queens' awaiting discovery. But there is no clear evidence to show whether she was still alive or not at the time of her husband's funeral.

And what are we to understand from the inclusion within the tomb of the two mummified foetuses? They are generally interpreted as being the stillborn children of Tutankhamen and his Queen. But there is, once again, a problem here that needs addressing. Are we to assume that every miscarriage of a queen resulted in the mummification of the foetus, which was then stored somewhere within the palace to accompany the king's eventual death? Or were they buried and then exhumed when their father died to be buried with him? What if, as was the case with many kings, they ruled for many years? Ramesses II, for instance, had hundreds of wives and ruled for sixty-seven years. Miscarriage and infant mortality must have been a common hazard. Are we seriously to assume that such a king stored all of these against the day of his eventual burial? It makes no sense. Some Egyptologists have suggested that the children in the tomb of Tutankhamen were not his, but were included symbolically to provide him with children in the afterlife. But again there is no evidence for this ever happening. Any such idea is based purely on speculation. Why two girls? Would not a son have been preferable? And surely one child would have been sufficient. Perhaps there is another explanation.

But the greatest anomaly of all, if you reconsider all of this archaeological evidence, is in the age of Tutankhamen himself. We know that he was around sixteen to seventeen years old when he died, and that he had ruled for nine years. This would have made him seven or eight at most when he was crowned. This means, if we count backwards through the previous reigns, that he would have been born around year 12 of Akhenaten. We know that for Akhenaten year 12 was very dramatic for many reasons (see page 88), including the eviction of Nefertiti and the public appearance of Smenkhkare.

We know that Akhenaten exiled himself to Tell el Amarna after he had first moved there and that no evidence is available to suggest that he ever left there again. As Akhenaten elevated Smenkhkare to co-regency in year 12, the two men must have known each other for some time beforehand, and thus Smenkhkare must also have been living in, or was a regular visitor to, Tell el Amarna. At any rate, when promoted by the King, he must have been living there. If Tutankhamen is the little brother of Smenkhkare, then at the very moment that his brother openly entered the bed of the King, causing the eviction and public humiliation of Nefertiti, Tutankhamen's mother was actually giving birth to him.

The picture that we must believe, then, is of a much older youth becoming the lover of the King of Egypt at the same time that this youth's mother was giving birth to a baby. Egyptian texts suggest that mothers breastfed their infants as long as they could – a practice still common in countries where weaning is often the riskiest time of a child's existence. The wisdom text of Ani, in the Cairo Museum, states that one should revere one's mother because 'she had her breast in your mouth for three years'. Thus, while Smenkhkare was dominating the palace, his mother must have been breastfeeding his baby brother around the place. In other words, we cannot imagine that Tutankhamen in any way jostled for the throne. There is no way that he could have decided to 'marry' Princess Ankhesenpaaten in order to take the throne. He was simply too young.

Was it his parents who pushed him forward? Since they had become the parents of the King through their son Smenkhkare, then surely their pictures or names as parents of a King should survive on pictures or inscriptions, and should have emerged during excavations in Tell el Amarna, if not from Tutankhamen's tomb. Amenhotep III had married a 'commoner', Tiye, and not only are the names of her parents written everywhere alongside hers, but they were also accorded a magnificent burial in the Valley of the Kings. Whoever they were, the mother and father of Smenkhkare and Tutankhamen were not just the parents of a queen, as were Yuya and Thuya – they were the parents of two pharaohs. So why have we found absolutely nothing about them anywhere?

The problems go deeper than that. By Tutankhamen's own state-ment on the Restoration Stela, the temples of the old gods (principally Amun) had been closed and abandoned to nature when he took the throne. Tutankhamen is said to have corrected all of this. He returned to Luxor; reinstated the festival of Opet; banished the Aten; brought back Amen; and confirmed it all by changing his and his wife's names. Are we supposed to believe that a seven-year-old boy really did all this? Even if you believe that it might have been possible (and seven-year-old boys then were essentially no different from seven-year-old boys now), then consider that this child had spent the whole of his short life brought up in the court of Akhenaten, alongside his powerful older brother Smenkhkare. The only religion he had ever known was that of the Aten. We are suggesting, then, that he had an interest in this religion to start with; that he then threw out the only thing he knew for the sake of something that had been finished twelve years before his birth; that he reinstated a festival that he knew nothing at all about; and that he threw out the religion of his brother's lover, the man to whom both he and his brother owed their thrones. What could have inspired him to act against the very brother and the King who had gained him the post of Pharaoh in the first place? It is clear that he could not have done any of this. It is not even convincing to suggest that he ordered someone to do it for him. Someone must have been controlling him. This someone knew about Amen and the festival of Opet; he must have been at least in his mid-twenties to have remembered what the old religion was about and to have lived through the seventeen years of Akhenaten's reign. It must also have been someone powerful, since he was in a position to control the King; and it must have been someone who disliked everything that had happened previously in Akhenaten's reign.

One of the problems with archaeology is that we who study it can easily distance ourselves from the core of our study – the people themselves. We deal with facts and material objects, and often we forget that we are dealing with flesh-and-blood people who were born, lived, had ideas and thoughts, relationships of love and hate, and then died. The facts obscure the reality. But around 3500 years ago, along the Nile Valley, a very real little boy of seven or eight, the age of children first attending school in some countries, played not with sand trays and wax crayons, but with gold regalia; listened not to stories of the imagination but to affairs of state from officials who, by virtue of his position, had to listen attentively to whatever he, a little child, 'decreed'.

In order for Tutankhamen to become King, his predecessor must have died. In this case, it was his older brother Smenkhkare. We know that Smenkhkare married Princess Meritaten, the eldest daughter of Akhenaten. As far as we can ascertain, since neither of them are ever heard of again, they must have died at the same time. We know that Meritaten was born soon after the start of her father's reign. Allowing Akhenaten's seventeen years of rule and Smenkhkare's two, this would have made her around nineteen years old; and her husband presumably must have been a similar age. It is highly unlikely that two nineteen-year-olds died of natural causes at exactly the same time. One must assume that someone who opposed everything Smenkhkare stood for must have removed them both. If this is the case, why did Tutankhamen become King at all? Why should someone kill the existing King – presumably because of his homosexuality and heretical views – only to replace him with that person's seven-year-old brother? We know of several occasions in ancient Egypt when the official line of kings died out and the throne then went sideways into the hands of a vizier or similar official – at any rate, into the hands of some very powerful man. We are suggesting here that a man powerful and influential enough to murder the King and Queen should then stand aside for a seven-year-old without the least right to the throne. It makes no sense.

When Tutankhamen was crowned, we know from inscriptions that as well as viziers, two extremely powerful old men were appointed viceroys to rule Egypt on the King's behalf, presumably until he was old enough to take control for himself. These two men were Ay, the brother of Queen Tiye, Akhenaten's mother; and Horemheb, Commander-in-Chief of the Egyptian army. Both of them ultimately became King of Egypt in turn. If either of them murdered Smenkhkare and Meritaten, then it is astounding that they allowed Tutankhamen to be crowned; both were ambitious, both highly intelligent. Ay became Viceroy of Upper Egypt, based in Luxor; Horemheb, Viceroy of Lower Egypt, based in Memphis. One of them could have had total power by himself – so why settle for only half?

And what of Tutankhamen? Who protected him? Who and where were his parents? Was public hatred of Smenkhkare so great that when he died, his parents were killed also? Where did all Tutankhamen's family disappear to? His older brother had aroused such hostility in the country that Tutankhamen would now have an uphill battle to restore Maat to Egypt. Now Smenkhkare was dead, and perhaps his parents too, did Tutankhamen have any other relatives left to help him? Was it they who were protecting him? Perhaps we should widen our field and search not just for Tutankhamen's parents, but for his other relatives.

Let us examine the facts as we have them so far. Smenkhkare had been publicly proclaimed co-ruler of Egypt, rising from the relative obscurity of his birth to the acquisition of such power from his royal male lover that he caused the downfall of the great Queen Nefertiti herself. We know someone strongly advised, if not controlled, his brother the little boy-King. Is it not likely that this would have been a member of his family? Without someone's support, Tutankhamen had, ostensibly, no right to the throne whatever, yet the evidence proves beyond a doubt that he was crowned in his own right. If his family had been removed, and the country was, as the Restoration Stela has it, so hostile, it is doubtful the boy would have survived his coronation at all. Clearly someone felt it was in their interests to back the boy's claim, despite his shaky background. If any of his family did indeed survive the death of Smenkhkare, now here they were encouraging the younger son, who had inherited the throne of Egypt from that older brother, to reject the very cause of the man who had promoted their family. What disloyalty for the cause they should surely have fought to protect! And how could the mere younger brother of a homosexual

141

commoner, who had interfered with the royal family to such an extent that the beloved Queen was ousted, claim any public support whatever?

Let us now consider Tutankhamen's position within the framework of the Egyptian state at the time of his crowning. How must Egypt have felt as a whole when a child, whose only link to power was through his older brother, was crowned King? As has been discussed, two of Egypt's previous kings (Tuthmosis IV and Amenhotep III) had both been young children at the time of their coronation. The rising power of the Hittites threatening Egypt's empire, combined with a period of inactivity under Akhenaten, meant that the need for an adult at the helm was never stronger.

It has been said that Smenkhkare was married to Meritaten in order to maintain respectability. There are no clues as to what happened eventually to her when Smenkhkare disappeared. And since Ankhesenpaaten married Tutankhaten, she clearly survived the harrowing events of the late years of her father's reign. There are no clues at all as to what happened to her younger sisters, Nefernefrure and Setepenre, but as little more is heard of them, they probably died in early infancy. So was there, from all of this, no more suitable heir to the throne than little Tutankhaten?

It is always hard to recreate the past. Monuments do not readily reveal feelings and emotions. But consider the situation. At the time of the death of Akhenaten, Egypt was plunged into chaos. The King's palace, away in Tell el Amarna, was remote. For many years the King of Egypt had been inaccessible to the people. Now the impostor Smenkhkare was presented for coronation and shortly thereafter vanished from sight, along with his wife, Princess Meritaten. Suddenly someone, we know not who, presented the impostor's child-brother for coronation – and despite the existence of a legitimate princess, it was considered a better situation than the crowning of a girl. The child was backed by strong supporters who could maintain the boy's public credibility.

Public reaction to Akhenaten's very public rejection of his beloved wife is unrecorded. Queen Nefertiti had played an important role within the city of Tell el Amarna, and illustrations in tombs and on the stones recovered from buildings show her everywhere with her husband, the two of them in close and warm embrace. It is hard to believe that his rejection of her aroused anything other than hostility from the citizens. And he did not reject her for just anyone, but he rejected her for another man.

In some cultures and at some times, homosexuality has been not only accepted but highly praised. There is no evidence at all for this in ancient Egypt. In 4000 years of texts, there is only one that even alludes to homosexuality, dating from the Middle Kingdom, which speaks of a general who was caught in the act of sneaking into the bedroom of the king. Of the many tens of thousands of pictures and inscriptions, there is no other allusion to homosexuality. If it had been accepted naturally, as in, for instance, ancient Greece, then there would have been no need to cover it up – references to homosexuality would surely abound. The lack of evidence suggests that either it was publicly deemed not to exist, or was so frowned upon that references to it were never allowed. The only other possibility is that homosexuality did not exist at all in ancient Egypt!

On a personal level, Akhenaten, if homosexual, must have struggled hard with his nature and agonised privately over his feelings. Despite all that, he put on a brave public face, married one of the most beautiful women of his time, fathered six daughters with her, and had them all depicted as the happiest family ever to sit on the throne of Egypt. By his very openness, Akhenaten opened himself to public approbation or criticism. Then, faced with true love for a member of his own sex – a serious situation in such a society and for the most important man alive in the known world at the time, politically speaking – he made what must have been the hardest decision of his life. Instead of keeping his feelings suppressed, he 'came out of the closet', throwing his wife out of the palace and welcoming in her stead young Smenkhkare. Akhenaten declared his true feelings in public, and in the ensuing turmoil his wife, Nefertiti, hurt, scorned and publicly rejected, flounced out of the palace into ultimate obscurity and death. How the public must have hated Akhenaten – and focused their hatred on the one who had caused it!

How, then, would those same people have reacted when the brother of the person who had caused such problems first took the throne and then, almost at once, caused religious chaos? It would be a brave person indeed who undertook all that. And yet we are to believe that the boy who did it was only seven years old. There is clearly a huge problem here to be resolved, and it all hinges on who, exactly, Tutankhamen was. If we can establish who his parents were, who supported him and why, and what motivated them to restore the old religion, we might then be able to understand a little of the enigma.

It would have been completely reasonable for people to feel upset. Ever since the tomb was opened and the body of Tutankhamen was revealed for the first time, people asked how he had died. The post-mortem examination of 1968 (see page 121) showed a thinning of the bone of the skull behind the left ear, a problem that the pathologist, R. G. Harrison, stated in his report, 'may have been caused by a blow to the back of his head and this, in turn, may have brought about his death'. It was not the first time that foul play had been suggested. Carter himself believed from the start that it was possible Tutankhamen may have been murdered because of the problems he faced and the civil disturbance recorded on the Restoration Stela. Even in 1998, this theory persisted when the author Bob Brier suggested that Ay, Tutankhamen's successor, killed the boy on no stronger grounds than that, as his potential successor, he had a motive. Did Tutankhamen indeed receive a blow to the head? And if so, what evidence is there to suggest whether the blow was accidental or deliberate? To stand any chance of finding out, we need to return to the same task of finding out who Tutankhamen really was.

A block found in Hermopolis, the modern Ashmunein, on the opposite bank of the Nile from Tell el Amarna, is now in the Brooklyn Museum. It has one of the few references to Tutankhamen as a child, referring to him as 'the King's son, his beloved'. This is vital evidence. We have seen that his regalia suggests that he was crowned alone and in his own right. This inscription confirms that. This would mean Smenkhkare and Tutankhamen, far from being the sons of commoners, were royal princes by birth. But whose son was he?

The Restoration Stela says that, 'His Majesty came to the throne of his father'. This suggests that his predecessor was his father. His predecessor was Smenkhkare. So was Smenkhkare his father rather than his brother? The only evidence we have so far as hard fact is that Smenkhkare existed, and that the body in Tomb 55 was closely related to Tutankhamen. There is nothing at all on or around the body to identify it positively. The body does not have to be his brother – going by logic, it could be his father. But if Smenkhkare was his father, who was his mother? The only woman found alongside Smenkhkare is Meritaten, the eldest daughter of Akhenaten and Nefertiti. We find their names linked together after year 12 of Akhenaten's reign; and we know that Tutankhamen was born around year 12. There is no positive evidence to show that they had not been married before year 12, so that would seem a possible solution.

However, if Smenkhkare had been married to Meritaten and they were Tutankhamen's parents, then Akhenaten would have been Tutankhamen's grandfather and Nefertiti his grandmother. If the body in Tomb 55 was indeed that of Smenkhkare, it suggests that he was about nineteen or twenty years old at the time of death. We know that Smenkhkare outlived Akhenaten for some small time; this period was, at the longest, two years. Working on this supposition, then if he had been nineteen years old two years after Akhenaten died, he would have been seventeen at the time of the King's death, and twelve in Akhenaten's year 12. We know that Meritaten was alive in her father's year 1, so she would have been eleven at the time of Tutankhamen's birth. This is, of course, just about feasible, but is not a comfortable solution. It means Smenkhkare was twelve years old at the time that Akhenaten took him as his lover. Again, feasible, but not comfortable. The question then arises – who was Smenkhkare? He must have been of exceedingly high birth to come to the attention of the King, and to be permitted to marry the King's eldest daughter.

There are, in fact, other solutions. It was considered polite in ancient Egypt to refer to anyone of the older generation as 'father' and 'mother', to anyone of your own generation as 'brother' and 'sister' and to anyone younger as 'son' or 'daughter', even though they were no blood relation whatever. So the reference to 'father' on the Restoration Stela may mean no more than 'he came to the throne of his predecessor'.

Since the reign of Smenkhkare is ephemeral in any case (it may be contained almost wholly within the reign of Akhenaten), could we consider Akhenaten to be his father? On his monuments, Akhenaten always refers to his daughters as – 'his beloved, of his body', exactly the same epithet as is used on the Hermopolis block with regard to Tutankhamen. But if that were the case, then why is Tutankhamen never shown in pictures at Tell el Amarna? The birth of a son to Akhenaten would surely have been a major event, since the succession could then be secure. Why are Akhenaten and Nefertiti shown consistently with a series of daughters and never with the son they needed so much to inherit the throne? And why, then, if Akhenaten was his father, did Tutankhamen turn so openly against him, first abandoning his father's city where he had been born and brought up, and then renouncing his father's *raison d'être*, his religion?

We need to be objective here. In fact, looking at the evidence of royalty from ancient Egypt, the children of the King are very seldom pictured during the life of their parents. Princes only assume a position of importance when they inherit the throne. And our evidence is fragmentary. After Tell el Amarna was demolished, the blocks were used for rubble and thousands of these, though retrieved in modern times, await study. It might be that one or more of them may indeed have pictures of Tutankhamen as a child on them. So on the face of it, the lack of pictures of Tutankhamen as a child is understandable, even unsurprising. What is not so usual, however, is the very frankness and open honesty of the scenes portrayed during the reign of Akhenaten (see page 53). Wherever the King and Queen go, they are accompanied always by their daughters. Akhenaten consistently refers to himself as ☥⊙🏠⊖ – 'living in truth'. So why, if his daughters are shown, was Tutankhamen not?

Referring once again to Chart A, it will be observed that if Tutankhamen was six or seven years old when he assumed the throne, he would have been born around year 12 of Akhenaten's reign. Assuming that Amenhotep IV (Akhenaten) took the throne after the death of his father Amenhotep III, then the only apparent candidates for Tutankhamen's parentage, if he was a royal son, are either Akhenaten or Smenkhkare.

Or so it seems. In fact, there is another possibility. It is quite feasible that Akhenaten did not come to the throne after the death of his father, Amenhotep III. It is quite possible that the two Kings may have ruled side by side as co-regents for some time. In fact, Tutankhamen's father could have been Amenhotep III. On the face of it, Amenhotep III died twelve years before Tutankhamen was born. Or did he? A granite lion that once stood outside the Temple of Soleb in Nubia, now in the British Museum, is one of the few pieces in that collection that bears the name of Tutankhamen, carved on top of the earlier dedication of the lion by Akhenaten. This says that Tutankhamen restored the lion 'for his father'. The original builder of both the temple and the lion is stated as being Amenhotep III Nebmaatre. So could this be an alternative possibility?

The evidence clearly now points to Tutankhamen being royal – a prince from birth. His father must have been a king. There are only three choices: Smenkhkare, Akhenaten, and, at the moment the least likely, Amenhotep III.

And so we begin the historical search for Tutankhamen.

CHAPTER FIVE

Amenhotep III and
Queen Tiye

A menhotep III Nebmaatre was crowned King of Egypt at the height
of the New Kingdom period. At this time, Egypt controlled a
peaceful and prosperous empire that needed little supervision and yet
yielded almost limitless quantities of 'tribute'. Few kings before him
had inherited such a strong position. He took the throne around
1400 BC.

Establishing absolute dates in archaeology always invites conten-
tion. In Egypt, until the past few years, we have been more fortunate
than many of our colleagues in parallel fields. In many instances they
have to rely on carbon dating, a method of measurement involving a
radioactive isotope, carbon-14, which is present in all organic material.
Measuring the C-14 still present in any organic sample gives a date for
the time when the sample died. This is only accurate to within several
decades, even centuries.

In Egypt, dating relies in the first instance on the reign-lengths of
kings. They had no starting-point in history to date back towards. The
state, however, maintained an official calendar based on an annual
cycle of twelve months, each subdivided into three weeks of ten days
each. Above these basic 360 days were five 'extra' or epagomonal days
on which, according to legend or theology, the principal deities Osiris,
Isis, Seth and Nephthys were born to the sky-goddess Nut (on the fifth
day, she rested to recover). The calendar thus comprised 365 days, but

they took no consideration of the quarter-day which we now incorporate into our leap years.

While officials within the government kept note of the date, the majority of the people – some 98 per cent – relied on the land to tell them. The most important day of the year for the ordinary ancient Egyptian was the rising of the Nile for the annual inundation – the day on which, literally, life began again. This day, back in the mists of time, had coincided quite by chance with the reappearance of Sothis, or Sirius, the Dog Star, one of the brightest stars in the night sky. Before this time the star had been hidden from view by an eclipse for a period of many weeks. There is no reason for this coincidence – it was just an accident of fate. Egyptologists have suggested that it happened every year; some astronomers, however, have suggested that due to the procession of the stars (the height of any star or constellation over the horizon, due to the tilt of the earth on its axis), this coincidence may not have happened annually. Both the Egyptian farmers and the state officials thus had the means to predict the arrival of the floodwaters. Everyone would watch for the reappearance of Sirius, knowing that very soon the inundation would begin.

The inundation marked the New Year in ancient Egypt, and with very good reason. For the previous weeks, Egypt, in the full height of summer, would have been parched, with temperatures rising to impossible heights while the Nile ran at a trickle. People would be on the verge of starvation, living on the last of the previous season's crops. The coming of the Nile flood meant life for the farmer – and income for the inland revenue and the government, as taxes were assessed on the height of the rise of the river. Let us reason, then, that some time at the start of Egyptian records, Sirius appeared in the sky, warning the farmers that the flood was due; and on exactly the same day, state officials declared that the New Year had begun. State officials were working on a calendar of 365 days, not 365¼ days. After four years, they would be declaring New Year a day before Sirius appeared; four years later again, and the two calendars would be two days out; and so on. This means that for most of the time, the people of Egypt would be busy going about their work in the fields while the state announced the New Year festival, which should have been the time of the inundation, at completely the wrong time. The two calendars coincided only once every 1460 years.

Because the arrival of the water was so vitally important, not only for the farmers but also for the inland revenue, important documents recorded the date on the state calendar when Sirius was observed on several occasions in Egyptian history. The state year was divided into four seasons, each being split into three months. Hence, any date would be written: 'year (number), of king (name), month (1, 2, 3, or 4), of (name of season), day (number)'. We have one text dated 'Year 7 of Sesostris III, fourth month of the winter season, day 16'. Another records that the rising of Sirius was observed in 'Year 9 of Amenhotep I, third month of the summer season, day 9'. Both of these occasions should have been on day 1 of the first month of the first season: they had 'slipped' because of the lack of the quarter-day. We know that the two calendars coincided in 139. We can then count backwards, in cycles of 1460 years, to know that the two systems coincided previously in 1323 BC, in 2783 BC and in 4243 BC (the year 0 did not exist, the calendars moving from 1 BC to AD 1). We can now count back in groups of four years to establish the exact year on which the two inscriptions above happened. The first would be around 1870 BC, and the second around 1540 BC. Knowing the lengths of kings' reigns in between, we can come to a very close approximation of exactly when a certain king ruled. If only the writers had informed us where the sighting of Sirius had taken place, we could have been exactly accurate. Because of the curvature of the earth, the reappearance of Sirius would have been seen some two days earlier in Aswan than it would have been in Memphis. This gives us an inaccuracy of around 10 years – still a considerably greater accuracy in dating than other methods, such as carbon dating, might allow.

However, as several scholars have realistically pointed out in recent years, this method of dating assumes that in 4000 years the Egyptians, who otherwise prided themselves on their accuracy, not only ignored the differences between the calendars but also never made any attempt to readjust them. If any single pharaoh on any one day had taken it upon himself to correct the error – to insist that the day on which the Nile rose was New Year's Day and that the civil calendar had to be adjusted accordingly – then the whole basis of our dating becomes rocky. The field of Egyptology is facing this contentious issue at this very moment.

In the light of this, to say exactly at what date in absolute history we must start our search is controversial, to say the least. If this problem were not enough to deal with, we also have to face problems caused by kings reigning alongside each other, as co-regents. The end results? 'Wobbles' in our dates.

Suffice it to say, then, that by conventional dating, Amenhotep III Nebmaatre was crowned King of Egypt around 1400 BC. Hayes lists the start of his reign at 1417; Peter Clayton, equally positively, says 1386, while Sir Alan Gardiner takes the middle course at 1405.

It is equally problematical to say exactly how long he reigned. One of our principal sources of historical data in this respect is Manetho, an Egyptian priest who, around 320 BC, was called upon by Ptolemy I to write an authoritative account of Egypt so that the new Greek/ Macedonian government had facts with which to work. Manetho's original document is long since lost; but copyists record that Amenhotep III Nebmaatre (whom they call, in Greek, Orus), ruled thirty-six years, according to Syncellus' copy; or thirty-eight years, according to another copy. Evidence from inscribed fragments found in his palace buildings at Malkata has examples of year 38.

We know that Amenhotep III Nebmaatre celebrated not one but three jubilees on the throne. The first, in his year 30, has led many scholars to presume that jubilees were held for the first time in a king's year 30. While this occasionally happens, it may not, of course, be the general rule. We can only say with confidence that it was so in the reign of this king. This jubilee was followed by a second celebration around year 34 and a third in year 37. W. C. Hayes, keeper of Egyptian Antiquities at the Metropolitan Museum of Art in New York, lists the discovery of seventy-eight inscribed wine-jar fragments bearing year 37 and another sixteen to year 38. He goes on to state, 'the probability that Amenhotep III lived long enough to witness the beginning of at least his 39th year on the throne'. This has since been reasonably established.

Amenhotep was the son of Tuthmosis IV Menkheprure, about whose reign we know little, although once again controversy has arisen as to how long he reigned. The highest reign-date given on objects found so far is year 8, although the Jewish historian Josephus quotes Manetho as saying that he ruled a few months in excess of nine years. The Chicago Institute, however, has published one text that shows he may have celebrated at least one and perhaps two jubilees, citing

evidence of other kings and suggesting that this shows he lived to
reign-year 33. Such a long reign seems quite out of the question. As I
have already pointed out, jubilees were not necessarily celebrated in
years 30, 33 and thereafter; and it is quite probable that Tuthmosis IV
Menkheprure ruled for some time alongside his father Amenhotep II
Aakheprure, so the references may well be to the jubilees of his father
that he shared. At any event, a reign of more than thirty years in
Egyptian history must be considered to be a long one. By experience,
the longer a king ruled, the more monuments would have been built
during his reign. There is virtually nothing major to survive from his
reign and thus it is safer to assume that Tuthmosis IV Menkheprure
ruled for only a very short period.

In a small rear side-chamber (room XIII) in the temple of Luxor, the
walls were once carved with reliefs depicting the birth of Amenhotep
III. Today, thanks to erosion of the reliefs caused by salts exuding onto
the surface of the stone, there is virtually nothing left to be seen.
However, copies of the reliefs and the inscriptions show that they
depicted Tuthmosis IV and his mother Queen Mutemweia on the night
of his conception. The body of Tuthmosis IV had been 'taken over' by
the god Amen-Re, so that although it seemed to her that it was her
husband who visited her, the child conceived that night was quite
literally the son of the god himself. The text calls Mutemweia 'the most
beautiful woman in the whole land', and she is given the titles 'the
hereditary lady, great in graciousness, the lovable one'. When the child
is born, it is the gods and goddesses themselves who deliver the baby,
while Amun says, 'Welcome in peace, my son of my body Nebmaatre',
handing him to Hathor, the cow-headed goddess and aspect of Isis, to
suckle him.

The Great Royal Wife of Tuthmosis IV Menkheprure most prominent
during his reign appears to have been his full sister, Wadjet, whose
name, written in a cartouche, has not yet been found before his year 7.
This, together with a reference to him being a 'child' in one text, has led
some scholars to suggest that he was only a little boy when he became
King, too young to take a wife before his year 7. His mummy, however,
when examined by X-ray in 1967, has been estimated as being around
thirty-five at death. This would mean either that he was a child when
he was crowned and ruled for thirty-three years; or he was in his late
twenties when crowned, and ruled the eight years that we can

positively identify. The third possibility, which cannot entirely be ruled out, is that the wrong mummy has been identified as the King. Only future DNA analysis will make the situation clearer.

About Mutemweia we know relatively little, except that most scholarly works list her as 'one of his chief wives'. A statue found in the temple of Dendera, about 60 miles north of Luxor, has an inscription describing Mutemweia in these words: 'beautiful is the very thought of her. She fills the two lands with joy, wife of the god, Great Royal Wife.' The same title is also to be found on an illustrated inscription, now in the British Museum, where she is described as 'the one who fills her role with the scent of her perfume, the Great Royal Wife, his beloved, who asks for a thing and it is done for her, Lady of Upper and Lower Egypt, Mother of the God'. From the second inscription, where she is listed as 'mother of the god' – that is, she has already given birth to the prince who has been crowned Amenhotep III Nebmaatre – it might be suggested that the title 'Great Royal Wife' became hers only towards the end of the reign of Tuthmosis IV, or was even added to her titles by her son. Perhaps Wadjet died soon after receiving the title. However, the first inscription does not refer to her as the 'Mother of the God' at all. Since this title was the highest any royal woman could receive (except, perhaps, for God's Wife of Amen), one must presume that Mutemweia was given the title 'Great Royal Wife' before she gave birth to the prince. Surprisingly, in later pictures of her alongside her son Amenhotep III Nebmaatre (such as that on the Colossi of Memnon), she is listed only as 'King's Mother'. For Mutemweia to have been the king's wife, logically her husband must have been crowned King either at the time of the conception or soon after, but certainly before the birth of the child. In other words, if we fit this into history, we know that Tuthmosis IV Menkheprure ruled for eight years. For Mutemweia to be the king's wife and Tuthmosis to be king, this event must have taken place after his coronation. Supposing that the conception took place immediately after the King was crowned; allowing nine months for the pregnancy, Amenhotep III Nebmaatre could have been no more than seven years old when he became king. If the conception took place months or even one or two years after the coronation, Amenhotep III would have been considerably younger.

This fact is highly significant. Since we hear nothing more of Mutemweia after the birth of her son, we may reason that she died at or soon after the boy's birth, certainly before he was crowned king. In Theban Tomb 64, the owner, Hekhernekhekh, is shown with the little prince Amenhotep. Hekhernekhekh is described as having been the 𓀀 of Tuthmosis IV Menkheprure, a term generally translated as 'tutor'. The same title is used on statues of Senmut, a senior official during the reign of Hatshepsut, in relation to the child he holds, Princess Nefrure. Since we have no proof whatever of any woman in ancient Egypt who was formally educated, the translation of this term as 'tutor' is highly questionable. Most words in ancient Egyptian terminate in a picture which demonstrates the general meaning of the whole word, a symbol we call the 'determinative'. In the case of 𓀀 this determinative is a female breast. The feminine version of the same word, 𓀀, is regularly translated as 'wet-nurse', but obviously this cannot be extended to the male form, as no male can by definition be a wet-nurse. Today, a very ancient tradition in Egypt states that any woman who breast-feeds another woman's child from birth is deemed an honorary mother of that child. The link is thought so strong that another true child of that woman cannot marry the one suckled, since they both sucked from the same breast and are thus to be considered blood siblings. In English, we might term this role foster-parent, even though the same blood tie is not seen to exist – foster-brother and foster-sister may marry. This would seem to fit the bill in the cases cited above: Senmut was likely to have been responsible for caring for the Princess Nefrure while her mother, King Hatshepsut, was about her business.

This being the case, we can then say that this Hekhernekhekh was responsible, in part, for the upbringing of Tuthmosis IV Menkheprure. It seems he lived long enough to carry on this role into the succeeding generation, for on the ceiling of the tomb, he is also listed as 'the 𓀀 of the King's son of his body, his beloved, Amenhotep', the future Amenhotep III Nebmaatre. His wife, Meryt, is listed on the tomb walls as, 'the 𓀀 of the King's son of his body', while on her knee is shown a child, recorded as 'The King's daughter of his body, Tiw'. It seems that this very trusted couple acted as foster-parents towards two successive pharaohs, both of whom inherited the throne when young. Titles in the tomb link Hekhernekhekh with Sobek and call him 'mayor' of the region that today we call the Fayum.

In other words, it would seem that this noble couple were instrumental in some way for taking care of little Amenhotep III Nebmaatre as an infant – who later, as a child, had at least one little sister. Since we do not hear any more of her, it is probable that she died in infancy. The link with the Fayum is also interesting. While it is, of course, possible that his father chose at random from his officials the couple most suited for the upbringing of the child, it is also possible that they were chosen in the region of the Fayum. We know of a palace-city in the region called Gurob (in Egyptian, Merwer), which was occupied, so excavation suggests, primarily by royal women. Indeed, it has been termed by Angela Thomas a 'harem-city'. It seems that it was founded in the Middle Kingdom, but came into its own during the Eighteenth Dynasty.

We know from records that the kings of the Eighteenth Dynasty were proud of their athletic prowess. Tuthmosis IV Menkheprure, like his father and grandfather, loved hunting; and we also know, by comparing images of the Nile between the Old and New Kingdoms, that hunting had become sparse along the Nile in the New Kingdom, probably as a result of over-hunting and fishing and the removal of hiding places for quarry along the Nile as trees were cut for carpentry, fuel and animal fodder. So the hunting kings went to the Fayum for small game, where ground cover was still thick and animals plentiful. They would have stayed in the harem-palace, entertained by their wives, and going out to the rich hunting-ground every day. In all probability, since Hekhernekhekh would have been in charge of the area in which the palace of Gurob lay, he would have served the king on his hunting trips, and probably came into the presence of the king in this way. The influence that could be exerted by such an official cannot be underestimated. During their formative years, the princelings would have been greatly influenced by their 'foster-parents', and the latter could be assured of incredible power and influence once the child became king.

So a little boy whose mother died at birth or soon after had people to look after him. But upon the death of his father, little Amenhotep III Nebmaatre was orphaned and alone. Like Tutankhamen later, he would have needed to rely heavily on the people around him.

The first years of Amenhotep III Nebmaatre's reign are recorded, quite exceptionally, in inscriptions carved on the back of a series of 'commemorative scarabs'. Real-life scarabs, large beetles also known as dung beetles, were revered by the ancient Egyptians. The scarab habitually lays its eggs in animals' dung, which it then rolls into a ball across the hot ground, pushing it along with its rear legs. As the eggs incubate in the heat, they hatch and emerge as larvae. The Egyptians perhaps never realised that the beetles had laid the eggs there in the first place, but imagined that here was a species that could reproduce itself miraculously out of a ball of dung. The name for the beetle, 𓆣 , was used in the ancient Egyptian language to mean 'to come into existence'. It had, and still has, an amuletic significance as the regenerator of life. A scarab placed over the chest cavity in the mummy was believed to bring the heart out of the chest for judgment just as the real scarab brought out its larvae from the dung.

A series of five 'news scarabs' was issued around the Egyptian empire until year 11 of the reign of Amenhotep III Nebmaatre (see Appendix C). The scarabs were inscribed with 'news bulletins' and must have been produced in large numbers, since they have been found in many different places. The series is unique. It is unclear how news was normally circulated through the empire, other than by way of letters or verbal reports from messengers or ambassadors. Clearly, Amenhotep III felt a strong need to send written information regarding his reign to other countries. One possibility is that they were intended to reassure dependent states that the young boy was capable of strong rule.

The second series, dated year 2, tells how the young King shot and killed ninety-four wild bulls in the region of the Fayum, probably organised by his protector Hekhernekhekh. It states that he was already associated with the 'Great Royal Wife Tiye'. Another series, undated, establishes his marriage to the Great Royal Wife Tiye, which therefore logically must have taken place in his year 1. Since it was generally the practice for a king to choose a Great Royal Wife at the time of his coronation, it would seem the most reasonable idea that Tiye 'married' him at this time. The marriage scarab announces: 'the Great Royal Wife Tiye, may she be given life. The name of her father is Yuya, the name of her mother is Thuya. She is the wife of a strong King whose southern boundary is at Karoi, the northern one at Naharin.' A wooden statue base, now in Hildesheim Museum in Germany, describes her as 'the hereditary Princess, great of praise, Lady of the

Two Lands, gracious of feelings, sweetly lovable, Lady of North and South, rich in splendours, delightful in adornments, Great Royal Wife Tiye, may she be given life.' The titles, and others similar, have led scholars universally to describe the match as a true romance.

Tiye's father, Yuya, counted among his titles 'the Hereditary Prince, Courtier, Sole companion, praised of the Good God (the King), confidant of the King, beloved of the lord of the Two Lands, Overseer of the Cattle of Min, Master of the Royal Horses, King's Lieutenant of chariotry, High Priest of Min at Akhmim, the Father of the God', while her mother, Thuya, is named as 'The King's concubine; Royal mother of the King's Wife, great Lady of the Harem of Amun, Great Lady of the harem of Min in Akhmim, Lady of the House, musician of Amun, one who praises Hathor'.

The titles of both are quite revealing and their inclusion on the royal scarabs is quite exceptional. Far from being of lowly birth, or, as even the *Cambridge Ancient History* states, a commoner, Tiye was very nobly born. Many books have pointed out that the King's usual choice of Great Royal Wife was made from his sisters and half-sisters. This is clearly untrue; as we have stated, Amenhotep's mother was herself a 'commoner'. The title itself only came into use regularly in the Eighteenth Dynasty, so our examination of the various women who filled the role is strictly limited. It is very clear, however, that while a sister or half-sister would easily fulfil the state and religious demands made of her, the choice of Great Royal Wife was up to the king alone. This being the case, Amenhotep III Nebmaatre's choice of a 'commoner' as Great Royal Wife is everywhere alluded to as one undertaken purely for love, especially since we know from several inscriptions (see Hekhernekhekh's above) that Amenhotep had at least one sister whom he could have chosen. This now needs to be re-examined.

We have seen that Amenhotep III Nebmaatre was only about seven years old when he became King, as an orphan. Although boys matured somewhat earlier in ancient times, thanks to the responsibilities thrust on them, especially in the case of kings, is it likely that a seven-year-old would have fallen so madly in love that he would have denied any who tried to overrule him? On the contrary, since Tiye was probably a few years older than he was, it seems more likely that the marriage was suggested to the King by her parents. Since, in the early years, her

accompanied by those of her father and mother, it
...ere openly proud of being the hand behind the young
...all but name. Indeed, later the King was, quite
...ve his parents-in-law an outstandingly rich burial in
...ey of the Kings.

So who were these people, Yuya and Thuya? Ahmed Osman, in his
...ook *Stranger in the Valley of the Kings*, has suggested that Yuya, by
virtue of the fine blond hair on his mummy, was of non-Egyptian birth,
and that he was none other than Joseph of Old Testament fame – the
dreamer of prophetic dreams. Should we be tempted to take the
account in the Book of Genesis to be as accurately factual as he
suggests, one might point out that Joseph's body, according to the Book
of Exodus, was carried back to its homeland by Moses during the
Exodus. In any event, the account is clearly incorrect, since we can trace
Yuya's family with relative ease.

The title of 'hereditary Prince/Princess' was, first, a title handed
only to the upper echelons of nobles in the land, while Yuya's links
with the King's horses and chariots makes his one of the top military
posts in the land. Far from being commoners, the family was one of
very high birth indeed. A *shabti* in the Metropolitan Museum of Art in
New York bears the inscription of one Yey, who bore exactly the same
titles as Yuya and thus was probably his father or grandfather.

The titles associate the whole family with the temple of Min, the
local god of the area of Akhmim. Min is invariably depicted as a
human, with an arm raised behind his back holding a 'flail' and with a
distinctive erect phallus. Across the river from the temple lies a
little-known site excavated in 1900, known today as Deir el Ballas. The
site, explored by G. A. Reisner, A. Lythgoe and F. W. Green for the
Hearst Foundation in California, has not been much written about; and
the material found there is still undergoing scholastic research. There
were two palace buildings on the site: the northern palace standing on
a low mound, and a southern palace on the top of a much higher hill
about half a mile away. Between the two lies a substantial cemetery.
The burials, in shallow pit-graves, bore inscriptional material, all from
the early Eighteenth Dynasty, although within the palaces several
column bases bore the names and titles of Mentuhotep Nebhepetre, the
great King of the Eleventh Dynasty. The names found in the graves
start with a single sealing with mud seals from the time of Amosis, first

King of the Eighteenth Dynasty, and then titles of successive kings proliferate until the end of the reign of Tuthmosis IV, with a few dating from the start of the reign of Amenhotep III Nebmaatre. The northern palace was massively built, with large wooden roofing rafters and staircases that clearly led to upper storeys. From the southern building came examples of wall paintings on plaster of an unusually fine type. The overall impression is of two clearly royal residences, the northern one so strongly fortified with tower-like constructions that it was obviously defensive, and the southern building more probably used as a residence. It has been suggested, with some likelihood, that they were palaces built during the Eleventh Dynasty as garrison-bases for royal troops trying to re-establish control over the breakaway areas of Middle Egypt; and then, towards the end of the Second Intermediate Period, they would have come into their own once more as military boundaries in the fight between the Thebans and the Hyksos. Like many military castles of the modern era in the northern parts of Europe, they would have fulfilled two purposes – royal residence and military stronghold. Although we know little about the palaces of ancient Egyptian kings, this surprisingly well-preserved site clearly demands future meticulous excavation to reveal its secrets. What is apparent is that the palace-site was well used in the period we are discussing. Certainly the principal palace used by the kings was in Memphis. Today, little can be found on that site from before the Nineteenth Dynasty. But we know the kings travelled regularly through their kingdom, and obviously needed somewhere to stay that was suitable for their status, private and well protected. With the royal family sometimes living at el Ballas, it is hardly surprising that they should come into regular contact with the family of the high priesthood of the temple on the other side of the river, and thus consider marrying into it.

Cyril Aldred, in his classic study of Akhenaten, has gone even further than this. He points out that Yuya bears the title of 'Father of the God', ⌷𓏤⌷𓊹. The word 𓏤 in this instance refers to the King and, when used in the New Kingdom, was invariably given to a man whose daughter has married the king. It means, in effect, the King's father-in-law. Exactly the same title is given to Yey, Yuya's father. Aldred suggests that Yey's daughter, who married a king, can have been none other than Mutemweia. This would seem to make good sense. If she were, indeed, a sister of Yuya's, it would be logical that, after the death of his sister, Yuya should step in to protect and care for his nephew, the King and thus promote a marriage between the two cousins. Going back a stage further, he suggests that Yey, Yuya's father, was the brother of Hatshepsut-Meryetre, wife of Tuthmosis III and mother of Amenhotep II. If this could be substantiated, then we have not a family of 'commoners' but almost a parallel royal family, a group of 'kingmakers' whose intermarriage with the Egyptian royal house would have made them a force to be reckoned with.

Even Thuya, his wife, bears important titles. The reference to her as the king's ⟨hieroglyph⟩ – often translated as 'concubine' – is intriguing. The word 'concubine' now implies formal mistress, although this translation has overtones of meaning not present in ancient Egypt. In some hieroglyphic inscriptions, the title of 'wife' and 'concubine' seem to be interchangeable, being used of the same woman within the space of a single sentence. Despite many assertions in the literature, the Egyptians were generally monogamous, with the exception of the King, who maintained a number of wives just as a god might. Of all inscriptions examined from tombs, temples and stelae, only five examples of plural marriages have been found, and they were in all probability consecutive and not contemporary. In any case, these all refer to men with more than one wife: there are no records at all of polyandry, or the instance of a woman with more than one husband, even in the case of the female kings. So, clearly, Thuya cannot have been married both to the King and to Yuya. The simplest explanation is that she was married to Tuthmosis IV Menkheprure as a minor wife, and that after his death she was freed to marry a highly ranked official. This would, then, account for her title as 'great one of the harem of Amun', perhaps also linking her with duties within Karnak.

We know, then, from the 'marriage scarab', that Tiye was the daughter of Yuya and Thuya. From the coffin of Thuya, we read also that she had a son called Anen, named as the 'second prophet of Amen'. The title 'prophet' is a translation of the Egyptian ⟨hieroglyph⟩, sometimes rendered as 'priest'. Both these translations are emotive, implying, as they do, links with religious mysticism. The implication is wrong', ⟨hieroglyph⟩ means simply 'servant'. The duty of these characters was not to act as a leader of services, nor as an intercessor between man and god, but rather to enter into the 'temple' daily to offer practical service to a cult image, ensuring that it was cleaned, dressed and fed as any servant might do for his master. Hence, while the post had duties attached to it and some variety of stipend it should not be thought of as a full-time religious appointment requiring, for example, initiation. The 'prophets' or, as I shall term them henceforth, the god's servants, were far more business managers than they were religious acolytes. Karnak, where Anen served, was a huge business enterprise, covering large estates, buildings, dockyards and many workshops as well as employing tens of thousands of staff at all levels (the Great Harris papyrus in the British Museum records daily transactions for the temple in the Twentieth Dynasty). Anen was second-in-command of this huge enterprise. None the less, it must tell us something about him that, even though his sister was Great Royal Wife and his nephew was Pharaoh, he never attained the lofty height of First God's Servant.

Beside Tiye and Anen, Yuya and his wife appear to have had another child, a second son called Ay. On a box in Berlin (numbered 17555, and probably found in Tell el Amarna or Gurob), Ay is listed with exactly the same titles as those of Yuya, together with 'his sister, the Lady of the House Tiye'. The titles he shares with Yuya and Yey alone are conclusive enough.

We have, therefore, a most remarkable family. Hailing from Akhmim and serving originally in the temple across the river from the royal palace, they provide three generations of kings of Egypt with wives, two of whom appear to have been Great Royal Wives. Yuya and Thuya have three children who are destined to reach dizzy heights – Anen in Karnak; Tiye, wife of the King and mother of the next King; and last but certainly not least, Ay, who in time was to become Pharaoh himself. The last two are distinguished by their ability, their devotion to their country, their intelligence and their ruthlessness, talents they assuredly inherited or learned in some part from their parents. It is hardly surprising, then, that at the start of the reign of Amenhotep III, Yuya and Thuya should take the boy under their wing and put pressure on him, if he needed it, to accept their daughter as Great Royal Wife. The simple fact that their names are carved alongside their daughter's in the first few years of the King's reign shows how very powerful they were.

It is uncertain where the new King was crowned. As part of Amenhotep's royal title, he uses the term 𓉐𓋴 – 'ruler of Thebes', the Greek misnomer for Luxor. This has suggested to some that he was crowned in the temple of Karnak. Most kings of Egypt were crowned in

Memphis under the aegis of the old god Ptah; but Tuthmosis III Menkheperre and Hatshepsut Maatkare had both set a precedent by being crowned in their home town, Luxor. It was probably to sanction these state occasions that the small temple to Ptah was added into the temple-precinct of Karnak. If he was crowned in Luxor, it is far from clear where he would have lived, for there are no buildings in the area that we can establish were palaces before his reign. Perhaps he stayed within the boundaries of the Karnak temple itself. But clearly the beautiful city of Luxor appealed to him, for over the next thirty-nine years of his reign he was to build extensively in the area, on a scale never to be matched until the time of Ramesses II in the Nineteenth Dynasty.

Within the first few years of his reign, Amenhotep III probably authorised building work by sending conscripts to the stone quarries to cut and move stone. Despite generalised statements from outside the field suggesting the stone was cut by slaves, we know from plentiful quarry inscriptions that the stone was cut by professional stone-cutters, rather than by unemployed field-hands during the inundation month. The stones were then moved to the building sites by gangs of naval men – soldiers recruited into ship's gangs – usually sixty men divided into four groups of fifteen. Two inscriptions in Tura, to the east of modern Cairo, dated year 1 and 2 of Amenhotep III Nebmaatre, record that 'His Majesty ordered the opening of the quarries anew in order to build his mansion of Millions of Years.' This building we would call today his mortuary temple. Lying on the west bank of Luxor, virtually nothing remains of it save two colossal limestone statues standing over fifty feet high and called popularly the Colossi of Memnon. The huge temple behind it, from its foundations the biggest ever to stand on the west bank, has been systematically removed, stone by stone, by later kings building their own temples. A stone that once marked the centre of the rear of the building records in hieroglyphs that, 'I made greatness without limit in gold, stone and every noble precious stone, without limit.'

At about the same time Amenhotep III Nebmaatre started to renew the temple of Mont in Karnak itself. He declared:

it is decorated throughout with electrum [a silver-gold alloy], its doors made with genuine [solid] electrum, it is adorned with every noble precious stone from the tax of the Southern land. All its floors are inlaid with gold, with doors of cedar, bound with Asiatic copper from the tax from the Northern lands. It is like the Horizon of Heaven – Owner of Silver, Owner of Gold. It combines every noble precious stone – it is a resting-place for the Lord of the Gods.

In charge of building works was Amenhotep son of Hapu, the Leonardo da Vinci of his age, whose reputation for genius remained intact for hundreds of years after his death. With people of this ilk working for him and a seemingly limitless purse, nothing was too much for the court of this new young King. Within the first few years of his reign he began new building work on a 'mansion' or 'temple' on the east bank. It was dedicated to marriage and sexual partnership of the sort that was probably starting to dawn for him with his new wife. Called the Opet (see page 55), it was in effect a honeymoon hotel where once a year the figures of the gods Amun and Mut could 'lie' in connubial bliss for several days. Called today Luxor temple, this most graceful of buildings is covered with reliefs of Amun showing him with an erect penis, a form that encouraged Amun to fulfil his godly duty with Mut. The use of the image of Min of Coptos, the local 'god' from about thirty miles north of the city, in a temple of Amen's in Luxor probably owes much to the influence of Yuya, Thuya, Ay and Tiye, who originally came from Coptos. So the King and his new wife could appreciate the new works, work was started, at the same time, on a *maru* or viewing-point, which was later to become a great palace.

Today, the site of Amenhotep's palace is lost beneath the sands of the west bank, and only vague outlines on the ground give the signs of where perhaps the most luxuriously appointed buildings of the age once stood. Excavated first in the period 1910 to 1920 by the Metropolitan Museum of Art, and more recently by teams from the British Museum, the site has been shown to have comprised many magnificent buildings, from a palace for the King in the south, a palace alongside for Queen Tiye and her officials, to a Middle Palace (see page 194) and a great festival hall. Today almost no tourists visit the site. If you were to go to the mortuary temple of Ramesses III at Medinet Habu, and from there take a taxi and drive southwards along a barely marked track, you would find yourself, bewildered and alone, standing at the centre of what was once a multi-storeyed building, its ceilings painted

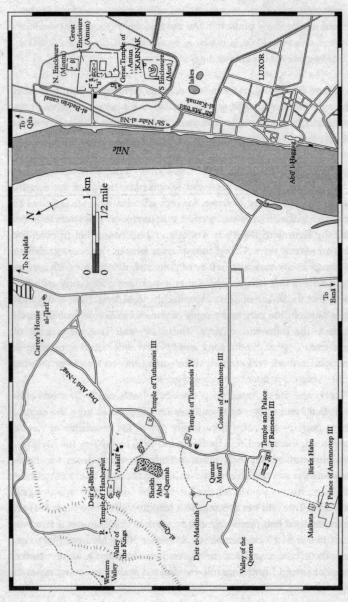

Luxor and the west bank today.

with the latest fashion in interior decorating 3500 years ago – Greek-key patterns and other geometric designs brought in from the Minoan civilisation, the walls plastered and painted in bright primary colours with scenes of reed-beds broken by leaping bulls and flying marsh-birds. Here once the young King lay with his wife; here once children were sired – at least two sons and four daughters; here once a revolution was born; and here once, in all probability, Tutankhamen slept, and died a young King.

Amenhotep, like his ancestors, was by all accounts a lusty youth. He hunted fearlessly, killing wild animals by the score, according to the records. He began building a huge pylon gateway in the temple of Karnak to his father Amen, a pylon that today stands only thirteen feet tall (the third pylon, see page 231). On it was recorded that 'he is patient, skilled in the use of his arm, wise in knowledge, he runs like the Aten, swift of stride, a star of electrum who flashes by in his chariot'. (Some of you will note the reference to the god worshipped by Akhenaten – the Aten. All will be explained presently.) At first, his time was occupied in home affairs. Then, in his year 5, word was brought to him of rebellion in the south. The Nubians, believed by Egypt since time immemorial to belong to them body and soul, were always quick to rise against any king they suspected of weakness. Amenhotep III Nebmaatre led his officers southwards, beyond the first cataract of Aswan. On a rocky outcrop in the Nile near Philae he had this inscription carved.

> Year 5, third month of the inundation season, day 2. His Majesty was informed that the Chief of Vile Kush had planned rebellion in his heart. His Majesty won a victory, achieving it on his very first campaign. He was strong of heart while killing and cutting off hands. Ikheny the Boaster was with his army, unaware of the lion that faced him, for Nebmaatre was a savage lion who grasped vile Kush in his claws.

Marching southwards to Semna, just below the second cataract, he was met by the loyal Egyptian leader of Kush, the viceroy, who ordered an army to be raised. 'The army was mustered and companies of troops were formed, starting from the fortress of Buhen going south to the fortress of Teroi. The strong army of Nebmaatre led them away again in only 1 day, in 1 hour – 740 heads, 312 hands total 1052.'

The victory introduced Amenhotep III Nebmaatre to Nubia. He presumably ordered the building there, close to his battle-site, of not one but two matching temples – one for himself at Soleb and another dedicated to Queen Tiye at Sedeinga. It is amusing to note that, despite Ramesside aversion to the kings of the Eighteenth Dynasty, Ramesses II was to copy this idea in the building of matching 'his-and-hers' temples at Abu Simbel. On Amenhotep III Nebmaatre's return, he recorded at Buhen that 'Year 5, First month of summer, he is beloved of the gods of Wawat (Lower Nubia)'. The campaign had lasted about four months, according to the stela cut on the island of Konosso at Aswan, 'having celebrated a great triumph on his first campaign of victory in the land of Vile Kush'.

On his return, he had his architects celebrate his triumph, and on his building works, victorious sentiments are carved everywhere. In the courtyard of the temple at Luxor he recorded, 'No foreign country has risen against him, but his might has subdued the Isles, every flat land and every hilly land who bring him tribute.' The mention of 'the Isles' is an intriguing one, as it probably refers to the Aegean Minoan civilisation. It certainly does not mean that he either visited Crete or sent a conquering army there, but throughout Egypt, pieces dating from his reign show a strong Minoan influence, as we've seen. Excavations carried out between 1984 and 1994 beneath the sea at Ulu Burun, southeast of Kaš off the southern coast of Turkey, have revealed a Bronze Age wreck dating precisely from this period in Amenhotep III Nebmaatre's reign. It had been loaded with copper and Egyptian pieces and sank while it was trading from port to port around the Eastern Mediterranean. It is clear that Cyprus, Syro-Palestine, southern Turkey and the Aegean were all on its trading route. Egypt controlled trade in the Eastern Mediterranean area at this time. Later, a story from the Ramesside era, *Wenamun*, relates how the eponymous hero, stranded at Byblos, mourns the passing of Egyptian maritime power. Despite excavation reports from the Ulu Burun wreck identifying a small gilded bronze figure found there as 'probably Resheph [a god in human form, with a feathered headdress], and thus Canaanite', the figure is recognisably Egyptian, and depicts Seth, a god associated with the Delta and with amuletic power over storms and rain – a good enough reason for the Egyptian crew to carry the figure on board. In all probability, then, Amenhotep's inscription referred to economic rather than military control.

Tiye gave birth to at least two sons who survived childhood: the oldest, Tuthmosis, named for his grandfather Tuthmosis IV, as was the usual practice in Egypt; and Amenhotep, named for his father. Among the daughters born to them was Sitamun, a princess who was soon to play a major role in her parents' life. The royal line thus seemed well established; but things changed dramatically after year 10. The King, by this time in his late teens and no doubt fully aware of his status, wealth and world standing, contacted the King of Mitanni and asked to marry his daughter. Just as he followed his father's example in choice of Great Royal Wife, it seems he was following the pattern of his father in this matter as well. The land of Mitanni, the exact boundaries of which still remain to be established, lies approximately where today we find Syria on the map. It seems that Tuthmosis IV, going by documents found in the area, had asked King Artatama for the hand of his daughter. Tushratta, Artatama's grandson, recorded, 'He repeated the message five times, six times but he did not send her. Then he repeated the message a seventh time to my grandfather and in reply he delivered her.' Now Amenhotep III Nebmaatre sent similar messages to King Shuttarna, requesting to marry his daughter. Negotiations took time, and eventually it was Tushratta, this girl's brother, who stated their demands: 'May my brother [Amenhotep] send untold gold; and may my father's power increase with me as my brother increases my favour, as my brother loves me in the sight of my country and in the sight of all my brothers.' Clearly Amenhotep III Nebmaatre obliged, for in year 10 the fourth series of news scarabs announce the arrival, with a retinue of 317 women, of Princess Giludkhipa. Many of these women would have entered the royal harem.

There is no doubt that Amenhotep was an uxorious man, and no doubt that Tiye had had to share his attention many times with other 'wives'; but the arrival of the foreign bride seems to have unsettled her. The fifth and final series of scarabs, issued the following year, shows Tiye making demands upon her husband. She begged that a lake be dug for her in Djarukha, near her home town of Akhmim; and despite its huge proportions, it was flooded and she was able to sail on it a mere fifteen days later. This bears all the signs of a woman distressed and a husband eager to please.

As the years progressed, it seems that Amenhotep III Nebmaatre lived off the fat of the land and, judging by images of him, his weight and girth increased dramatically. A headless statue of him now in the Metropolitan Museum in New York shows him plump, his arms barely touching in front of him. He wears a long pleated over-robe – ideal for disguising his size, but still, a woman's robe. He was the first man to adopt the wearing of this over-robe.

At some point, their elder son Tuthmosis was sent northwards, probably to Heliopolis, the traditional 'finishing school' of crown princes. What happened next is unrecorded; but Tuthmosis vanished from sight forever. It is clear that he died around this time. His tomb is undiscovered, but probably lies in unexplored quarters of Saqqara, the necropolis of Memphis. Suddenly, the younger brother was thrust into line as heir to the throne. Unprepared and totally unsuited for the role, Amenhotep seems to have been a dreamer and an intellectual, totally unlike his warlike ancestors, and more interested in his books than in hunting.

In year 30 of his reign Amenhotep III Nebmaatre celebrated his first and greatest jubilee festival In his palace at Malkata, hundreds of jar-sealings were found recording the date. Kheruef, the steward of the Estates of Queen Tiye during the reign of Amenhotep III, records in his tomb: 'the *sed* festival which he celebrated on the west of No [Luxor]'. On the west wall of his tomb, registers show the King and Great Royal Wife Tiye leaving the palace, acclaimed by crowds, while eight princesses greet them. Rows of singers and dancers go before them. It seems the festivities included a trip north to Abydos, where the King ceremoniously erected a *djed* pillar, symbol of renewal of life, in the presence of sixteen princesses. For his organisational skills, Kheruef was awarded the Gold of Honour – heavy gold broad-collar necklaces awarded only to a king's closest advisers and officials. Khaemhet, nicknamed Mahu (overseer of the granaries of Upper and Lower Egypt), received the same award at the same time, and so must have shared in the organisation of the festival with Kheruef, although the overall management of the event was undertaken by the Vizier of Upper Egypt, Ramose.

Celebrations spread throughout Egypt. Deep in Nubia, at the now completed temple of Soleb, the *sed* festival is recorded showing Amenhotep III Nebmaatre and Tiye 'while performing ceremonies of the first *sed* festival of His Majesty in the Palace "House of

Rejoicing"'. The earliest date for the festival is the 'Fourth month of winter, day 26', while in a small temple of Amenhotep son of Hapu, he records that the last date of festivities was the 'Third month of summer, day 2'. The celebrations had lasted for eight months, and the jar-labels from Malkata show most jars for the events contained a type of beer called ⎯⎯⏀🦶⌒. This beer, made with soaked barley-bread, was later fortified with dates, the sugars in which fed the fermentation and resulted in an exceptionally potent brew much higher in alcoholic content than anything classified today as beer. Clearly, the festival went with a swing.

The second festival, in year 34, was also celebrated at Malkata. This time a huge columned hall was added to the palace, with other buildings alongside. But there were fewer jar-labels bearing the date; no tomb references have yet been found; and four out of five of the labels were for stored meat. When the third and last jubilee took place in year 37, it was a meagre, insignificant event. Although Kheruef took part in the festivities, according to his tomb paintings, there were none of the celebrations shown for the first event, while from Malkata we find only twenty-seven jar-labels, all discovered within the king's palace.

The conclusion is inescapable. The joy and euphoria surrounding the first festival had dwindled to nothing by the time of the third. Why should that be?

It has been thought for many years now that Amenhotep IV Nefer-kheprure Waenre (Akhenaten) did not inherit the throne when his father died, but in fact may have shared the throne with his father as a co-regent. It is often said that this theory was first proposed by Cyril Aldred in 1974, but the notion is in fact a venerable one. Rex Engelbach, in an article in the *Journal of Egyptian Archaeology* in 1911, proposed the theory that the two Kings were co-regents for eleven or twelve years; John Pendlebury, when digging at Tell el Amarna in the 1920s, accepted an overlap of eleven years; George Steindorff in 1941, preferred twelve years; while, in 1951, Hayes accepted a co-regency as a matter of course when he describes the palace of Malkata as 'built for the King's eldest son Akhenaten and occupied by him previous to and during the first five years of the long co-regency with his father'. Recently, the notion has been attacked on many fronts, and despite the evidence, many scholars still insist that the two reigned successively. In his classic book,

Ancient Egyptian Co-regencies, W. J. Murnane lists the evidence he believes may support a co-regency. However, many of the references he cites where the two Kings are pictured together are quite reasonably dismissed by scholars, who point out that frequently a son is shown making offerings to a parent who is dead. Some references are harder to dismiss. For example, he quotes from a graffito found at Meidum: 'Year 30 under the majesty of the King of Upper and Lower Egypt Nebmaatre . . . who caused the man to rejoice in the place of his father who established his inheritance in the land'.

Many of the absolutely incontrovertible pieces of evidence have been neglected or overlooked completely. If you go to the temple at Karnak at around three in the afternoon on any day, when the rays of the sun fall obliquely over the walls, you will see images carved lightly on Amenhotep's third pylon. These images are invisible at other times of the day, and are indeed only clearly visible for a period of around thirty minutes. In the pictured scenes is a huge boat, with one large figure carved in raised relief standing on it. Only the lower half of the figure survives. Behind this one stands another figure, more slender than the first, carefully chiselled out at a later date, but so carefully that the outline can still be seen. In the oblique light of mid-afternoon, even the hieroglyphs, faintly carved, many deliberately removed, can still be read.

The large figure in these images is Amenhotep III Nebmaatre; the smaller, his son, Amenhotep IV, later Akhenaten. The inscription below reads:

> He commanded his son to appear, rich in magnificence, this King who brought him into being, being his son. He united with his beauty, he hands over to him his daily plans to do the things that are beneficial. He has elevated the wonders of the one who brought him into existence . . . [below the damaged figure] I am his eldest son, who came into existence through him [name hacked out]. I rule by his agreement, I join with his strength, I take possession of his power . . . I am the son who will do good for the one who begot him.

The scenes show Amenhotep presenting his son to Amen in the temple. The images seem clear enough. But when did this happen?

Theban Tomb 55 seems to provide the answer. This tomb belonged to Ramose, the vizier who served during the first *sed* festival of Amenhotep III Nebmaatre. Yet Ramose had disappeared before the second festival, when his place as vizier was occupied by another. He is never mentioned again, and thus clearly died some time between year 30 and 34 of Amenhotep III Nebmaatre's reign. The tomb of Ramose comprises one large rectangular chamber leading to an unfinished back chamber. The burial shaft lies in the southwestern corner of the room. As one enters the room, one's eye is caught immediately by the long mural that adorns the left-hand (southern) wall. This depicts the funeral procession of Ramose, with friends and family carrying his personal possessions into the tomb while mourners weep over his burial. Later, to the immediate left and right of the entrance door, one sees the exquisite raised-relief carvings that cover the walls on each side. These richly detailed carvings are uncoloured except for the black-lined eyes of the figures; and it is these eyes that first catch the attention and draw the viewer in to look more closely. Detailed images, never bettered in Luxor, show Ramose with his wife, his brother and sister-in-law, their parents and other relatives. Only after the eye has absorbed all of this beauty does the opposite wall summon attention. Here the work was started, but never finished. Line drawings, some roughly and quickly sketched, adorn the walls. And finally, in these scenes, the full story is told. For here, in one place, Ramose is shown in standard Eighteenth-Dynasty form – rotund, bald and leaning on his staff of office. Next to this portrait he is shown as curiously distorted, with an elongated head, pointed chin and swollen belly – very like portraits of Akhenaten, in fact. Ramose is shown under a balcony where Amenhotep IV Neferkheprure Waenre (Akhenaten, that is) and his Great Royal Wife Nefertiti hand him the Gold of Honour. The inscription below reads: 'The garland for your father, Re-Horakhte, given life, who rejoices on the Horizon in his name of Shu, which is the Aten'. This inscription is actually the first title given to the Aten.

The curious thing is that Akhenaten was never depicted in this distorted manner until around years 4–5 of his reign. Let us consider the possibilities. Ramose, the great vizier who organised the first *sed* festival, dies between year 30 and 34 of Amenhotep III Nebmaatre's rule. His tomb is cut, but one wall in the entrance chamber is left unfinished. About eight or nine years elapse, then the old King dies.

His son, Amenhotep IV, comes to the throne and around four years later, introduces a new style of portraiture, and new titles for his god. Around twelve years have now elapsed since Ramose died; yet an artist returns to the unfinished tomb of the vizier, paints on it Ramose in a form he would never have recognised, shows him receiving gold from a king he never knew, and then left the tomb again with it unfinished. This makes no sense whatever. The only reasonable explanation for the existence of the scenes are that Ramose knew and was rewarded by Amenhotep IV. Since he disappeared after Amenhotep III's first jubilee and before his second, this would make the two events concurrent. When Ramose died between the jubilees of Amenhotep III, Amenhotep IV was already King and the new artistic style was established. In other words, we have here a clear co-regency.

This immediately makes many things clear. For example, we have now identified the mummy of Queen Tiye as the 'elderly lady' found in the tomb of Amenhotep II in the Valley of the Kings. This body, previously identified as Hatshepsut, was re-examined in the light of the discovery of a lock of hair bearing the name of Queen Tiye in the tomb of Tutankhamen. The hair is distinctive; rich, thick and auburn in colour. A section of the lock was compared microscopically with the hair of the mummy and found to be identical. What is more, not only does the body physically resemble those of Yuya and Thuya, Tiye's parents, but Thuya's hair is also luxuriant and the same auburn colour. Now we know that Amenhotep III Nebmaatre ruled for thirty-nine years; and that he married Tiye at the start of his reign. We know that she started bearing him children within the first ten years of his reign, and that she was around eight or nine years old when she married him. We know that she lived through the reign of her son Amenhotep IV; and that she died before Tutankhamen, since the lock of her hair labels her as  – literally, 'true of voice' – meaning she had undergone the judgment of the dead. This means she was dead when the lock of hair was prepared. A gilded wooden panel found in Tomb 55 bearing, as Davies recorded, Tiye's name and titles, showed her under the rays of the Aten, while the title of the Aten in hieroglyphs was of the variety introduced around year 8 and changed in year 12 of Akhenaten's reign. Scenes dated in year 12 of Akhenaten do not show her, so presumably she died then. If there was no co-regency between Amenhotep III and Akhenaten, then we need to add all these years together: 9 (age at marriage) + 39 (years of her husband's reign) + 12 (years of her son's reign), and we arrive at an age for her, at death, of 60. If, however, there was a twelve-year co-regency between the two Kings, as the evidence suggests, then she would have been only forty-eight years old at death. Not only does the mummy identified as hers suggest an age of the mid-thirties (which may be a little too low, as we've seen), but the hair is naturally auburn, while her features and the condition of her teeth are certainly not those of a woman of sixty – in ancient Egypt, a very old age indeed. An age at death in the region of the mid-forties is more feasible, given the condition of the body.

Other facts also point to the same conclusion. We know that in his year 12, Akhenaten initiated a huge festival to which all members of the empire were invited. These celebrations make sense if he were celebrating his sole rule for the first time. There is no precedent for such a ceremony otherwise and it is hard to explain what the celebrations were for if not for a move to single rule. In addition, one of the Amarna letters (number 27) is damaged at the beginning, although all scholars today agree that it must start 'year x + 2'. Since it is from the reign of Akhenaten, who ruled seventeen years, it can only be reconstructed as 'year 12'. The letter from Tushratta, King of Mitanni, greets the new King: 'Tiye, the Great Wife of Nimmuria (Nebmaatre) your mother knows all things; all of them have been seen by Tiye your mother – the messages that your father caused to be addressed to me; ten times more than with Nimmuria your father shall we be friendly'.

We know that Tiye accompanied her son to Tell el Amarna, and from the letters it appears that she took responsibility for foreign affairs during the late years of her husband's reign. It was undoubtedly she or her ministers who transferred the letters of the foreign office archive to Tell el Amarna. It would seem from this that monarchic responsibility may have been split between the two Kings, giving Tiye at Amarna responsibility for links with neighbouring countries while Amenhotep III retained control over home affairs, dominated during his late years with celebrations of his jubilee festivals.

Once Tiye moved to Tell el Amarna to supervise her son, it seems her influence in Malkata naturally declined. In year 34 of Amenhotep III's reign, he had built a second huge palace there called the 'Middle Palace', where inscriptions bearing the name of her daughter Sitamun proliferate. Now, however, she is found with the title 'Great Royal

Wife'. Although much has been made of this by various writers, it may well be that the marriage with his daughter was a routine one of state, since the principal Great Royal Wife Tiye was absent most of the year in her son's palace in the north.

By this time Amenhotep III was clearly ill, as can be seen from his mummy. The mummy was identified as his by a wooden docket tied on a rope around its neck. These handwritten dockets were used by Pinnedjem, the first priest and his son Herihor from the temple at Karnak to identify the kings when they tidied up royal tombs in the Valley of the Kings over a century after they had been robbed by the marauding Nubian army just after the death of Ramesses VI. The mummy was found in the royal cache, and is that of a grossly obese man with extremely bad teeth that must have caused him misery in his old age. That this is a true picture of Amenhotep III might be confirmed by a letter from him to Shuttarna of Mitanni, asking him to send 'the healing statue of Ishtar of Nineveh'. Statues of him from this time show him wearing voluminous gowns and with folds of fat around his midriff. These images, together with the handing over of some of the reins of power to Tiye, all adds up to a man in sudden and great decline. So was it, as some have suggested, also a sign of moral and physical decline that he married his daughter Sitamun?

We have pictures from the tombs at Tell el Amarna that show Queen Tiye sitting with her son and his wife, Nefertiti, with a little girl behind her, named as the Princess (King's daughter) Beketaten. This girl is never seen with Akhenaten and his wife, so she cannot be their daughter, nor can she be Tiye's, as she would have been beyond the age of child-bearing when the girl appears. Beketaten disappears from view as quickly as she appears, and it is impossible to escape the conclusion that this child might be the daughter of Amenhotep III Nebmaatre by his own daughter the Great Royal Wife Sitamun. Even though Sitamun is listed as 'Great Royal Wife' from year 34 onwards, in the celebrations of the third *sed* festival of Amenhotep III shown in the tomb of Kheruef, it is only the figure of Great Royal Wife Tiye who is present; and in many places where Sitamun's name appears she is listed as 'the Princess, Great Royal Wife Sitamun, born of the Great Royal Wife Tiye, may she live'. It is clear that the two women lived peaceably side by side. From a personal point of view, one cannot but admire a woman who took all of this in her stride, and still managed to support her son as well as running foreign state affairs. In fact the choice of a daughter as Great Royal Wife was completely acceptable; cohabitation between her and her father, however, is more questionable.

Although it is wrong to draw too many extreme conclusions, the facts seem to add up as follows: that around year 27 of Amenhotep III Nebmaatre's reign, following the death of his elder son Tuthmosis, the younger son Amenhotep, being deemed unsuitable, probably even by his parents, for sole royal office, is crowned co-regent in Karnak. Three years later the old King celebrates his first jubilee; and shortly afterwards his son leaves Luxor in search of a place of his own. He is accompanied by his mother, Tiye, in charge of foreign affairs as her husband becomes increasingly infirm. In her absence, but without ousting her in any way, Sitamun is promoted to Great Royal Wife status and given large estates in Malkata. By the time of Amenhotep III's second jubilee, many officials have left Luxor, some following the new rising star of Amenhotep IV; by the time of his third jubilee, the old King, sick, obese and abandoned by most of his court, celebrates his festival relatively quietly; and in his thirty-ninth year, finally dies.

As Cyril Aldred and others have suggested, all of this evidence points to a twelve-year co-regency between Amenhotep III and Akhenaten. This would mean that Akhenaten was crowned in Karnak in the twenty-seventh year of his father's reign, and that the first twelve years of Akhenaten's reign were therefore alongside his father. We know that the year of Smenkhkare's appearance and the birth of little Tutankhaten was the same year 12 of Akhenaten's reign. This would mean that Smenkhkare's elevation and the birth of his younger brother took place in year 39 of Amenhotep III's reign. This would mean that it is possible the inscription on the granite lion in the British Museum is correct (see page 146) – that Amenhotep III could be Tutankhamen's father. There is little chance, though, that Tiye could have been his mother, for by year 39 of her husband's reign she was at least in her very late forties if not her fifties. Since Sitamun was made Great Royal Wife around year 27 of Amenhotep III's reign, it would be more feasible, at first glance, that Sitamun would have been Tutankhamen's mother.

As we've seen, many have thought that Smenkhkare and Tutankhamen were brothers, and we have established that there must be at least a twelve-year gap between their births. This means that Smenkhkare would have had to be born around year 27 of the reign of Amenhotep III – in other words, immediately after Sitamun was promoted to Great Royal Wife. We know that at his coronation, Amenhotep III was no more than seven years old. Although we do not know how old Tiye was at the time of her royal marriage, we must assume that their first child could not have been born for at least four years (making the King eleven years old). Sitamun was not the first child of Amenhotep III and Queen Tiye. If she was the second-born, and we allow time for the pregnancy with the first child, then a short gap, then pregnancy with the second child, this would mean that Sitamun was born no earlier than year 6 of her father's reign, and perhaps even after that. In year 27, she would have been twenty-one or a little younger. Her father died in his year 39, making her around thirty-three years old or younger at his death – of a reasonable age to bear the child Tutankhamen.

Let us examine this suggestion again for what it is. If Smenkhkare and Tutankhamen were the sons of an incestuous relationship between Amenhotep III Nebmaatre and his own daughter Sitamun, this would make Amenhotep IV – Akhenaten – the half-brother of both Smenkhkare and Tutankhamen. So when Akhenaten rejected his beloved wife Nefertiti, not only was he declaring his love for another man – but that man was also his brother.

How much more can we accuse Akhenaten of? Nothing like this was ever attested in Egyptian history. From the whole 4000 years of ancient Egyptian history, nowhere is there any hint that homosexual relationships were considered acceptable; and the suggestion of such a relationship between a king and his brother would have been quite unthinkable. So we now have a man who was grossly deformed, reviled all state religion, introduced heresy and disturbed the essential Maat, persecuted those who followed a different path, and then publicly rejected his 'beloved wife' and six daughters – and all for the sake of a public physical relationship with his own brother. Can any of this really be true? Even when I was seven years old, and reading the story for the first time, I began to wonder if there was not an alternative explanation. There has to be another answer.

CHAPTER SIX

Akhenaten and the
Religion of the Aten

—

As we now know, the period in which Tutankhamen was born, grew up and died was dominated by the new religion introduced by Akhenaten. Tutankhamen came to the throne at perhaps one of the most politically unstable periods that Egypt had ever had to face. Externally, the Hittites had regrouped and placed their entire loyalty in a single King who thus had the authority to challenge Egypt within its empire; internally, loyalties and ideologies split the country in two. Even Tutankhamen's very identity was challenged, since he was born Tutankhaten, and although his coronation name remained always Nebkheprure, feelings evidently ran so high in Egypt that he felt the need to change his birth-name to Tutankhamen. The time just after his coronation must have been a tense and critical one as the public – most of all the highly ambitious courtiers around him – waited to see what his first move would be. Would he back Akhenaten's heresy, or turn against it? Had it not been for the heresy, the temples of the 'old gods' would not have been abandoned and the young King would not have been forced to choose. If some writers are correct in believing that the young King *was* eventually murdered, then surely the principal motive is to be found in Tutankhamen's determination to restore the religion of Amen. In so doing he clearly must have challenged some very powerful men.

After the death of Tutankhamen, the throne was taken for a short while by Ay, Tiye's brother; and it has often been suggested that he had the ideal motive for murder – the crazed ambition of a commoner to take the throne, no matter what the cost. When Ay died only four years later, without an heir, the crown was then seized by Horemheb, the Commander-in-Chief of the Egyptian army based in Memphis, who staged a military coup. The edict he issued at the time of his coronation shows that he put the country under tight military control. He started a campaign to eradicate the very existence of Akhenaten, Smenkhkare, Tutankhamen and Ay. He demolished their buildings, using palaces and temples as rubble for his own buildings; he usurped their reign-lengths into his own, pretending that they had never been crowned at all; and he erased their names either by chiselling them out or, more often, by overcarving his own. Historically, though, we must have some sympathy with his cause, for he had justification for his actions, did he not? After all, this corrupt royal family had eroded the moral and religious stability of the country for many years. In other countries, and at other times, there were to be bloody revolutions fired by less cause than Horemheb had. The next dynasty carried on with his campaign of vilification with increased ferocity. In an attempt to regularise his hold on the throne he married the Lady Mutnodjmet, Nefertiti's sister. But despite her efforts to bear him a child, it was to no end. He died childless, and thus handed the throne to his best friend in the army. Henceforth, under the Ramesside pharaohs of the Nineteenth Dynasty, Akhenaten was 'the great enemy'.

This chaos and division was all caused by the religion that Akhenaten steeped himself in. What exactly was this?

The Egyptians were always quick to adopt any new deities that came along. Such characters as Astarte, Dagon and Resheph, all Canaanite deities, were adopted speedily into the Egyptian religious framework. In more modern times, first Christianity and then Islam were also quickly accepted, and their precepts devoutly followed, despite fierce persecutions and pogroms. So what made Akhenaten's religion so unique that it was not only rejected but vilified? The overall reason that archaeology has given is that it was monotheistic, as opposed to the polythesim so favoured by the Egyptians. But then so was Islam in Saudi Arabia in the seventh century – and despite its problems, it caught hold and still flourishes today. So why did Akhenaten's religion fail so spectacularly?

The nature of ancient Egyptian religion is highly complex and its study is completely different from other areas of their culture. In every other field of learning, the Egyptians were essentially conservative. Their rules of society were guided by the single fact that as long as you followed the accepted and established ideology, you could not be faulted if anything went wrong. In mathematics, engineering, education, medicine – in all fields of learning – someone had written down the exact route a student had to take to solve a problem. This even included the very words that must be spoken at certain points. The student was taught to follow this guidance to the letter, and to then expect that nothing could go awry. The result of this was intellectual standstill in most areas of culture. Things simply never moved forwards, as the very notion of innovative research was denied them. History has recorded that this was the province of great geniuses, such as Imhotep, Hordjedef, Amenhotep son of Hapu and Khaemwese. But once these revolutionary new ideas had been tried, tested and accepted, progress once more ground to a halt. One of the only fields of ancient Egyptian culture that changed and adapted through the ages was their religion.

In the fourth century BC, the traveller Herodotus, in search of Greek roots, described the Egyptians as 'religious to excess, beyond any other nation'. But what is religious belief? If you walk around a ladder, if you consider a black cat crossing your path to be lucky, if you wear a St Christopher's medal, if you always do, wear or carry a certain thing at certain times to give you confidence or luck – is that religious belief? It is certainly strong; it will motivate all your actions. Is that not a belief akin to spirituality? And what is religion? If you believe in the strength of your football team – if you wear its colours, chant 'liturgies' on the terraces, play music and sing to its success – where, in terms of historical evidence, is the difference between that and a 'religious cult'? Imagine, in thousands of years' time, given that video recordings are still available, trying to comprehend the differences between a pre-match warm-up on the football terraces and a gospel choir. Both groups are wearing colours; both groups are singing and clapping with enthusiasm and passion; both groups sway to the rhythms. Where is the difference, except in what they believe?

In fact, distinctions between beliefs are often almost impossible to draw, the more so when you must rely on imperfect evidence, such as trite, standardised inscriptions on royal monuments. If a king is described as 'the great god', is this flattery or a literal truth? Archaeology finds it easy to define 'how' an object was made, but virtually impossible to say 'why', without being subjective. Every object we find is interpreted according to our twentieth-century knowledge and our own prejudices. In most archaeological fields, when an object is defined as being 'of religious, cultic or symbolic significance', it would be more truthful to say 'purpose unknown'. For example, Egyptian collections in museums are filled with little figures, some made of faience, others of bronze or even wood. They are, we are assured, deities. But are they? Little figures of Taweret (in Greek, Thoueris) resemble a pregnant hippopotamus, a figure often found in the houses of ordinary people in ancient times. She is described almost universally as a goddess. This decision was presumably made by applying knowledge gained in the last century about Greek and Roman beliefs. In these ancient cultures, inscriptions confirm that deities had small votive, or offering, figures made to resemble them. But is the same true of every ancient society? Is it fair to colour everything with our own stereotyped belief that, as all ancient societies were pre-Christian and 'pagan', they must all be similar, and all images must be 'gods'? Could there be another explanation? In the case of Taweret, where was her temple? Where her priesthood? Where her cult? She had none. But people believed in her. Today, you may believe equally in your copper bracelet as a treatment for rheumatism, or in Manchester United. It still does not make them gods.

Today, in Egypt, the principal religion is Islam. The majority of Moslems are Sunnite. Yet in many ways, their beliefs are 'non-standard'. Of course, the practice of every religion varies from country to country as it is adapted to conform to traditional local customs. But in Egypt even today, many of the local, private beliefs come not from Islam but from very ancient customs. This should be no surprise, nor should it be vilified as 'pagan', any more than our own use of trees and evergreen plants at Christmas, eggs at Easter and celebration of growing things at Harvest Festival (a truly non-Christian occasion) should be rejected. On the contrary, these festivals offer continuity and, with it, the confidence and comfort that comes with familiarity.

So I have witnessed often in Egypt a local village woman, shrouded and anonymous, silently offering up her newborn child to the carved image of a 'goddess' on the wall of a temple. Ask her why, and she cannot tell you, except that 'the woman is good and has power'. Similar things were witnessed and attested regularly by Omm Seti, the elderly Englishwoman who lived out most of her life at the temples of Abydos. The Egyptian people are Moslem – but sometimes other ideas and beliefs, just as strong, may intervene. There is a common belief, even in the highest echelons of Egyptian society today, in the Evil Eye. You might, perhaps, call it a curse. In any case, it can be put on you accidentally or deliberately. If someone openly admires your possessions, your achievement, your child – then the Evil Eye will take it from you. If someone accidentally crosses your path at certain stages in your life, it may render you childless later. If someone hates and despises you, the use of hair, nail-clippings, part of your clothes – all can be used, buried secretly with the right invocations, to bring chaos and doom to the one hated. All of this is carefully defined and deeply believed and there are set routines, offered by people regarded as spiritually gifted, who can change your fortune by applying certain remedies. But they are not religion.

The same, then, applies to ancient Egyptian belief. As Joyce Tyldesley has written,

> although the ordinary people owed an official allegiance to the state gods, they were far more likely to worship the less-exalted and more familiar local gods, while folk-religion, including magic, superstition and witchcraft, played an important role in the life of peasant communities.

It is probably this that made Herodotus declare the ancient Egyptians to be 'religious to excess'.

Pre-Amarna religion

To understand how different the new religion of Aten was, we need first to understand orthodox religious beliefs during the Eighteenth Dynasty. For a start, we need to break their beliefs down into different sections instead of looking at them as a whole. For example, there were, first, the 'household deities' such as Taweret, whose function was purely amuletic. Their images would be worn either to bring luck or to avert evil, especially in times of crisis or ill health. These figures, without cults, could be considered more amulets than 'gods', even used as part of medical procedures, so let us put them aside first.

Then there were the 'local gods'. These were different in every single town and village. Each was believed to be the *ka* (see page 95) of a local figure who had once lived and died in your town. The Egyptians believed that if you built them a stone house, put inside it a figure that they might recognise and then offered it food, drink – all the things a *ka* needed – then the *ka* would doubtless return and respond to some of the reasonable requests that you might put to it in return. These stone houses in Egypt we call 'temples'. The translation is a bad one, coloured by nineteenth-century beliefs that 'pagans' worshipped in 'temples'. The ancient Egyptian word for these buildings was ⌐▯△⌐, which means 'the home of the god'. Even its very floor plan was that of a large private house. In fact, there were no 'services' held here; you did not sing or pray or praise; and the 'god' was kept in secret, hidden, dark within its sanctuary, approachable only by his servant. The people of the town would have been aware of the existence of the figure; indeed, they were probably employed on the land owned by the 'temple' and occasionally, with increasing frequency, the image might be withdrawn from the silent blackness of its sanctuary, placed within a shrine-cabin, mounted on a tiny boat that could be carried by four or six men, and walked around the periphery of the 'temple'. On these occasions, often translated as 'oracles', ordinary people could put a question to the 'god'. Scenes show great rejoicing when this figure appeared among the people. Similar things happen today, for example in many Catholic countries, when the figure of a saint or some holy relic is processed through the town. No doubt the people believed in the power of the figures and felt ownership towards them. But were these figures gods – any more than the processed saints of today are gods? It is more likely that they were regarded as intercessors with the principal god.

Sometimes a local boy along the Nile 'made good'. From time to time, the natural line of kings would die out and the throne would pass to the most worthy successor – often a vizier or army leader. This new king, coming from a certain town, naturally owed allegiance to his own local figure and 'temple'. He might go into the local 'temple' himself to thank the *ka* of the one who had brought him to this place, and, in thanks, would make offerings or give tribute. But this was no longer the attention and tribute of an ordinary man – it was that of a king, elevated by coronation to the very status and company of an immortal himself. Only the king owned the produce of quarries and the gold; only, then, the gifts of a king could amount to huge wealth for the local temple. So it was with the elevation of Ptah of Memphis, when the first King built his palace there, that Ptah became one of the first 'national' gods of Egypt. Later, in the Fifth Dynasty, several kings elevated the cult of Re in their area of Heliopolis. Later still, the kings Mentuhotep of the Eleventh Dynasty briefly elevated the cult of Mont at Medamud; and the kings of the Twelfth and the Eighteenth Dynasties raised the status of Amen, their own local deity in Luxor.

Once these 'gods' achieved national status, just as the king was no longer on the same spiritual or physical level as his subjects, so their cult-figures were imbued with new powers. They were credited with the creation of the world and everything in it, and the continued maintenance of it, day by day. To them were attached a succession of creation myths, or cosmologies. These cosmologies should not be understood, as some try to suggest, as a complex morass of ideas all current at the same time, but rather as an ever-developing series of ideas, built one upon the other, each taking responsibility for creation one stage further as one family of kings replaced another. The cult within the temples changed to suit the new ideas. As Gay Robins and others have pointed out, the kings, within the sanctuaries of their elevated gods, now undertook ceremonial to ensure that the positive sides of creation should be maintained, though, being secret, the actual nature of the ceremonials are now lost to us.

By propitiating the cult image, then, a king ensured the maintenance of Maat. Maat, as we have seen, is often pictured as a female with an ostrich plume in her hair, and represented equilibrium, the very balance of Nature. Truth was only one aspect of her duties. She was the order that emerges from Isfet, or chaos; she was the primeval force of creation that needed maintaining. Not all she represented was good. To achieve balance, some things need to go wrong in order that right can triumph. But just as the *ka*s of local figures needed feeding by their servants, so the king, the ultimate servant (his title in Egyptian, ⫴⫾, means 'servant', although we translate it as 'majesty') had to feed the balance of the world, Maat. If he failed, Isfet would return, and the Nile would not flood, and the cosmos would collapse. The king maintained

Maat with the assistance of such concepts as *hu* and *sia* – empirical knowledge and instinctive perception, neither of them any use without the other. As servant to the national god, then, the king was literally in charge of the order of world. What he did while in the sanctuary concerned no man in Egypt; all they knew was that the things he did directly ensured their continuing existence. If he did not do them, the floods might not return. They relied on him and his knowledge unquestioningly.

So, what exactly did the ordinary Egyptian believe in? Herodotus speaks of witnessing cults of 'the god whose name cannot be spoken'. The rites he describes and the beliefs attached to them are clearly those of Osiris, the lord of the afterlife. This figure, enshrined in mythology as a murdered demigod, brought back to life briefly by his sister-wife, Isis, in order to father Horus, was deemed to rule over life after death. After your death and the resurrection of your body by means of the Opening of the Mouth ceremony (see page 97) Osiris would preside over your trial where he would ask your *akh* to declare the sort of life you had led. Every lie your tongue spoke would literally weigh down your heart with guilt. The heart could then be weighed, so that no one, not even god, condemned you – you condemned yourself by your own words. To this extent, then, the one god in ancient Egypt recognised by all men and feared universally was Osiris, sometimes alluded to in texts as the 'Lord-of-All'.

To sum this up, if any one ancient Egyptian could be brought back and asked in what he believed, he would undoubtedly have responded 'god', by which he meant Osiris. This leaves ancient Egypt neither polytheistic nor pagan. These attributes were given to the local figures by early Christians, who were eager to proselytise and quick to condemn. The life of the ordinary Egyptian was ruled first by his locality, where he frequently worked for the local temple, behind whose walls something went on – what, he neither knew nor really cared, except that the figures there worked for him, and on occasion, when publicly processed, he might get close enough to gain some benefit. In his daily life, he and his family used amulets for healing and protection, and believed implicitly in them. Somewhere, perhaps many miles away, the king of Egypt maintained the national 'temple' with wealth but that was only to be expected, since within those walls, the very nature of Egypt, the world and the cosmos were maintained. Most of this had nothing to do with him; the only thing he feared was the ultimate judgment of god – Osiris – the one figure who ruled his daily actions through fear of hellfire and damnation. In fact, the average ancient Egyptian believed primarily in Osiris, as Herodotus recorded.

Taking it further, orthodox Egyptian religion was essentially monotheist, even before the time of Akhenaten. To demonstrate what I mean, compare these two short translations of texts.

> Father of the gods who created Mankind, who made the animals . . . and all the plants that sustain the cattle . . . Lord of the rays of the sun that give light . . . You are the only one, the one who created all that exists, the Sole One who made everything that is. He is the one who made fields for cattle, the fruit tree for Mankind. It is he who made the fish in the river and the birds in the skies, it is he who gives breath to what is in the egg and keeps alive the offspring of the serpent.

> Your love is great, immense. Your light brightens up all faces, your brightness gives life to hearts when you fill the Two Lands with your love. Holy god who created himself, who made every land, created what is in it, all peoples, herds and flocks, all trees that grow from the soil.

Both of these are 'hymns'. One is taken from the hymn to the Aten, the 'heresy' of Tell el Amarna. The other was written to Amen of Karnak, three generations earlier, during the time of orthodoxy. So which was which? History declares the failure of the religion of the Aten to the fact that it was monotheistic and unsettling to the Egyptians. But these two pieces show how inconsistent that idea is. The first piece was dedicated to Amen, the second to the Aten – but both express identical sentiments. It is evident that the revulsion felt towards Akhenaten was not primarily because he headed a monotheistic religion that was alien to Egyptian ideas. The notion of monotheism is purely a modern concept. So how true, then, are the other statements about him – that he was an obsessive and heretical iconoclast, who had invented the new religion himself? Just what problems did he leave behind for Tutankhamen to resolve?

Our knowledge of the religious views of Amenhotep IV came, in the first place, from excavations at Tell el Amarna. The city was surrounded by boundary stelae demarcating the exact area of land it was to cover. The King called the site Akhetaten – 'the Horizon of the Aten'.

There are fourteen stelae, all with similar inscriptions, eleven of which say that the King visited the site on the thirteenth day of the fourth month of winter in year 6 of his rule. Exactly a year before this day, they state,

> One was in Akhetaten in a carpeted tent made for His Majesty in Akhetaten, the name of which was 'Aten in Content'. The King appeared mounted on a great chariot of gold, like Aten when he dawns on the horizon and fills the Two Lands with his love. Setting out on the fine road of Akhetaten on the first anniversary of founding it, which his Majesty had done in order to make a monument for his father the Aten ... Making a great offering of bread, beer, large and small cattle, poultry, wine, fruits, ⌇⌇⌇ [possibly a narcotic drug, or alternatively, incense] and all kinds of goodly plants on the anniversary of the founding.

It thus seems that Amenhotep IV Neferkheprure Waenre had first found the new site for his new palace-home the same day the previous year, year 5 of his reign, which would have been year 32 of the reign of Amenhotep III Nebmaatre. It has been said that he came here, to a deserted site that belonged neither to god nor man, after being forced out of Luxor by the priests of the temple of Karnak, who could not stand his heresies within their province.

Yet we now know this site was not his first choice. It seems that, after his coronation as co-regent, one of the duties he was sent first to fulfil was a journey not north, but southwards, into Nubia. Inscriptions and pictures at Soleb and Sedeinga, the Nubian temples between the Second and Third Cataracts, at northern and mid-Sudan, built for his father and mother, record the celebrations of Amenhotep III Nebmaatre's first jubilee in his year 30. It seems that they sent their son here to order and oversee the carvings, carry the news and organise the celebrations. To do this, young Amenhotep IV seems to have stayed in the nearby town of Sudla, called today Sese, at the foot of a large rock promontory, Gebel Sese. Although local town-dwellers call the site Gami, for some reason it was identified by early archaeologists as Sesebi, a name which has since stuck. The site was first identified as an ancient site perhaps by the German Egyptologist Karl Lepsius, who drew a site-plan of it in his *Denkmäler*, published in 1849.

The importance of the site was fixed during the Nubian Survey in 1967, in preparation for the building and opening of the proposed High Dam at Aswan.

Excavations were carried out in two seasons, 1936–37 and 1937–38. The initial season's work comprised, first, mapping of the outstanding features, and then an examination of some of the most important sections. This occupied just fourteen weeks' work, from 1 November to 17 February. The second season was even shorter, for some of the team's time was spent at the neighbouring site of Amara West. Brief notification was published in the *Journal of Egyptian Archaeology* for each of the two years of excavation, outlining the extent of work done. The work was carried out by members of the Egyptology Department at Liverpool University, led by Professor Aylward Blackman, his assistant, H. W. Fairman (later Professor in the same department), F. W. Green and J. G. Griffiths, although sickness kept Blackman away during the second season. After the sites had been excavated artefacts were sent back to England for distribution to contributing museums. However, no full excavation report was ever published. The material from Sesebi remains in disparate Egyptian collections around the world, while the photographs and field-notes await full study.

It was clear from the start, however, that here was a town, within a boundary wall, dating from the time of Amenhotep IV and later usurped by Seti I. Within the town three 'temple' areas were identified. At least one of these was, in all probability, a palace-type residence for the king rather than for a 'god'. At two corners of the town wall were found intact foundation deposits, pits covered by slabs of stone containing small items left at the time that the wall was first laid out. On the underneath face of each slab were inscribed the cartouches of Amenhotep IV Neferkheprure Waenre, and objects in the pits all dated from the very early part of his reign. Two similar pits were found in the centre of the town. The buildings within the walls were found to be scattered. The centre part, for example, seems never to have been built on at all, while other buildings were heavily altered in later years, and part of the town appears to have been destroyed by fire. Throughout the town, pictures and names confirmed the identity of Amenhotep IV as the probable builder of the town. There was no evidence found to suggest any earlier occupant of the site. Under the three temples, foundation deposits of the same kind as the town's were found, while the 'central temple' comprised an open courtyard, where the stone blocks, coated with plaster, bear the first form of the name Amenhotep gave to the Aten, together with his title, ⟨⟩ – Amenhotep the God, Ruler of Luxor. This title, which copies and then adds to that of his father, is of the very earliest type, showing it was carved soon after his coronation, while another epithet, ⟨⟩ 'Shining like the Aten', has still not been found elsewhere.

Perhaps the most remarkable find, uncovered on 14 January 1937, was the entrance to a subterranean crypt below the temple, its walls formed by fine stone blocks carved in sunken relief. It is the only one of its kind ever found in a pharaonic temple, the nearest equivalent being the crypt below the Ptolemaic temple of Dendera. Here is depicted Amenhotep, already in the somewhat distorted shape that was to become the norm in portraits of him, making offerings to the Aten who is pictured as a falcon-headed god with the sun-disc worn as a headdress. This deity is one of a panoply of gods that the King is offering to. He stands with Shu, the 'child' of Amen; Geb, the son of Shu; Atum, primeval god of creation; Osiris, lord of the afterlife; and Maat. All of them were associated with the cosmos.

It is clear that here we have the very beginnings of the religion that he was to extol. The name of the Aten is written in hieroglyphs alongside the figure, together with the first-ever full version of his name, ⟨⟩ – 'Re-Horakhte is venerated on the horizon in his name as Shu, which is the Aten'. It is clear that the Aten was not originally conceived as a sole god, but rather as one specific aspect of the sun. The theological statement also equates Aten to other gods, while the picture shows that he was originally not conceived as 'faceless', without an image. In fact, both picture and text show that Aten is but one aspect of Re-Horakhte, the sun.

The early name of the Aten, written here as a simple text, was to assume great importance as the years went by. It was first enclosed within a cartouche and then, as the ideas about Aten developed, it was to change twice more. Eight blocks that once belonged to shrines within the temple of Karnak, later used as rubble, used the same title without the cartouche but added the epithet ⟨⟩ , 'which is in the *sed* festival'. This is contemporary with, and presumably added during, the celebration of Amenhotep III Nebmaatre's first *sed* festival in Luxor. Later, in year 8 of Akhenaten, the name was changed finally to [hieroglyphs] . The exact translation of this has been hotly argued by scholars. After the word 'it', meaning 'father', is a sun-disc invariably read as 'Re'. The inscription would then mean, 'May Aten live, ruler of the Two Horizons, venerated on the horizon in his name of Re the Father who is the Aten.' Clearly the names of Re-Horakhte and Shu from the first series of titles have been removed, suggesting a move to outlaw the names and images of other gods. If that is the case, one wonders why the name should include 'Re the Father'. Does this not deny the exclusivity sought? It is more likely that the sun-disc is not to be read as Re any more, but as Aten, and that in this instance it acts as a determinative for 'it', so it would mean, 'May Aten live, ruler of the Two Horizons, venerated on the horizon in his name of the father who is come as the Aten.'

The pattern we have, then, is that Amenhotep IV, from the start of his reign, is keen to find a place in which to establish his new beliefs. These beliefs, however, are only slowly emerging. After his coronation he travels south to Nubia to assist with the jubilee celebrations of his father. Here he founds a city nearby, and builders work on the King's images of his new god. The Aten at this stage is simply another falcon-headed deity who lives and works alongside other gods. This suggests that the religion was not intended primarily to be monotheistic, as so many people have suggested. Probably because the region was so remote, or more likely because it was in Nubia and not Egypt, he decided that his city was unsuitable. So he returns to Luxor, celebrates his father's jubilee, and then sets out, this time in the opposite direction, to find a place within Egypt itself where he can devote a place exclusively to the Aten. It is clear that he felt that Luxor belonged to Amen. He needed a place that belonged to no god. When he found it, he dedicated the site to Aten, marked its boundaries, began building work and finally moved in. Having now somewhere of his own to live, he sets to work on finalising his theologies. Finally, around year 8 of his reign, he changed the name Aten to its later variant, removing the names and images of all other gods.

But did he do that at all? We have seen that monotheism was more the rule than the exception in ancient Egypt, with other figures being either amulets or local protectors. So did he need to outlaw the others at all? It is, in fact, a commonly held misbelief that Amenhotep IV outlawed other deities. Although the central temple in Tell el Amarna was built to the Aten, this was a common town plan throughout Egypt. In any town site you might expect the name and image of only one local 'god' to predominate. A quick look at the excavation report of the British team, *City of Akhenaten, I*, shows that virtually every house the team excavated had figures within them of other gods.

House no.	Date excavated	Artefact
0.49.23	1922	scarabs
		2 monkeys
0.49.23	1922	Hathor head
K.51.1	1922	Bronze Isis plaque
		Isis head with disc
K51.2	1922	Bes amulet
M.50.15	1922	Bes amulet
N.49.12	1921	2 faience Bes figures
N.49.12	1921	Eye of Horus
N.49.20	1921	Bes, clay, painted red
0.47.17	1922	Isis figurine
0.47.18	1922	Isis figurine
0.49.22	1921	Scarab with sphinx carved on

Among other pieces found in the same years were a head and image of Hathor, the cow-headed reincarnation of Isis, painted on a bowl; three figurines of Taweret; a plaque with a curly-horned ram and the name of Amen; a plaque with a cow and the name of Hathor; and innumerable Bes figures and Horus (*wadjet*) eyes. Similar finds were made in subsequent years.

In other words, despite protestations that the King tried to make his god exclusive, the evidence suggests that little really changed in the Egypt of the time. Exactly the same kinds of figures are commonly found as on any site elsewhere; and the Aten simply replaces the local god of the other towns. In archaeological terms, what should be read from this is that Amenhotep IV Neferkheprure Waenre needed to find an unoccupied site in which to found a 'temple' for the god to whom he was dedicated, the Aten. In creating this, he was creating yet another local god of the ilk discussed previously. There is no evidence to suggest that he insisted on Aten worship exclusively throughout the new city. On the contrary, it seems, from the figures found, that either there must have been a local factory turning out figurines for the people or the figures were imported onto the site in bulk to satisfy local demand. Neither of these options could have been kept secret from the King who ruled the town. Both suggest that the King, far from forcing his ideas on others, led ideas that people could either follow or not, as suited them. This is far from the heretical, iconoclast image usually drawn of him.

And what of that other claim – that Akhenaten's move away from Luxor was forced upon him by the powerful priests of the temple of Amen of Karnak? Once again, from both the archaeological evidence and from our knowledge of Egyptian religion, this can be demonstrated to be nonsense. Firstly, and most importantly, the temple of Karnak at the time of Amenhotep III Nebmaatre was not the building that we see today. If you remove from a plan any of the buildings erected during the Nineteenth Dynasty and after, you are left with a small sanctuary, with a set of pylon gates erected by Amenhotep III only a few yards in front of it. The great columned halls, the huge open courtyard, the southern pylons – none of these existed in his time. In other words, although the temple was in the process of being enriched by the kings who lived in the area and habitually visited there, it had not reached either the wealth or the power that it achieved under Seti I Menmaatre and Ramesses II Usermaatre Setepenre. On the contrary, inscriptions from both the temple of Amen at Karnak and from the palace-city of Malkata show conclusively (see page 170) that Akhenaten lived there, entered regularly into the temple and even built extensively there.

Besides this, the thought of the 'servants' of Amen forcing out a king is totally untenable. It is, metaphorically, the tail wagging the dog. The servants of any master obtain their jobs, and their livelihoods, because the lord employs them. If the lord chooses not to employ them, or to redeploy them, or if he chooses to move home and live elsewhere, that is his choice. In this instance, Amenhotep IV chose to find a 'home' for his own deity, but left his father, the senior co-regent, behind him in Luxor. The 'temple' of Amen would therefore continue to be served as long as Amenhotep III Nebmaatre lived and chose to support it. If the young king moved away and consequently removed much of the revenue from the area, there was nothing whatever that the 'servants' could do about it. Without the presence of the king, the 'temple' would indeed become neglected and abandoned. But that was not because the 'priests' forced him out. Logically, if they wished to remain rich and powerful they should have done the opposite – persuaded him to stay.

In other words, under no circumstance whatever was Amenhotep IV forced to move. The archaeological evidence from Sesebi, plus the King's own declarations on his boundary stela, make it quite clear that he simply wanted to find a place of his own. Material from the city shows that he did not force this view on those around him, but rather offered his views open-handedly.

So what of the other notions? How heretical was he? Where did his ideas come from? What exactly was the Aten in the first place?

In general terms, the Aten, during the occupation of Tell el Amarna, is depicted as a sun-disc, with a uraeus – the rearing hooded cobra seen on the front of a royal crown – at the front, and rays emerging from it, each terminating in a hand. These hands are often shown holding the looped-cross hieroglyph meaning 'life' to the noses of members of the royal family. The King wrote 'hymns', or, rather, descriptive poems, to his god, and these were carved, in a short or a long version, in several of the tombs cut into the walls of the cliffs to the back of the plain of Tell el Amarna (see page 194). These poems are remarkably similar, all scholars agree, to Psalm 104, reputedly written by Moses. This has led many to suppose that either Moses and the Jews were in Egypt at the time of Amenhotep IV and thus 'converted' him, or even that the King himself was Moses. While it may well be true that the Exodus happened at the time of the decline of Tell el Amarna, there is no truth whatsoever in the rest of it. Linking Amenhotep IV with Judaism or Christianity is a purely subjective exercise.

Some people have suggested that the impetus for the whole movement came from Queen Tiye, who constantly supported her son in everything and is seen in pictures from the Amarna tombs accompanying her son into the temple for the morning ceremonies. One writer, working out that the name of the Great Royal Wife Nefertiti means, in hieroglyphs, 'the beautiful woman has come', has suggested that Nefertiti was a foreigner who thus brought the new religion into the country with her. We know that Nefertiti was as Egyptian as her husband. And I shall demonstrate that the religion had been there for a long time. Like many things concerned with the story of the period, much of this business of a new religion is nonsense.

Often it is said that it was the very nature of the religion of the Aten that was hostile to the Egyptians, rather than that it was purely monotheistic and outlawed every other god. Because the Aten was the physical disc of the sun in the sky, it was on view to everyone and thus lost the secrecy attached to other Egyptian cults. More importantly, it has been said, the cult had no allowance for life after death. In denying Osiris, it also denied traditional burial and mummification, the promise of eternity. Since no cemetery has been found in the city, it has been said that the citizens of Tell el Amarna, at death, had their bodies shipped back home for burial. The sun-based religion was undeveloped and ultimately selfish. It failed because it made no provision for many aspects of religion that were important to the ordinary people.

Once again, we have here statements that are inherently wrong. For a start, in Tomb 1, belonging to Huya – Overseer of the Royal Harem, Overseer of the Two Treasuries and Steward of Great Royal Wife Tiye in Tell el Amarna – one of the walls in the main hall is carved with a picture showing Huya in an anthropoid coffin, standing upright before mourners. The process of mummification, the use of an anthropoid coffin, and standing for mourning – all these are linked with the old belief associated with judgment by Osiris. The layout of the tombs is identical with the traditional layout encountered in Luxor – and the provision of a tomb at all, as the home of the *ka*, is in accordance with old and traditional beliefs. Moreover, in nobles' tombs in Luxor, it was never the habit to picture gods or goddesses, though reference might be made to the king who was being served and to the name of the local god. Here, exactly the same pattern is followed, with scenes of everyday life, pictures of the King, and the name of the Aten. Even more illuminating has to be the provision, within the royal tomb itself in the *wadi* at the back of the site, of sarcophagi fragments and *ushabti* figures to accompany the burials. It seems that even Akhenaten, the very author of the cult, was mummified and buried in accordance with Osiride tradition. There is nothing different at all here in any provision for the dead.

As far as the lack of a cemetery goes, we have here a major and glaring error. The map of Tell el Amarna usually used in publications goes back to the one provided by the British excavation team of 1921 to 1933. This shows more of the extent of their excavation than it does the

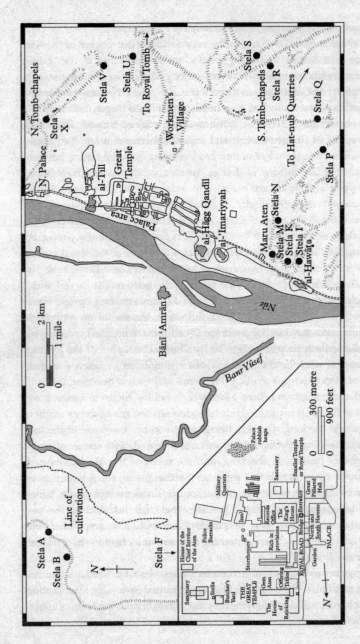

Tell el Amarna (location of boundary stelae).

extent of the city. In fact, when Akhenaten founded his city and laid out his intentions on the fourteen boundary stelae, three of them (see map on page 194) were placed on the west bank of the Nile opposite the main city. His intentions are clear. The city boundaries enclose not just the east bank but the west as well. The siting of the west bank boundary stelae today has been little studied but is hugely informative. The northernmost stela lies at the southern edge of Tuna el Gebel, the necropolis of El Ashmunein, and encloses, between it and the river-bank, a quarry that most certainly provided some of the stone for the building of Tell el Amarna. But a question should have been asked at some time: if the city is on the east bank, why did the King need a western boundary marked? If today you stand in the late afternoon, as I have often done, at the western stelae, carved from the cliff, and look down at the sandy strip between the cliff and the fertile strip, you can clearly see the regular indentations that mark grave sites. Logically, the most promising site for a cemetery in ancient Egypt has to be near a town-site on the periphery of the desert. Here, on the west bank, adjacent to the older cemetery site of El Ashmunein, we have the ideal spot, but no one has examined the site to this day. If we are to understand what the religion of the Aten meant to ordinary people, we need to check their graves – not in Luxor, but in Tell el Amarna. Perhaps this site, more than any other, should be excavated sooner rather than later.

The contradictions published with regard to the understanding of sun-religion in ancient Egypt have been a constant source of amazement and often amusement to me over the years. If we go back to the earliest corpus of religious texts in Egypt, the Pyramid Texts, carved in a series of pyramids at the end of the Fifth and beginning of the Sixth Dynasties, it is clear from both the content of the 'chapters' and the style of the language that they encapsulate a series of beliefs spanning hundreds, if not thousands, of years. It seems that these traditions were largely verbal, but that towards the end of the Old Kingdom, a decision was taken to write them down for the first time. In the earliest texts (recognisable from their content but also from the structures of the language used in them), sentences designed to be recited over the king's burial, referring to the king being buried in a grave in the sand, urge him, 'protect your face', 'keep the sand off your face' and 'do not allow your head to be separated'. In the second series, the king's spirit is now to be associated with star-groups, especially some of the stars in Orion and Sothis (Sirius), whom he is urged to join on a papyrus raft, going among them not as a supplicant but as a conqueror. He is even urged not simply to sit among them, but to hit them, even to cannibalise them.

Only in the final stages, the latest of the texts, is he urged to join the sun on its passage across the sky. These beliefs are concurrent with the writing of the texts themselves, in the Fifth to Sixth Dynasties. The sun-god in this instance is Re; but in Egyptian thinking, the sun goes through many transformations through the day. In fact, if you visit the Nile Valley, you can judge the transformations easily for yourself. There is, first, the time of early dawn, as, over the eastern hills, the infant sun slowly climbs over the horizon, offering a little light but no heat. Then, as it leaves the land behind, the heat strikes, as strong as the blow of a fist. One moment Egypt is cool and shrouded with mists; the next, the heat of the sun dissolves them, the air clears, and intense heat strikes. From eleven until mid-afternoon, the sun becomes increasingly fierce – so much so that most locals have a siesta, and even schoolchildren rush home at lunchtime in time to miss the full heat. From midday to three, streets become quieter, the earth and the air burn while the sun becomes the centre of existence. In the late afternoon, after three, the sun seems to get larger in the sky as the heat reduces and gentle breezes blow in from the north. At sunset, the sky is painted scarlet briefly until, like a light switching off, the sun suddenly disappears from view into the western hills.

The Egyptians saw each of these phases as an aspect of Re. At dawn, as he rose, he was Khepri; as the sun rose higher above the hills in the morning, he was Re-Horakhte, Re who was Horus of the two horizons (Horus being the lanner falcon who, like the sun, streaked across the sky); or as Re-Horemakhet (Re as Horus on the Horizon). At its fullest noon-day height, it was the Aten; and in the late afternoon as it is set, it became Atum.

Surprisingly, in a country so dominated by heat and light from the sun, sun worship was far rarer than many people suggest. Egyptian religion (see above, page 181) was dominated by secrecy, which itself gave power into the hands of the ones allowed into the presence of the image. But the sun was open and visible to all. While it was a power to be reckoned with, it was not an exclusive image. In fact, Re only became popular towards the middle of the Old Kingdom. The so-called Westcar Papyrus in Berlin purports to tell of the coming of this new religion. Cheops (Khnum-Khufu), the Fourth Dynasty builder of the Great Pyramid at Giza and father to many children, should surely have been assured of a long existence on the throne of Egypt for his sons and grandsons. But it was not to be. The papyrus tells a tale of magic – how a magician or wise man is summoned to the King, who asks him where the ultimate wisdom of the universe, the scrolls written at the beginning of time by the god Thoth, were to be found. These forty-two texts, if found, would give humanity the answers to every question they would ever need to ask. The magician tells the King that, although he knows where they are – and they are protected by virtually undefeatable magic in the form of immortal serpents – it is 'not you, nor your son, but the eldest of the three boy-children who are in the womb or Ruddjedet, the wife of the servant of Re of Sakhbu'.

These three boys, so history leads us to believe, were the first kings of the Fifth Dynasty. These kings built their pyramids close to each other at Abusir; and, remarkably, also built a series of sun-temples not far away, at modern Abu Ghurab. These solar temples are approached, like the pyramid complexes, up a long causeway. A portal then leads to an open courtyard dominated by a *benben* stone, a prototype obelisk made of many smaller stones rather than, as with later obelisks, being cut from a single stone. Storehouses around the open courtyard seem to have contained animals and plants which were presumably to be offered to the sun as it rose from behind the *benben*. It seems from these two pieces of evidence, therefore, that these three kings, coming from an area of Egypt dedicated to Re, began the cult of the sun in the Fifth Dynasty. The temples, like the cult, were abandoned at the end of the Old Kingdom.

When we examine the cosmologies of the national gods of Egypt, not only do they come in succession and represent the home towns of their proponents, but they also tend to give their name to the king himself. The habit of naming your child after the local god was a normal practice. So, for example, the kings of the Eleventh Dynasty, coming from the Medamud area north of Luxor, took the name of their local god – Mentuhotep (meaning Mont is content); kings of the Twelfth Dynasty took the name Amenemhet (Amun is Foremost) after the local god of Luxor. Hence the kings of the Fifth Dynasty took names ending in 're', (such as Sahure), and from that time on all successive kings of Egypt adopted the title 〰⊙ , or Son of Re.

In fact, we can see that the change to the religion of the sun, or Re, started earlier than the Fifth Dynasty. The successor of Cheops was called Djedefre (or Redjedef, depending how the name is read). The throne was then usurped from him by Khafre, or Chephren, and his successor was Menkaure, or Mycerinus. All three of these names terminate in 're', the name of the sun-god. From this it would seem that the sun-based religion was followed by several of Cheops' sons. At this distance in time, it is impossible to say how the populace reacted to a change in theology led from the top. However, life was different during the Old Kingdom. At this time the king was truly seen as a living god. It is likely that the new religion may well have been limited to the topmost echelons and did not cause the problems its resurgence was to cause during the New Kingdom.

In other words, the solar revolution of the Eighteenth Dynasty was not the first time that it had happened. The whole thing was merely a reflection of what had occurred centuries before in the Fourth and Fifth Dynasties, except that attention now turned to the Aten, or the point of the sun at noon, as a metaphor for god the creator. But in most ways, the practice of the two religions seems almost identical. Akhenaten claimed to be the son of the sun-god, just as, from the Fifth Dynasty on, all kings claimed to be the Son of Re. Even the open construction of the temples of the Aten in Tell el Amarna and in Karnak were direct copies of the solar temples of Abu Ghurab, dominated by a *benben* stone that was almost identical. It is, in this context, interesting to note that the head of a statue, now in Cairo Museum, made of greywacke, a hard grey stone, and found at Abu Ghurab, wears exactly the same flat-topped 'crown' adopted in Tell el Amarna by Nefertiti, and has been described variously as either the head of Userkaf, first ruler of the Fifth Dynasty, or Neith, tutelary goddess of Lower Egypt. Under the circumstances, it is hard to understand why such a religion should have aroused any opposition at all.

The sun-cult of the Fifth Dynasty was unsuccessful, perhaps for the lack of power it renders to its followers in that the sun is open to all. In any event, although the cult became a secondary one in Egypt after that time, in two respects it persisted. The first is the insistence of the kings on the title Son Of Re. The second is the continued domination of Heliopolis, literally 'the City of the Sun'. The cult of Re was centred in Heliopolis, (today a northern suburb of Cairo). Here the acolytes were not called servants but 'seers' – literally, in Egyptian, the ones who see, or, rather, observe. Here, according to all texts, was the ultimate seat of wisdom. It was to Heliopolis, as the seat of higher education along the Nile Valley, that successive generations of crown princes came to learn the wisdom that would guide them as maintainers of Maat. It was to Heliopolis, we know, that Amenhotep IV's elder brother went before his disappearance; and, presumably, after Prince Tuthmosis died, it would be reasonable to expect that Prince Amenhotep, later Amenhotep IV, would have come there to learn. At any rate all the signs – from the construction of his temple to the design of Nefertiti's crown – point to a strong influence from the teachers of the Re temple of Heliopolis on the impressionable Prince, even if they were not the direct source of his ideas.

In the New Kingdom, frequent links or syncretisms were established between pairs of gods, one of which was invariably Re. So, for instance, we find Sobek-Re, but, more importantly, Amen-Re. Divine syncretisms are complex; but to explain them simply, they might be compared to town-twinning. For example, my own home town of Yeovil in Somerset is twinned with Herblay in France, and Tanusstein in Germany. This does not take anything away from any of the three towns. They maintain their own existence; but the uniting of them creates another, separate entity, celebrated by the things they have in common and providing a unity between them. So it was with Amun and Re; the syncretism did not erase the existence of either Amun of Karnak, nor Re of Heliopolis, but created a united force that drew from the strengths of both. This, therefore, does not and never could mean that Amun of Karnak was an element of the sun. His very name means 'hidden' or 'secret', and his home, the sanctuary within the centre of Karnak temple, was its darkest, quietest and most secret part – the very opposite of sun worship.

In other words, in the Eighteenth Dynasty, Egypt had already seen, lived through and survived a period of pure sun worship. It acknowledged various stages of the sun's passage over the sky as aspects of Re who centred on Heliopolis which was, first and foremost, a place of advanced learning. Re was united with Amun, forming occasional solar aspects for the king in his role as living god; but it had never achieved the national status of, say, Ptah or Amun. The temple of Karnak, small though it was at this time, belonged to Amun the Secret, and not to the sun.

So by the time of Amenhotep III Nebmaatre, if not before, the concept of Aten, the sun at its highest point, was a common one. We find references to the Aten as the physical sun-disc throughout Egyptian history. But we do need to make a distinction. In its usual aspect, the Aten is purely the disc of the sun visible in the sky at midday and not a deity in any respect. But it is clear from the hymns written to Aten by Amenhotep IV Neferkheprure Waenre that this is not what was meant in his case. He describes Aten as his father, as the giver of all life on earth. Aten is the father of all creation, of all the races on earth, even Egypt's enemies, and the maker of all animals, plants, birds and fish. So Amenhotep IV describes *not* the sun-disc but, rather, the power of god behind it. What he is describing is not the sun itself but the might of god, using the sun as a metaphor. He is saying you can no more look upon the face of god than you can look upon the face of the sun in Egypt at midday. Just as the sun's power is omnipotent and omnipresent, manifest to all, so also is god who gives life to everything on earth, and just as you feel the physical thrust of the sun through its rays at midday, so the power of god the lifegiver can be felt all around. The King did not, therefore, worship the sun; he worshipped god, but unlike any god in Egypt that had gone before, this was a god without a 'graven image', who was shared by all men. Was it in this virtually Judaic ideology that the heresy lay? Who inspired the ideas in him? Did they, as some say, come from outside Egypt?

Amenhotep IV, after expressing these ideas, changed his name. He abandoned the name Amenhotep, given to him at birth after his great-grandfather Amenhotep II and his father Amenhotep III, taking instead the name Akhenaten – the living spirit of the Aten. At the same time he changed the name of his wife from Nefertiti ('the beautiful woman has come'), to Nefernefruaten Mery Waenre ('How beautiful are the beauties of the Aten, the beloved of Waenre'). He would invariably, from this time onwards, refer to himself in inscriptions not as the ruler of Egypt, with his name in cartouches, but usually simply as Waenre, the second part of his coronation title, written without adornment or epithet of any kind. Instead it was the name of Aten that he inscribed in cartouches. In other words, Akhenaten virtually resigned the kingship in his own eyes, handing it over instead to god.

How revolutionary, then, were his ideas? As we can construct it from the evidence, he was not originating the theology at all, but just rewriting an old idea. Secondly, he copied designs from those times into his own, adapting them on a grander scale. His religion, far from being inherently heretical, was in fact strictly orthodox. The evidence of other gods from Tell el Amarna shows clearly that he did not force his religion on those around him in his new city, although equally clearly many did follow him, and revered both him and his family with a reverence that seems to have made *them* the local gods. He appears to have devoted himself totally to his own ideas that were no more monotheistic than any other aspect of local religion in Egypt at the time. Only in some aspects were his ideas different. First, this was a god without an image; secondly, it could be shared by everyone, and not kept as the private privilege of the initiated few; and thirdly, he declared himself the son of the Aten – almost the son of god. The revolution, then, was not so much in the religion, as in the person of Akhenaten.

It has often been stated that the followers of Akhenaten and the Aten religion were iconoclasts, moving from town to town, excising the names and images of the old gods wherever they could. From the discoveries at Tell el Amarna, it is hard to defend this view archaeologically. After all, if he did not exert the exclusivity of Aten in his own town that he founded specifically for the Aten, it is hard to see how iconoclasm of the type often suggested took place. In fact, we know that Akhenaten, after moving into his new city in year 6 of his rule, probably never left it again. Charismatic power, such as he clearly exerted over those who knew him, can inspire fundamentalist zeal. If excisions *did* take place, they were not necessarily done to his order. Recent discoveries from the same period in Saqqara show that, although some of the idiosyncracies of the Amarna style of art reached there, the appearance of other local gods and the gods associated with the afterlife were in no way affected by what was happening further south.

In fact, if you examine the evidence carefully, you will find that positive evidence of iconoclasm is lacking. In order to prove that an inscription or image was chiselled out by Akhenaten's Atenists, you need one of two things – either a declaration that this had been done and by whom (literally, a signature), or alternatively, that the name had been cut out and later overcarved by a later king. In this last respect, several instances are cited where inscriptions were later restored, often by Seti I Menmaatre, who deemed his reign the ⟨hieroglyphs⟩, or Repeater of Births – literally translated as the renaissance. In other words, after the cataclysm of the Eighteenth Dynasty, Seti I Menmaatre undertook to bring Egypt back to normality. In fact, where Seti re-dedicates there is no clear evidence that the names of the old gods had been excised. One example frequently quoted by authorities as proof of iconoclasm is the removal of the name of Amen on the tops of the columns in the open courtyard of Amenhotep III Nebmaatre in the temple of Luxor. There is no doubt at all that the names have been chiselled out; but, equally, there is no proof of when that was done. To read these inscriptions, you now need binoculars; and to excise them, you would have needed to have put up scaffolding. What was the point, if the inscriptions could not be read easily from the ground? Especially when the names, pictures and epithets of Amen lower down, at eye level, were left intact? We know that during modern times, the temple was filled with sand – almost to the tops of the columns in the open courtyard. The traveller Lady Lucie Duff-Gordon relates in her diaries that she owned a house built on top of the walls of the temple. After a journey south to escape the cold of winter in Luxor, she returned to find part of her house had collapsed into the space between the columns below. In other words, there is no reason whatever why the names should not have been erased at any time later in history, perhaps even as late as 200 or 300 years ago, when local Moslems may have objected to the pictorial images of the old gods in the hieroglyphic inscriptions of the names Amenhotep (Amen) and Nebmaatre (Maat and Re). Stones bearing both the names and titles of Akhenaten and his god have been found in Luxor and Karnak; there is evidence of both a temple and palace built by him in Memphis and there was substantial building within Karnak itself. As I have already shown, several notable pieces, including a sceptre from Tutankhamen's tomb, bear the names of Aten and Amen side by side. As a result, I can find no conclusive archaeological evidence whatever that proves irrefutably that the Atenists were iconoclasts by order.

To summarise so far: we have here a king who decided of his own volition to move away to find a place of his own. He did not force his ideas on anyone but allowed some of the old ways to continue under his very nose. His religion was derived from a much older version of the same thing, in part taught to him at the flourishing temple of Re in Heliopolis. Indeed, from the very name of the Aten, it was only an aspect of Re. Far from being iconoclasts, there is no evidence anywhere else of the religion being forcibly spread. In addition to this, we have already discovered that for twelve of the seventeen years Akhenaten ruled Egypt, he ruled alongside his father. So his influence, in any case, would have been limited, certainly so long as his father was alive. And so long as his father was alive, then the temples of Karnak and Luxor would continue to be served and endowed by the old King. Any 'heresy' in Karnak should have been after year 12.

If all this is true, where did the ideas of heresy begin? In the first instance, it had to be laid at the door of Horemheb who, in his edict and through his usurping of the Restoration Stela of Tutankhamen, making the boy-King's words into his own, claimed that the temples had been abandoned and the gods had, as a result, turned their backs on Egypt. However, from the rest of his words, he was primarily describing civil disorder. We know from his destruction of their places and names that Horemheb hated the Amarna royal family. We can be certain that he instilled, or at least shared, this hatred with the succeeding dynasty of kings. What we do not know is what triggered the hatred.

Horemheb was a military man first and foremost. It is clear that he was ultraconservative and deeply feared the effect the abandonment of the old ways would have on Maat, the order of the state. In fact, his tomb, when it was discovered, was found to contain a bewildering array of figures of gods and goddesses, as if he were trying desperately to propitiate the gods – *any* gods, no matter their relevance – to counter the negligence of Akhenaten. It seems he did not display any specific reverence to any one god, but rather, in a panic, appealed to them all to restore favour to Egypt.

Before he became King, he was apparently prepared to die and be buried in Memphis. His Memphite tomb, rediscovered by the expedition led by the Leiden Museum and the Egypt Exploration Society in 1975 following the removal of blocks in 1843 by Karl Lepsius, was long known to depict Horemheb as the General of the army, undertaking attacks on his Hittite enemies. In the reliefs he shows great personal venom. These scenes are unprecedented in the tomb of an official. While a king is frequently shown smiting foreigners – and many of those scenes are symbolic of his power rather than representational of an actual battle – the officials were not. But here, in one scene, he is shown dealing a foreigner a right upper-cut.

In summary, Horemheb appears to have been a fiercely patriotic warrior irritated equally by non-Egyptians and by lack of internal civil control. The evidence from his tomb shows that he feared the divine but had no clear picture of what that represented. He was evidently not by nature a theological man. The word 'heresy' is never mentioned anywhere.

But we can go further than this. A statue of Horemheb in the Metropolitan Museum of Art in New York bears a carved inscription on its base. On the right side, hieroglyphs read: 'May your *ba* come forth each day to see Aten.' A stela of his in the British Museum (no. 551) states:

> The hereditary Prince Horemheb says, 'Hail to you, the one who is splendid and skilled, Atum-Horakhte. You are risen on the Horizon of the sky, praise for you is in the mouth of everyone, because you are beautiful and young like Aten in the arms of your mother Hathor.'

Both inscriptions were carved during the reign of Tutankhamen. Both show that, certainly during the reign of Tutankhamen, the cult of the Aten was not banished as many have claimed. They also suggest that even though Horemheb later utterly demolished all material proof that Akhenaten ever existed, and even though he placed reliance on every traditional god of Egypt, he did not outlaw the Aten totally. The evidence proves beyond a shadow of doubt that the objections Horemheb and the kings of the Ramesside period had were *not* directed at the Aten, but towards Akhenaten himself. Their inscriptions allude to him as a criminal, an enemy or as a rebel. They do not refer to him as the father of an unacceptable cult, nor as a pervert. They were not banishing the Aten, but Akhenaten.

The second, and probably the most influential, source attesting to the existence of heresy lies squarely at the door of early Egyptologists.

My references to the objectiveness of archaeologists, above, are exceptionally pertinent here. The nineteenth century was the time of the gentleman-archaeologist. Few people could afford the time for the leisurely pursuit of the past. Even fewer could afford the journey to Egypt and the huge financial investment that a dig might entail. The attack of Darwinism on the Church shook the world of academe and the Establishment to the core. Many of the older families expected their sons to enter the Church, so they were sent to Egypt, a stop on the Grand Tour, to try to prove that the Bible was true. They went in search of Joseph and his multicoloured coat; of Moses and events in the Exodus. When Edouard Naville, in 1883, found evidence in an inscription on a broken statue for the cities of Pithom and Ramesses mentioned in the book of Exodus, it was seen as striking a blow for the Church – the historicity of the Pentateuch could clearly be relied upon. Creation was vindicated.

The Church traditionally saw Egyptians as the worst sort of polytheistic pagans. Were they not the nation that had enslaved the Hebrews? And did they not worship animals? In the evidence from Tell el Amarna they saw Judaistic and Christian links – the imageless god who created the entire world and its creatures, who was the very epitome of peace, brotherhood and equality. Some described Akhenaten as a Christ-like figure, even as a forerunner to Christ himself. The rejection of Akhenaten, thus, *had* to be interpreted as religious – the temporary and satanic victory of pagans over the true religion that had come to man too soon. The removal of Akhenaten's name and buildings was equated with the pogroms that true religions had always suffered. Had not those other pagans, the Romans, done exactly the same thing to the Christians a millennium and a half later? The more links that were found between Atenism, Judaism and Christianity, the more 'obvious' it became that it was revulsion of the religion that lay at the core of it all.

The definition, then, of the Atenist heresy has derived not from those who destroyed it in the Eighteenth Dynasty, but rather from those who found it and tried to interpret it in their subjective understanding of what was important.

Final evidence that the nature of the religion of Akhenaten was not the root cause of the destruction of all things to do with him must be taken from the wisdom text of Amenemope. This text, which survives on a complete papyrus in the British Museum, dates from the Rames-side period, the time during which, according to most sources, Atenism was rejected as a heresy and reviled. In Chapter 7, a piece encouraging man not to seek after material wealth, the writer adds, 'Pray to the Aten when he rises, saying, "Give me well-being and health." He will give you your needs for this life and you will be safe from fear.' You do not pray to the sun in the hope of a reply giving you promises of well-being. Moreover, were it to be addressed to the sun, the word used would be Re. Clearly the reference here is to the Aten as Akhenaten envisaged it, as a spiritual entity. In other words, it was not Aten which was rejected – but Akhenaten. The hatred that followed him was not, therefore, religious, but personal. Knowing that Tutankhamen tried to restore the balance of Egypt after his coronation, it becomes vital to establish exactly what the objection to Akhenaten was.

Let us now add the final academic brick to this wall. Scholarship is united in that the change in the nature of Aten from sun-disc to spiritual figure took place in the early reign of Tuthmosis IV. Until that time, references were made to the Aten as just one aspect of the sun in its course. At the start of the reign of Tuthmosis IV Menkhe-prure we find a reference to him going into battle 'with the Aten before him'. After this, references to Aten as a 'deity' proliferate.

One of the few things we know about Tuthmosis IV Menkheprure is that, just before he became King, he had a strange experience at Giza. Between the paws of the Sphinx stands a granite stela, the bottom half, unfortunately, so badly damaged that nothing of the original inscrip-tion remains. The top half tells how, one day, Prince Tuthmosis was hunting by the pyramid when, 'at the time of noon', he sat down in the shade of the Sphinx and fell asleep. In his dream, Re-Horemakhet, the divinity whom the Sphinx represents, appeared to him and 'was speaking to him out of his own mouth, as a father speaks to his son'. The Sphinx complained of the sand that had accumulated around him, and begged Tuthmosis to clear it away. The Prince 'understood the words of the god but kept them secret in his heart'. (For the full text, see Appendix D.) It is clear that Tuthmosis undertook the task of clearing away the sand since the stela, today called the Dream Stela, stands on the bedrock in front of the Sphinx.

The usual interpretation of the text is that the Sphinx promised Tuthmosis the throne if he would carry out the clearance of the sand.

Recently, other Egyptologists, encouraged by media interest in the restoration of the Sphinx, have added to this story, saying that the Prince was not the legitimate heir of his father, Amenhotep II. One scholar has embroidered this even further, suggesting that Tuthmosis, in order to inherit the throne, had killed the rightful heir and 'invented' the dream to legitimise his position in the eyes of the people. In fact, all of this is clearly problematical. For a start, Tuthmosis bore the name of his grandfather, the great Tuthmosis III. As I have pointed out, it was always the custom of Egyptian kings to name their first son after their father – thus names would skip a generation. Tuthmosis, by definition and proof of his very name, was the eldest son of the previous King. Even if this were not enough, we have the evidence of his own words at the start of the inscription on the stela: 'The beautiful son of Khepri, beautiful of features, like his father, who came into the world perfect, equipped with the shape as Horus, because he was the first-born'. Tuthmosis cannot have been clearer – he was Horus, the first-born.

Archaeologically, the only thing that might suggest that he had siblings was the discovery in 1901, in the tomb of Amenhotep II in the Valley of the Kings, of a broken *shabti* on the floor of the tomb, amid much debris, bearing the name and title of Prince (literally, King's Son) Webensennu. Nearby, on a wooden ship, lay the unwrapped body of a young man. With no more evidence than this, the body was declared probably to be that of Webensennu who was another, previously unknown, son of Amenhotep II and thus a brother or half-brother of Tuthmosis. In fact, the identity of the young man has not been discovered. Even had Webensennu been a brother of Tuthmosis (and there were the reburials of several other kings within the tomb, any one of which may have been associated with the *shabti*), the idea that Tuthmosis was a younger son, without the right to inherit, or that Tuthmosis had led a murder plot to remove him, is the work of novelists, not historians. The evidence of the name of Prince Tuthmosis and his insistence that he was the first-born should be sufficient.

The Dream Stela text never uses the word 'if' – as in, *if* you clear the sand *then* I shall give you the throne. It simply states that Re-Horemakhet appeared to Tuthmosis and spoke to him, requesting that he cleared the sand. There is simply no 'cause and effect' in the text whatsoever. There is nothing at all within the text that makes Tuthmosis' claim to the throne conditional on his clearing the sand. The notion that it *was* conditional has been mooted by Egyptologists seeking to find a reason for the existence of the stela in the first place. The argument is simply that Tuthmosis cleared the sand, inherited the crown, and thus placed the stela to prove to posterity that he had carried out his promise and that Re-Horemakhet thus protected his kingship.

So if Tuthmosis *was* the rightful heir to the throne and did not need the Sphinx to promise it to him; and if he then cleared the sand around the Sphinx – the question must be asked, why was the stela placed there? If he had wished simply to explain to posterity that he had cleared it, there was no need to bring the god into it. It would have been a mammoth undertaking, and worthy of recognition in a stela text. We need to rely simply on the words and the facts, and not on some ideological interpretation. The fact is simple and clear. Tuthmosis had the stela carved because the god appeared to him in a dream. The proof that this actually happened, he cited, was that the god made a request which he then later fulfilled. The amazement of the Prince in relation to the dream is apparent, since according to the text itself, the Prince kept the message secret in his heart, probably because he thought no one would believe him. Tuthmosis had had a divine revelation: the god had appeared to him and spoken to him. This made him a person of huge consequence. When, later, an identical thing happened to Moses when he heard the voice of God in a burning bush, it made of Moses a prophet, a messenger of God. Why should it be different for Tuthmosis IV Menkheprure?

Perhaps we may see in this some reason for other things we have already come across. For example, in the text in the temple at Luxor that talks of the divine conception of Amenhotep III Nebmaatre by his mother, Queen Mutemweia, it says that the body of his father, Tuthmosis IV Menkheprure, was filled with the spirit of Amen-Re – not Amen, the dark god of Karnak, but Amen-Re, the syncretic god linked with the sun. Is it just possible that the story of the dream is not metaphorical, but a true one? That Tuthmosis IV Menkheprure really did feel, after his encounter with the divine on the plateau of Giza, that he been transformed by the experience – that he was, as the Sphinx had told him, with the mouth of a father to a son, the very son of Re-Horemakhet?

It is often said that such an experience was a common one, and that kings of Egypt regularly related the story of their divine conception. In reality, there are only two such instances – this one, and the story of the conception of Hatshepsut as told on the second terrace of her temple at Deir el Bahri. In the case of Hatshepsut, her insistence on her divinity is easily understood. She was the stepmother and sworn regent of the infant Tuthmosis III as well as being a woman. She openly usurped the throne from him, on the strength of a revelation she had had in Karnak, when, so she said, Amen told her she was literally 'his son'. She needed to relate the tale in order to legitimise her claim. But what need did Amenhotep III Nebmaatre have to legitimise his claim? He was the lauded son of his father and mother and rightful heir to the throne. He had no need to claim that his father had been subsumed, on the night of the conception, by the spirit of god.

All the archaeological evidence, now accepted by Egyptologists, is that the reign of Amenhotep III Nebmaatre is almost as full of references to Atenism as is that of his son Akhenaten. Even the palace of Malkata, built before Akhenaten was born, carried the title, 'the splendour of the Aten', while the ship on which Tiye sailed on her lake in year 11 was entitled, 'the Aten shines'. South of the great temple of Karnak is the delightful smaller temple of Amun's consort, Mut. She is always pictured either as a woman, arms protectively around her plume-crowned husband Amun, or occasionally as a vulture – $\text{\Large$\cap$} \, \text{\small$\cap$} \text{$\m$}$ which has the sound 'Mut'. Yet around the temple area were placed an estimated 600 statues of the goddess Sekhmet by Amenhotep III Nebmaatre. Sekhmet was the consort of the sun-god Re; and to confirm this, the sun-disc surmounts the heads of each of the statues. Why should such an overwhelming set of images of the wrong goddess have been placed in the temple of Mut? One suggestion has to be that Amenhotep III Nebmaatre was encircling it, re-dedicating it, to the worship of Re by the addition of the consort-figure.

It would seem, therefore, that this new religion was a deviation from the norm within the very heart of the royal family. So Tuthmosis IV Menkheprure saw and heard a god, and was told by him that he was his son. This information was passed down to the next generation, when his son Amenhotep III Nebmaatre also believed himself to be the son of god through the possessed body of his father. Young Prince

Amenhotep, the son of Amenhotep III and Queen Tiye, must have known all of this from infancy. No doubt they discussed the matter. But there is no doubt that Amenhotep was a dreamer, an idealist. Unlike the previous generations, he took the matter seriously. It seems that even his parents realised he was in need of preparation for kingship and, soon after the death of his older brother, presented him as co-regent within Karnak. But was he actually a heretic?

The answer is, overwhelmingly, no. It is we who have made him into a heretic. He was the follower of an aspect of religion inculcated in him from childhood because of the experience of his grandfather, Tuthmosis IV Menkheprure. The religion he followed was no heresy, just the logical progression of thought from the appearance of the god of the Sphinx to his grandfather at Giza – the name he gave to the Aten, after all, was, 'Re-Horakhte who celebrates on the horizon in his name of Shu [sunlight] which is the Aten'. By definition, the Aten was no more than a manifestation of Re-Horakhte – who was the deity associated with the Sphinx. In other words, we have clear archaeological evidence of a private divine belief within the royal family that for two generations, as Tuthmosis wrote on the Dream Stela, 'he kept secret in his heart'. Only Amenhotep IV finally let that secret out. And by doing so, by rejecting the material world and showing his loyalty to the very real divinity who had appeared to his grandfather, by separating himself from the political world of plot and counter-plot, by removing himself to Tell el Amarna and living out his life there, he cultivated many bitter enemies.

Akhenaten was no heretic – just a confused and obsessed man who, like some New Age traveller, wanted to live life in peace and solitude. But his attitude must have aroused great hatred. The hatred that Horemheb and the Ramessides expressed against Akhenaten was caused not so much by religious offence against the heresies that he stood for, but rather against his ineptitude, his simple unsuitability for the kingship. When they tried to erase his memory, it was not because of his heresy, but to try to re-establish Maat. After all, Akhenaten had ignored all the tried, tested, established methods for supporting the cosmos. He had not undertaken the rites that kingship demanded of him. By so doing, he had endangered the very material of the world in which Egyptians lived. It was little wonder that they hated him; and little wonder, also, that Tutankhamen's reign was fraught with terror.

As I questioned at the start of this chapter, would Tutankhamen go along with the ideas of Akhenaten? Would he, too, be a weakling on the throne, splendid in his isolation? Or would he have the strength to pull Egypt out of the morass of chaos into which it was sinking? Many powerful officials waited to see what would happen next.

CHAPTER SEVEN

Evidence from
Tell el Amarna

Meticulous examination of archaeological evidence, as we have seen, may often reveal quite a different story from the one that might be expected. In other fields of archaeology, scholars may have relatively little material to work on. This leaves them free to interpret the evidence as they may. Archaeology becomes discursive. But in Egypt it is a different story. We have so much evidence that at times it becomes almost overwhelming. Simply assimilating all the evidence, omitting nothing and then relating it all together to make sense of it is a daunting task. The problems we face today in the field remain twofold: first, the subjective judgments of scholars in the past who, faced with far less material evidence than we have today and without the means of understanding it, came to questionable conclusions that are still often blindly followed; and secondly, those people outside the field who come in to review the evidence, but with little knowledge to back up their enthusiasm. As a result of these problems, much work is repetitive, with nothing new to offer; while the material that is new is often totally inaccurate. Scholarly work, on the whole, finds a limited reading market, while wild theories, usually based on nothing but intuition, reach a wide readership. It is, after all, more 'exciting' to read suggestions, for example, that hidden secrets await discovery under the Sphinx, than it is to read a masterly account of tombs that have already been discovered, even though analysis of which are revealing new discoveries. These discoveries may be such things as re-dating the reign of a king by one or two years. These finds, which are archaeologically more important than the first sort, unfortunately excite few but the professional scholars.

Few topics in ancient Egypt have roused as much passion and generated as many theories as the story of Akhenaten and his successor Tutankhamen. Millions of words have been written about them over the years; but the majority of this work is either out of date or is grossly inaccurate and based purely on speculation. Works extolling the foreign origins of Nefertiti, linking Akhenaten with Moses and exploiting the curse of Tutankhamen are more prolific than serious archaeologically based works.

As 'time-detectives', Egyptologists are duty-bound to examine and constantly review every last detail of evidence as it appears – to extract, so far as we are able, the heart of the matter. I have often said that in this respect the field is like life itself – if you tell a lie, the odds are you will be caught out. So it often is with our subject: where evidence exists that does not fit the arguments being proposed, the common method of dealing with it is to omit it altogether. I started in the field when I was only seven years old, by picking up a book by Leonard Cottrell. By the time I was nine I had taught myself hieroglyphs; and I have been steeped in the field ever since. To this end I am able to refer to the actual evidence that the Egyptians left behind at first hand, without the need for translations, which are often inaccurate, coloured by the subjectivism of the translator.

Understanding hieroglyphic inscriptions is at the very core of Egyptology. Some colleagues excavate in the field; some work in museums; others work freelance, lecturing and writing books. But all need to be fluent in the language of the ancient Egyptians. Yet beyond all translations, beyond the study of all objects and all pictures, opinions start to creep in. Many people entering the field for the first time as students find these varying opinions extremely confusing. As I've said, I am frequently faced by people perplexed by the morass through which they are expected to wade, who ask, 'But what can I actually believe, when all the books tell completely different stories?' My answer to them is always to rely on your own judgment and on no one else's. Look at the evidence for yourself. Examine, even in translation, the words of the Egyptians themselves, study their pictures closely, and try not to rely on someone else's conclusions. And if, like a detective, you follow the clues meticulously, the answer at the end should become clear of its own accord. If any of the clues do not fit, suddenly there will be an insurmountable problem, and the chain of evidence must be unravelled once more for the flaws in the argument to be identified. Liars will always be caught out: some fragment of the evidence will not fit.

So far, then, using the evidence of written texts from my own translation (thus avoiding other people's opinions, but relying on the evidence of the Egyptians themselves), I have tried to review the material without the overlay of bias produced by out-of-date or fringe writers. In this way I have produced evidence that suggests that although Tutankhamen may have been the child of Amenhotep III Nebmaatre and his daughter-wife Sitamun, this would also have made the relationship between his older brother, Smenkhkare, and the King, Akhenaten, an incestuous as well as a homosexual affair. If the censure directed towards this latter couple had been so great, why was the equally incestuous relationship between Sitamun and her own father not also the cause of hatred? Why should the one relationship be accepted and the other outlawed? In view of the animosity exhibited by Horemheb and the Ramessides towards Akhenaten, these are problems that deserve attention. I have also shown that the weight of archaeological evidence suggests that Akhenaten was not the heretic and religious fanatic that some have supposed. On the contrary, the development and theology of his religion were strictly within the usual Egyptian practices. Nor was he manipulated, as some have suggested, by a 'powerful priesthood of Amen' based in Karnak. On the contrary, it is clear that even had they objected (which it was not their place to do), there was nothing they could do about it anyway. In fact Akhenaten, as co-regent with his father, simply wanted a place of his own. He tried Nubia first; but in dissatisfaction he returned to Egypt, travelled north, and found a site on which he could build his new city. Here he relaxed with his beloved wife and their children. Either here, or in his father's palace-city of Malkata in Luxor, Tutankhaten was born and raised.

We have established that a maelstrom of hatred surrounded the eccentric King, in all likelihood centred upon the powerful officials and nobles whose careers were being placed in jeopardy by his actions. Let us review their situation. Put yourself, as much as you are able, into their place. The new King is crowned and intends to move himself and his court away into total isolation. He is a weak-minded fellow, with none of the strength that a king of Egypt needs. Should you remain behind and serve the older King – a King who must, by virtue of his age, surely die before the younger one? Do you choose to stay behind with the setting sun? Or do you follow the rising star, knowing, as you do, that it may require you to be exiled physically from the heart of Egypt, from government circles? Whatever choice you make will bring you problems. One solution that must have occurred at some point may have been to remove the younger King altogether – to assassinate him. It must have tempted some nobles. But Egypt was not imperial Rome. In Rome, men were simply men; in Egypt, when a man became king he was lifted from the normal ranks of men to become of like nature with the 'gods', ancient spirits of superheroes. On them, the structure and maintenance of existence depended. It is astonishing to realise from study that in all the thousands of years that the Egyptian civilisation survived, not one king can be proved conclusively to have been murdered by anyone except their own wives. Given the wealth and power that devolved upon some individuals, it is all the more amazing that a man of genius should sit back and serve a weaker, less intelligent man simply because of what he had become. But this is the case.

So probably they were stopped by this tradition of royal divinity. At any rate, there is every indication that trouble was brewing, centred strongly in the army. Until the Eighteenth Dynasty, Egyptians were reluctant soldiers. Even the very word, in hieroglyphs, for 'army' and 'soldier' use determinatives of foreigners, suggesting that in the very earliest times, most of the army were mercenaries. Models of soldiers found dating from the Middle Kingdom depict regiments of foreigners. Egyptians today have and always have had a passionate love for their country, and an innate desire to die and be buried there, not in some far-flung forgotten country fighting for someone else's cause. Things changed dramatically, however, at the start of the New Kingdom. The desire to oust the Hyksos united Upper Egypt as it had seldom been united before. Inscriptions show how men followed bravely behind their generals and fought for honour, while behind them, at home, their women, too, rallied to assist, sending supplies, fresh soldiers and arms to their menfolk while keeping the country united in the cause. The kings that succeeded them now put together a permanent, standing army comprising professional officers, trained for the first time in the use of weapons and battle tactics. Although the bulk of the infantrymen might be conscripts, called up to serve as part of the annual corvée, the chariotry and their officers were all trained and well-equipped fighters. The headquarters of these regiments was in Memphis, Egypt's capital and permanent home of the government.

During the combined reigns of Amenhotep III Nebmaatre and his son Amenhotep IV Neferkheprure Waenre, the Hittites to Egypt's north consolidated their power and began to attack Egyptian territory. The professional army was ready and willing to attack. But neither the old King nor the new seem to have given the orders. The army sat and sulked, chafing at the bit, while the monarchy, complacent and divided, did nothing. When Tutankhamen became King, therefore, the division he encountered was not just among the officials waiting to see where his loyalties lay within Egypt; the army waited also to see whether or not he would lead them against their bitterest enemies, the Hittites. All of this was surely a lot to ask of any six-year-old boy.

Let us now return, then, to the statement on the Restoration Stela of Tutankhamen on which it says that he 'came to the throne of his father'. We can be certain, through evidence from his tomb, that Tutankhamen was indeed born to inherit the throne in his own right. If Amenhotep III Nebmaatre was not his father, then could his father have been Akhenaten himself? The possibility must be considered. More to the point – was Akhenaten physically capable of being a father at all? His appearance as shown in the art of the time has led some to believe otherwise.

This question has arisen frequently over recent years in the light of the curiously distorted and deformed images of the King. Statues, relief-carvings and paintings depict him with a distorted, grossly elongated skull; a pronounced, jutting jaw; a thin neck; heavy lips and eyes; an almost female bust and slender waist; fat hips around a swollen stomach, often with a marked lack of genitalia; and spindly calves and legs. If the representations show him as he really was, then this was a man in trouble. When you see his pictures, your response is purely subjective – either he appears fascinating and mysterious, or distinctly ugly and grotesque. Sir Alan Gardiner described images of him as

> Frankly hideous portraits, the general fidelity of which cannot be doubted. The elongated head slopes from a long thin neck; the face is narrow, showing a prominent nose, thick lips and rounded protruding chin; the body with its sunken chest, swelled-out stomach, wide thighs and slender calves is the reverse of virile. In the sculptured reliefs, Akhenaten as he later preferred to call himself is often shown lolling effeminately upon a cushioned chair, yet the standing colossi from the peristyle court at Karnak have a look of fanatical determination such as his subsequent history confirmed only too fatally.

Hardly the words of a dispassionate historian. Yet like him or loathe him, you cannot ignore him. Walking up the stairs in the Louvre Museum in Paris, and the sightless eyes of his colossal bust follow you wherever you move, the sneer on his face seeming to be for you personally.

So how much of our opinion of Akhenaten is based not on written evidence but on instinctive reaction to his portraits? Can you tell a criminal by his face? Can you declare Akhenaten morally corrupt and fanatically religious – because he looks it?

One of our problems in examining the art of the period is Akhenaten's insistence, in all of his inscriptions, that he is $\stackrel{\rightarrow}{?}$ ⊜ 𝕂 ⊒ , or 'living by truth'. If this is the case, it must be argued that no healthy man could possibly look the way he does. Surely, he must have been ill. But what disease could have had such a terrible effect? Egyptian art is well known for its 'cardboard' stereotypes, stiff and formalised images that have led many art historians to decry it as childish, almost not worthy of the title 'art' at all. The figures shown on walls all appear the same – eternally young, slender and good-looking. But the truth was, inevitably, different. Often, when we examine the mummies of the dead, they bear no resemblance to the artistic image. Queen Ahmose-Nefertari, for example, was always shown as slender and young, yet her mummy shows that she died very old, and nearly bald on the top of her head, and had buck teeth and congenital scoliosis, or a twisted spine, which had given her a pronounced hunchback. The dream is often far from the reality. So, by the same token, how far can the images of Akhenaten be trusted? It would be unique in Egyptian art to find someone represented as worse than they were in real life, especially a reigning king.

For many years, Egyptians put Akhenaten's appearance down to inbreeding within the royal family – the result of generations of incestuous brother–sister marriages. We can now be certain, however, that Tuthmosis II, Tuthmosis III, Amenhotep II, Tuthmosis IV, Amenhotep III and even Akhenaten himself were not the products of inbreeding but of marriages between a royal father and a non-royal mother. Even if the non-royal mothers, as we have suggested, came from within the same family, there is still no basis whatsoever for suggesting that Akhenaten was deformed because of a bad genetic mix. Indeed, problems of this sort are often accompanied by mental impairment, and there is emphatically no evidence of this. A stela at Aswan that was dedicated to his two sculptors, Bek and Men, insists that it was the King himself who instructed them on the way in which he wanted all his artistic work carried out. 'The overseer of works in the Red Mountain, the assistant and pupil whom His Majesty himself taught, the chief of sculptors for the many monuments of the King in the House of Aten in the Horizon of the Aten'. The hymn to the Aten, reputedly written by the King himself, would show him to be a person of deep perception and understanding, with great sensitivity and a gift for words, and with a desire for universal peace and understanding.

Some medical specialists who have studied images of the King have suggested that he may have suffered from a tumour of the pituitary gland. This tiny gland, situated at the base of the brain, releases hormones that control growth and sexual development. The growth of a tumour here results in Fröhlich's syndrome, sometimes called acromegaly. One medical dictionary defines the condition as follows.

This is a long-term progressive disease due to the over-secretion of a growth hormone, usually from a benign tumour. The [effect of the] disease, which affects adults, who cannot grow taller as their limb-bones have fused the growing ends to the main shaft, is to distort the other bones, the hands and feet enlarging and thickening. The skin becomes coarser and fleshier so that the face gets a bloodhound look. The bones of the face broaden, the lower jaw emerges and the brow becomes over-prominent. The nose widens and the tongue enlarges. Acromegalics are prone to

> arthritis, blood pressure and often diabetes . . . Pressure on the pituitary
> gland also causes interference with sexual functions. If the tumour spreads
> upwards it can press on the optic nerve and eyesight may be damaged.

The problem is the opposite of dwarfism, whereby the secretion of hormones is restricted. Since dwarfism was a well-known condition at all times in ancient Egypt, a pituitary disorder with the colourful and seemingly accurate description of Akhenaten's appearance seems likely. However, acromegalics are rendered totally sterile. Egyptologists have suggested that this was the reason why, in many statues where the King is depicted totally naked, he is shown without genitals. The argument is frequently repeated in serious books on Akhenaten to this day. But if Akhenaten did indeed suffer such a terrible condition, not only does it make his marriage with the exceptionally beautiful Nefertiti and her apparent total devotion to him hard to understand, but it means that he could not have fathered any of the six daughters that Nefertiti had, much less Tutankhamen.

Let us imagine this scenario. It is a startling one. Here we have a weak and obsessed man, thrown onto the throne of Egypt by his parents in order to train him for office as much as might be possible, married to one of the most beautiful women of all time, yet permitting her to be unfaithful to him not once but many times. He accepts her continual pregnancies by another man, then claims each daughter born to him as 〔hieroglyphs〕 – 'His beloved, of his own body'. After accepting his own sterility and her frequent unfaithfulness, after twelve years he forcibly ejects her from the palace to replace her with a male lover. And Smenkhkare, as the brother of Tutankhamen, was – if not his son, as he was sterile – a child perhaps of Nefertiti's by another man.

So Akhenaten was a deformed, sterile, obsessive, compliant with the immorality of his Great Royal Wife and, at the same time, filled with homosexual urges for his own son. Or was he? Just how far can we take this story?

If we shy away from such a characterisation, deeming it too extreme and in any case not proven by the evidence, we are back to square one: the art itself. As we've seen in the case of Queen Ahmose-Nefertari, art can be deceptive. No one would ever expect to meet a woman who looks as Picasso depicted them! Nor could you tell the time from Dali's 'melting' clocks. Art, after all, conveys emotions, ideas, or metaphors, and different artists have handled this in different ways. So why should we place such reliance on art to give us a faithful 'snapshot' of its subject, rather than a portrait filtered through the artist's eye?

Is it not possible that in the portraits of Akhenaten we are seeing a style of representing the King that is as extreme as Picasso's during his Cubist period? This idea is borne out by radical changes in the way he was depicted. The images of Akhenaten as 'deformed' seem to proliferate the moment he moves to Tell el Amarna. The carvings at Sesebi, which echo the style, suggest that it was being formed, along with his theology, from the very start of his reign. This suggests that from the start, Amenhotep IV Neferkheprure Waenre felt dissatisfied with virtually every aspect of traditional life in Egypt. He changed his and his wife's birth-names; moved away from both Luxor and Memphis and built a new city to his own design; introduced a new aspect of religion; and brought the written language up to date, matching the writing with the spoken idiom. Is it surprising, then, that he should also have dismissed the traditional art form?

The art form of Amarna evolved over time. At first it can be seen to develop from hints of distortion of Sesebi into the virtual caricatures of Akhenaten's early years at Tell el Amarna. Then, during and after his festival of year 12, the images soften, become less dramatic. By the end of his reign, the images of Akhenaten have become stereotyped. A *shabti* bearing his name, found in the tomb of the royal *wadi*, is so formalised that it could represent any royal character of the mid-Eighteenth Dynasty – it has no distortions whatsoever.

It should be obvious by now that what we see in Akhenaten's portraits is a new art form that he himself appears to have introduced. Examination of the carved pictures of the period show that every one of the people in Tell el Amarna share the same odd shape. And Gay Robins has proved that the Amarna images follow a new, mannered style. Traditional artists in ancient Egypt relied on a standard grid of squares, each one based on the size of the clenched fist of the person depicted. This grid, which we call the canon of proportion, lays down for the draughtsman exactly what part of the body must be drawn where. The standard grid was eighteen squares, measured from the base of the foot to the hairline. Other aspects of the figure – for instance, chest and waist size – were defined exactly within the grid. This, naturally, makes all the figures look the same, although there were occasional differences, especially in the facial features, that break up what might otherwise be a monotonous regularity. Robins has shown conclusively that in the Amarna period, a grid of twenty squares was used. The artists apparently used much the same shapes as before, but adapted them to the new, longer grid. The effect was to stretch the figures considerably, but only in some parts of the anatomy.

There may, however, also be other things that changed the outline of figures. In this period men abandoned their usual kilts, which were either plain and smooth or vertically pleated, in favour of a horizontally pleated one. These garments were made of linen, and experiments have shown that the material takes easily to pleating without the use of starches or other fixatives. When a horizontally pleated garment is wrapped around the waist and tied at the front, several things happen. First, the waistband at the back rises up higher, while the hemline drops as the horizontal pleats sag. The knot made at the front cannot adequately cover a man's genital area; so the material drops below the navel, and must be made more decorous by the use of a tapestry-sash, carefully tied around the top of the kilt. In order to stop the kilt from falling down, it must be secured tightly around the waist, and this tightness, and the fall of the horizontal pleating, make the kilt flare out around the hips and cause the stomach to protrude over the tight waistband. So some of the wideness in the hips and thighs, and the swollen abdomens of Akhenaten and other figures of the period, must be due to the kilts that they are wearing.

It is also interesting that in the early years at Amarna, the skull-shapes of the royal family were shown as markedly distorted. As we've seen, similar distortions can be found in the actual skull measurements of Tutankhamen. We know that Tutankhamen was of royal descent, so no matter who his father was, it seems highly likely that the peculiar shape of his skull was inherited. So the skull-shape in the Amarna art, although grossly exaggerated, presumably by the use of the taller grid, is to some extent an observed feature of the subjects.

The distortion of human subjects in Amarna art throws up another problem: it is often difficult to recognise exactly who is who in the pictures. In many carvings, Nefertiti Nefernefruaten is shown as distorted as her husband. Indeed, if the only images we had of Nefertiti were the relief carvings, and not the famous painted bust in Berlin, we might not deem the Queen such a rare beauty. Most of the scenes from

Tell el Amarna are undated. As a result, we who study the period have become 'daughter-counters'. We know that Nefertiti and Akhenaten's first daughter, Meritaten, must have been born at the very start of his reign, because on the boundary stelae at Tell el Amarna that date from his year 4, she is constantly shown in company with her parents. The so-called Stela K on the east bank of the site, also dated year 4, shows an addition – the tiny figure of the second daughter, Meketaten. Thus she must have been born during year 4. Stela A on the west bank, dated year 6, has the tiny figure of a third daughter, little Ankhesenpaaten – as you'll remember, she was later wife of Tutankhamen. By the time of the festival of year 12, six daughters are being shown, so three more must have been born between years 6 and 12. Thus in order to put the art from Tell el Amarna into sequence, the most common method, when dates are lacking, is to count the daughters present, and thus get us a good enough idea of the right date for the piece.

Using this method we can tell that the greatest exaggeration in the new style of art took place in the first years that Akhenaten and his family lived at Tell el Amarna. Then, comparing the images of the King and Queen on the boundary stelae with the images of the festival of his accession to sole rule around year 12 in the tomb of Meryre II, a courtier in Tell el Amarna, it can be seen that the figures become less exaggerated, softer and more traditionally Egyptian in the intervening years. Some of the exaggerated features, such as the extended skull and swollen stomach, are still present. Perhaps by year 12 the artists had become more familiar with the use of the new grid and had learned to adapt the human figure to a more acceptable shape. It is clear that the exaggerations were deliberate, however. In the Cairo Museum and other institutions, fragments of stone or broken pottery from the period that bear sketches, called ostraca, show how, using trial and error, the artists tried to get the strange head shapes exactly right.

But we still need to know why these odd proportions were adopted. They are far from flattering either to the King or the Queen. Instinctively, one tends to think that they would have objected to being so grossly caricatured; but since such efforts were being made by the artists to get the 'distortions' exactly right, we have to presume that they were desirable. We now know that in Tell el Amarna it was the Aten whose name was enclosed within cartouches, thus making him the ruler of the city, while the names of Akhenaten were written as if he were an ordinary person; so it is possible that the art was an attempt to demean the King in comparison with the god. Against this it must be argued that the inscriptions say clearly that it was only the King who was the messenger, even as the son of the god, so the distortions should have been limited to him and his family. But they were not: they included all the citizens of Tell el Amarna.

It is also difficult to tell who is who in Amarna art because of damage, a lack of inscriptions and carving techniques. The scenes in Tell el Amarna, whether in the tombs or in the city's buildings, are tiny and lightly carved, with the human figures, as usual in Egyptian art, apparently indistinguishable from each other. Very often the figures are unnamed, with the exception of the royal family. In cases where a noble is shown being rewarded, the names of the recipient and his family may be left out. Even worse, in instances where there are few inscriptions or where the inscriptions have been damaged, there is a very real problem in trying to figure out which figure is male and which is female. Without names it is frequently impossible to tell which Princess is which; in some cases, it is virtually impossible to tell which is the King and which is the Queen.

Over the years scholars have worked hard, studying the Amarna images closely to find clues to point us in the right direction. For example, Nefertiti is frequently shown wearing the tall, flat-topped crown that she seems to have adapted from its use either by Neith or by Userkaf (see page 198). If she wore the crown in order to symbolise Neith, she is taking the form of a goddess, protectress of Lower Egypt. Inscriptions in the tombs of the nobles from Luxor for the mid-Eighteenth Dynasty regularly give 'divided' titles – where, for example, Anen, brother of Tiye and Ay, is called 'the mouth of the King of Upper Egypt and the ears of the King of Lower Egypt'. The significance of these inscriptions may have been missed. Study has shown that these split titles only occur during the late reign of Amenhotep III and Akhenaten. Usually they have been read as mere repetitions referring to the same King. Given the long co-regency between the two Kings, it is more likely that Anen and many others were recording the actual facts: that they served offices between the two courts. In Anen's case, this would mean that he attended and listened in the court of Akhenaten, and then reported back all that was happening to Amenhotep III in Luxor. These inscriptions suggest that for the period of the co-regency, the monarchy of Egypt was split fully between two courts, each King having full responsibility for one area of Egypt. So if Nefertiti was showing herself as protectress of Lower Egypt, this was only logical, as it was the section of the country that her husband ruled. If, alternatively, Nefertiti wore the flat-topped crown to copy that of Userkaf, she was showing herself as the representative of the solar religion. Both roles are feasible and understandable. It is in fact likely that she wears the crown as a combination of both elements.

There are other, smaller, points that assist us in recognising the pictures from Tell el Amarna. The King and the Queen are always shown wearing sandals, a type of shoe then worn by few others. The King's robe generally finishes at mid-calf or ankle-height, whereas the Queen's sweeps the floor. Going by this, we can tell who we're looking at when all we have are pictures of feet on the recovered stones from the buildings of Tell el Amarna. It has been discovered that different wigs or hairstyles are adopted regularly by different characters. Similarly, in the inscriptions, certain epithets or descriptive phrases are used that indicate who the person is, even where the actual name is missing. For example, Nefertiti Nefernefruaten is always described as ⟨ hieroglyphs ⟩ – 'the beloved of Waenre'. It appears so regularly it is like part of her name.

These visual and written identifiers, which appear even in the unusual art forms at Amarna, led Cyril Aldred to make a most remarkable discovery. He found that by studying carved reliefs of the King and Queen, the back of the Queen's neck is invariably concave, while the back of the King's neck is very distinctly convex. He applied this finding when he examined the colossal statues in the Broad Hall at Amarna that scholars had identified as Akhenaten. It should be understood that the statues bear no names except the cartouches of the Aten. It had long been observed that the statues were of two distinct types. One shows the person kilted, the other apparently naked and without genitals. It was this last series that led some scholars to doubt the sexual capabilities of the King. Aldred was now able to prove without question that although the first series showed Akhenaten, the second series in fact showed Nefertiti. In hindsight, given the close, loving relationship of the King and Queen, it should have come as no surprise that both should have been represented. So where figures of the second type were apparently naked, it was presumably because the Queen was wearing the typical tight-fitting sheath dress favoured by women at the time while the 'lack of genitals' simply means a lack of the male variety. All this means we can dismiss any speculation about the King being sexually deficient.

In the light of all these findings, how does Tell el Amarna itself now appear to us? Surprisingly, as mentioned in the last chapter, careful study shows there is little evidence to support the spread of religion from Tell el Amarna. Likewise, there is little evidence that the Amarna style of art was adopted outside that city except where royal building work was undertaken. Excavations at Saqqara at mid-Eighteenth Dynasty level do not show that the same distortions were adopted there as they had been further south in Tell el Amarna. We have references to buildings of Akhenaten's in Heliopolis and Memphis from the Amarna tombs of the nobles, but neither of these sites can be dug down to Amarna levels.

Today, virtually nothing remains of the buildings in Tell el Amarna except faint lines and very low walls marking their outlines. The city was laid out, as were most in Egypt, along one main street running parallel with the Nile. Today, villagers in the area call it Sikket es Sultan, or King's Road. The road was not paved, but rather made of gravel-like stones trodden to form a hard surface. It is narrow – just wide enough for the wheels of one chariot.

Buildings were then drawn out to front on to this main street. The town-plan appears to have been deliberately and carefully conceived (see page 194). Since the area had never been settled, the King could design the town to include the most up-to-date features. Priority was given first to the placement of the royal buildings. Then the most important nobles had their choice; then the lesser nobles and so on. The poorest people had to squash in their houses wherever there was the space, sometimes using the outer walls of a larger house as one of their own. To the north of the main city there was a broad sewage ditch, designed to carry away the effluent from the great city houses. Along the banks of this, the very poorest slum houses were clustered.

The centre of the plain was occupied with the Great Temple, the 𓉐𓉐𓏏𓇳 . The back of the temple was oriented exactly towards the royal *wadi* at the back of the cliffs that bordered the plain. At dawn, as the sun rose on the eastern horizon, it would appear over the *wadi*, bordered on each side by the cliffs, thus 'drawing' the hieroglyph for ◎ on the landscape. Since Akhenaten called his city ◎ or 'The Horizon of the Aten' one cannot help but think that it was this very feature that drew him to the deserted place in the first instance.

Directly to the south of the temple were the storehouses and magazines, the so-called temple dependencies. South of this was the royal palace itself. The palace was divided into two principal sections by the main road. To the east of the road were the private quarters, with columned halls, floors and walls painted with Nilotic scenes, leading to smaller chambers and ultimately to a series of six tiny rooms adjacent to each other. These rooms had alcoves within, each with the remains of a 'platform'. It is impossible to resist the idea that these were the bedrooms for the little princesses. Adjacent to them, one small room, with plastered and painted walls and floor, was found to have random splashes of colour, resembling paint-marks left by small brushes being wiped across the surfaces. This led to the notion that it was the girls' playroom.

Next door to the private quarters, to the south, lay another temple, smaller than the Great Temple, although still of substantial size. It appears that this was for the personal use of the King and his family, although depictions in the nobles' tombs show the royal family participating in the daily rituals in the Great Temple.

From the private quarters, a bridge led across the main road to the public part of the palace, dominated, behind a wall that screened off the road, by a huge columned courtyard filled with colossal statues of the King. As we know, there are pictures showing the King and Queen handing out gold to loyal nobles from a balcony. Some have suggested that this balcony was on the bridge over the road – so that as the royal family went from their home to 'work', they would immediately be on public view. This seems unlikely, however. Pictures of the palace carved on the walls of the tombs of the officials cut into the eastern cliffs suggest that the 'Balcony of Appearances' was at the front of the royal private quarters, much like the balcony of Buckingham Palace in London. Also to be found on this side of the road was the throne room; and, divided from the rest of the palace by gardens, the harem, or women's quarters.

Behind the temple dependencies was a cluster of buildings that archaeologists have identified as public buildings, including the 'foreign office', where tablets in cuneiform were found; a building with clusters of wine-jars, thought to be an inn; and 'military' quarters, which are more probably the police headquarters, within which the Medjai, or security forces, were housed. These security forces are seen in all the pictures, protecting the royal family at every turn, and on permanent guard throughout the city. The palace buildings are shown as being patrolled strictly around the outside, while every time the King or a member of his family appears in public, they are surrounded by large numbers of armed guards on every side. One is left with the feeling that the King must have felt distinctly insecure even within his own lifetime. Were it not for the destruction of everything to do with him after his death, you might accuse him of paranoia; but the continual presence of security guards in great numbers makes you feel uneasy. It suggests that the threat was a real and tangible one.

Somewhere around this area was presumably the house of Queen Tiye, whom we know from inscriptions had substantial estates in Tell el Amarna, with a large staff. In charge of them was Huya, whose titles included Stewardship of the Estates of Tiye as well as Overseer of the King's Harem.

From here, a narrow road led to the east of the plain where the workmen's village was situated. Here, the permanent workforce that built the city was housed. Once again, pictures in the nobles' tombs show that this road, running to the rear of the Great Temple, was flanked with forms of sentry-boxes, with what appears to be chain-link fencing between, manned as always by the security guards.

To the very north of the plain was a separate establishment, called by archaeologists the Northern Palace. Excavation shows it was well-appointed, with beautifully decorated rooms, once again a suite of six small rooms, arguably for the princesses, and, at the centre, a large pool. Roots in and around this suggest, as many painted scenes from the period confirm, that the pool stood in a tranquil garden site, surrounded by trees and flowering shrubs, the water filled with colourful fish, lotuses and perhaps even turtles.

Matching this, to the south of the plain, was the *maru*, or viewing-site. This building was inaccessible from the city because the main road stopped well to the north, and so was only approachable by river. Within the main building the rooms were exotically painted and decorated with glazed tiles representing bunches of grapes suspended near the ceilings. Outside and to the rear there were beautifully planted gardens. Here, among the trees, there was a series of small buildings made of quartzite, the hardest stone found in Egypt. The translation of the Egyptian word for these is 'sunshades', and they were dedicated to each of the royal ladies. Although Thomas has described it as a harem, it seems more likely to have been an escape from the hustle and constant public gaze to which the women were subjected within the main city.

The entire city seems to have been well-conceived. From the palace, according to the images in the tombs, steps led down to a prosperous and thriving quay filled with ships bringing news and supplies into the city. The streets were lined with trees and plants; this feature even seems to have been a priority of the planners. Overall, the finished city would have been cool, delightfully organised and with the scents of a thousand flowering plants and trees to fill the air.

Around the bay of cliffs behind the city were cut the tombs of the King's prime officials. In the centre of the cliffs was the *wadi*, within which the royal tomb itself was cut. To the north are to be found, among others, tombs to Huya, Overseer of the Royal Headquarters of Tiye; Meryre II, who undertook the same duties for Nefertiti; Meryre I, Chief Servitor of Aten in the Great Temple; and Penthu, the Royal Physician. To the south were cut the tombs for Perrennefer, the royal craftsman; Mahu, the police chief; Ramose, Commander of the Army; Nekhpaaten, the vizier; May, who was Steward of the House of Waenre in Heliopolis; Paatenemheb, Overseer of Works in the City and Commander in the army; and last, but certainly not least, the tomb of Ay, God's Father and Overseer of the King's Horse.

The buildings, after having been laid out, had plaster footings and floors laid over the sand on which the walls were erected. The lowest part of the walls, probably submerged below the sand, was of sun-baked mud-brick. But above this, most of the walls of the principal buildings were made of stone. The stone, generally limestone, was cut on the west bank opposite, while finer stone came from Tura in the north, as quarry inscriptions there attest. Some sandstone was used, cut in the quarries of Gebel Silsileh.

According to the boundary stelae, the King found and claimed the site for his new city in year 4 of his reign, and presumably returned to Luxor while building work got underway. One year later, it seems that he returned to stay and dedicated the city to the Aten. On the exact anniversary of that day, in year 6, he revisited the boundaries, giving orders for the final stelae to be cut marking the periphery of his city; and the stelae add in a colophon, or ornamental tailpiece, that he renewed his oath never to go beyond those boundaries in year 8. It would appear, therefore, that by year 5 at the earliest, and year 6 at the latest, the entire city was complete. The speed of the building work, given the sheer scale of the site, is virtually incomprehensible. The organisation required on this lonely and deserted site to cut and move the stone, to put it into place and decorate it, to lay out all the buildings – and more than that, to feed and clothe the workers involved – cannot be less of a task than the building of the great pyramids of the Fourth Dynasty.

Today, it is hard to gain access to the site because it is in the heart of the politically unstable area of Middle Egypt. Even when it is possible to go there in safety, there is virtually nothing to be seen. It is hard to imagine the three-dimensionality of the city merely going by its foundations and the carved pictures we have of it, with the two-or perhaps even three-storeyed buildings, the huge, full-sized pylon gateways before the temple, and the gates, walls and columned halls of the palace buildings. Bearing in mind the ephemeral nature of the plaster footings between the foundations and the walls, and the use of relatively thin layers of plaster on the surface of the sand to form the floors, these huge buildings were, in effect, floating on 'rafts' rather than rooted into the rock. It could well be that the builders had to adapt their usual methods to ensure the work progressed at the remarkably rapid rate that the King demanded. Another oddity about the buildings lies in the stones used for them. These are curiously small. Most buildings in Egypt make use of massive blocks, but in Tell el Amarna, the building stones were just three hand-spans wide. Because of this peculiarity the Amarna blocks are called *talatat*, which means 'three' in Egyptian Arabic. They can easily be carried and put into place by one man; and presumably they were specifically ordered by the King so that the workers could construct the buildings as quickly as they could possibly manage.

The *talatat* were cemented into place using plaster. Only when the surface was completed was it carved all over with scenes. The carving was, like the stones, small in scale: the hieroglyphs are simply carved and tiny. More importantly for us, the scenes did not follow the lines of the stones, but rather crossed over them, the relief-carvers working on the wall as a whole rather than being guided by the stones that formed the wall. Afterwards the whole wall was painted white, and the images and hieroglyphs were picked out in bright colours on this background.

Inscriptions found around the city date from year 5 onwards, confirming that this was the first date of occupation. One inscription was dated year 17, crossed out and replaced with year 1. This is universally accepted as the date of the death of Akhenaten and the succession of the next King. All over the site the names of members of the royal family appear, although examples of the last three daughters of the King and Queen – Nefernefruaten Tasherit, Neferne-frure and Setepenre – are rare. These daughters probably did not live long after birth. The title of Smenkhkare, who, as King, seems to have taken the throne name of Ankhkheprure Djeserkheprure, also appears many times. And so, too, do the names and titles of Tutankhaten Nebkheprure and of the Great Royal Wife Ankhesenpaaten. These last seem to date only to years 1 and 2 of his reign. Inscriptions of year 1 and 2 cannot refer to Akhenaten, since the city was founded only in his year 4; so it seems, then, that since the names of Tutankhaten abound in the city, years 1 and 2 refer to him. But after that, there is nothing.

The city functioned for around 15 years, as the inscriptions appear to show, until it was finally abandoned when Tutankhaten left for Luxor. The King's presence was the only reason for the existence of the city in the first place. There had never been any buildings on the site previously because it was unable to sustain them. The area was too isolated, too unapproachable from either north or south to function independently. It was ideal for Akhenaten's purposes, but for his successors its location made it intolerable. Excavation suggests that, on the day when the last citizens finally walked out, they simply left everything behind them as it was. The sculptor walked out leaving behind finely carved heads of the royal family, masterpieces of his craft, in his studio. Even the foreign office archives, that most vital source of foreign policy during those years of isolation, were simply abandoned. There is no evidence of any force that impelled the people to leave. There had been no fire, and there is no evidence to suggest an attack. It simply died when the last King left.

At the start of Horemheb's reign, this new, military King decided, as we have seen, to erase all sign of the family he detested so much. His men moved onto the site and, with a dedication and organisation equal to that of the workers who built it, carefully dismantled it, stone by stone, shipping the *talatat* blocks over the river to the city of Ashmunein. Here they were systematically used as rubble for building pylons and courtyards for Horemheb's new temple, built to appease the abandoned gods of Egypt.

Yet Tell el Amarna was not the only site where building took place

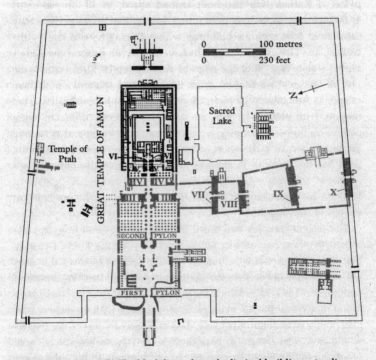

The temple of Karnak. The black lines show the limited buildings standing during the reign of Amenhotep III; the lighter lines show buildings which were added only over later centuries.

during the reign of Akhenaten. Despite the oft-held insistence that the priests of Karnak forced the King out because of his heresies, and Horemheb's insistence that the temples were all shut when he took the throne, we now know that Akhenaten built substantially in Luxor – and mostly within the very precincts of Karnak itself. Yet if you visit the site today, vast though it is, nothing from the Amarna period can be seen. As Redford said, 'So complete and thorough was the destruction wrought by the Pharaoh Horemheb, whose reign terminated the Amarna period, that literally no stone was left upon another.'

It appears that the ninth pylon at Karnak, built by Horemheb, was packed solid in its core with *talatat*. Later, hundreds more emerged from the rubble-core of the pylons of Luxor temple, and of the temple of Mont in Medamud. Later investigations proved that the second pylon of Karnak was also built around *talatat*. In all, an estimated 45,000 *talatat* or more have been found. Inscriptions on them show they came from four separate buildings within Karnak temple itself – the earliest, the Gempaaten, seems to have been built around the King's year 3 – also year 30 of the reign of Amenhotep III Nebmaatre – the year of the great *sed* festival. From these rescued *talatat* we now have images of Amenhotep IV Neferkheprure Waenre also celebrating a *sed* festival, with pictures of him, his wife and Princess Meritaten being carried on litters, celebrating with the traditional gods, and even, like his father, wearing the short, diamond-patterned cloak traditionally used for the festival. It appears, then, that while the older King's festivities took place largely on the west bank around the palace of Malkata, his son celebrated his father's anniversary on the east bank, in the temple of Karnak.

The second complex was called the Tenimenu. Stones from this site invariably show servants at work, together with the kind of storage that is typical of palaces, although Donald Redford believes this does not necessarily show that the Tenimenu *was* a palace. We know of buildings in Malkata in which the young King's cartouche is regularly found, implying that his main place of residence within Luxor was in his father's palace; but it is likely, despite Redford's assertions, that he would need somewhere to base himself for the work involved with preparing for the festival on the east bank. In any case, the Tenimenu is proof of Amenhotep IV's personal presence within Karnak. On some of the stones, he and his wife are shown with two daughters. This proves

Talatat blocks from Akhenaten's temple buildings within Karnak have been restored and are now on display in Luxor Museum. Here, the king, alone under the rays of the Aten, supervises building work.

that they must have been decorated after year 4, when their second daughter Meketaten was born; and before year 5, when he left Luxor for Tell el Amarna. Since the *sed* festival took place in year 3 of his reign, this shows that the Tenimenu, and perhaps some of the other buildings, were occupied by the young King even after he had instigated work on his own city. So much for being driven out of Luxor.

The third building, the Rwdmenu, comprised stones showing the King and his wife making offerings in a large, open-roofed building filled with offering-tables, sometimes termed 'altars'. This building is probably to be identified with the Gempaaten (see below). The fourth and final building, the Khut-benben, 'House of the Benben Stone', is undoubtedly a copy of the obelisk-dominated courtyard that we have seen in Tell el Amarna and Abu Ghurab, presumably copies of the original temple to Re in Heliopolis.

In the early days, Karnak, Luxor and Medamud all had buildings dedicated to the Aten. Later research showed that the stones all came from the same four buildings within Karnak; and that in every case Horemheb had moved them to their new sites to provide rubble. So not only did he systematically and methodically dismantle every building, even removing traces of their foundations in most cases, but he was even prepared to have the stones shipped miles away to ensure that not even one should be left on view. This man's hatred was astonishing.

When the stones were found by archaeologists the thought of reassembling some 45,000 of them to restore four buildings was too daunting even for consideration, so the stones were simply stored away in safe compounds until some solution was found. In 1965 Ray Winfield Smith, a retired American government official, decided to put together a team to study the *talatat*, using a computer to do the hard work. The notion was to number and then measure each *talatat*, noting the exact measurements where a line of carving cut each edge, and to feed this data into the memory of a computer. The computer, within seconds, was then able to establish which block matched with which others. The scheme was remarkably successful, and in some instances large numbers of blocks could be matched in theory, then studied. In this way the whole relief was restored, and one wall of these restored *talatats* now stands in the magnificent Luxor Museum.

But where were these buildings originally situated? From 1975 onwards a team led by Donald Redford dug immediately behind the eastern outer wall of the temple of Karnak. Here they found the remains of square column-bases, once surmounted by square-profile columns, and so ideally suited to the use of *talatat* blocks. These columns were mounted into a colonnade behind which stood a wall, again carved in relief. The temple, which proved to be an open courtyard just like the Great Temple at Tell el Amarna, would have been some 142×218 yards, with its internal columns flanked by colossal statues of the King and Queen, presumably alternating around the outside. This building proved to be the Gempaaten, built for the celebration of the jubilee. It would have been approached via the processional route through the temple, and would, in effect, have become the focal point of Karnak. In other words, the entire temple would have been re-dedicated for the Aten, with the earlier tiny sanctuary of Amen thus turned into a nondescript and unimportant chamber in the middle of the temple, not towards the back, as it should have been. Once again, the building work must have been tremendous. The majority of the sandstone blocks came from Gebel Silsileh. The cutting of the stones and their transport to the site was the province, as always, of military groups while the actual building must have involved virtually every man in the region of Karnak.

Once again, the archaeological evidence defeats the myths that have grown up about the whole period. The organisation of work in the first years of the reign of Amenhotep IV Neferkheprure Waenre was vast. It meant that squads of army-men were virtually permanently employed in supervising the transportation of stones from quarries to the prime building sites of Tell el Amarna and Karnak. The dates suggest that, soon after he was crowned, the young King first went south to Nubia to start off the celebrations there for his father's festival; then returned to Karnak to organise the building of the structures there. In his year 4 he sailed north with his most loyal followers to find and dedicate the site of Tell el Amarna. He then returned to Luxor, where building work continued unabated. Getting together the gangs of builders' alone was a vast enterprise.

Far from being 'rejected' and 'cast out' as a heretic from Luxor, then, this King, either vigorous and intelligent himself or served by men who had these qualities, planned and then carried out one of the most ambitious building programmes Egypt had ever seen. Had Akhenaten's buildings survived, they would have outranked in number and size anything of Ramesses II Usermaatre Setepenre, who is called by posterity 'the Great' for the constructions he built. Perhaps we need to revise our opinions of Akhenaten yet again. Since it was Horemheb who demolished his works, the buildings of Akhenaten still stood in Karnak when Tutankhamen reinstated the worship of Amun but made no attempt to demolish the buildings of Karnak. These would still have stood as reminders of the religion of the Aten. In other words, he adopted an evenhanded approach, bringing back the festivals which the local people so loved while maintaining the religion in which he had grown up. All he had to do was to lower the priority of the Aten and make it one among all the other gods. In doing this, he was conforming to the usual Egyptian attitudes, accepting any deity that came along into the huge pantheon of gods that seemed to stretch the length of the Nile.

We must now ask what force drove Horemheb to these astounding acts: dismantling Akhenaten's buildings; moving the stones to sites far away and using every one of them for rubble; restoring the temple of Karnak to its original form and restoring the sanctuary and statue of Amen within; and, in doing so, according to his Edict, placing the country under tight military control. Why did Horemheb erase even the reign-years of his predecessor on the throne, and thereafter only ever refer to him by allusion?

The nature of the Edict suggests that Horemheb's campaign may not have been universally popular. It was vindictive, yet totally thorough. Horemheb succeeded in blackening the name of Akhenaten to such an extent that even today, 3500 years later, it is hard to understand what it was like before he took control. By carefully considering the facts, we now see that Akhenaten may have been a very popular figure during his life, yet remained frightened at the possibility that someone might take action against him, if we take the strong security forces he had everywhere with him into account. That someone was surely Horemheb. Yet what was it that drove this old soldier to such lengths? Horemheb must have known Akhenaten. What event made the King of Egypt and the Commander-in-Chief of the army such bitter enemies?

CHAPTER EIGHT

Akhenaten and Nefertiti

—

T he picture that is slowly emerging from the historical evidence, while light years away from the accepted – and false – tale I repeated in Chapter 3, is still indistinct. From the established age at death of Tutankhamen, allied with his reign-length of nine years, we can understand that he was about six or seven when he was crowned King – an age that accords well with the size of some of the objects found in his tomb. Many of the objects, together with several inscriptions, tell us that he was the son of a king. But which one? All the evidence points to Tutankhaten being born around year 12 of Akhenaten. His predecessor on the throne, Akhenaten, ruled for seventeen years, twelve of which were shared with his father Amenhotep III Nebmaatre. Since Amenhotep III Nebmaatre died during the year that Tutankhamen, as he later chose to call himself, was born, he could have been Tutankhamen's father. If he was, Tutankhamen must have been born within a few months of his death. But the crux of the accepted story was that Tutankhamen was the younger brother of Smenkhkare, who was the male lover of Akhenaten. Yet it is precisely at this point that we start to stumble. For if Tutankhamen was a royal son, so must his brother have been. And whoever their father was – whether Amenhotep III or Akhenaten – we have the added problem of incest. In any case, it means that Tutankhamen did *not* take the throne solely because of his relationship with Smenkhkare, but rather because he was in direct line for the throne.

Yet in many respects the evidence is already becoming contradictory.

We know from the images carved on the walls of tombs at Tell el Amarna and in Karnak temple, that, until his year 12, Akhenaten was the epitome of a dedicated husband and family man, utterly besotted by his wife. And yet in that turbulent year 12, she was evicted and died in solitude of a broken heart, her place taken by Smenkhkare, Tutankhamen's older brother. If Tutankhamen and Smenkhkare were the sons of Amenhotep III Nebmaatre and Sitamun, the old King's daughter, then they were Akhenaten's brothers (as they were all sons of the same father) as well as his nephews (as they were sons of Akhenaten's sister). This means that Akhenaten publicly rejected his wife to make his brother his paramour. If this had been the case, then it is altogether strange that Sitamun, as Queen, nowhere records the much-vaunted title 'King's Mother'. Since Tutankhamen was born at almost the exact time that his brother, Smenkhkare, was made joint ruler with Akhenaten, then if Sitamun was indeed their mother, she would have been alive to witness the elevation of one of her sons to the throne and would thus have been expected to take the title.

If this is not the case, and Akhenaten was the father of the two boys, then why are they never shown in the company of their six sisters? The only obvious explanation is that Nefertiti was not their mother. It would be quite usual for a King to have had many wives, and children by most of them. It seems strange, then, that even if they were not born to the Great Royal Wife, they were not depicted anywhere, in any of the court scenes at any time. We have pictures of the little Princess Meketaten at Tell el Amarna. The King is shown everywhere with his daughters, fondling and kissing them when they are babies, teaching them to drive chariots and, as they grew, he is depicted as accompanied by them everywhere he went. There is now enough reconstructed *talatat* available, complete with carvings, to make it seem odd that the two little boys are not pictured anywhere. They must have been born and brought up either in Malkata or in Tell el Amarna, and most certainly they would have spent the greater part of their lives in Tell el Amarna. But apart from the one reference to Tutankhamen found on a block in Ashmunein, there is no real record of either of them anywhere.

Now, it is not up to us to make judgment on moral grounds using modern values over facts that happened so long ago. If Amenhotep III married his daughter and had children by her, it is not for us to decry him. It happened, we cannot change it, and it is our duty simply to note the facts. Likewise, if Akhenaten took as his lover either his brother or his son, again, it is not for us to comment. Yet we know, thanks to the analysis of the Amarna style of art, that we cannot always rely wholly on the evidence that we have. We can now say safely that Akhenaten was neither deformed nor sterile, despite his bizarre portraits. Thus he did not have to be cuckolded by his Great Royal Wife Nefertiti, and the children she had were, without any shadow of doubt, her husband's. We can also say, by virtue of his writing, his architectural and artistic work, and his organisation of the labour for vast building projects in Sesebi, Tell el Amarna and Karnak, that he was a highly intelligent man and must have been respected by many of his subjects. He was quite capable of making his own decisions. So what was it, in year 12, that drove him to reject Maat, and drive out his Great Royal Wife and the mother of his children, in order to declare his passion for one of his closest male relatives? After all, whether brother or son, he would have had a close relationship with them in any case. He could have made them co-regent without driving Nefertiti out and without making a private incestuous passion public. There must have been something that happened to force him to this point.

The pictures from the *talatat*, showing the constant presence of security guards around him and his family, demonstrate that even at the start of his reign Akhenaten felt physically threatened, even within the safety of his own isolated city. His rejection of Nefertiti, a publicly respected woman and a great beauty, must have caused even greater problems for his safety. The army, led by Horemheb, already irritated by the advances of the Hittites against Egypt's borders but given no royal order to attack, then used by the King to carry stone for his building work, must have been doubly angry. Was it not foolish, then, for Akhenaten to jeopardise the little favour that he enjoyed?

To tread back over familiar ground, we know that Amenhotep, as Akhenaten was called when he was born, would have been brought up within his mother's and father's palaces. The principal palace was undoubtedly in Memphis, but indications suggest that much of their time as a family would have been spent in Malkata, the royal palace in Luxor. His father had built the extensive palace complex early in his reign at about the time Deir el Ballas was abandoned. No doubt this was setting an example that his son would later follow when he abandoned Luxor in favour of Tell el Amarna.

We do not know exactly where or when the Prince was born. We know that Amenhotep III Nebmaatre was only a child himself when he became King, and that Queen Tiye was not much older. We also know that by year 10 of his reign, Amenhotep III was sexually active, since he summoned the Princess Giludkhipa of Mitanni to Egypt, with her 317 women, to marry. In fact, we have written evidence from the north that he married at least seven foreign princesses. One letter from Amenhotep III Nebmaatre to a prince who lived in Gezer, south of Jerusalem, says:

> I am sending you the Chief of the Army together with goods, in order to fetch beautiful women . . . total women 40, amounting to 40 debens of silver for each woman. Now send me beautiful women, but none with harsh voices.

This shows that by year 10 at the latest, the King and his Great Royal Wife would have been capable of having a child. We also know that Akhenaten had an older brother. We could calculate that, if Akhenaten were born around year 10, and his older brother had been born, for the sake of argument, two years earlier, this would have made Amenhotep III Nebmaatre around fifteen at the birth of Tuthmosis and seventeen at the birth of Amenhotep – both reasonable assumptions. Tiye would have been a little older.

It might appear from our perspective that the Great Royal Wife had much to put up with from her apparently lascivious husband, but in ancient Egypt a strong King such as Amenhotep III Nebmaatre may have had many wives. That Tiye was not altogether happy with the arrival of the foreign princess is suggested by her demand for the lake the following year, and the speed with which her husband completed it (see page 167). The siting of the lake is also informative, since Djarukha was near Tiye's home town of Akhmim rather than in her husband's palace in Luxor. We have no indication that Deir el Ballas palace was still occupied in year 11 of Amenhotep III's reign. So where was she staying, and why? Is it all indicative of a growing apart of the Queen and her husband?

After the death of Tiye's elder son and the coronation of her younger son in year 27, evidence suggests that her husband the King was increasingly incapable of carrying out his duties. It is unheard-of for a

Great Royal Wife to take over such an important matter as foreign correspondence, but the fact that she did so, and in her own name, is certain from the foreign correspondence addressed to her son when he inherited the throne in year 12. Was it the decline of her husband's health and stability that persuaded Tiye to leave Luxor and travel with her son to Tell el Amarna? Although we use the term 'elderly', Amenhotep III Nebmaatre would still have been only around thirty-four years old when his son was crowned. It all suggests some form of premature senility, and one questions the possibility of either something such as Alzheimer's disease, or even, knowing his lifestyle, perhaps some degenerative sexually transmitted disease.

In any event, Tiye joined her son and daughter-in-law in Tell el Amarna soon after the young royal family moved there. She was given estates in her son's city, honoured by Akhenaten and Nefertiti in public, and clearly carried out public duties as well as organising foreign affairs while she was there. It would seem that when she left Luxor, after Tell el Amarna was completed in year 5 of Akhenaten's reign and year 32 of Amenhotep III Nebmaatre's, the old King needed someone to fulfil her state duties in Luxor and thus elevated his daughter Sitamun. Yet it was always Tiye who took priority; and in the jubilee festival of year 37, Amenhotep III Nebmaatre is shown accompanied by the Great Royal Wife Tiye. Of the Great Royal Wife Sitamun there is no sign. So either the younger Queen stood aside when her mother was around, simply standing in for Tiye when she was in Tell el Amarna, or she died before the old King's third and final jubilee. Another intriguing bit of information is that, on the deaths of Yuya and Thuya, Tiye's parents, most of the objects from the tomb are dominated by Sitamun, although often showing Tiye present. Clearly Sitamun was close to her maternal grandparents and at the time of their deaths, given that their names both appear on the knob of a chest from the tomb of Yuya and Thuya, Tiye and her daughter carried the role of Great Royal Wife simultaneously.

Towards the end of his reign, Amenhotep III Nebmaatre, who from his mummy and images of him appeared obese and ill, sent northwards for yet another princess from Mitanni. The old King of Mitanni had died and had been replaced on the throne by his son Tushratta, Gildkhipa's brother. Tushratta, however, did not welcome the Egyptian King's request at first. It seems Tushratta had sent an emissary to the

Egyptian court to see how his sister fared, but the emissary was unable to recognise her. The Egyptian King now requested permission to marry Tushratta's daughter as well, but the King of Naharin prevaricated.

> You want to marry my daughter, but my sister, whom my father sent to you, is with you although no one has seen her of late, or knows if she is alive or dead ... You said to my messengers when your wives were together standing in front of you 'Your Lady is before you.' Now my messengers did not recognise her. Does my sister really look like this?

It is understandable under the circumstances, fearing that the King of Egypt was trying to trick him, that Tushratta tried to delay the sending of his daughter Tadukhipa. Negotiations almost collapsed with arguments about the girl's dowry. But finally, Tadukhipa was sent.

> My brother has enriched me ten times more than my father. My son-in-law is to be married in Luxor in the presence of the statue of the god. Is it not in this way that Tushratta, though living far away, arranges the marriage of Tadukhipa, consenting to the desire of Nimmuria the Egyptian?

Finally, in a letter dating to the end of the reign of Amenhotep III, it seems the lady had finally arrived. 'To Nimmuria King of Egypt my brother by letter thus: Peace be to you, and to your household, to the Lady Tadukhipa my daughter, to your wife whom you love, be peace.'

It seems that the letter was probably sent as the Princess left and before the King had had news of her arrival.

Amenhotep III Nebmaatre was to die at about this time, so it is uncertain whether Tadukhipa ever was married to the old King. If she was, and joined his harem, it could not have been for very long. Clearly, on the death of the old King, Tadukhipa, and presumably some of the other younger wives of Amenhotep III Nebmaatre, must have been sent to Tell el Amarna to join the younger, now sole, King Akhenaten Neferkheprure Waenre. Tushratta wrote again to Egypt: 'To Niphuria [Neferkheprure], my brother whom I love, peace. To the lady Tiye and to Tadukhipa my daughter your wife be peace. To your children, to your family, peace.' It seems that Nefertiti the Great Royal Wife thus had competition, just as Tiye had had years earlier.

Here we have a new element in the story of Tutankhamen. For if Tadukhipa was sent from the court of Amenhotep III to marry Akhenaten on the death of the old King, she would have joined Akhenaten around year 12: the very year that Nefertiti was banished and the King apparently revealed his true sexual preferences. How did Princess Tadukhipa fit into all of this domestic turmoil?

From the very start of his reign, it seems that Amenhotep IV leaned heavily on his mother Tiye and her brother Ay. Although we have no evidence that Ay accompanied the young King Amenhotep into Nubia to Sesebi to see the celebration of the old King's festival in the temple of Ay's sister Tiye, it is certain that he accompanied him on the journey north to Tell el Amarna in year 4. Ay was given a large house within the main part of the city, and the prominent position and large size of the tomb of Ay shows that he must have been one of his royal nephew's most loyal supporters. Inscriptions in his tomb call him:

The fan-bearer on the right of the King, Master of all his Majesty's Horses, the Royal Scribe, his beloved, the god's father Ay.

He says:

I am one praised by his Lord in the course every day. My praise increases from one year to the next because I am excellent in his heart. He increases my rewards as much as the sand, because I am the first of the nobles over the Common People. The fan-bearer on the right of the King, his great friend, the one who can go right up to his Lord, the true Royal Scribe, his beloved one, the god's father Ay.

He even, touchingly, leaves a message for us, his attempt at immortality.

O you who still live upon the earth, all the future generations that shall come into existence, I shall tell you about my way of life and I shall speak to you of my rewards. You shall remember my name because of the things I have done, for I was a good person when I was on earth.

Pictures carved on the walls show him being rewarded with several of the broad-collars, known as the Gold of Honour, at the same time by Akhenaten and Nefertiti.

Ay's wife was Teye, about whom we know very little except that she was also rewarded with the Gold of Honour by Akhenaten and Nefertiti – a singular honour for a woman. We also know that she was the [hieroglyph] (possibly foster-mother) of Nefertiti. The identity of Nefertiti has been much discussed. However, in the tomb of Ay and Teye in Tell el Amarna, mention is made, and images shown, of their daughter Mutnodjmet. Mutnodjmet is frequently pictured in scenes of the royal family carved in the nobles' tombs at Tell el Amarna. Here she is shown always in the company of two dwarves, but with no mention of a husband. She is always shown looking after the six royal Princesses and she is always recorded in inscriptions 'the sister of the Great Royal Wife'. Nefertiti herself is referred to in texts as 'the hereditary princess, greatest one in the palace, fair of face and beautiful of the two plumes, great of joy, at the sound of whose voice everyone rejoices; possessor of charm, great of love, the one who makes the Two Lands contented'. The titles suggest that she was of very noble birth indeed, and the link with Mutnodjmet, her sister, could not be clearer. In addition we have the title of Ay as [hieroglyph], 'God's father', a title, as we have seen before, that meant at this time father-in-law of the King – that is, his daughter married a king.

Given all the facts, it seems beyond any reasonable doubt that Nefertiti was Ay's daughter, Tiye's niece and thus Akhenaten's cousin. This would make absolute sense, knowing, as we do, of the close links already forged between the two families. We can equally be sure that Ay's wife Teye was not Nefertiti's mother. The title [hieroglyph], as we have seen, seems to mean foster-mother. Presumably Nefertiti must have been born to another mother. But if Teye had fed her as an infant, as the breast-determinative implies, she would have seemed to Egyptian society as good as Teye's daughter, although Teye would not have been entitled to the honours due to the mother of the Great Royal Wife of a King.

Thus we are drawing the net closer. If we are right about the date of Akhenaten's birth, then in year 27, when he was crowned King, he would have been about sixteen or seventeen years old – once again a reasonable assumption and an ideal time to be crowned co-regent. We might also presume that Nefertiti was about the same age as her new husband. For the first time for several generations, Egypt thus had a crowned King and Queen who were not children and were thus not dependent on someone else to guide them. We know from the *talatat* blocks from the Gempaaten in Karnak temple that by year 30 Amenhotep III Nebmaatre's reign and year 3 of Akhenaten's, they were already accompanied by their first daughter Meritaten. Since their second daughter, Meketaten, appears in year 4, we must assume, allowing time for a pregnancy, that the infant princess was born earlier than year 3; and thus Nefertiti and Akhenaten were presumably married at the time of his coronation, she being chosen, as was the usual practice, as Great Royal Wife at the same time. We know that the young King went southwards to Nubia after his coronation; but there are no references there to the Great Royal Wife, suggesting that she had stayed behind in Luxor. This may well have been one of the reasons that persuaded her husband not to settle in Nubia but to return north to collect her and find a more amenable place in which to bring up his young family.

So we now have a family picture. And what a family! There is Tiye, highly intelligent and quite capable of running state affairs, putting her national duty before the pressures placed on her by her husband's way of life; Ay, again of supreme intelligence and intensely loyal both to his son-in-law and to his daughter; and then Nefertiti. And it seems that Nefertiti inherited all her family's intelligence and ambition, with a little extra. For in the *talatat* blocks so far recovered from Horemheb's buildings, more than 60 per cent of the scenes show Nefertiti in preference to her royal husband; while in the [hieroglyphs], the open-air temple built in Karnak for the Aten, virtually every scene shows Nefertiti, and so far only two show her husband. In several of the pictures, instead of wearing the twin-plumed crown of the God's Wife of Amen, or the flat-topped crown we are more familiar with, she wears the true crown, as if she were King of Egypt.

It is often said that the crown of Egypt was the double crown, the linking of the white crown of Upper Egypt and the red crown of Lower Egypt. But this is untrue. The double crown, seen in most of the ancient pictures of Egyptian regalia of the time of the unification, began not as two separate crowns but as one unit. The reason for this becomes apparent if the crown is turned onto its side; for there, clearly, is to be seen the *wadjet* eye, the healed eye of Horus. References to the magical power of the double crown in the pyramid texts thus become understandable. In fact, in an article published in 1982 W. V. Davies, now

Keeper of Egyptian Antiquities in the British Museum, traced the origin of the *khepresh* crown, commonly (and incorrectly) called the War Helmet or the Blue Crown, back to the skull-cap of Ptah of Memphis. Because Ptah, the originator of the *khepresh* cap, was traditionally the celebrator of the coronation since the founding of Memphis at the start of Egyptian history, it seems thus logical that it was this *khepresh* crown that represents the state of the monarchy, while the double crown merely represents the political unity of the Two Lands. Davies states that 'there is good evidence to support the view that the *khepresh* in its fully developed Blue Crown form functioned as the symbol of coronation and thus of legitimate succession'.

The statement is clear, and the pictures of Nefertiti from ⌷⌷⌷⌷ in Karnak, wearing the Blue Crown are also conclusive. Nefertiti is showing herself to be crowned ruler of the country. To emphasise the point even further, in several reconstructed scenes from the *talatat* blocks, she is shown, mace in hand, in the stereotypical view of a pharaoh clubbing a group of foreigners. In another scene, while Nefertiti sits enthroned upon a dais, a string of foreign captive women, Nubian and Asiatic, are presented to her as captive males are regularly presented to kings.

For the first time the picture of this royal family changes dramatically. Was this why Akhenaten rejected Nefertiti in year 12? Was she having herself depicted in scenes as above her station? Were her ambitions favoured by her husband? Or was she doing it all without his consent?

Wherever Nefertiti is depicted in Tell el Amarna, she is shown in company with her royal husband and her daughters. There is never any mention of any son at all. This is hard to reconcile with the evidence so far presented. If Tutankhamen and Smenkhkare were brothers, and if Tutankhamen was born around year 12 of Akhenaten's reign, while in the same year his brother was old enough to come to the Pharaoh's bed, then Smenkhkare must have been born at least at the start of Akhenaten's reign, if not before. This being the case, Smenkhkare would have been Akhenaten's and Nefertiti's first child; and as Crown Prince and heir to the throne, surely he would have been shown in pictures if his younger sister, Meritaten, received such a prominent position in depictions of her parents. Besides this, if Nefertiti was his mother, being the Great Royal Wife appointed at the time of her husband's coronation, we would have to suggest she bore not two but three children in her first four years of marriage. This would then make Smenkhkare eleven years old at the time of Akhenaten's downfall.

The whole reconstruction is now starting to become totally untenable. As I said several chapters back, if you tell a lie, you will be caught out. The time will come in the examination of a false hypothesis when nothing fits and the whole matter needs unravelling to try to find the point at which it all went wrong. That point is now with us.

Pictures of the early years at Tell el Amarna show Nefertiti bearing a succession of daughters for her husband. It is hard to say at what point her husband became concerned, or even if he ever did become concerned, about the lack of a male heir. At any rate, the pictures are very informative. Right from the start, Meritaten is shown sharing ceremonial and state occasions with her mother and father, while her little sisters hang back, often being looked after by their aunt, Mutnodjmet. Scenes show the little girls driving their own chariots along the main street of Tell el Amarna, while in Tutankhamen's tomb there were writing palettes belonging to both Meritaten and her younger sister Meketaten. It seems that the King and Queen, quite remarkably, were bringing up their daughters to be in every way equal to a son, being educated in aspects that girls would never usually venture into. Never had a woman before been depicted driving a chariot, let alone a group of princesses, accompanied by their parents who, in one tomb, are shown openly kissing in the street in their chariot while their daughters drive behind them. At the same time Meritaten, given her more important status, is being groomed as heir to the throne.

The whole thing is quite remarkable. From the images, it is as though Smenkhkare and Tutankhamen did not exist at all, while everywhere six girls take pride of place. And then, quite suddenly and dramatically, everything changed.

The royal tomb at Tell el Amarna lies far up a *wadi*, or dried-up river-bed, to the back of the plain of Tell el Amarna (see page 194). Its shape bears many basic similarities to the tomb of Tutankhamen, although on a larger scale. The entrance passage sloped downwards to where there was once a second door. In this passage were found twenty-five pieces of *shabti* figures inscribed for Akhenaten, all of the normal, conservative Eighteenth Dynasty style. Between the two doors, a side entrance to the right leads to a separate suite of passages and rooms which, as Geoffrey Martin has indicated, match in size and number the main complex of the tomb. Within the chambers at the end of this side complex were found pieces of sarcophagus with the titles of the Queen. It would thus seem that the tomb is made up of two adjoining yet equal sections, the first, main section for the King, and the side complex for the Queen.

Next to the second door in the main passage is yet another, very small group of rooms, labelled a, b and g. The pictures carved on the walls of these rooms, which are badly damaged, have been the subject of huge amounts of scholarly debate. In chamber g, the body of Meketaten is shown lying out on a bier with, quite remarkably, her mother and father, leaning on each other for support, crying uncontrollably. Behind them, courtiers fall to the floor and raise their hands, their grief pouring from them. The picture is unique. Nothing else ever carved in Egypt even comes close to the drama of the scene. Dr Martin, however, drew attention to one of the courtiers standing behind the grieving parents, who is shown clutching a baby. He suggests that Meketaten died in childbirth. Since the only likely candidate for father of the child was her own father, Akhenaten, just as Amenhotep III Nebmaatre had married his daughter Sitamun, he suggested that Meketaten had thus been 'married' to her father, become pregnant and bore the baby. She evidently died in childbirth and, since the date is right, identifies the child as Tutankhamen. But here we have a problem. If, as seems the case from all the evidence, Meketaten was born in year 4 (and two of the boundary stelae of year 4 do not show her at all, so it must have been late in year 4 when she was born), she can only have been seven and a half years old, or at the very most eight, at the time of her death. If the child survived, which from the picture it seems to have done, (and if it was Tutankhamen, of course, it did), then allowing a minimum of eight months for a viable pregnancy, she could only have been six and a half or seven when she 'married' her father and conceived the child. This, of course, is quite impossible; with the best will in the world, a girl of that age is not likely to have achieved puberty. In fact, the baby is not identified; and since we know that Nefertiti herself was bearing children up to year 12, there is no reason why the child should not be Meketaten's baby sister, the youngest child, Setepenre.

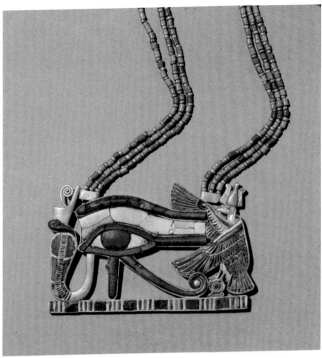

A pendant from Tutankhamen's tomb in the shape of the 'wadjet' eye, the healed eye of Horus. It was designed to focus good onto the wearer

The lid of an ivory-inlaid box shows Tutankhamen sitting in a garden with his wife, Ankhesenamun, dutifully at his feet

This unusual pectoral depicts the King as Osiris between Wadjet, the cobra, tutelary goddess of Lower Egypt, and Nekhbet, vulture protectress of Upper Egypt. It was clearly not made to be worn during life, but specifically for use after death

There are few pictures of Tutankhamen on Egypt's monuments. Here the King is shown, carved in raised relief, on one of the walls of Luxor temple. Horemheb later overcarved his own name, in one of his attempts to obliterate memory of the boy-king

The back of the Golden 'Throne' shows Tutankhamen, seated below the rays
of the Aten, the god he is supposed to have proscribed. The scarf at the back of
the Queen's neck is curiously not joined to her crown, suggesting that
the images·and the names were overcarved. So why was the disc-and-ray
icon of the Aten not also overcarved?

Amenhotep III placed this granite lion in front of his Nubian temple of Soleb. Later overcarved with the name of Tutankhamen, it now stands in the statue gallery of the British Museum

Uraei, the rearing-cobra emblems of a King's regality, support the back of Tutankhamen's golden throne, in between bars that bear his throne-name, Nebkheprure

In the burial chamber of Tutankhamen's tomb, this painting shows Ay, crowned and with his name already in cartouches, as King of Egypt at the time of Tutankhamen's funeral. This is unique in Ancient Egypt; a new King, by rights, should not have been crowned until after the burial of his predecessor

This image of Tutankhamen and his queen is invisible until the alabaster lamp is lit from within

The damage to the back of Tutankhamen's mask shows lots of missing blue glass where it was once stuck to the foot of the gold coffin

The lid of the coffin from Tomb 55 shows curiously altered features. The female head has been cut from another lid and adjoined to the front of another, shortening it

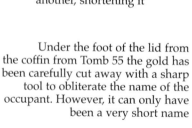

Under the foot of the lid from the coffin from Tomb 55 the gold has been carefully cut away with a sharp tool to obliterate the name of the occupant. However, it can only have been a very short name

One of a series of four solid gold coffinettes found in Tutankhamen's tomb, containing his internal organs removed during the mummification process. The coffins do not resemble the boy-King, and the names within were altered, showing, like many other objects in the tomb, that they had been borrowed – from adjacent tomb 55

Horemheb, while still Commander-in-Chief of the Egyptian army, being rewarded with the Gold of Honour, probably during the reign of Tutankhamen. Once he became King, he did everything he could to remove all evidence of the previous royal family. From the Memphite tomb of Horemheb, now in Leiden

We know, from references in the tomb of Amenhotep III Nebmaatre in the Valley of the Kings, that Meketaten was alive at the time of his funeral, since Meketaten was named in one fragment found in the tomb without the usual terminaten 𓏏𓏤𓊹𓏏 – 'True of Voice' – which would have shown she was dead. So it seems that within a very short time of each other, first Akhenaten's father, then his second daughter, died. The King's world must have been torn apart; and being now alone, in sole control of Egypt while isolated in Tell el Amarna, he must have seen the need to secure the throne into the next generation. So he chose Smenkhkare. The young man, having been chosen, sat openly at Akhenaten's side, and is shown being 'cuddled' by him (the Paser Stela). And, to legitimise his hold on the throne for the future as well as to 'cover up' his embarrassment, Akhenaten had him married to his eldest surviving daughter, Meritaten.

Inscriptions from the Northern Palace show that the most common name found there was that of Nefertiti. So as has been repeatedly suggested, the Queen must have moved here when she retired. What must her father, Ay, have thought of it all? How must he have felt at the public humiliation of his daughter, who had had such a glittering future? Had Ay encouraged her in her ambition in Karnak? Was this a father-and-daughter conspiracy for control that went wrong? Did Akhenaten see the plans Nefertiti clearly had for educating her daughters so that they might succeed her, thus founding a line of female pharaohs? And what of Tiye? Her name is found on objects in the burial of her husband, so she clearly outlived him. How did she face up to the banishment of her niece in favour of Smenkhkare, whoever he was?

In the last years of Akhenaten's life, we have relatively little information. There are very few descriptions at all of the last two daughters of the Queen, Nefernefrure and Setepenre. Perhaps they died soon after birth. Similarly, Nefernefruaten Tasherit ('Junior') also disappears from view. Her name has been found on a piece in Byblos, and it has been suggested that she was sent there to make a diplomatic alliance for Egypt in the face of the oncoming Hittite army. This seems unlikely. In the time of Amenhotep III Nebmaatre, a foreign prince asked for the Egyptian King to send him a daughter to marry, but Amenhotep was adamant. 'It has never since the beginning of time been the custom for a daughter of the King of Egypt to be given to anyone.' It is hard to see that policy changing, even given the radically new views of Akhenaten. In all probability, Nefernefruaten died young. We know, again from foreign letters, that at this time the plague was raging around the Middle East. It is possible that several members of the royal family in succession may have swiftly succumbed to some infectious outbreak.

At the end of Akhenaten's reign, there were only two daughters left: Meritaten, married to Smenkhkare; and Ankhesenpaaten. A block found in Hermopolis names a child, ⌗𓈖𓏏, his beloved of his own body, Ankhesenpaaten Tasherit. Once again the possibility has been mooted of a consanguineous marriage between Akhenaten and the third of his daughters. But there is no evidence. The epithet 𓂋𓏤𓈖𓏏𓏥 simply means 'the little girl'. Perhaps it was an epithet for Ankhesenpaaten after her sisters died, making her the youngest survivor.

And so, after seventeen devastating and incident-filled years on the throne, Akhenaten died. It is just at this time, then, that General Horemheb makes his first clear appearance on the national stage. Of his background we have very little knowledge. While he was general, serving in the army of Tutankhamen and the Ay, he had cut for himself a fine tomb at Saqqara. This was rediscovered by the Leiden Museum and the Egypt Exploration Society team in 1974, although blocks and statues from it had been removed earlier by Lepsius' Prussian expedition. There is no evidence at all of his parentage from there, except that we find his first wife was called Amenia. She seems to have disappeared just before Tutankhamen became King, to be replaced by Mutnodjmet, Nefertiti's sister. This seems to have been a clear move by Horemheb to secure some title to the throne. Did he try to take the throne at the death of Akhenaten? We have no evidence. Yet Smenkhkare and Meritaten, who do take the throne, lived to rule for only a matter of three years at the most before they, too, disappear at the same time. The coincidence is almost too much. It seems more than likely that they were removed.

In Tell el Amarna, Tomb 24 belonged to a man called Paatenemheb, the son of one of Akhenaten's greatest supporters other than Ay, Ptahmay. Paatenemheb is called 'Royal Scribe, Overseer of all works in Akhenaten, Army Commander of the King of Upper and Lower Egypt'. The titles are strongly reminiscent of those of Horemheb later.

On a statue of Horemheb and Mutnodjmet as King and Queen, now in Turin Museum, a long inscription on the back pillar says:

> The heart of the King was pleased with his work, agreeing with his decisions. He made him Lord of the land in order to maintain the law of the land as hereditary Prince. He was unique, without an equal. All the plans for the Two Lands came from his hands. Everyone agreed with what he said when he was summoned by the King. Now the palace fell into a rage, and he answered back to the King.

Could this, then, be one solution? That Horemheb was, indeed, Paaten-emheb, son of Akhenaten's friend Ptahmay, who argued with the King? The titles of the two men are very similar. Replacing Paaten in his name with Hor (Egyptian for Horus), thus Paatenemheb may have become Horemheb, leaving the palace because of a major problem. The inscription on the statue is also unique, as are many aspects of this whole business. Never on any other occasion is the temper of the King mentioned, or even alluded to. So what had caused this row? Was this the reason for Horemheb's hatred of the royal family?

In 1975, excavation in the Memphite tomb of Horemheb revealed a chamber containing fragments of a coffin with the name and titles of Mutnodjmet, together with some of her human remains. Among these latter pieces was found a section of her pelvic girdle. Pathological examination of it in 1976 showed it was quite badly notched. This, it was suggested, showed that she had attempted to give birth to several children, but without success, as Horemheb died childless. One particularly deep scar shows that she may have died in childbirth.

It is a sad reflection of her life that, having spent a good deal of her youth looking after her sister's children, she should then marry a man who seemed above all to want her solely for the legitimacy she might bear to him and their children. The statue of them in Turin shows she lived long enough after the death of her sister Nefertiti to take the title of Great Royal Wife of Horemheb herself. But unlike her forebears Tiye and Nefertiti, there are no pleasant words spoken of her on her husband's statue. Then, having failed to give him the child he so desperately needed, when she died he had her buried in the tomb he had had cut for himself as a soldier, before he became King. After taking the crown, he had a royal tomb cut for himself in the Valley of the Kings. There was neither provision nor mention there for the woman who had failed him. She was given a fine, though not a royal, interment hundreds of miles from where her royal husband would later lie.

There are now too many contradictions in our reconstruction of the historical events leading up to the life of Tutankhamen to make any sense of the story at all. Something has gone very wrong somewhere. There is only one element in the story left to investigate: we must now turn our attention to Smenkhkare, the brother of Tutankhamen. After all, if it had not been for him, the boy would never have become king at all. Or would he?

CHAPTER NINE

The Elusive
Smenkhkare

The historical evidence we have collated concerning the three generations previous to Tutankhamen still does not make much sense, even when everything has been put together and carefully analysed. No matter what arrangements are made within the family tree, the evidence seems to point to Akhenaten's total degeneracy. If Akhenaten and his whole family *were* so degenerate, it would not be surprising if the opposition they aroused did not result in murder at some point. Yet there is no evidence for that anywhere beyond mere supposition.

We know that Akhenaten died around his year 17, but we have no way of knowing how he died. From the fragmentary evidence in the royal tomb, we can take it that there was a state funeral for him, which would at least have involved the thousands of people who lived in Tell el Amarna. If foul play had been involved in Akhenaten's death it was too well hidden at the time for us to hope to discover it without the evidence of his mummy.

We know that Smenkhkare and Meritaten inherited the throne after his death, that they ruled only a short time and then both disappeared. When Ankhesenpaaten, the third daughter of Akhenaten and Nefertiti, married Tutankhaten, logic suggests that she must have had some right to the throne to bestow upon her husband – in other words, she must have been the eldest, if not the only, daughter surviving. It thus follows that her sister Meritaten must have been dead. We know Meritaten was born around year 2 of her father's reign, which would have made her about fifteen when her father died and her husband came to the throne. If Smenkhkare ruled around a year, she was thus sixteen when she disappeared. Her disappearance at such a young age, and at the same time as Smenkhkare, seems suspicious. The tomb of Meritaten has never been found and, once again, without her mummy we do not have the concrete evidence needed.

But we do, of course, have the body of Tutankhamen, and the postmortem of 1968 showed a thinning of the skull behind the left ear that, Harrison suggested, 'could have been the result of a blow to the head'. So was he murdered? It has often been suggested. But to prove it we need three things: positive forensic pathological evidence; a motive; and a murderer. As for the first, we shall delve further into the postmortem evidence in the last chapter. We may have found the motive in the background of the whole period. But who was the murderer? If indeed Smenkhkare and Meritaten were murdered, perhaps the same person was involved. But if someone murdered Smenkhkare and Meritaten, why did they allow Tutankhaten to live long enough to inherit the throne, only for the murderer to strike again nine years later?

We need to know more about Smenkhkare. All we really know so far is that he was the older brother of Tutankhamen. Since the Hermopolis block (see page 144) shows that Tutankhamen was a king's son, logic dictates that Smenkhkare must also have been royal. And no matter which king was his father, here we have the almost insurmountable problem again, for he can only have been Akhenaten's brother or his son.

The problem with the inscriptions

The publication of the first ever Egyptian hieroglyphic grammar by Jean-François Champollion in 1836–41 opened new doors in the study of ancient Egypt. Champollion's work was published posthumously by his older brother, Jacques-Joseph. This older brother had wanted to accompany the Napoleonic expedition to Egypt in 1798, but for some still unexplained reason was turned down. He seems to have passed his passion for all things Egyptian to Jean-François, who to this day is generally regarded as the first decipherer of hieroglyphs.

But this distinction is not strictly accurate. While Champollion did publish the first grammar and dictionary, the credit for recognising that the symbols were not mystical and symbolic, but actual letters representing sounds, must go to Thomas Young, of Milverton in Somerset. Young published his first commentary on the contents of the Rosetta Stone, and the decipherment of the royal names on it, written in hieroglyphs, in 1815 – more than twenty years before the publication of Champollion's grammar. After corresponding with Champollion, eight years later, in 1823, Young published his *Hieroglyphical Literature and Egyptian Antiquities, including the author's original alphabet as extended by M. Champollion*. While not by any means a bestseller, and still little known today, this work had a profound influence on many scholars.

One of them, the mathematician George Butler, was appointed Headmaster of Harrow in 1805 at the age of thirty-one. He studied hieroglyphs with Young, becoming his good friend. Butler was captivated and enthused by Young's work on hieroglyphs, which he then, in turn, passed on to many of his pupils at Harrow. Among these was the sixteen-year-old John Gardner Wilkinson, who joined the school in 1813. Butler taught Wilkinson all he had learned. In 1821, possessed of independent means, and encouraged in his love for things Egyptian by several friends, Wilkinson travelled to Egypt and remained there, copying pictures and inscriptions wherever he went, for the next twelve years.

Wilkinson first visited Tell el Amarna in 1824. It is uncertain what drew him to the spot, for there was no published description of this isolated plain before his time. Perhaps it was mere chance. At any rate, he entered several of the nobles' tombs that were already open, and over the next few years he made hand-copies and 'squeezes', or impresses, of the scenes that he found there. In 1837 he published some of these scenes in his renowned and popular series of volumes, *Manners and Customs of the Ancient Egyptians*. The distinctly strange people who appear in the reliefs from Tell el Amarna were a revelation, and more and more people wanted to see the site for themselves.

Wilkinson's introduction to hieroglyphs by Butler now proved very fruitful. It appears that merely by copying and studying so many inscriptions, he had learned how to read and understand much of the ancient Egyptian language long before the publication of the first grammar. In 1828, he published his *Materia Hieroglyphica*, a list, in hieroglyphs and translation, of the principal gods of Egypt, and of the kings in order of succession.

Before Wilkinson's book, the only list of ancient Egyptian kings available to scholars was via Manetho (see page 151), where the names of the kings had been transcribed into Greek. Wilkinson now published the names for the first time in ancient Egyptian. At once it could be seen that the two lists bore little resemblance to each other. He left it to later scholars to try to match up the two lists, but at least he presented the serious scholar for the very first time with a workable structure for ancient Egyptian history, and in the words of the Egyptians themselves.

It was Wilkinson, then, who first identified the strange King of Tell el Amarna. He called him Khuenaten, and his successor, Smenkhkara.

One of the first copyists to go to Tell el Amarna, intrigued by Wilkinson's discoveries, was Nestor L'Hote, a draughtsman who was one of Champollion's best friends. He was followed soon after by Achille Prisse-D'Avennes. The latter noticed similarities to the Tell el Amarna pictures in the relief carvings on the ninth pylon in Karnak – the gateway built by Horemheb, which years later was found to be stuffed with *talatat*. Karl Lepsius, who visited the site in 1842, added more to the available information in the way of copies of inscriptions in his publication of 1849, *Denkmäler aus Ägypten und Äthiopen*, in which examples of the names of the King, his family and the succession were added to Wilkinson's list. With so much information now available, scholars could start work analysing the inscriptions for the first time without having to go to Egypt.

By this date, it was already fully understood that each king of Egypt had had not one but five separate names, each representing a different aspect of his kingship. Three of these names were rarely used. The 🦆☉ name, which was given at birth, was written together with the picture of a pintail duck with a sun over its back (meaning 'son of the sun') and shown within a cartouche, an oval shape in the form of a rope knotted at the end. This was the name that most people had already begun to identify with each king. For example, Ramesses, Seti and Amenhotep were all birth, or 🦆☉, names, and were already known to the public. Next, to distinguish between different kings with the same names, numbers were added – as, for instance, with Amenhotep III; although in fact the Egyptians them-selves never did that.

The 𓇓𓇌 name, though regularly included in standard titles, was cast aside by the man when he became king. At the time of his coronation, he received another name that was unique, in all history, to him and him alone. This name, written in a cartouche below two pictures, one of a reed and the other of a bee, seems from the Amarna foreign archive letters to have been pronounced 'insibya'. This name often seems complex to the general reader today, but it was the name by which the Egyptians knew their king. For example, Ramesses II's insibya name was Usermaatre Setepenre – quite a mouthful.

We have little idea today how the ancient Egyptian language was pronounced – most of the information on this aspect of the language has long been lost. The Amarna foreign correspondence was not, however, written in hieroglyphs, but in cuneiform, written as wedge-shapes that were imprinted into a wet clay tablet that was then baked. But cuneiform is not a language in itself; it is merely the name given to the shape of the letters (just as, for example, the Russian style of writing today is called Cyrillic.) The language expressed by the letters was Akkadian – the language of Akkad in Syria. The Egyptian scribes, when writing the letters, had had to put down names as they heard them rather than how they were spelled. So, for example, Amenhotep III, whose insibya name was Nebmaatre, is referred to in the letters as Nimmuria; Amenhotep IV, whose insibya name was Neferkheprure Waenre, was addressed as Niphuria; and Tutankhamen, whose insibya name was Nebkheprure, was called Nibkhuria.

Unfortunately, at some time towards the end of the nineteenth century, as the general public became more interested in Egyptology, translators began to write the 𓇓𓇌 names of the kings in every instance. So, for example, if there was an inscription with a cartouche bearing the name Nekheprure, it would almost certainly be published as Tutankhamen. Of course this is not what the hieroglyphs actually say, but the theory goes that general readers will immediately identify the name 'Tutankhamen', but would never recognise 'Nebkheprure'. In all the books it says that Carter identified Tutankhamen's tomb by the seals on the outer mud door which bore his name. In fact, they bore the name 'Nebkheprure'. But as long as we are certain that the two names refer to the one king, such inaccuracy surely does not matter.

The same thing goes for place names. For example, we know that the city built by Akhenaten was called Akhetaten. We also know it more familiarly by the name Tell el Amarna, although this name was a mistake and no such place actually exists. If an inscription in hieroglyphs reads ⌁, a book would generally publish it as Tell el Amarna.

This bad habit continues to the present. Readers will have noticed that in this book I always include both names of each king. While tedious to some extent, it is a more accurate method of recording the names. At least the use of both names indicates exactly who is meant, where the use of only one may be misleading. As you will see, the confusion that results by publishing one name, when the hieroglyphs actually say another, can lead us into very troubled waters indeed.

By the start of the twentieth century, the existence of the Amarna kings was well attested, though Khuenaten's name had been corrected to Akhenaten, and their order on the throne had been established. Also familiar at this time was the name of Akhenaten's wife Nefertiti, even though in Tell el Amarna her name had been most often written as either Nefernefruaten Mery Waenre, or Nefernefruaten Mery Akhenaten, where 'Mery' means 'beloved of'. It seems that she was given the name Nefernefruaten at the same time that her husband called himself Akhenaten, when the couple moved to Tell el Amarna. To be correct, then, we should say that Nefertiti was married to Amenhotep IV Neferkheprure Waenre; while Akhenaten was married to Nefernefruaten Mery Waenre. Waenre, half of the insibya name of Akhenaten, was the name commonly used for the King in and around the city.

It may intrigue many people to point out that when the King changed his name from Amenhotep to Aknehaten, he was changing his birth name, not, as many assume, the name by which he was known as King. The change of the birth name would never perhaps have been realised by the majority of people alive at the time. His throne name, Neferkheprure Waenre, not only was not altered in any way at the time of the change of his other name, but also remained unaltered throughout his reign. Bearing in mind the fact that he was supposed to have banished all other gods, the Aten being the sole god, it is instructive to realise his names were Neferkheprure Waenre, and that his last two daughters by Nefertiti were named Nefernefru*re* and Setepen*re*. Hardly support for the monotheism theory.

It had also been discovered that the King and Queen had had six daughters. In front of the names of each were routinely written the words, 'the King's daughter, of his own body, his beloved', sometimes with the additional phrase 'born of the Great Royal Wife Nefertiti Nefernefruaten beloved of Waenre'. The daughters appeared gradually, in an easily ascertainable order. Thus, the eldest was Meritaten, followed in turn by Meketaten, Ankhesenpaaten, Nefernefruaten Tasherit, Nefernefrure and Setepenre. As for Smenkhkare, when he was crowned co-regent by Akhenaten in year 12, he was given the throne name Djeserkheprure. After the death of Akhenaten, when he came into sole rule, another name was added – Ankhkheprure. With both names the addition of the phrase 'Mery Neferkheprure' – 'beloved of Neferkheprure' (the insibya name of Akhenaten) – is added.

In the early days, evidence for Smenkhkare's existence *per se* was scanty. His part in the drama was reconstructed bit by bit over many decades in what today appears a most alarming way. Let us examine the evidence chronologically.

Most of the pictures within the nobles' tombs in Tell el Amarna were found to be limited to scenes of the royal family, their life around the town and pictures of the town itself. But there were some unusual scenes. In the tomb of Meryre II, for example (Tomb 2, see page 194) both Nestor L'Hote and Achille Prisse-D'Avennes had copied the same carved relief picture in the main chamber. Although very badly damaged, it shows a king and queen, the cartouches for whom had been destroyed. Recent examination by scholars concur that they should be restored to read 'Smenkhkare Djeserkheprure' and 'The Great Royal Wife Meritaten'. When, later, the British epigraphers Nina and Norman de Garis Davies copied the pictures faithfully from the walls of the tombs, they restored these cartouches in a corner of the illustration. It was inferred from this picture that Meritaten had married young 'Smenkhkare', since they were standing together and had their names in cartouches. From the style of the names it was inferred that they were married at the time of his rise to the co-regency. Since she took the title of the Great Royal Wife, her husband must have been King; and thus it was also inferred that Smenkhkare must have been the next King after Akhenaten. But it was clear that this Smenkhkare was not a

member of the main royal family. He must have been someone important if Akhenaten had allowed him to marry his eldest daughter and put
him in line for the throne. The picture encouraged scholars at the time
to understand that the line of the succession must thus have been
passed down through the King's eldest daughter, so that whoever she
married, she thus endowed with the crown of Egypt.

Other scenes in the tombs often showed Akhenaten's mother, Queen
Tiye, finding equal favour as the King and Queen under the rays of the
Aten. It was already 'known' that she was a 'commoner'. The Restoration Stela of Tutankhaten said that at his accession the gods had turned
their backs on Egypt. This, in turn, suggested that it was the religion of
his main predecessor, Akhenaten, which had upset the balance of
society. The ideas about the Aten were said to be very different from
those of the old gods. Yet at the time, Akhenaten was being portrayed
by archaeologists as deformed and weak-minded. People began to
question whether his ideas were his own, or if he had got them from
elsewhere. Since Tiye was a 'commoner', some suggested that it was
she who had taught her son the new religion.

As nineteenth-century scholars began to translate texts, especially
the *Great Hymn to the Aten* (see Appendix E) found in the tomb of Ay,
similarities began to be drawn between Akhenaten, Moses and even
Christ. In the very religious atmosphere of academe at the time, the
King was seen as the first monotheist. Scholars knew that monotheism,
or any radically different religious theory, has historically led to violent
opposition, even persecution. Akhenaten had, for instance, founded his
own city. It was 'obvious' then, that the pagans had forced him out.
Since his city had been ultimately destroyed and his name deliberately
cut out from many monuments, talk of zeal resulting in 'religious
persecution' grew, and came to be accepted without question. Akhenaten was seen as a man before his time, promoting proto-Christian
doctrines in a pagan, polytheistic society that was not ready for him. In
the minds of scholars he became the purveyor of heresy.

Odd pieces in Tell el Amarna were also found, naming a little-
known King called Tutankhaten Nebkheprure. It was uncertain who he
was at first. Once again, from the cartouche for his name, scholars
deduced that he must have been a king. In the temple of Luxor, fine
images carved on the wall of the colonnade bearing the name and titles
of Horemheb were found to have been carved on top of the names of

Tutankhamen Nebkheprure, while relief carvings showed the celebration of a remarkable Opet festival carried out by this King. It was at once inferred from these that the little-known King, having been born, named and raised in the religion of the Aten, had at some later point turned his back on the heresy and fully restored the religion of the old gods.

Meanwhile, in 1906, Kurt Sethe, Professor of Egyptology at Göttingen, had published a magnificent compendium of texts of the period, *Urkunden der 18 Dynastie*. This made all the known texts of the period available for study by all scholars, not just the texts accompanying pictures. It could now be read, in the text of the Restoration Stela, that Tutankhaten, who was married to Ankhesenpaaten, the last surviving daughter of Akhenaten (since Smenkhkare and Meritaten had disappeared), had been faced with religious chaos in Egypt at his coronation. Scholars were scandalised, but not surprised, to hear how Tutankhamen had had to restore the old gods and turned his back on the Aten. It could now be said with certainty that Akhenaten's monotheistic religion had upset the whole country. It could also now be seen that Tutankhamen, like Smenkhkare before him, had inherited the throne by marrying the late King's daughter.

Yet this Tutankhamen was an ephemeral King. It was found, for example, that on the king lists carved by the first Ramesside kings, the names of Akhenaten Neferkheprure Waenre, Smenkhkare Djeserkheprure, Tutankhamen Nebkheprure and Ay Kheperkheprure were all omitted. The throne, according to them, had passed directly from Amenhotep III Nebmaatre to Horemheb Djeserkheprure Setepenre. The mystery deepened. We knew those missing kings existed, but for some reason that very existence was being officially denied them. It was certain, if Horemheb could add all the reigns together and include them as his own, that Smenkhkare and Tutankhamen could have ruled only a very short time each. Since they were unknown in the city of Tell el Amarna, and never pictured with the rest of the royal family, it was inferred that they must therefore be related: brothers, presumably, both inheriting the throne because of their marriages.

It must be emphasised at this point, however, that nowhere, ever, do the inscriptions actually call either one the brother of the other. What hold, then, did Smenkhkare have over Akhenaten, that he allowed a nobody to become the next king of Egypt? Sinister plots began to be voiced.

It was in January 1907 that more information about the whole period suddenly and unexpectedly became available. First, Davies discovered the pit in the Valley of the Kings (see page 42) that contained eight jars, each with the name Nebkheprure (Tutankhamen) on its shoulders. The pit was in total disarray, with the jars packed around with wads of soiled linen. Inside each pot were the remains of a meal and a papyrus collar, stitched with petals, seeds and berries. Davies was convinced he had found the tomb of Tutankhamen. Shortly afterwards, he and his team entered the tomb of Horemheb. He had his 'excavation reports' of the two finds published together in 1909, even though by then, most Egyptologists were totally convinced that the 'tomb' of Tutankhamen was no such thing.

According to Davies, then, two more 'unknowns' had been 'checked' on his list of missing Eighteenth-Dynasty kings – Tutankhamen and Horemheb. Akhenaten was surmised to have been buried in Tell el Amarna, so no tomb was expected for him in Luxor. That left only Smenkhkare Djeserkheprure to be found. The discovery, six days after that of the pit, of Tomb 55 just across the valley floor from the magnificent tomb of Ramesses VI Nebmare-mery-Amen, excited even more attention. Right from the start it was known that Tomb 55 dated from about the same period as the pit, Tomb 54, since the outer mud door bore the seals of Nebkheprure (Tutankhamen). Inside, across the rubble-strewn passage, lay two wooden panels. Ayrton noted that one of them, covered in heavy gold foil, bore the name of Queen Tiye. The name was enough to convince Davies that he had found the tomb of the famous Queen. The artist Harold Jones drew a hand-copy of the carvings and the inscriptions. Davies, however, found the panel worthless, so he left it where it was, allowing everyone to walk across it until very soon it crumbled to dust. The passage led to a chamber, almost identical in size and shape to Tomb 62, the tomb of Tutankhamen Nebkheprure. In this, however, water had seeped into the tomb over the centuries, causing immense damage. There was a body in the tomb which had originally lain in a coffin, on a very low bed. These beds were habitually placed within a sarcophagus; but the sarcophagus was missing, and no traces of fragments were found in the tomb. The floor was covered with rubble. Only perfunctory photographs were taken, and a few handwritten notes. Davies' interest was in finding and then emptying the tombs as quickly as might be arranged in order to move on to the next. As the concession he held entitled him to a generous share of the finds within any robbed tomb, he could thus remove some of the objects and sell them to defray excavation costs. A unique golden vulture collar that lay around the neck of the mummy was one thing he took and presumably sold, as it turned up weeks later at a dealer's in Luxor.

The bed had collapsed, throwing the coffin onto the floor, and the lid had been jolted aside, revealing the mummy underneath. The existence of the vulture collar, which would have been placed over the outer bandages, suggests that the bandaging at this point was intact. It was noted that the coffin lid had been altered substantially. The bottom part of the lid was clearly royal, since it was gilded and bore the familiar *rishi*, or feather patterns, all over it. But the face on the lid, which seemed to be female and clearly came from quite a different coffin, did not fit. It had been cut short, and the bottom sections of the wig were missing, thus foreshortening the lid by two or three inches. A false beard and a uraeus – the rearing cobra, worn by kings and queens on the front of their headdresses – had been added. More mysteriously, down the front panel of the lid where the name should have been, a sharply cut rectangle of wood showed where the gold had deliberately been cut away. Similarly, gold rectangles had also been cut off the footboard. For some reason, it seemed as if the identity of the person in the coffin had been deliberately hidden.

The examination of the human remains was badly mishandled. From the available notes it seems probable that by the time the remains arrived in Cairo for examination, most of the unwrapping of the bandages and considerable damage to the body itself had already been done. Davies sent what remained to Cairo, via Weigall, as being the remains of Queen Tiye. A short time later, the pathologist Elliot Smith wrote back saying the remains were not those of an old woman, but of a young man. The age at death was estimated to be around twenty.

Scholars immediately set to work to solve the mystery of the coffin's occupant. None of the objects within the tomb really helped. A set of canopic jars, containing viscera of the deceased, bore lids with sculpted heads that were clearly female but seemed to be unnamed. Four bricks bore the name Neferkheprure Waenre. Two jars were found, a greenish one with the titles of Amenhotep III Nebmaatre, and an obsidian one with the name of the same King, together with Queen Tiye. Tiye's name, beside being on the wooden panel, was also found on a fragment of wood; while the entire tomb had clearly been filled and then sealed by Tutankhamen, whose name had been found on the outside. Since the body was young and apparently male, it could not be Tiye. Nor could it be Amenhotep III, since he had ruled for thirty-nine years. It also seemed that it could not be Akhenaten, since he ruled for seventeen years and was married and a father shortly after his coronation, although several scholars still, to this day, call the remains those of Akhenaten. Davies, to his death, refused to take any notice of the pathology report, and claimed it in his excavation report to be Queen Tiye. In any event, the body of an elderly lady, found in the tomb of Amenhotep II, has since been identified as Tiye on the basis of the lock of hair in Tutankhamen's tomb.

This apparently left us with a mummy and a tomb of a young man of the time of Tutankhamen whose identity had been deliberately removed. By a process of elimination, it was inferred that there was only one person it could be. It had to be Smenkhkare. Even though the name was found nowhere near or even within the tomb, scholars were almost united on the identification. The obliteration of the name of the coffin lid again excited much comment. It was clear that it was a reburial, not an original burial, since so few, poor and disparate objects were found in the tomb; and the reburial must have taken place in the reign of Tutankhamen. This made sense if it were his brother's body. But why hide its identity? Clearly Tutankhamen had something shameful to cover up. Evidently the boy-King had buried his brother, wanting the remains to be safe, yet fearing, for some reason, that if they could be identified they might be destroyed. Everything suggested that Tutankhamen must have been protective because Smenkhkare must have done something to upset popular opinion.

Against this background it is inevitable that when the first real excavation was carried out in Tell el Amarna by Ludwig Borchardt in 1913, there was a general expectation as to what needed to be found. They were looking for more information about Smenkhkare, especially what it was that could have caused embarrassment to his successor. But Borchardt's work was cut short by the First World War. In his time there, one of his most important discoveries was the workshop of a sculptor called Tuthmosis. There he found several heads, including the

sculptor's great masterpiece, the painted head, now in Berlin, identified as Nefertiti. In view of my comments, however, regarding the need
for accuracy and care in naming finds from Egypt, it should be noted
that the head bears no name. While the headdress is the one worn by
Nefertiti, it must be added with caution that we cannot say it was worn
exclusively by her. Since, for example, Meritaten inherited all of her
mother's roles in Tell el Amarna, it is just possible that the head might
be of her. In the same workshop were found a series of mysterious
'masks' made of plaster and moulded from life. In fact, they are not
masks at all, since masks must be concave, and these faces are convex.
Since they were in the workshop of the sculptor who produced royal
statuary, it was deduced that these must be moulds taken from life
masks of the royal family, used by the sculptor to get a realistic image
of his 'sitters' when they were not able to sit for him live. Scholars were
quick to identify them: an elderly woman 'must' be Tiye; a long-
chinned individual 'must' be Akhenaten himself; an elderly man 'must'
be Ay; and a sallow-looking youth 'must' be Smenkhkare – the first
image of the young man.

And so we come to 1921 and the start of excavations in Tell el
Amarna on a large scale by the Egypt Exploration Society (see above,
page 194). During the 1921–22 season, substantial excavation work was
carried out at the Maruaten, the Southern Palace, where, in the gardens
behind the main columned house, fragments of quartzite, remains of
small kiosks called, in hieroglyphs, 'sunshades', were found smashed
into tiny pieces. Many of these fragments were devoid of inscription or
were relatively uninteresting. But a few told a different story. Blackman, in his excavation report, wrote the following.

The personality of Akhenaten has made so strong an appeal to modern
interest that no new fact about him can be considered unimportant. And
from the El Hawateh (Maruaten) ruins we have been able to recover not
only a vivid picture of how the pietist King took his pleasures, but also a
new and unsuspected light upon his domestic life which he paraded with
such insistence.

Here, as elsewhere, the inscriptions, like the sculptured scenes, are of a
monotonous uniformity; the titles of the Aten and of the King are
repeated ad nauseum with the conventional epithets and praises, and on
all the monuments Queen Nefertiti was represented as sharing in the act

of worship and taking a place second only to that of the royal ministrant. But here, as nowhere else, the Queen's name has in nearly every case been carefully erased and that of her eldest daughter written in palimp-sest upon the stone, her distinctive features have been blotted out with cement, her features recut and her head enlarged into the exaggerated skull of the Princess Royal. This alteration is most thoroughgoing in the case of the little temple and the island kiosks – a group of buildings which seems to have been called 'The Shadow of Re' [i.e., sunshades]. In the entrance hall, it is limited to the more conspicuous places, but the intention is still the same. The ownership or patronage of the precinct was transferred from mother to daughter either during the former's lifetime or on her death. But Nefertiti, if alive, could hardly have agreed to so public an affront, nor would her death have been seized upon by so devoted a husband as an occasion to obliterate her memorials; are we to suppose that things were not so happy as they seemed in the royal household, and that a quarrel so serious as to lose the Queen her position, put an end to the idyll which had long been the standing theme of the court artists?

The discovery in the Northern Palace of considerable numbers of inscriptions bearing the name of Nefertiti sealed the argument. The name and titles of Smenkhkare were found after year 12. Clearly the huge royal argument implied by the palimpsest (overcarved) inscrip-tions on the Maruaten fragments actually happened. Nefertiti, the greatly beloved, had been thrown out, replaced by her daughter Meritaten. Meritaten was part of the conspiracy, since she later married Smenkhkare; and since Smenkhkare was described as Mery Waenre, it did not take long to put the links together. Clearly Smenkhkare and Akhenaten were lovers. Akhenaten had argued with Nefertiti, who had then fled to the Northern Palace. Since she was never heard of again, evidently she had died. Meritaten, then, either by choice or by force, first replaced her mother in the central palace; and then married Smenkhkare to cover up her father's misdeeds as much as possible. Smenkhkare had introduced his little brother into the palace. After the death of Akhenaten, Smenkhkare and Meritaten took the throne for a short while before being removed. Ankhesenpaaten was the only person left from the royal family, so she was forced to marry Tutankhaten, who thus inherited the throne. Later, having returned to

Luxor, he restored the old religion and changed his name to Tutankhamen. He then arranged for his brother's body to be reburied in the Valley of the Kings. Given the nature of Smenkhkare's relationship with Akhenaten, Tutankhamen naturally had Smenkhkare's identity deliberately hidden, in fear that someone may find, recognise and then destroy the body.

Now that the facts were known, searches were made for more evidence to back up the claims. It was soon found. A stela of Paser in the Berlin Museum showed the effete couple together, one pouring wine for the other, and tenderly caressing each other. A statue in the Louvre, strongly Amarnan in style but bearing no resemblance to anyone within the royal family, was also identified as representing Smenkhkare. Other attributions followed. In Cairo a coloured ostracon, or pot-sherd used for inscribing, of an Amarnan male leaning on his staff, and a woman offering him a lotus, was identified positively as Smenkhkare and Meritaten. In the space of a few years any painting, relief carving or statue from the Amarna period that could not be immediately identified as one of the recognisable characters of the period was captioned as 'probably Smenkhkare'.

It all began to make sense. And so in 1922, after these facts had been elicited by scholars, the discovery of the tomb of Tutankhamen excited professional interest not for the gold but rather for the information we might at last get as to his identity, and thus the identity of Smenkhkare. But of course, there was no information. Scholars were disappointed; and though strange theories were now put forward by 'fringe' scholars, it seemed that, within the field, the trail had finally gone cold.

In 1961, suddenly and unexpectedly, new information appeared. In his classic history of Egypt, *Egypt of the Pharaohs*, Sir Alan Gardiner added a footnote:

Recently published vases in the Metropolitan Museum of Art and the British Museum name a lady Kiya who is described as the 'greatly beloved wife' of King Akhenaten ... This is the first explicit evidence that the heretic King possessed in addition to his officially recognised Queen Nefertiti a concubine who was presumably one of many.

Of course, it should have been obvious. Meryre II is described throughout his Amarnan tomb as 'The Overseer of the Royal Harem of the Great Royal Wife Nefertiti', while pictures within tombs and excavation within the Great Palace had shown extensive harem buildings. Of course, every king of Egypt had many wives, and many of them were probably shown in pictures; but without the means of identifying them, they remained anonymous. Why shouldn't Akhenaten have had many wives? It had occurred to no one as a potential area for research, simply because the love between Akhenaten and Nefertiti was everywhere so explicit and so strong until the arrival on the scene of Smenkhkare. Now specialists began to dig deeper. From 1971 onwards, articles began to appear in journals all over the world in which the name, titles and images of Kiya were shown to be more common than hitherto suspected. She was now found to be described as ⸢hieroglyphs⸣ – 'the Great Favourite, wife of the King who lives in Truth Neferkheprure Waenre, Kiya, the goodly child'. Pictures were now found of her. She could be recognised by a distinctive wig, sometimes described as a Nubian wig, which was short but fell to long points at each side of her face; and she often wore recognisably large earrings.

Among scholars, the discovery of a second wife, and presumably more besides in the harem, resulted in questions about the nature of Akhenaten. The trail began and ended with Smenkhkare. And all at once suspicions were aroused. If you now quickly glance backwards through the earlier material in this chapter, you will find, time and again, the phrase 'it was inferred'. In fact, almost the whole of the story of Smenkhkare had been built up on a series of implications. Each one seemed reasonable by itself; but taken together the whole account relied more on assumptions than on archaeology. As Egyptologists became more sceptical, demanding solid evidence rather than 'purple prose', the archaeology of the Amarna period suddenly seemed filled with more questions than answers.

By 1973, John Harris and Julia Samson were both hot on the archaeological trail of Smenkhkare. Examples of pictures showing Smenkhkare with Akhenaten were now subjected to closer scrutiny, and Harris subsequently published incontrovertible evidence that, on the Paser Stela, the figure with Akhenaten could not be Smenkhkare. Although the two figures were unnamed, he pointed out that until the discovery of the Maruaten palimpsests, the two figures had been identified as Akhenaten and Nefertiti. It was only later, when scholars actually wanted to find Smenkhkare, that the attribution was changed. Harris also pointed out that a king always had his name carved in two cartouches, while the Great Royal Wife's name would be in one. There were three empty cartouches on the Paser Stela, proving that here was a king and queen and not two kings, which would have required four cartouches. Other reliefs and pictures were found to be the same. Ultimately, not a single image of Smenkhkare was actually named, while for different reasons, the unnamed ones hitherto positively stated to be Smenkhkare were brought into disrepute. By 1974 there were no pictures at all that could be positively identified as images of Smenkhkare.

Attention turned next to the inscriptions. Samson pointed out that after year 12 of Akhenaten's reign, the year that Nefertiti disappeared from the records, Egyptologists had assumed that her title of Nefernefruaten Mery Waenre had been adopted by Smenkhkare. Since Nefertiti had vanished in year 12, after that year it was reasoned that the names could not be hers, and must therefore have been given to her replacement, Smenkhkare. So wherever the title of Nefernefruaten Mery Waenre was found in the last part of Akhenaten's reign, it was published by scholars as 'Smenkhkare'. Yet the actual name 'Smenkhkare' very rarely appears in inscriptions. For example, Samson cited that there was not a single mention of Smenkhkare by name on any of the 45,000 blocks from Hermopolis and Karnak; yet wherever the name Nefernefruaten Mery Waenre appeared, it was automatically published as Smenkhkare, even though it was actually the recognised name of Nefertiti. There were actually far more examples of 'Ankheprure', the other title Smenkhkare adopted after he was crowned in his own right following the death of Akhenaten, and in many of these cases the name was actually written 'Ankhetkheprure' – oddly, as 't' indicates it was a woman's name. References in Manetho (see page 151) actually stated that a King succeeding 'Orus' (to be identified as Amenhotep III Nebmaatre) was called 'Achencheres, his daughter'. Scholars had taken this to mean 'Akhenaten', and put the gender down to the effeminate portrayals of him. But perhaps 'Achencheres' was actually 'Ankhetkheprure'; and perhaps this character was a woman.

In the light of these speculations, the inscriptions in the tomb of Tutankhamen on part of a box now needed reconsideration. In these,

'Ankhkheprure Mery Neferekheprure' appears in one cartouche; 'Nefernefruaten Mery Waenre' in the second; and 'Great Royal Wife Meritaten' in the third. Scholars argued that Smenkhkare Ankheprure must be male if 'he' had a Great Royal Wife; that the identity of the body in Tomb 55 was clearly that of a young man, to be identified as Smenkhkare; and that the coffin in that tomb, although made for a woman, had been masculinised by the addition of a false beard and a uraeus. In fact, none of these arguments is acceptable in the face of the evidence. Many kings of the New Kingdom appointed their daughters as Great Royal Wife without ever cohabiting with them. As stated earlier, the rank of Great Royal Wife was first and foremost one of state, and may be equated with that of a mayoress. A king needed a Great Royal Wife for the cults of the goddesses to be observed; and if that king were female, there was still the need for a Great Royal Wife, just as a mayoress would still be appointed if the mayor was a woman. The image in the tomb of Meryre II is cited, as we have seen, as evidence that Smenkhkare and Meritaten were married; but the mere fact that they are pictured together does not amount to evidence. On the reconstructed *talatat* from Karnak, Nefertiti is shown with Meritaten behind her in almost every picture, and there is no suggestion that they were married. The body in Tomb 55 was identified as Smenkhkare by elimination, not by positive identification; and the notion that only royal men wore ceremonial beards is untrue – Hatshepsut for example is frequently shown wearing one, and, despite her images, she was entirely female.

In other words, as Samson stated, 'There is as yet no valid evidence that a youth called Smenkhkare ever existed.' All the archaeological evidence was now suggesting more and more strongly to many scholars around the world that Smenkhkare Ankh(et)kheprure was none other than Nefertiti herself. After all, the names Nefernefruaten Mery Waenre were hers in the first place; it was only assumed that they were given to Smenkhkare after year 12 because Nefertiti had disappeared. And it is this disappearance that still perplexes scholars to this day. All sorts of explanations are given to try to get round the problem; and serious scholars still tend to accept that Smenkhkare existed only because of the disappearance of Nefertiti and the body in Tomb 55. Nefertiti's disappearance had, after all, been proved by the palimpsest fragments from the 'sunshades' in the Maruaten, as the excavation report had concluded. Once again, it seemed as if the trail was completely cold.

In 1976, I was a volunteer in Bolton Museum, working on the cataloguing of the Amarna material there. The ancient doings at Amarna intrigued me, and I spent many months at this and other museums looking at the smallest fragments of stone and pottery to see if anything had been overlooked. The Bolton Museum had made substantial contributions towards the Egypt Exploration Society's excavation of Tell el Amarna in the 1920s and 1930s, and in return had received a proportion of the finds in the distribution, once all the pieces had safely arrived in England. Because contributions had been made to the society from institutions all over the world, the distribution of finds was a complex business, as the society had to ensure that each contributor received finds in proportion to their subscription.

As I said at the start of this book, the Bolton material had been logged into the museum's day book as 'Miscellaneous objects: Tell el Amarna', and had sat there ever since. This was nothing unusual. Museums are generally understaffed, and sometimes years pass before a specialist arrives who has the expertise required to identify the objects correctly. So I had a massive job in hand, giving the objects numbers, measuring each piece and trying desperately to find words that would absolutely identify each fragment for succeeding keepers. On the whole, it was a tedious and repetitive business, enlightened every so often by a little find that made it all worthwhile. Baked terracotta moulds, used to make grape-clusters for decorating the palace, came out by the score. Every now and then, a fingerprint would adorn one of them, and at once the romanticism within me came to the surface. After all, every fingerprint is unique; and for a split second time stood still, as I communed with some unnamed individual who had died thousands of years before I had been born.

So I didn't expect much when, at the bottom of one box, I came across a pile of purplish-red fragments – pieces of stone smashed into tiny pieces, the biggest being no more than three inches long. Each stone bore some sort of inscription on at least one face, while some, presumably from a corner, might have partial inscriptions on two faces. Most of the sixty-one fragments were part of a larger picture, showing part of a sleeve, a foot, a hand. But a few bore hieroglyphs. When pieces are found during an excavation, any pieces with hieroglyphic inscriptions are given extra attention by the excavator. Copies are usually made of them, and published; so it should be possible to find these fragments easily within the excavation reports, whereas the less interesting fragments may only be listed under the umbrella heading 'miscellaneous pieces'.

I was not disappointed. Ten of the fragments bore palimpsest inscriptions. And not only that: I gradually realised, to my astonishment, these were the very fragments found in the Maruaten 'sunshades' upon which the whole notion of Nefertiti's banishment was based. The discovery of such supremely important fragments in a provincial museum in Britain was staggering. By rights, they should surely have gone to one of the major subscribers to the fund. And one look at the distribution list showed at once what had happened. During the distribution, the fragments had been assigned to Boston Museum in the United States; but the list was either misread or, more likely, the label on the box had been mistyped by an anonymous volunteer. In any case, the fragments had made their way to Lancashire, where they had collected dust for half a century.

On reading the palimpsests, it seemed for a moment as if my heart would stop beating; the inscriptions carved on the top were those of the Princess Meritaten, 'his beloved of his body'. But the names and titles below were not those of Nefertiti. They were of Kiya. Here was the clearest example yet found of the titles and names of Kiya, the 'Great Favourite' (⌣) of the King. Time stood still as I took in the enormity of what I had found by accident. For fifty years, if scholars had wanted to examine these fragments – the very heart of the identity of Smenkhkare – they would have applied to the Boston Museum, where, of course, no one would have been able to find them. Yet here they were – proof, if anyone had wanted to look, that Nefertiti had not been banished in year 12. The person who had disappeared, and been replaced by Meritaten, was Kiya.

The implications of these inscriptions is thus beyond any further dispute. The myth of Nefertiti's fall from grace was based entirely on these few palimpsests. In the original excavation report, the archaeologist had done what he should not have done: instead of merely recording the finds and leaving the analysis until a later date, he had gone looking for evidence to prove why Smenkhkare had come to power. Because he had looked for it, he presumed he had found it. In the 1920s, on-site conditions would have made it impossible to investigate the palimpsests carefully, and in any case, at that time it was presumed that Akhenaten had only one wife. The title King's Wife was clear – it was taken for granted that it was Nefertiti.

Now, the full sequence of the misunderstanding could be fully seen. The name Smenkhkare had led archaeologists to assume the existence of a male co-regent; they had then looked for pictures and found what they thought they were looking for; they had mistakenly published names as Smenkhkare when they were not; then the palimpsests gave them evidence for the disgrace of the Queen; and the identification of the body in Tomb 55 could follow without dispute.

But as we now know, the reality is quite other. In year 12, Kiya disappeared and was never heard of again. Presumably, she died, and her place was taken in state circles by Meritaten. At around the same time, Amenhotep III Nebmaatre also died, leaving Akhenaten, who was totally unsuited to the role, as sole King. Not wanting to leave Tell el Amarna, where he had comfortably cocooned himself, he had his beloved Nefertiti Nefernefruaten Mery Waenre crowned co-regent, giving her the title Smenkhkare Djeserkheperre. She had then left for Karnak and, probably, Memphis, to reassert royal authority where it mattered. Images there show she had chosen her eldest daughter as Great Royal Wife, and thus as her acknowledged heir. In the meantime, back in Tell el Amarna, Akhenaten's attention turned to the 'Great Favourite Kiya', who died very soon afterwards. After his death, Nefertiti took the throne in her own right as Ankhetkheprure, with the expectation that her daughter would succeed her.

For the first time, then, we can see Akhenaten as he truly was. Smenkhkare (as a man) never existed. Nefertiti was never banished. Akhenaten had thus raised the love of his life, Nefertiti, to supreme power – as might have been expected. In this, she was following the example set by the great queens of the Eighteenth Dynasty – Tetisheri, Ahmose-Nefertari, Ahhotep and Hatshepsut.

So now the mystery of Tutankhamen can also begin to be addressed. He was indeed royal and the son of Akhenaten, since he is never titled 'King's Brother', which he would certainly have been had he been the son of Amenhotep III Nebmaatre. This gave him unquestionable right to the throne when there was no one else alive. And it also explains why there is no reference to his parents, his birth and childhood, or his 'brother' in his tomb. His parentage was taken as read, since he was the son of the previous King, Akhenaten. The Restoration Stela was factually accurate: he did indeed come to the throne of his father. And Smenkhkare was not mentioned because Tutankhamen bore no relation to Nefertiti.

Who, then, was his mother? And, more important, whose is the body in Tomb 55?

PART THREE

THE REAL
TUTANKHAMEN

CHAPTER TEN

The Life of Tutankhamen

O ur search for the roots of the boy-King has been unexpectedly – and absolutely – successful: we now have incontrovertible archaeological evidence for the true story of Tutankhamen, and can recreate the events of his life and death.

But first we need to step back again, to the time of Tuthmosis IV. He was Crown Prince, according to his own words, the eldest son of his royal father Amenhotep II. As we have seen, just before his coronation he went hunting at Giza, where he fell asleep under the shade of the Sphinx and dreamed a dream. In the dream, he had a vision of the divine. God appeared to him and complained about the sand that had gathered around him. God identified himself as Re-Horemakhet (in Greek, Harmachis), an aspect of the sun. When Tuthmosis awoke, he hardly believed what had happened. He returned to the palace, 'keeping the secret in his heart' until later, when he was able to fulfil his promise and cleared the sand around the Sphinx. After being crowned King, he promoted the worship of the sun, on one occasion leading his army into battle with the symbol of the sun as his totem. He recorded the incident as 'going with the Aten before him'.

The King's dramatic divine revelation on the plateau of Giza had a profound effect on him. It appears that he felt himself 'reborn' or, to take the words of both his son and grandson, the very son of god. After all, Re-Horemakhet had said to him, 'Look at me my son Tuthmosis. I am your father.' In all likelihood, Tuthmosis believed this to be the actual truth. Some time soon after his coronation, he visited one of his lesser wives, Mutemweia. Although we cannot yet be certain, it is possible that she was a member of a prominent family from Akhmim in Middle Egypt. That night the couple conceived a child. When, in due time, his son was born, the story of the revelation must have been related to him from time to time, no doubt by Tuthmosis himself. As we have little evidence of her after the birth of her son, Queen Mutemweia perhaps died, either in childbirth or soon afterwards. Like many royal children, Prince Amenhotep would have been looked after and tutored by others. Among the courtiers who took responsibility for him, Yuya and Thuya were prominent. The former was in charge of the royal horses, the latter, from her titles, may have been one of the lesser wives of Amenhotep II who, after his death, had married again.

During his childhood, Prince Amenhotep must have divided his time between the many royal palaces throughout Egypt. Although Memphis was where the royal family spent the most time, they also lived for some of Prince Amenhotep's youth in Deir el Ballas, across the river from Coptos, where stood the temple of Min, and Yuya officiated at the regular daily ceremonies there. As a boy, Amenhotep would probably have been taken there by his father. Deir el Ballas was primarily a military, defensive building, the 'frontier post' that his ancestors had built during the occupation of the Hyksos 200 years earlier. Although still strong, the royal apartments were already old and in a state of disrepair.

Yuya and Thuya had several children whom Prince Amenhotep would have come into contact with regularly while staying here, whether he were related to them or not. Of the two sons, Ay and Anen, the former had both intelligence and ambition. Anen was later to be appointed Fourth 'Priest' of Amen in Karnak, rising to the post of Second 'Priest' before his death. Considering his blood-relationship to the throne, this is surprising. Such a rank could be expected to be filled by any official; a King's relative would be expected surely to rise to the highest rank. That he did not suggests he may have lacked some of the drive of his siblings Ay and Tiye.

The mummy of Tuthmosis IV, if correctly identified, does not as yet give us any clear indication of how this king died, save that he appeared somewhat emaciated. Kings of Egypt were well supplied with food, so unless he suffered from anorexia nervosa (and there is little evidence that such conditions existed in antiquity), he may have suffered some wasting disease, or a painful or debilitating illness that made eating difficult. His emaciation does bring religious asceticism to mind, but that would be reading far more into the situation than evidence permits.

Prince Amenhotep ascended the throne when he was only, at the most, seven years old. Within a short time – perhaps at the coronation itself – Tiye was married to the King and given the role of Great Royal Wife. The first series of 'news scarabs' that were issued at the start of his reign prominently lists the names of Tiye's parents – evidence that they were behind the marriage of their daughter to the King. Given their young age, it was most certainly not an affair of the heart, but was more likely coldly manipulated by Yuya and Thuya. Unlike any other royal in-laws in ancient Egypt before or after, the persistent listing of the parents' names in every inscription that named their daughter assumed them immortality and earned them a royal burial at their deaths in the Valley of the Kings. Yet there is no suggestion that this marriage was either forced or unsuccessful. The two concerned had known each other since childhood, and they seemed to have worked well together until their deaths.

The young Amenhotep III Nebmaatre was richer than any other King before him, and in any other kingdom of his time. He ruled over a vast empire bequeathed to him by his ancestors, and these conquered peoples remained loyal and peaceful, certainly in the earlier part of his reign. The King was served by many great men, among whom was one of the great geniuses of Egypt, remembered in legend centuries after his death. This was Amenhotep son of Hapu, in tombs frequently given the nickname 'Huy', and he took charge of the King's building work, which was to prove extensive. For the first time for many decades, large quarrying expeditions were sent to almost all of the workable quarries in the land – Aswan for granite, Hatnub for alabaster-calcite, Tura for compacted limestone and elsewhere for regular limestone. Improvements were made to the temple at Karnak, with the building of a new pair of pylon gates. Probably in thanks for his happy marriage, he built the exquisite temple of Luxor a mile south of Karnak, for the celebrations of the divine marriage of Amun and Mut. In here, carved reliefs show Amun with an erect penis, the so-called ithyphallic form in which Min of Coptos is shown. Coptos was Tiye's home town.

Directly across the river from this magnificent 'honeymoon home' of Amun, the King gave orders at first for a *maru*, or viewing place, to be built. Although little evidence remains to show exactly what this first building was like, if it was like other *maru* built in Egypt, it was probably a compact but lavishly decorated palace with uninterrupted views across gardens, fields and the river to the new temple on the other side. All of these buildings were originally brilliantly painted in vivid primary colours. Luxor, in this era, must have been a vision of colour, now lost to us. The *maru* was extended until it became the palace-city of Malkata. Here were palace establishments for the King, the Great Royal Wife, his lesser wives and his children. There were estates for each of them, overseen by ranks of highly paid officials who seem, from their tomb paintings, to have participated in a life that was a whirl of parties.

From the start of the King's reign, his afterlife was being prepared for. Almost at once, work started on his own tomb, and probably a smaller one for his Great Royal Wife in an adjoining valley – what was to become our Tomb 55. Amenhotep III Nebmaatre also ordered work to begin on a place for his offerings to be made after death, the so-called 'Temple of Millions of Years', or what we today call his mortuary temple. From the descriptions of it, it was covered lavishly in gold and precious stones, while its immensely high gates, fronted by colossal coloured statues of himself, dominated the whole of the west bank.

Once Tiye had reached puberty, if not before, the marriage between them became a real one and she began to bear him a succession of healthy sons and daughters. No matter what problems they faced, Tiye remained consistently loyal to her husband and to Egypt until the end of her life. The children must have been told about the divine revelation experienced by their grandfather, although how each took the story is impossible to gauge. Amenhotep III Nebmaatre undertook his own commemorations of the event. In the new temple of Karnak, he ordered a carving showing his conception when his father, imbued with the spirit of god, visited his mother, thus making him the literal son of god. He forebore to carve images of the sun-god he clearly revered himself within Karnak temple, although he ordered a great ring of more than 600 statues of Sekhmet, the divine consort of the sun-god, erected around the temple of Mut on the east bank, just a little south of Karnak. His loyalty to the sun-god grew, and he called more and more frequently upon the name of the Aten, the most powerful aspect of the sun at its highest point in the sky. He even named his new palace after the god. However, he remembered his state duty to Maat and made certain that all the other gods who protected Egypt were served also.

The King still carried out the rituals required of him within the temple of Amun. In the heart of the temple of Karnak he had a new sanctuary built, home to the state of Amun, where every day he carried out secret rituals that recreated the First Time, the time of the Creation – rites that ensured the safety of Egypt and the continuation of Maat.

We know nothing at all as yet of his elder son, Prince Tuthmosis, except that he was appointed heir to the throne by his parents. He was sent away from home when he was quite young to attend the House of Re in Heliopolis for tuition. While he was there, quite unexpectedly he died, and was probably buried in Memphis. His tomb has not yet been found. The younger brother, Amenhotep, was now the natural heir to the throne; in fact, he may well have been Amenhotep III Nebmaatre's only remaining living son, as we have no indication of any other. This boy had evidently taken the Aten of his grandfather and father strongly to heart, but as events were to show, was clearly unsuited to the demands of kingship. But the King and his Great Royal Wife seem to have had no choice in the matter.

In year 10 of his reign Amenhotep III Nebmaatre, master of the richest country in the Eastern Mediterranean, the man who could have anything he wanted, decided to extend his harem by marrying a princess from Mitanni. In this he followed the example of his father, securing continued peace and unity with his northern territories through marriage. Princess Giludkhipa arrived in Egypt shortly afterwards, dowry gifts having been formally exchanged. She brought with her a large number of female attendants, many of whom undoubtedly followed their mistress's example and married the King. The King had by now become quite a ladies' man, and letters show that he was on the lookout for beautiful women wherever they might be found, even paying for some to be sent to him.

Although it was the regular practice of Egyptian kings to have an extensive range of wives, it seems that by the following year his Great Royal Wife Queen Tiye was starting to feel restless. A news scarab of year 11 says that her royal husband ordered the cutting of a huge lake for her near her home town in Middle Egypt. A few days later, she sailed on it in the royal barge, named, once more, for the Aten, the King's personal and private deity.

Prince Amenhotep must have been an intelligent and charismatic boy. Many people clearly were attracted to his ideas, whether for the sake of the boy's zeal or for his character – or perhaps, more likely, because they knew that he would one day be King and would raise their positions if they showed their loyalty in his youth. Among his greatest supporters was his uncle, his mother's brother, Ay. It seems likely that Ay was genuinely fond of the boy and may have agreed with his notions about the Aten, just as, 2000 years later, Abu Bakr followed *his* nephew, the Prophet Mohammed. Ay and his wife Teye had several children, although it seems probable that Ay had been married before. This other woman seems to have borne him a daughter, but must have died in childbirth, since Teye is listed as the girl's stepmother. Ay and Teye went on to have another daughter, Mutnodjme. The two girls, Nefertiti and Mutnodjme, were close, and regarded each other as full sisters. It seems that Nefertiti was the more beautiful of the two, and inherited the ambition of her father and his family. They must both have spent considerable time with their cousins, the children of their aunt, Queen Tiye, and the King. Nefertiti became attached to the young Prince Amenhotep. Whether this was initially the result of family pressure is hard to say. In Egypt to this very day, the friendship of young cousins is encouraged, in the hope that they will marry one day. But it is clear that this striking young woman had more native ambition than the Prince, whose imagination was gripped more by religion. It is probable that in any decisions that were to be made, she would be the one who would have taken the lead. Partly brought up by her powerful Aunt Tiye, she thus had a good model of strong womanhood to emulate. Bearing in mind how she later treated her daughters, there is a good chance that she had been formally educated by her family, something very rare indeed for a girl in ancient Egypt.

In year 27 of his reign, Amenhotep III Nebmaatre presented his son Amenhotep in Karnak temple for acceptance as co-regent by the gods. The young King was given the royal name Neferkheprure Waenre, a name that seems to have been pronounced 'Niphuria'. We have no means of knowing if he had already married his cousin Nefertiti before his coronation. The evidence for marriage is, in any case, almost non-existent in remains from ancient Egypt. Clearly the two young people were meant for each other, since they shared a great love that was publicly demonstrated. At the coronation, Nefertiti was acclaimed as the new Great Royal Wife.

Inscriptional evidence (see below) from the Theban tombs of the period suggests that the old and new kings, no doubt aware of the schisms that a joint rule within one city might cause, agreed very sensibly to establish two separate areas of rule: Upper Egypt, based in Luxor, ruled as before by Amenhotep III; and Lower Egypt, based elsewhere, ruled by Amenhotep IV Neferkheprure Waenre. To this end, officials were appointed either to one court or the other; or in some cases, given authority to commute and report between the two. Two viziers were appointed, one for Upper Egypt, the other for Lower Egypt. At around the same time Nefertiti became pregnant with her first daughter.

Very soon after his coronation, the younger King was sent south into Nubia in anticipation of his father's coming jubilee festival. In year 30, Amenhotep III Nebmaatre would celebrate his thirty years as King, and his younger co-regent seems to have been authorised to record the great event. Amenhotep IV visited his parents' temples at Soleb and Sedeinga, founding a small settlement nearby where he and his men could live, near Gebel Sese, the site today known as Sesebi. Here he was free for the very first time to take total control and allow his deep loyalty to the Aten to show. Unlike his father, who did nothing overtly to upset the status quo and kept his personal loyalties relatively quiet, the young King felt no such restrictions. In Nubia he was at liberty to develop his ideas, to elevate Re-Horakhte in the person of the Aten. His theological ideas were still not fully developed. He had artisans in his new town represent the Aten as a falcon-headed figure, the traditional image of a sun-deity since the start of Egyptian history. The Aten was also shown on equal status with the other major gods of Egypt.

At what point exactly his theology developed more fully, and whether or not he was supported and encouraged in this by the officials who surrounded him, is impossible to say from the evidence we have. We do not know whether he was accompanied on this trip by his uncle Ay, but as the young King's self-appointed guardian and as Tiye's brother, it would have been remarkable if he were not there.

Amenhotep IV Neferkheprure Waenre eventually returned to Luxor to rejoin his wife Nefertiti and, probably, their first child, the Princess Meritaten – 'His greatly beloved daughter, of his own body'. The King was self-evidently an extremely proud father. He was already determined to do as his father had done, to establish for himself his own palace in a new place. His intention was to devote this place to the one god who had ever revealed himself to humankind, the Aten. To accomplish this, he needed to find a place that belonged to no other god. In the meantime, the jubilee celebrations of his father's year 30 were marked by eight months of joyous revelries and festivities, in which he participated fully. During these months the young King built extensively for his father within the temple of Karnak on the east bank. The fact that he had already told his parents his intentions to leave, and Tiye's determination to accompany him, can be seen by Amenhotep III Nebmaatre's elevation of his daughter Sitamun to the office of Great Royal Wife at the time of the festival, which would allow her to undertake the responsibilities of the office when her mother was no longer there. It is probable that these decisions were shared by both the King and the Queen, so that the highly intelligent Tiye and her brother Ay should stay by her son's side to guide and protect him. It was probably around this time that Tiye began to take a hand in foreign affairs, if she had not already done so before.

As soon as the celebrations of year 30 were over, Amenhotep IV Neferkheprure Waenre, now in the fourth year of his reign, sailed northwards to find a suitable place for the new palace-city he was planning. On his journey he was accompanied and supported by some of his ministers, prime among whom was his uncle, Tiye's brother Ay. Others must have included his architects, Bek and Men, and the twin artists Suti and Hor, all of whom recorded later that the King had instructed them personally. Swearing to 'Live by Maat', he encouraged a new style of art based on a grid of twenty squares. At first these carvings and paintings appeared distorted, almost like caricatures. They emphasised personal characteristics the young King undoubtedly had, but to an uncomfortable degree.

After sailing a little north of his mother's home town, he arrived at a deserted, cliff-ringed plain on the opposite bank of the Nile from the ancient city of Ashmunein. Here he swore on the first morning to build a magnificent city, laid out to the most modern design. He took a hand in deciding the plan of the city and designing the buildings. He naturally gave priority to building the main temple, dedicated to the Aten, which he modelled on the temple to Re in Heliopolis. After choosing the site for his own home and official palace buildings, the next available prime sites were taken by his officials. He appointed a full team of them to take control of the building works required, and no doubt instructed army commanders to take charge of stone-cutting and removal of materials to the site. Wanting the work to progress as fast as humanly possible, he decided to order the stones for the work to be cut unusually small, so that each stone could be carried by one man. There can be no doubt, whatever his identity or name at the time, that Horemheb would have had a major part to play in this work. The King founded a workmen's village at the back of the plain to house the permanent staff of builders, decorators and carpenters. The King decided that the following year, on the exact anniversary of his departure, he would return to find the city had progressed far enough to enable him to move in. It was a hugely ambitious target.

The King thus returned to Luxor for a time to tell everyone what he had found and what he planned. There was so much involved in building on his new site that much of the conscripted annual labour of the whole of Egypt would have had to take part in the building or supply in some form or another. No one could have been ignorant of his ideas during this period. In the course of this year, as they waited to move northwards, his wife Nefertiti bore their second child, once again a daughter, whom they named Meketaten.

The nature of the political arrangement between the two co-regents was uncertain. Throughout Egyptian history, co-regencies were always difficult for both partners. Courtiers would have to serve one king or the other, not both, and there would consequently be jostling for position, no doubt accompanied by threats. It is, however, intriguing to note from the inscriptions in tombs of many officials of the period that these people spoke of themselves in reference either to 'the King of Upper Egypt' or 'the King of Lower Egypt' – suggesting, in other words, that there were two distinct characters involved, not one. For example, Kamose, son of a man called May, and, from his titles, probably the father of May, who was head of security in Tell el Amarna, calls himself 'leader of the regiment Nebmaatre – the Aten Shines . . . royal ambassador and seal-bearer of the King of Lower Egypt'. Userhet (buried in Theban Tomb 47) says of himself that he was '. . . reliable for the King of Upper Egypt, honest for the King of Lower Egypt', and also 'the hereditary Prince and Noble whom the King of Upper Egypt loves and the King of Lower Egypt loves'. Theban Tomb 226, belonging to an unnamed *mn'y* (guardian) , describes himself as 'the eyes of the King of Upper Egypt and the ears of the King of Lower Egypt'. Similar inscriptions have been found in many tombs of the period on the west bank at Luxor. Is it not possible that they may be recording a truth? That the kingdom was quite literally split in two, with Amenhotep III Nebmaatre undertaking control of Upper Egypt, while his son, living in the north, not only took control of Lower Egypt but also managed all foreign affairs. This, of course, would be fitting for the King in whose jurisdiction the northern coastline fell.

The reason, then, that Tiye travelled north with her son may have been entirely political rather than personal. Her husband, Amenhotep III Nebmaatre, had avoided any difficulties by allowing two separate court establishments to be set up, each in control of a different area, with his wife as his representative in the other court, controlling foreign affairs. When letters started to pour into Egypt from beleaguered members of the Egyptian empire, which were under threat of attack from the Hittites, it may not have been the responsibility of Amenhotep IV Neferkheprure Waenre to respond. If indeed the control of foreign affairs was in Tiye's hands, then it would have been up to her to mobilise the army.

On his arrival in his new city, the first thing the King did was to change his birth name to Akhenaten, although the name by which the Egyptians knew him remained unchanged. His wife changed her name to Nefernefruaten. He also gave a full royal title to the Aten, giving him twin cartouches and thus kingship within the city. Since the King considered himself to be the son of god, he was thus carrying out true filial duty. Shortly after their arrival, the Queen gave birth to their third child, another girl, whom they called Ankhesenpaaten. Were they becoming worried that they may never have a son?

It is unclear what the rest of Egypt felt towards this radically different new couple. No doubt animosity was raised in some quarters. At any rate, the young couple felt under threat even within the apparent security of their new city, for the constant and heavy presence of security guards is shown in all pictures of the place. Who did they fear? One possibility was the Commander-in-Chief of the army, Horemheb, one of the most powerful men in all Egypt. As a professional army officer stationed in Memphis, he would have been eager to lead his forces northwards against the Hittites, no doubt wanting to cover himself and his army in glory. But Akhenaten lived only for peace and brotherhood, while Tiye presumably gave no orders. The only clear indication of work that the army undertook during this time was the cutting and moving of stone. Such work must have rankled when there were military affairs to be considered. Since there is no direct reference to Horemheb in Tell el Amarna (unless he was Ptahmay's son, Paatenemheb), it must be assumed that he lived permanently in Memphis; but by virtue of his position, he must have known the young King personally and must have visited the city of Tell el Amarna regularly. According to his own words on his statue in the Turin Museum, on one occasion 'the palace fell into a rage'. Was it over military inaction? By his later actions, Horemheb was a fierce patriot and supporter of law and order. It is highly likely that he felt Akhenaten's inaction treasonable. At any rate, the King felt need to protect himself and his family at all times.

Soon after they moved into the new city, the King began to reform even the written language. The spoken language of the Egyptians had moved far away from the old-fashioned language used in writing. He seems to have ordered that the language should be written down exactly as it was spoken, as we have here the first instances of what we today call 'Late Egyptian'. It seems that around this time Yuya and Thuya, his maternal grandparents, died, although we do not know who died first. Because of their royal connections, Amenhotep III Nebmaatre gave orders for a tomb to be completed for them in the Valley of the Kings. Both of the Great Royal Wives, Tiye, their daughter, and Sitamun, their granddaughter, attended the funeral and gave lavish gifts.

We know from letters that towards the end of the reign of Amenhotep III Nebmaatre, plague was raging in the lands to the north of Egypt. We also know that at this very time, Amenhotep III Nebmaatre was sending regular deputations to secure the hand of Giludkhipa's niece, Tadukhipa, in marriage. Was the plague carried into Egypt in this way? For in the traumatic year 12 of Akhenaten, which was also year 39 of Amenhotep III Nebmaatre, first the old King died, with Princess

Meketaten's name on some of his funerary objects; but then the little Princess herself died soon afterwards, aged around eight or nine. Presumably she was buried in the chamber of the royal tomb at Tell el Amarna that bears her image, although no remains of her body have been found there.

Now Akhenaten was in sole charge of Egypt for the first time. Although his mother was still alive and at his side, the responsibility for kingship was his and his alone. There was now an urgent need for a royal presence in the two traditional centres of Luxor and Memphis. Akhetaten, or Tell el Amarna, was far too remote to serve as an active head of government. What Akhenaten's reasons were for not going himself are unknown. The pressure for him to leave his city must have been tremendous at this time. If nothing else in his life shows his unsuitability for the role he had inherited, it was his refusal now to move to answer Egypt's need.

Whatever his reasons, Akhenaten decided to stay where he was. Instead, he had his wife elevated to the role of co-regent, and his eldest daughter Meritaten appointed Great Royal Wife to her. The two of them then moved away to reassert royal authority in the rest of Egypt.

It was at this point, no doubt, that the younger wives from the harem of Amenhotep III Nebmaatre joined the royal household at Tell el Amarna. From pictures of the palace buildings, there were already harem quarters there, but there is little evidence to show that Akhenaten ever took great notice of anyone other than his Great Royal Wife, for whom, as pictures and inscriptions show, he had a profound love. It is at this point that the King's Great Favourite, Kiya, comes into the picture. Who exactly was she? Pictures now positively identified as her show her with pointed features, a distinctive wig falling in sharp points on each side of her face, and huge earrings. There are two distinct possibilities. In conversations that I had with the Egyptologist Cyril Aldred shortly before his death, he suggested that the name Kiya had a lot in common with the names of the Akhmim family – Yey, Yuya, Thuya, Ay and Tiye. He thought there was a possibility that she was perhaps a cousin of the royal family. The other possibility, and one which I and others consider much more feasible, is that she was none other than Tadukhipa, Kiya being an abbreviation for her name, which would have been pronounced Tadukiya given the evidence of pronunciation on the Amarna letters. There are two small, but significant, clues that may support this. In the tomb of Tutankhamen there are two pieces – an iron-bladed dagger (see page 108), and a bracelet inset with a large amethyst scarab – that are of northern and not Egyptian origin. Both of them are embellished with gold granular work, for which there is no evidence in Egypt itself but seems to have originated from Mitanni, Tadukhipa's home. The gold sheath of the dagger has distinctly non-Egyptian hunting scenes in raised relief. Both pieces are too precious to be simple trade items. In all likelihood, these were part of a Mitannian dowry. Tutankhamen had no apparent link with Giludkhipa, but we know from letters that Tadukhipa arrived after the death of the old King, and married Akhenaten instead at exactly the same time that Tutankhaten was born; so the dates, if nothing else, seem to fit.

The boy Tutankhaten was born while his grandmother Tiye was still living. In the royal tomb at Tell el Amarna, we have already discussed the death scene of Meketaten in chamber g. But in the chamber nearest the passage, chamber a, there is another death scene, showing another lady, not Meketaten. The lady is seen standing in a distinctive bower, like a garden pergola, with columbine-like plants curling around the supports. This building, as Jac and Rosalind Janssen have pointed out, is recognisable as the type of place in which Egyptian women gave birth. So this woman has just given birth and died. Objects found within the chamber bore the names of Kiya; these objects were later to reveal her very existence to scholars. Thus the child picture in the arms of a courtier in chamber g may indeed be Tutankhaten, as he was at first called, but since the mother could not have been Meketaten, who was too young, it seems most likely that it was Kiya.

If this is true, then after Nefertiti moved away with her eldest daughter, Tadukhipa, or Kiya, became the King's Favourite, as her titles record. She bore the King a son, Tutankhaten, but died almost immediately afterwards. So Tutankhaten lost his mother at birth. Almost as if to confirm this, a tomb found in 1998 by Alain Zivie in Saqqara bears the titles of Maya, a lady described as the 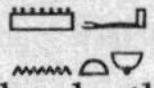 of Tutankhaten. Whether she was literally his wet-nurse after the death of his mother is hard to say. The title can, as I have shown, mean 'foster-parent' or 'guardian'.

One thing is certain. Nefertiti Nefernefruaten now had a rival for her daughters. By this time, she had not only accepted that she was her husband's rightful heir to the throne, being his appointed co-regent, but she had already decided upon her own heir, her daughter Meritaten. She even had another daughter in reserve, Ankhesenpaaten. In other words, she was well on the way to establishing a hereditary line of female pharaohs. While there had been several female kings before her time, most of them had simply filled a temporary vacuum between the death of one king and the appointment of another recognised male heir. Only Hatshepsut had been different, taking the throne as a woman but proclaiming that she was a man. In many of her titles, Nefernefruaten Mery Waenre did exactly the same thing, calling herself by a male name and so confusing archaeologists for many years. But the Gempaaten at Karnak, built after her coronation and following her return to Luxor with her daughter, makes it quite clear that she could see no difference between male and female; and that she fully intended to make the monarchy, henceforth, a female preserve.

Horemheb, the professional, patriotic soldier, now had reason to feel very alarmed. First Tiye, in control of Egypt's foreign affairs, refuses to order the army to march against Egypt's enemies. Now, with Nefertiti's ambitions, he is faced with the prospect of an unending line of female kings. It is at this point that he makes his own ultimate intentions totally clear. By marrying Mutnodjme, Nefertiti's sister and Tiye's niece, he allies his blood with the royal family in the hope of providing an heir to oust the female King.

But what of Tutankhaten? He was born after Nefernefruaten had been crowned and moved away, and was thus no challenge to her directly at that moment. But he was Akhenaten's son and heir, and if Akhenaten were to die, he would have had greater right to the throne than Nefertiti after Akhenaten's death; and his very existence directly challenged her intention to crown her daughter after her. Someone needed to protect the boy. From his tomb come two clues. First, the lock of his grandmother Tiye's hair shows that he must have been close to her as a child. Even though she died before he did, the hair was a touching *memento mori*, and he must have known her as a child for the hair to have been included among his personal items. The second is a series of five *shabtis* bearing the name of Nakhtmin. On a statue of Nakhtmin, now in Cairo Museum, he describes himself as 'the hereditary Prince, noble, seal-bearer of the King of Lower Egypt, great of praises in the Royal Palace . . . the royal scribe, commander of the army, Nakhtmin . . . for the *ka* of his mother, the servant of Min, the musician of Isis, Yuy'. Not only was Nakhtmin a colleague of Horemheb's in the army, he was also, in all probability, yet another relative of Ay and Tiye, since his titles, and the name of his mother, show exactly the same form as all the others in the family. The names in the tomb of Tutankhamen show that they were both very close to the boy. One cannot think of a better protector and supporter for the child than Tiye and her brother Ay, together with a relative, Nakhtmin. It is interesting to note that around the time of Tutankhaten's birth, work ceased on the planned tomb of Ay in Tell el Amarna. Various reasons have been suggested for this. But in all probability, the birth of a son and heir would have resulted in Ay's support turning away from his ambitious daughter and towards Tutankhaten. Perhaps he saw that the day would come when he would return with the little boy to the heart of affairs in Memphis and Luxor, making the completion of his tomb in Tell el Amarna unimportant.

The reference to Tutankhaten as a king's son was found on a block in Hermopolis, while no mention has been found of him in the Karnak *talatat*. This would seem to show that he was raised and recognised by Tiye and Ay's relatives in Tell el Amarna and thus kept out of the way of Nefertiti and Meritaten in Karnak. Yet his very existence must have been an ever-present threat to her and her ambitions.

From his tomb, the writing palettes suggest that he used some of the things belonging to his absent older half-sisters, Meritaten and Meketaten. Yet as we've seen, the palettes are virtually unused. The prolific number of bows, sticks and throw-sticks, plus the chariots, the hunting-gloves and the depiction of him on the feather-fan base chasing ostriches with his pet dog, all suggest he was an active youth more interested in hunting than in formal education, and more like his grandfather Amenhotep III Nebmaatre and his great-grandfather Tuthmosis IV than his father. So long as he remained in the tightly secure city of his father, he was safe. But when Akhenaten finally died in his year 17, leaving Tutankhaten, a child of five, the kingdom must have seemed totally insecure. It is clear from the inscriptions that, initially, Nefertiti Nefernefruaten claimed the throne as Ankhetkheprure Djeserkheperre, with her eldest daughter at her side. But their victory was only short-lived: for they both disappeared at the same time.

Without their tomb, any idea of what happened to them can only be speculative and unsupported by any evidence whatsoever. The fact that two people disappeared suddenly and at the same time must appear highly suspicious. It is highly likely that they were removed from office, perhaps even assassinated. If this were to be the case, then it was not for heresy that they were removed, but for their proclaimed intention to feminise the throne of Egypt. Egypt now lay between the hands of two devious, ambitious and Machiavellian old men. Ay, in the south, protector of the little boy who was the final hope for his family, and Horemheb, the Commander-in-Chief, with the army behind him and Nefertiti's sister as his wife to strengthen his hand. Whoever controlled Tutankhaten controlled the throne. The little boy became a political pawn in the hands of powerful players.

After the disappearance of Nefertiti Ankhetkheprure Djeserkheprure and of the Great Royal Wife and heiress Meritaten, Tutankhaten was taken under some protection to Karnak temple in Luxor to be crowned King, as his royal title shows. But the temple here, as the *talatat* remains show, was still dominated by the large precinct of the Aten at the rear. The destruction of these buildings did not take place until after Horemheb had been crowned; and since the Opet festival was not restored until after Tutankhaten had changed his name, which was to happen a few years later, the coronation took place in a bewildered environment, recorded truly by Horemheb on the Restoration Stela. The coronation itself was, no doubt, stage-managed by the two older men. After the little boy's coronation, these two men then made an unholy agreement, reducing Tutankhaten's role to that of mere figurehead, while Ay took the title of Regent of Upper Egypt, based in Luxor, and Horemheb Regent of Lower Egypt, based in Memphis. It seems that these two elderly men, poles apart politically – the one the protector of the King, the other the sworn enemy – had agreed to divide all real power between them. For the coronation, the Restoration Stela announces Tutankhaten Nebkheprure's intentions to quell civil disorder and renew the cults of the national gods. Only, of course, they could have been neither his own intentions nor his words. This little boy, only six or seven years old, was no doubt more interested in hunting than in political and religious affairs. Even if he had some little knowledge of the problem, his upbringing meant that he would know nothing whatever of the old god Amun; and the temple of Karnak had been 're-owned' as a consequence of the building of the Gempaaten. The little King must have been as completely bewildered as everyone else.

It is quite obvious that someone was in overall control. The words and intentions on the Restoration Stela were all Horemheb's. Later, when Horemheb seized control and became King in his own right, he took the words on the stela back again to himself by overcarving his own name. The intentions were clearly his, *not* those of Ay. Not only was Ay the brother of the deceased Great Royal Wife Tiye, and so had accompanied her through all the problems of the courts of Luxor and Tell el Amarna, but he had also been Akhenaten's most vociferous and lauded supporter. Pictures from the city and from his tomb show him receiving honour after honour, laden down with the weight of gold that Akhenaten awarded him. The euphoric testimony to him in his tomb, together with the carving on the walls of the full version of Akhenaten's hymn to the Aten, could not have made his feelings for Akhenaten any clearer. In other words, for probably at least thirty years he had been in the very centre of the royal family and had supported them even in their worst hour. His house, estates and tomb in Tell el Amarna show that he was one of the city's most important inhabitants after the King himself. Either he was the most devious, Machiavellian hypocrite who ever lived, saying one thing for more than three decades while thinking quite another; or, and more likely from what we know of him, he was the most devoted protector of all the royal family.

At Tutankhaten's coronation, then, the two men cut up the land equally between the two of them. This was an astute move on Ay's part. Once the boy had been crowned, he would be protected by the transformation of power that the crown gave to its holder. Once crowned, the child was safe. But first, Ay had to ensure that Tutankhamen *was* crowned, and that Horemheb, with his higher titles and legitimate claim via his wife, did not step in first. Horemheb was a deadly threat to the succession. By apparently plotting with the General and agreeing to share power with him, he effectively secured his agreement to the crowning and thus disarmed him. Once Horemheb swore to be Regent for the young King, he also agreed to protect him from harm.

The Restoration Stela says that after his coronation the young King promised to restore the statues of the old gods while 'in the palace of Aakheprure'. Gay Robins has identified this as being the palace of Tuthmosis I in Memphis. This suggests that the Restoration Stela was actually written there. It may mean that Horemheb took the boy to Memphis for a time. On the other hand, it may only show that the stela was composed there; and for that, Tutankhaten need not actually have been present. Memphis was the home of Horemheb. Even if Tutankhaten had been taken there by Horemheb he would have been safe: Horemheb would have protected him just as any loyal noble would protect the crowned King of Egypt.

Soon after the coronation, the large number of dated inscriptions in Tell el Amarna from years 1 and 2 suggest that Tutankhaten was returned there, probably by Ay, for his own safety. During this time he took Ankhesenpaaten as his Great Royal Wife, as one of the chests and the Golden Throne affirm. Around his second year, being then about eight years old – a little child by our reckoning but old enough, at least in ancient Egypt, to begin to understand – his responsibilities slowly dawned on him. He thus finally left his father's city, the only home his wife had ever known since birth; and together they sailed with his men once again to Luxor where, with Ay's help as Regent, he restored the Opet festival and returned the worship of Amun to Karnak. However, he did *not* demolish his father's great temple there, which, from its size, would have virtually doubled the size of Karnak. But his regalia shows him to have been even-handed: he restored the old gods without completely banishing the Aten. Probably due to a suggestion of Ay's to respond to public demand, he changed his name to Tutankhamen and that of his wife to Ankhesenamun. The people of Luxor would have loved the return of the festival and all the free food and drinks that entailed. In one swoop, the young King had placated both sides.

It seems that as soon as Tutankhamen and Ankhesenamun left Tell el Amarna, the heart of that city stopped beating forever. The restoration of the Opet signalled clearly that the King would never return to his place of exile. So the citizens simply left. Some probably returned to Luxor; some probably left the country. What happened to all of the faithful Atenists, those who had been drawn in by the charismatic power of Akhenaten, we do not know. They simply vanish from sight. Scholars have suggested that they drifted back to their original home towns and readapted to the old religion. But this seems oversimplistic. Seldom in history, when people have followed a charismatic religious leader, do they find it easy simply to forget all that has happened and revert to ways that had become anathema to them.

Now the young King and Queen, their favour restored, were free to enjoy life to the full. We do not know where they lived within Luxor, but undoubtedly the palace buildings of Malkata must have beckoned them and been in good order. Tutankhamen gave orders for a mortuary temple to be built for himself alongside that of his grandfather Amenhotep III Nebmaatre on the west bank. Surviving statues from here show it must have been as magnificent a structure as his grandfather's temple. Inscriptions from Gurob show that the young Queen stayed there, probably while her royal husband went hunting in the Fayum, like his forebears before him. We cannot be certain whether he had a large harem of wives, nor how uxorious a man he was. Certainly, as he reached his teen years, there was every likelihood of him having numbers of wives, as was the common practice.

At some point in the middle of his reign, Tutankhamen gave orders for the Overseer of Works in the Place of Truth (that is, the overseer of the tombs in the Valley of the Kings), Maya, to arrange for a reburial. It seems likely that he chose the tomb cut for his grandmother, Queen Tiye. Since her body was found later in the tomb of Amenhotep II, it is possible that it was placed there secretly by Tutankhamen at the time of the reburial. Wherever he moved her body in the first place, it certainly ended up there eventually. The body that was reburied in her tomb was presumably carried into the valley with the utmost secrecy, and with little or no ceremony; and fearful of its identification, the King gave commands for the names of the coffin and the funeral pieces to be deliberately and carefully cut out.

The nature of the epithets in the inscription on the front of the coffin lid and the coffin foot found in Tomb 55 can only refer to one person, even though the name was removed: Kiya. Even the spaces left by the deliberate excisions can only have contained a name as short as Kiya. The coffin lid was changed, a uraeus and beard added to denote her regality. Yet at the postmortem in 1907, and again in 1967, the remains were declared to be those of a 'young man'. In 1978, Pedro Costa produced an article in which he measured the frontal sinuses of the body in Tomb 55 and compared them with statistical figures from other human remains. He measured both normal and acromegalic skulls of both sexes. Although he declared ultimately that the body *was* male, the figures show this is not necessarily so – the heights of the sinal cavities fall exactly diametrically between the figures either of a normal man or of an acromegalic woman. When the X-rays of the skull were compared with those of the skull of Tutankhamen, they were found to be identical in every way. What is more, the bodies shared exactly the same blood group, A 2 MN. There is no doubt that they were closely related. But the skull of Tutankhamen is very far from being a normal shape. There is, thus, a chance of acromegaly here; and if that is the case, this would make the body in Tomb 55 female. There is one more clue to support this. The epithet of Kiya was [hieroglyphs]. The last two words, 'the young one', are masculine. This could mean that Kiya was a masculine-looking woman. If that is the case, then the problem would be resolved.

The identity of the body in Tomb 55 could be solved once and for all by the extraction and analysis of DNA, which will still be present in the teeth and in the long bones. If the chromosomes do prove that they are of a woman, then the body is likely to be Kiya. If, on the other hand, they are male, the problem remains to be solved. However, there is still one young man whose body is missing – Tuthmosis, the elder brother of Tutankhamen's father, Akhenaten. Perhaps it may be his. The hiding of the identification, at any rate, is a puzzle. Tutankhamen had no known need to hide the identity of his father's brother. It is equally uncertain why he should have tried to hide the identity of his mother, unless public opinion forced him. What should have caused this remains a mystery.

At any rate, even if the identity of the person is hidden from us, Tutankhamen knew whose the body was; and if it *was* that of his mother, it would make perfect sense. Kings of Egypt traditionally buried their mothers close by them, instead of letting them lie near their husbands. It would then account for the order to cut his own tomb alongside that of his mother. The tomb of Tutankhamen lies right next to Tomb 55, a few paces away. Despite what has often been said in books, there is no indication whatever that the tomb was ever intended for anyone else. On the contrary, its location suggests that it is the spot that Tutankhamen would have most wanted, next to the resting place of his mother. There is no suggestion anywhere in the tomb or on any of the objects that the tomb was even intended for Ay. Until he was crowned, his place for a tomb would have been among those of the other nobles on the hillside facing the Nile. His final resting place was close to that of Amenhotep III Nebmaatre, his brother-in-law; and there is no suggestion there that the tomb might have been made originally for Tutankhamen.

And so Egypt drew a breath and started at last after many years to find its balance again. But the troubles were not yet over. There is no clear evidence at all that the young King led any military expeditions abroad; but in the Memphite tomb of Horemheb, carved by the Commander-in-Chief and viceroy while he was serving Tutankhamen, the General is shown leading varieties of Nubian and Asiatic captives into the presence of his King. Did Tutankhamen order the forays? Or did Horemheb now make his own decisions? Whatever the case, the Hittites in the north were daily gaining ground at Egypt's expense, and Horemheb, judging from the reliefs within his Memphite tomb, objected strongly.

In all probability, as Tutankhamen reached his mid-teens, Egypt rustled in anticipation. A stela of Maya at Liverpool University says how, in Tutankhamen's year 8, Maya, the man responsible for reburying the occupant of Tomb 55 and for cutting a tomb for his royal master, was sent 'from Elephantine to the delta' on the King's behalf to collect taxes. Was it a sign of growing unrest? Or was it, more likely, that the King was collecting money for an expedition against the north? It shows, in any case, that the great riches of which his grandfather Amenhotep III Nebmaatre had been so proud must have been completely dissipated during the years of crisis, and that Tutankhamen had found his treasury relatively empty.

Whatever the reason for the taxation, no campaign ever materialised. Within a few short months, the King was dead and Egypt once more teetered over the abyss. Now, truly, chaos loomed, for there was no true heir to the throne except the widowed Queen, last surviving daughter of Akhenaten. And we can be certain of one thing. Queen Ankhesenamun would never be crowned if Horemheb had any say in the matter.

The King was dead. Long live the King! But how had he died? And which King would be crowned next?

CHAPTER ELEVEN

The Death of Tutankhamen

—

We have traced the King's life through the surviving evidence. But why did he die so young, and suddenly? That the death of the King was totally unexpected is shown at the very least by his poor and extremely hasty interment. The tomb is not what would be expected for a king of the Eighteenth Dynasty.

On his death, there was no one left to inherit the throne. He had no children to survive him. The succession to the throne was therefore open to the pretenders. The two most important men in the kingdom during his short life and at his death remained his two Vice-regents, Ay and Horemheb. Surprisingly, given Ay's royal connections, Horemheb's titles proclaim that he was the senior partner. He also, of course, had overall control of Egypt's army. It was not beyond the bounds of credibility that he would use his rank and his control of the army if he had to seize control by force.

It has long been suggested that Tutankhamen was murdered. The X-ray of his skull taken during his postmortem in 1968 made that a strong possibility, given Harrison's comments. The motive for murder was clearly twofold – despair over the state of the country, and raw political ambition. But who could have perpetrated the deed?

There is one thing for certain. If it had been Horemheb, he would have taken the throne afterwards. As the man who had the army to back him, and with titles that outranked anyone else, if Horemheb had indeed killed the King, Ay would never have stood a chance.

But Horemheb did not succeed. It was Ay who took the throne next. So could Ay, then, have murdered the King? Based on the evidence of a supposedly lost ring-bezel long known to have been in Berlin, it has been suggested that he did. On the ring, the names of Ay and the widowed Ankhesenamun are linked, suggesting that after the death of Tutankhamen, Ay married the widow and thus inherited the throne through her. Yet this ring was not excavated. It is totally unique, and came from an extremely dubious source. It was first seen in the hands of a dealer in Luxor known in professional Egyptological circles to be the purveyor of many items of very doubtful authenticity. Percy Newberry saw it there but did not acquire it for himself. He himself doubted its authenticity.

Ay had been known from his days in Tell el Amarna to be married to Teye; and in his royal tomb in the Valley of the Kings, this same Teye is still shown loyally at his side. Bob Brier suggests that this is evidence for a state marriage forced on the widowed Queen by the old man, who then disposed of her and returned to his original wife. But a lack of evidence is no evidence at all. It is far more likely, given the dubious status of the ring-bezel, that no such 'marriage' ever happened in the first place. For such a ring to exist, at least one and presumably more moulds would have had to have been made. It is totally inconceivable, given the exhaustive search for evidence over the last century relating to this highly complex period, that only one ring had ever been made; that then only one example of such a ring survived; and that that one should have fallen, quite by chance, into the hands of such a dealer. Ring-bezels bearing kings' names are relatively common from the New Kingdom onwards. It is quite inconceivable that not even a broken sample of the same ring should have been found before now. We can comfortably ignore this as evidence.

While excavating the capitol of Boghaz-koi, from the time of Mursilis II, a record was found in the Hittite archive. The Hittite King referred to letters sent to his father. Apparently sent by the widowed Queen Ankhesenamun in Egypt, it is said to have read, 'My husband is dead and I do not have a son. They say that you have many sons. Send me one of your sons and I will make him my husband.' Not unreasonably, bearing in mind the state of war between Egypt and the Hittites, Mursilis's father seemed not to trust the request. According to Mursilis, he sent one of his men to investigate further. The widow wrote a second time. 'Would I have written to you if I had a son whom I could marry? My husband is dead and I will not marry a commoner! Send me your son and I will make him King.' The offer was too much to resist. According to the Hittite record, Prince Zannanzash was despatched with a retinue of officials. But they never arrived. Ambushed on Egypt's northern frontier, they were slaughtered to a man.

In recent, sceptical times, it has become fashionable to decry the evidence as second-hand, untrustworthy and thus probably false. Yet Mursilis, in writing about relations between his country and Egypt as they worsened in the Nineteenth Dynasty, had no need to lie in the state records of the Hittites. After all, the letters presumably would have still survived. We must therefore take the account on face value. Someone, according to the account, was threatening the Queen, someone who terrified her and whom she called 'a commoner'. Using the evidence of the ring, many have claimed that it was Ay. But the Queen explicitly says, 'I will not marry a commoner!' This word is derogatory and refers to someone of the lowest social class. Bob Brier never states exactly who Ay was, but we do know he was Ankhesenamun's grandfather. Is it likely that she would refer to her own grandfather in such a way? In fact, there would seem to be only one person she might rank as 'commoner' or 'servant' – logically, Horemheb. But since Horemheb evidently did *not* murder the King, as he would then have succeeded him, we seem to be back at the beginning.

We now need to ask whether the King was murdered at all. Let us consider the forensic pathological evidence. The autopsy held by Harrison in 1968 was the first time any evidence at all regarding the King's death was found. In the original examination in 1925, it had already been noted that the King's head had been shaved, but there was no external sign of any trauma. The X-ray now showed up the thinning of bone behind the left ear. There was no fracture involved, although, as we've seen, within the skull there appeared to be a small fragment of bone. Harrison never stated where he thought this bone had come from, but in any case, pathologists who carried out future examinations all agreed that it was likely to be postmortem damage. It did not come from behind the left ear, where the bone was intact. The thinning of the bone could only have been by pressure from below – perhaps a subdural haematoma, a sort of swelling caused by blood, or something similar.

Damage of this sort does not happen quickly in the skull of a developed young man of around sixteen or seventeen. Neurological pathologists agree that after a blow, it would take between three and four months, if not longer, to thin the skull bone of a mature young adult male to such an extent. A haematoma in this spot would not necessarily have caused a lack of consciousness. A person struck behind the left ear would subsequently have suffered dizzy and sick spells, persistent though intermittent pains in his head, and probably interference with his vision, perhaps in the form of flashing lights, until finally the pressure would have brought about unconsciousness.

Let us then apply this evidence to the case in hand. If we consider the notion that Tutankhamen had been murdered, it then presupposes four things. First, the murderer had to strike his victim in the most unlikely spot, behind the ear and not, as might have been expected, on the top of the head. Secondly, the blow was not enough to kill the victim, yet the would-be murderer walked away without finishing the job, either then or later. Thirdly, since the victim survived, there was a good chance that he would have seen the would-be assassin and could thus accuse him. And finally, it means that the victim not only survived the attack but lived some considerable time afterwards. In all, it would have been a totally inept piece of work; and because the victim survived for such a long time and medical knowledge was so minimal in ancient Egypt, it is doubtful if the two events – the blow and the death – would have been linked. In other words, in Egyptian eyes, even if he had been deliberately hit on the back of his head, it is doubtful if his subsequent death could be called murder at all.

So murder is out of the question. No one could have made such a deliberate attack on the King's life and allowed him to survive without considerable repercussions. So could the King have died from an accidental blow to his head? We know that he enjoyed hunting. Could a blow from, say, a throw-stick have caused the problem?

At this point I need to repeat one almost insignificant fact which has seldom been used in the argument before. The king's head was fully shaven, and the only hair on it – a microscopic amount – had grown after he died. The Edwin Smith Papyrus, often miscalled 'The Surgical Papyrus', deals, in fact, with the treatment of traumatic injuries and fractures. There are several cases of head injuries cited, and the prognosis and treatment depended almost completely on whether the wound was 'open' or 'closed'. In some cases the symptoms appear to be the same, except for the state of the skin above the injury. Today we would diagnose the same problem and apply the same treatment in both cases. A fractured skull is a fractured skull, whether the wound is open or closed. But in ancient Egypt, according to the Edwin Smith Papyrus, if the wound was open, the physician would have to say, 'This is a problem against which I shall struggle', whereas if the skin was undamaged, he would say, 'This is a problem that I cannot treat', and send the patient away, presumably to die.

So if Tutankhamen had received a blow to his head, whether deliberate or accidental, the first thing the doctors would want to ascertain would be the nature of the injury. They would have shaved his head to see if there was an open wound, and where exactly it was. If, as indeed we know, they found nothing external, then there was nothing further they could have done.

If the King had been conscious at the time of the examination, he would have been able to point out the exact spot on his head where he had been hurt. There would have been no need to shave his entire head. So the fact that his head was indeed shaved completely seems to imply that the King must have been unconscious and unable to identify the exact problem for himself. The doctors, having shaved his head once and ascertained that there was no visible injury, had no need ever to shave it again. One did not routinely and regularly shave the head of a King without good cause. If there was no open injury the first time, then in the weeks that followed there would have been no need to shave his head again – the diagnosis of open or closed wound would not have changed.

Indeed, all the other royal mummies have their hair intact, even when it is thinning on top. In one case, a balding Queen was given a hair-weave of dyed string to try to restore her hairstyle. The shaving of Tutankhamen's head is the one most significant clue we have as to the cause of his death. If the King had been hit on the head and was unconscious, he would have had his hair shaved off. But we know from the thinning of the skull bone that he survived afterwards for many months. During that time, the hair would have regrown and there would have been no need to shave his head again. This means, simply, that the King cannot have suffered a blow to the head of any kind. Instead, the King was examined by doctors while unconscious, then died almost immediately afterwards. It may indeed already have been too late when the shaving was done.

All the evidence can have only one possible explanation. The King must have developed a swelling of some kind under his skull behind his left ear. The thinning of the skull could have been caused by the pressure within an artery building up, but was most likely the result of some kind of tumour. As the swelling grew, it would have exerted equal pressure on both the bone of the skull, causing the bone to thin, and on the brain itself. Tutankhamen would have known nothing of it at first. As weeks passed and the pressure intensified, he would have suffered pains in his head, severe enough to complain about, while his mobility might from time to time have been affected. Those around him would have been aware that he had head pains, so that when finally the King fell unconscious, they would have known to investigate. It would have been to no avail; there would be no surface sign of the problem. Once he had fallen unconscious, there would be little hope of his recovery. His shaved head shows that he died within minutes, at the most an hour, after being carried in for investigation. Tutankhamen, without any doubt at all, died suddenly and of natural causes.

The discovery of Tomb 54, the pit in the Valley of the Kings published by Davies as being the King's tomb, is most illuminating. The soiled rags found within the bottom of the pit, stained with the residues of resins, together with bags of natron, all show that they were used in the mummification process. The mummification would not, of course, have been carried out within the pit itself. But it must have been carried out somewhere nearby for the cloths to be disposed of here. This is quite unprecedented. After the death of a member of the royal family or a rich noble, the body would be taken first, and quickly, to the 𓉐𓈖𓏤𓉻 , the House of Cleansing. The flowers in the tomb and on the floral necklaces in the jars in the pit show that Tutankhamen died around March or April. In Egypt it starts to get hot round that time, and decay sets in quickly, so it would have been vital to act fast. The evisceration process, which involves the drawing out of the brain and the internal organs followed by partial drying in natron, is messy and extremely unpleasant. It was therefore usually carried out well away from people, but either in or near the mortuary temples on the

Nile side of the range of hills where the Valley of the Kings lies. No similar cache of mummification material has ever been found in the Valley of the Kings. We know of 62 tombs, and one of those, Tomb 5, in all probability contained hundreds of burials, so the odds would be very much in favour of having found more of such material if it existed. The only remains of a mummification found in the Valley have been those of Tutankhamen.

The evisceration and drying process completed, the body would then be transferred to the ⌐⌐, the House of Beautification. This is where the costly resins, the specially prepared bandages and the amulets would be placed, with due regard for ritual. This, no doubt, would have been a semi-public affair, where at least relatives or highly placed nobles would have been able to leave gifts. The rite would have involved many people directly. The thought that such a process should have been carried out in the remote and dusty desert, in the Valley of the Kings, is quite untenable.

If all of this were not proof enough of a secret mummification for the King's body, the X-rays of the skull of Tutankhamen show that when the final processes were underway, and hot, melted resins were being poured over his head and body, some of them entered through the nose, from the place where the brain had been removed. This is quite usual. What is more of a problem in the case of Tutankhamen is, as we've seen, that these resins, as they cooled, formed two separate levels within his cranium. The first, logically, is at the back of the skull. This pool of resin would have formed when the King's body was laid out horizontally on a table. Inexplicably, the second layer is at right angles to the first, inside the top of the skull. This can only mean either that the King's body at some point was suspended upside down by his feet for long enough for the resins to harden; or, more likely that his neck was still soft after the drying process, thus allowing his head to fall backwards off the edge of a table. On the whole, I prefer the second explanation.

This all indicates beyond any doubt that the mummification and wrapping of the King's body was both secret and extremely hurried. Clearly the first process, the drying out, had scarcely begun for the head to be able to fall backwards during the application of the resins. The eight jars found within the pit, Tomb 54, each containing the remains of a funerary meal for one person, indicate that at his burial there were only eight people present. Within the tomb, the wall in the

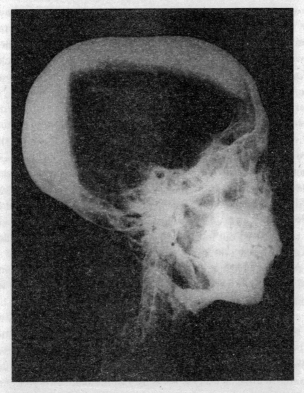

The X-ray of Tutankhamen's skull, taken during the postmortem examination in 1968, shows the area behind his left ear where the bone is extremely thin, caused by prolonged pressure below the skull. Also apparent are the two curious layers of resin, forming a sharp right-angle at the top and back of the skull.

burial chamber adjacent to the 'Treasury' is painted with the funeral procession, which shows twelve people involved, two of them the viziers of the time. Gifts in the tomb indicate that Ay, the Regent; Maya, the Overseer of Works in the Valley of the Kings; and Nakhtmin, the General related to Tiye and Ay, must also have been among those present. Both in the mummification and in the burial ceremonies, the evidence is not at all indicative of the splendid, ritualistic preparations nor public funerary procession that might be expected for a King.

305

Taking into consideration the fact that much of the material within the tomb was either broken (the furniture), out of date (the wine), wrongly assembled (the beds and the gilded shrines) or borrowed (the sarcophagus, the lids of the Canopic chest and the gold coffinettes within), it all adds up not to the usual royal burial of a relatively unimportant King, but a deliberate cover-up.

Let us try to understand the situation at the time of his death. When the young King died suddenly and unexpectedly within the palace in Luxor without an heir, political crisis would have loomed. There were two strong contenders for the succession, neither of them royal but both with strong claims. These were Ay in Luxor and Horemheb in Memphis. In Egypt, news travels extraordinarily quickly. Even if the news of the death had not been carried officially to Horemheb, there is every chance of him hearing by the 'grapevine'. We know for a fact that Ay took the throne after Tutankhamen. This means, since Horemheb was the senior candidate for the post, that Ay would have had to keep him out of the way for as long as possible. The evidence for the mummification suggests that this is exactly what happened.

It all suggests, then, that Ay ordered that the death of the King be kept secret for as long as possible. To stop news of a royal mummification being carried north, the mummification took place secretly within the Valley of the Kings. Since it had to be done exceptionally quickly, there was not time to prepare the King's body fully. The drying process was cut short, so the King's body was not hard when the bandaging and application of resins took place.

The tomb then had to be filled. How could Ay have done that without alerting his colleague in the north? It seems that, first, he acquired pieces that would not be missed – furniture from the King's childhood, for example. It would have been relatively easy to move smaller objects – the King's personal jewellery and clothing, throwsticks, and bows and arrows – without causing alarm. But the larger objects would have been more of a problem.

We stated above that the sarcophagus was too small for the King's coffins – that they had to be chiselled at the foot for them to fit inside the sarcophagus. The sarcophagus itself was clearly borrowed. The inscriptions on it have been shown by Marianne Eaton-Kraus to have been overcarved, the original name being Nefernefruaten. Clearly this sarcophagus cannot have been removed from the royal burial at Tell el Amarna to the Valley of the Kings at the time of Tutankhamen's death. In fact, it came from Tomb 55. The bed that held the coffin within the burial chamber of that tomb was found on the floor, the sarcophagus was missing and there were no signs to suggest it had been destroyed. In fact, measuring the length of the coffin lid from Tomb 55 proves it would have fitted perfectly within the sarcophagus in Tutankhamen's tomb. The gilded panels taken from the dismantled shrine of Tiye and found on top of the rubble in the passage into Tomb 55 would have been ideal 'sledges' for the sarcophagus and other heavy items to be removed and slid into the adjacent tomb of Tutankhamen. The lid for the sarcophagus, which was in any case broken, was no doubt found somewhere abandoned nearby and painted in a futile attempt to make it match the base. It seems from the original names on the sarcophagus that when Tutankhamen had ordered the reburial to be done from Tell el Amarna into Tomb 55, the sarcophagus containing the remains of Kiya, if that is who the occupant is, was found to be either damaged or missing, so that the exhumation party used one cut for Nefernefruaten Nefertiti instead. It is ironic, is it not, that Tutankhamen's body should thus lie for his eternity, until archaeology interrupted his rest, inside the sarcophagus of the woman who may have challenged his very right to inherit the throne in the first place?

It was probably during this reburial that the two mummified bodies of the infant girls found in the tomb may also have been moved into Tutankhamen's. There is as yet no definitive evidence that they were the King's own children. In fact, the odds are against it, as it is highly unlikely that the mummies of such children would have been stored against the day the King died. It is quite possible, however, that they are Princess Nefernefrure and Princess Setepenre, half-sisters of Tutankhamen by Nefertiti. There is no evidence of their surviving their birth for very long. Even though pictures exist of them, Egyptian art frequently depicted babies as children. It is possible, then, that when the reburial party went to Amarna, they also removed two tiny mummies that they found in the same place. When objects were being transferred from Tomb 55 into Tutankhamen's tomb, they were moved too.

Reeves has now proved that the Canopic lids that were found in

Tutankhamen's tomb, yet did not resemble him, were indeed made for Kiya, whose name was carefully erased when the lids were reused for Tutankhamen. The gold coffinettes were also hers. All these things must also have been taken for Tutankhamen's burial from Tomb 55. Interestingly, there was still a set of Canopic jars with lids within Tomb 55 when it was found. The faces on them are those of a very young woman – probably Meritaten. It seems that the reburial party sent to Tell el Amarna brought back with them as much as they could find, regardless of who it had originally been made for.

The removal from storage of the royal mask and the coffins must, however, have alerted suspicion. It would have been impossible to hide the death of the King for a moment longer. At this point, one expects that Horemheb should have made his way southwards with great haste to ensure that he got to the crowning ceremony before Ay. Clearly, he did not arrive in time, since Ay took the throne. In fact, part of the answer lies within the burial chamber of Tutankhamen itself. Painted on the long wall opposite the entrance into the burial chamber is a unique scene. It shows Ay carrying out the ceremony of the Opening of the Mouth. It has regularly been stated that he performed this duty as Horus did for his father Osiris, thus making himself the King's heir. But it is nothing of the sort. In fact, not only is Ay shown wearing the royal crown and the uraeus, but his name above his head is written within a pair of cartouches. He did not perform the ceremony in order to inherit the throne – he performed it as the next King, already crowned. This is absolutely astonishing. This is the only royal tomb in which the successor is pictured already crowned and named. By tradition, the next king of Egypt could not be crowned until after his predecessor was sealed within his tomb, the royal seals on the door being the last time they would have been used. Ay had broken this tradition and been crowned even before the burial chamber in Tutankhamen's tomb was painted. This is all the evidence needed to prove conclusively that Ay managed Tutankhamen's secret burial deliberately to ensure that he was the successor.

After Tutankhamen died, therefore, Ay arranged for the King to be mummified secretly and hastily within the Valley of the Kings, where none could suspect anything, while presumably announcing to the official world of the court that the King was merely ill. During this time he ordered minor pieces to be collected together to be placed within the tomb. News of the removal of the mask and coffins for the dead King would have spread along the Nile Valley to Memphis like wildfire. The King's body was put within the coffins and placed within the tomb with only eight officials present; and as the objects were being crammed in, painters attempted to paint scenes on the burial chamber wall, too hurried to clear up either paint drips or sooty rings from their lamps, and unable to gauge the scale of the figures, which thus appeared squat. As this was happening, Ay was secretly crowned, presumably within Karnak. To tell Horemheb – and posterity – that his position was established at the time of Tutankhamen's burial, he had the proof painted on the burial chamber wall.

What, meanwhile, of Horemheb? What kept him away so long that Ay had the opportunity to achieve all of this? No doubt he had eventually heard of Tutankhamen's death. But tradition meant that no King could be crowned until his predecessor was sealed within his tomb. And that gave him time.

The letters apparently written by the widowed Queen Ankhesenamun to the Hittites seem totally incomprehensible, given the state of war between the two nations at the time. It would have been unthinkable to make a Hittite prince the king of Egypt. And yet this seems to be exactly what she suggested. The only excuse for the letters is that she felt threatened by someone. Horemheb, Commander-in-Chief of the army and Regent of Lower Egypt, would have been aware of anything leaving Egypt and going abroad. No doubt he would have intercepted all the mail. The fact that the Hittite party was expected in Egypt and that it was then ambushed and wiped out shows that Horemheb, as leader of Egypt's military forces, was well aware of the correspondence and knew exactly when and where the Prince would arrive. Upon the official death of Tutankhamen, his place should have been in Luxor, claiming the right of successor. Yet at the very moment that he was needed, at the very instant that Ay was taking the crown from him illicitly, Horemheb was sent on a wild goose-chase northwards to stop Hittites taking over his beloved Egypt.

So why – if Horemheb was the 'commoner' whom Ankhesenamun feared, and who watched and monitored her every move – did Ankhesenamun write the letters in the first place? If she was being threatened it would have been sheer folly on her part to write to the very people that the man who was threatening her hated, and to invite them to rule

Egypt. She would have known full well that Horemheb was in a position to make sure they never reached Egypt. The knowledge of what she had done would then harm her position even more in Horemheb's eyes. She could have expected severe retribution for such treason. In fact, the letters are so extraordinary that I doubt that Ankhesenamun wrote them in the first place, or, if she did, that they were her own idea. I suggest the whole thing was a ploy by Ay, deliberately orchestrated to buy himself the time he needed.

The devious tactics evidently worked well. Down south in Luxor, Ay presented himself to Karnak temple and had himself crowned Pharaoh while on the opposite bank, preparations were still underway for the secret burial of Tutankhamen. By taking the crown, he was protecting the throne until his very last gasp for the family he had served all his life. There has to be a strong suspicion that Ankhesenamun was not even alive at the time of the burial, or she could have been the next ruler. In any case, her grandfather Ay would hardly have attacked his last surviving granddaughter.

So, while this extraordinarily devious old man carried out the last rites in secret for his great-nephew, he misled his opponent deliberately into believing that Egypt was under threat. Horemheb rode north to intercept the Hittite party. By the time he did finally arrive in Luxor, it would all have been too late. The tomb of Tutankhamen was already sealed and hidden, and Ay was already crowned.

And so it was virtually all over. Horemheb, loyal and patriotic Egyptian that he was, could not have attacked the living King, as this would have been a blow against Maat. Instead, he simply bided his time, knowing full well that Ay would die very soon. Ay, in fact, survived only four years, holding onto his son-in-law's ideas until the very end. He took no action in shutting down the Aten temple in Karnak; he may even have celebrated within it.

When Ay finally did die, Horemheb wasted no time in taking the crown at last. The old Amarna family was now all dead, and Horemheb began to ensure that they would be quickly forgotten. Despite the challenge involved, he dismantled the Karnak buildings and the great city of Tell el Amarna, until 'not one stone stood upon another'. He and his friend-in-arms, the future Ramesses I (probably to be identified with Rames, a man who was at Horemheb's right hand during the reign of Tutankhamen, according to his Memphite tomb), decided that never again would any of that family be mentioned by name. The names of all of them – Akhenaten, Nefertiti, Tutankhamen and Ay – were omitted from the official records. And in this lies, if there is any need for it, the final proof that Ay could never have killed the one he sought to protect. If indeed Ay *had* removed any of the family of the previous king, he would have won the favour and support of Horemheb and Ramesses who wanted to obliterate them from history. And Ay's name, far from being omitted, would have been proudly carved on the walls of the king lists.

From the time of his coronation onwards, Horemheb deliberately destroyed everything to do with them. Later, it was probably he who ordered the destruction of the tomb of Ay, his hated adversary. The body of Ay has never been found. Perhaps it too was destroyed.

And so, everything that told of the turbulent period and the family at the centre of it had gone forever. Posterity would never even know of their existence. But Horemheb overlooked one thing: the lost tomb of Tutankhamen. We know he overcarved his name on the King's mortuary temple and statues. So why did he not destroy the tomb also? Then the devastation would have been complete and this book could never have been written.

The tomb of Tutankhamen had, in fact, been entered twice by robbers, probably within months of it being sealed. In charge of resealing was the man who had built it in the first place, the Overseer of Works in the Place of Truth, Maya. We also know that Maya was at the secret funeral, no doubt one of the eight who had their last lonely meal together in the silent valley as the tomb was being completed, the remains of their macabre feast sealed forever into the pit, Tomb 54. In Tutankhamen's tomb, a little wooden statuette of the dead boy bore Maya's name, the final gift to the King from the man he had trusted to cut his last resting-place.

In the sixth year of Horemheb's rule, the same Maya was still in his office as overseer of the royal tombs. A graffito of his, scrawled on the wall in the tomb of Tuthmosis IV, shows that King Horemheb ordered him to check the tomb and reseal it, presumably after it had been robbed. Maya was the one man who knew exactly where Tutankhamen was buried; and he served the one man who would have wanted to know that location, in order to destroy it as he had destroyed everything else from the period. Yet Maya never told the secret. Against all the odds, the simple tomb of Tutankhamen survived until 1922, almost 3500 years after Maya had sealed it.

Tutankhamen had rested silently in darkness while the Greek and Roman civilisation came and went; while the Arabs arrived and converted Egypt to Islam; while Egypt yielded to conqueror after conqueror. When at last it gave up its secrets, it was as much a testimony to a friendship as it was to a king. For Maya, the man Tutankhamen trusted, took the final secret with him to the grave.

APPENDICES

APPENDIX A

Family Tree

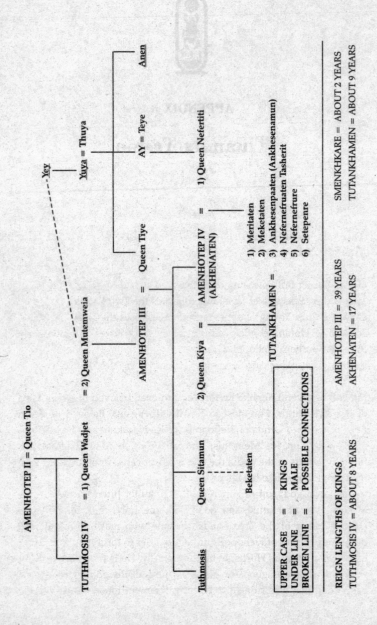

AMENHOTEP II = Queen Tio

TUTHMOSIS IV   = 1) Queen Wadjet

= 2) Queen Mutemweia

Yey

Yuya = Thuya

AMENHOTEP III   =   Queen Tiye

AY = Teye   Anen

Queen Nefertiti

AMENHOTEP IV
(AKHENATEN)   =   1) Queen Nefertiti

1) Queen Nefertiti   =   1) Meritaten
2) Meketaten
3) Ankhesenpaaten (Ankhesenamun)
4) Nefernefruaten Tasherit
5) Nefernefrure
6) Setepenre

2) Queen Kiya   =   TUTANKHAMEN =

Queen Sitamun

Beketaten

Tuthmosis

UPPER CASE	=	KINGS
UNDER LINE	=	MALE
BROKEN LINE	=	POSSIBLE CONNECTIONS

REIGN LENGTHS OF KINGS
TUTHMOSIS IV = ABOUT 8 YEARS

AMENHOTEP III = 39 YEARS
AKHENATEN = 17 YEARS

SMENKHKARE = ABOUT 2 YEARS
TUTANKHAMEN = ABOUT 9 YEARS

APPENDIX B

The Restoration
Stela

Year 1, fourth month of Akhet, day 19, under the Majesty of:

Horus: Strong Bull, pleasing of Births
Two Ladies: Effective of laws, who placates the Two Lands
Golden Horus: Young of appearance, who pleases the gods
Son of Re: (Horemheb, Beloved of Amen) [carved over 'Tutankhamen, Ruler of Southern Heliopolis']
Insibya: (Djeserkheprure Setepenre) [carved over 'Nebkheprure']

May he be given Life, like Re forever and ever, Beloved of Amen Lord of the Two Lands, Foremost in Karnak (Ipet-esut), Beloved of Atum Lord of the Two Lands of Heliopolis; of Re-Horakhte and Ptah-south-of-his-wall, Lord of Memphis; and of Thoth, Lord of Hieroglyphs [literally, words of the gods] the one who appeared upon the throne of the living Horus, like his father Re.

The good god, son of Amen, son of Kamutef [literally, Bull-of-his-Mother, title of Horus], the good son, the holy egg whom Amen created, father of the Two Lands, the one who makes the one who made him, the *ba*s of Heliopolis united in order to form him, to be King forever and ever, as Horus, living immortally. He is the effective King who did what was good for his father and all the gods. He restored everything that was ruined, to be his monument forever and ever. He has vanquished chaos from the whole land and has restored Maat to her place. He has made lying a crime, the whole land being made as it was at the time of Creation.

Now when his Majesty was crowned King the temples and the estates of the gods and goddesses from Elephantine as far as the swamps of Lower Egypt had fallen into ruin. Their shrines had fallen down, turned into piles of rubble and overgrown with weeds. Their sanctuaries were as if they had never existed at all. Their temples had become footpaths. The world was in chaos and the gods had turned their backs on this land. If an army was sent to Djahy to extend the boundaries of Egypt, it would have no success. If you asked a god for advice, he would not attend; and if one spoke to a goddess likewise she would not attend. Hearts were faint in bodies because everything that had been, was destroyed.

Now some days after this His Majesty appeared upon the throne of his father and he ruled the 'Two Banks of Horus' [Egypt], the Black Land and the Red Land being under his authority and every land bowed down before his might. Now His Majesty was in his palace which was in the House of Aakheperkare, being like the Sun in the sky, and His Majesty carried out the works of this land and everything the Two Lands needed every day. Then His Majesty considered in his heart and looked for something which would be effective for his father Amen. He made the holy statue out of genuine electrum, giving to it more than had been done before. He made his father Amen 13 poles long, the holy statue being made of electrum, lapis lazuli, turquoise and every noble and precious stone, although the Majesty of this holy god had only been 11 poles long before. He also made Ptah-south-of-his-wall, Lord of Memphis, his holy statue of electrum, 11 poles long, the holy statue being made of electrum, lapis lazuli, turquoise and every noble and precious stone, when the Majesty of this noble god had been only 7 poles long before. His Majesty made monuments for the gods, making their statues from electrum from the tribute of the foreign lands. He renewed their sanctuaries as his monuments forever and ever, endowing them with offerings forever, laying aside for them divine offerings daily, laying aside bread from the earth. He added great wealth on top of that which existed before, doing more than his predecessors had ever done. He allocated *waab*-priests, God's Servants and the heirs of the Chiefs of the Cities to be the sons of wise men whose reputation is established. He has enriched their tables with gold and silver, bronze and copper without limit. He has filled their storehouses with male and female workers and with His Majesty's booty. He has added to the wealth of every temple, doubling, trebling and quadrupling the silver, gold, lapis lazuli, turquoise and every noble and precious stone, together with byssus, white linen, ordinary linen, oil, fat, resin, 𓎡𓏤𓎼𓏤 [incense or possibly a narcotic drug], perfumes and myrrh without limit.

His Majesty, Life Prosperity Health, has made quays for the river from new wood from the hill-slopes from the pick of Negau, inlaid with gold, the tribute of foreign countries, so that they might decorate the river. His Majesty, Life Prosperity Health, picked male and female servants, musicians and dancers who had been women of the palace, their cost being charged to the palace and to the treasury of the Two Lands. I shall have them protected and guarded for my ancestors, the gods, in the hope that they will be contented, by doing what their *kas* wish while they protect Egypt.

Now the gods and goddesses of this land are rejoicing in their hearts, the Lords of the temples are in joy, the provinces all rejoice and celebrate throughout this whole land because good has come back into existence. The Ennead [the nine gods of Luxor] in the temple, their arms are raised in adoration, their hands are filled with jubilees forever and ever. All life and might is with them, and it is for the nose of the mighty King Horus, repeater of births, beloved son of his father Amen Lord of the gods, who made the one who made him, the King of Upper and Lower Egypt, his eldest son, the true and beloved one who protects his father who begot him. His Kingship is that of his father Osiris son of Re, the son who is good to the one who begot him, plentiful in monuments, rich in wonders, the one who makes an accurate monument for his father Amen, fair of births, the King who has established Egypt.

APPENDIX C

The Scarabs of Amenhotep III

Series 1

Long live: Horus, Strong Bull, Appearing in Truth
Two Ladies: the one who establishes laws and pacifies the Two Lands
Golden Horus: Mighty of Strong-Arm who subdues Asiatics
Insibya: Nebmaatre
Son of Re: Amenhotep Ruler of Luxor.

The Great Royal Wife Tiye, may she live long.
The name of her father is Yuya,
The name of her mother is Thuya.
She is the wife of a mighty King. His southern boundary is at Karoi,
   his northern one is Naharin.

Series 2

Year 2, under the Majesty of [titles as above, Series 1]
Great Royal Wife Tiye, may she live.

The wonders that have happened to His Majesty. His Majesty was informed 'There are wild bulls in the desert in the district of the Fayum' so His Majesty sailed north on the ship 'Rising-in-Truth' by night. A good journey started, he arrived safely in the Fayum in the morning. Then His Majesty appeared upon his chariot, the entire army behind him, the officers and men of the whole army and the young men with them were commanded to watch over the wild bulls. Then His Majesty gave orders that the bulls be rounded up into an enclosure with a ditch. Then His Majesty rode out against these wild bulls, the number being 170 wild bulls. The total which His Majesty took on the hunt on this day – fifty-six bulls. His Majesty waited four days to give rest to his horses and then His Majesty appeared again on his chariot. The number of bulls which he took on the hunt – forty wild bulls. Total number of bulls ninety-four.

Series 3

[Titles as Series 1]
Great Royal Wife Tiye, may she live.

The number of wild lions which His Majesty took with his own shooting, starting from year 1 down to year 10 – 102 wild lions.

Series 4

Year 10 under the Majesty of [titles as Series 1]
The Great Royal Wife Tiye, may she live.
The name of her father is Yuya,
The name of her mother is Thuya.
The wonders that were brought to His Majesty (life, prosperity, health).
The daughter of Shutarna, King of Naharin – Giludkhipa.
Women of her household – 317 women.

Series 5

Year 11, 3rd month of Inundation day 1 under the Majesty of [titles as Series 1]
The Great Royal Wife Tiye, may she live.

His Majesty commanded the making of a lake for the Great Royal Wife Tiye in her town of Djarukha. Its length is 3700 cubits, its width 700 cubits. His Majesty celebrated the opening of the lake in the 3rd month of Inundation, day 16, when His Majesty was carried in the royal ship 'Aten Shines'.

APPENDIX D

The Dream Stela

———

The King: King of Upper and Lower Egypt, Lord of the Two Lands, Menkheprure Tuthmosis Appearing in Crowns[?], given life

Making [an offering of?] divine water

The Sphinx; Horemakhet

Words spoken: I have given life and power to the Lord of the Two Lands Tuthmosis Appearing in Crowns

Words spoken by the Sphinx: I have given power to the Lord of the Two Lands, Son of Re; Tuthmosis, may he be given life.

[Left:] Giving honour using a *nemset*, or , pot

Given life stability and power like Re

Words spoken: I have given power to the Lord of the Two Lands Tuthmosis Appearing in Crowns.

[Between the two inscriptions:] Words to be spoken; I have caused Menkheprure to appear upon the throne of Geb; Tuthmosis Appearing in Crowns, in the Office of Atum.

Year I, month 3 of Inundation season, day 19 under the Majesty of:
Horus: Mighty Bull – perfect of crowns
Nebty: Established in kingship like Atum
Golden Horus: Strong with power, the one who has defeated the Nine Bows.

Insibya: Menkheprure
Son of Re: Tuthmosis

Appearing in Crowns, Beloved of Horemakhet;

Given life, stability, power, like Re forever.

May the Good God live, son of Atum,
The protector of Horakhte,
Living image of Lord-of-All;
A King whom Re brought into existence;
The powerful offspring of Kepri
As beautiful of features as his father,
Perfect likeness who came forth in his forms of Horus as first-born,
King of Upper and Lower Egypt, beloved of the gods,
The Lord of dignity among the Ennead,
The one who purifies Heliopolis and pacifies Re,
The one who has renewed the temple of Ptah,
The one who has given Maat to Atum,
Who has given it to the One-south-of-his-wall;
The one who has erected monuments of offerings to Horus
Who created everything that exists;
The one who seeks out for that which benefits the gods of Upper and
    Lower Egypt
The one who has built temples out of fine stone
Who has renewed all their offerings,
The son of Atum, of his own body
Tuthmosis, Appearing in Crowns, like Re,
The offspring of Horus on his throne
Menkheprure, given life.

Now when his Majesty was still a royal child like Horus in the [Marsh of the King?], his beauty was like a protection [consolation?] for his father. Everyone looked at him as if he were the god himself. The army rejoiced for love of him. All the royal children and all the courtiers were under his might because he flourished. He repeated his daily custom [?], his power being like that of Nut's son.

Now he would take his pleasure, he would keep fit in the desert of Memphis, on both north and south sides, shooting at a target of copper and hunting wild lions and wild animals while riding in his chariot. His horses were faster than the wind, along with one of his followers while no man could see them.

Now it so happened that he used to allow his follower to rest near the wonderful monument of Horemakhet, the one which is close to Sokar of Rostaw, to Renenutet of Tamut near the pyramid, to Mut, Lady-north-of-the-wall and South-of-the-wall, to Sekhmet, greatest one of the desert; to Seth, elder of magic, the sacred place of the First Occasion in the region of the Lord of Kheraha and to the holy way of the gods of the Horizon west of Heliopolis.

Now the statue of Khepri, the very great one lay in this place, the one great in power, sacred in mysteries, and the shadow of the sun fell in front of it. Now the citizens of Memphis and every other town which neighboured it used to come out to it, their arms raised to venerate his face, bringing a great many offerings for his *ka*.

Now it happened one day that Prince Tuthmosis set out galloping at the time of noon. He relaxed in the shadow of this great god and sleep overcame him just at the time that the sun was at its height. Then he discovered the Majesty of this Great God was speaking out of his very own mouth, just as a father addresses his son, saying, 'Look at me, gaze at me, my own son Tuthmosis! I am your father, Horemakhet Kepri Re Atum who gives you kingship on earth over the living. You shall wear its White Crown and its Red Crown on the throne of Geb the King's Son. To you shall belong the land, its length and breadth, all that the Eye of the Lord-of-all illumines. All the growing things from the land shall be yours; all the great tribute of every foreign land. Yours shall be a reign of many years [literally, great in years].

I look to you, my heart is yours; you belong to me. My state is that of one in trouble, all my limbs are broken and the desert sand is covering the place in which I sit. I have waited to have you carry out that which is in my heart for I know you, saying, 'You are my son and my protector. So come nearer! I am with you and I am your adviser!'

He ended these words. At this the Prince was amazed when he had heard these [words?] . . . He understood the words of the god, but he kept them secret in his heart, saying instead, 'Come, let us go to our palace and let us give offerings for this god! Let us bring cattle, plants and all kinds of offerings for him, let us give praises to those who have gone before us.

325

The Great Hymn to the Aten

Splendid you rise in heaven's lightland,
O living Aten, creator of life!
When you have dawned in eastern lightland,
You fill every land with your beauty.
You are beauteous, great, radiant,
High over every land;
Your rays embrace the lands,
To the limit of all that you made.
Being Re, you reach their limits,
You bend them [for] the son whom you love;
Though you are far, your rays are on earth,
Though one sees you, your strides are unseen.

When you set in western lightland,
Earth is in darkness as if in death;
One sleeps in chambers, heads covered,
One eye does not see another.
Were they robbed of their goods,
That are under their heads,
People would not remark it.
Every lion comes from its den,
All the serpents bite;
Darkness hovers, earth is silent,
As their maker rests in lightland.

Earth brightens when you dawn in lightland,
When you shine as Aten of daytime;
As you dispel the dark,
As you cast your rays,
The Two Lands are in festivity.
Awake, they stand on their feet,
You have roused them;
Bodies cleansed, clothed,
Their arms adore your appearance.
The entire land sets out to work,
All beasts browse on their herbs;
Trees, herbs are sprouting,
Birds fly from their nests,
Their wings greeting your *kà*.
All flocks frisk on their feet,
All that fly up and alight,
They live when you dawn for them.
Ships fare north, fare south as well,
Roads lie open when you rise;
The fish in the river dart before you,
Your rays are in the midst of the sea.

Who makes seed grow in women,
Who creates people from sperm;
Who feeds the son in his mother's womb,
Who soothes him to still his tears.
Nurse in the womb,
Giver of birth,
To nourish all that he made.
When he comes from the womb to breathe,
On the day of his birth,
You open wide his mouth,
When the chick in the egg speaks in the shell,
You give him breath within to sustain him;
When you have made him complete,
To break out from the egg,
He comes out from the egg,
To announce his completion,

327

Walking on his legs he comes from it.

How many are your deeds,
Though hidden from sight,
O Sole God beside whom there is none!
You made the earth as you wished, you alone,
All peoples, herds, and flocks;
All upon earth that walk on legs,
All on high that fly on wings,
The land of Khor and Kush,
The land of Egypt.
You set every man in his place,
You supply their needs;
Everyone has his food,
His lifetime is counted.
Their tongues differ in speech,
Their characters likewise;
Their skins are distinct,
For you distinguished the peoples.
You made Hapy in *duat*,
You bring him when you will.
To nourish the people,
For you made them for yourself.
Lord of all who toils for them,
Lord of all lands who shines for them,
Aten of daytime, great in glory!
All distant lands, you make them live,
You made a heavenly Hapy descend for them;
He makes waves in the mountains like the sea,
To drench their fields and their towns.
How excellent are your ways, O Lord of eternity!
A Hapy from heaven for foreign peoples,
And all lands' creatures that walk on legs,
For Egypt the Hapy who comes from *duat*.

Your rays nurse all fields,
When you shine, they live, they grow for you;
You made the seasons to foster all that you made,

Winter to cool them, heat that they taste you.
You made the far sky to shine therein,
To behold all that you made;
You alone, shining in your form of living Aten,
Risen, radiant, distant, near.
You made millions of forms from yourself alone,
Towns, villages, fields, the river's course;
All eyes observe you upon them,
For you are the Aten of daytime on high.
You are in my heart,
There is no other who knows you,
Only our son, Neferkheprure Waenre,
Whom you have taught your ways and your might.
[Those on] earth come from your hand as you made them,
When you have dawned they live,
When you set they die;
You yourself are lifetime, one lives by you.
All eyes on [your] beauty until you set,
All labour ceases when you rest in the west;
When you rise you stir [everyone] for the King,
Every leg is on the move since you founded the earth.
You rouse them for your son who came from your body,
The King who lives by Maat, the Lord of the Two Lands,
Neferkheprure Waenre,
The son of Re who lives by Maat, the Lord of crowns,
Akhenaten, great in his lifetime;
[And] the great Queen whom he loves, the Lady of the Two Lands,
Nefer-nefru-Aten Nefertiti, living forever.

Suggested Reading

It would be impractical to list here all the references which were alluded to within the text of this book as many are to be found in obscure Egyptological journals and frequently in languages other than English. The following books will be of interest and their specialised bibliographies will provide further information.

Aldred, Cyril, *Akhenaten, King of Egypt*, Thames and Hudson, London 1988.

Carter, H. and Mace, A., *The Tomb of Tutankhamen*, Dover Publications, London, 1985.

Cooney, J.D., *Amarna Reliefs from Heliopolis in American Collections*, Brooklyn, 1965.

Davis, T., *The Tomb of Harmhabi and Touatankhamanou*, London, 1912.

Gohary, J., *Akhenaten's Sed-festival at Karnak*, Kegan Paul, London, 1990.

Kemp, B. *et al*, *Amarna Reports*, Egypt Exploration Society, London, 1980 on.

Khouly, A. and Martin, G.T., *Excavations in the Royal Necropolis at El-Amarna*, Cairo, 1987.

Martin, G.T., *The Hidden Tombs of Memphis*, Thames and Hudson, London, 1990.

Martin, G.T., *The Memphite Tomb of Horemheb*, Egypt Exploration Society, London, 1990 on.

Murnane, W., *Ancient Egyptian Coregencies*, Chicago, 1977.

Peet, Woolley *et al*, *The City of Akhenaten* (3 vols), Egypt Exploration Society, London 1923 on.

Perepelkin, I., *The Secret of the God Coffin*, Moscow, 1978.

Petrie, W.M.F., *Tell el Amarna*, Egypt Exploration Society, London, 1894.

Redford, Donald, *Akhenaten the Heretic King*, Princeton University Press, Princeton, 1984.

Reeves, Nicholas, *The Complete Tutankhamun*, Thames and Hudson, London, 1995.

Samson, J., *Amarna, City of Akhenaten; Nefertiti as Pharaoh*, Aris and Phillips, London, 1978.

Smith, R. and Redford, D., *The Akhenaten Temple Project*, Aris and Phillips, London, 1976.

Index

Abu Ghurab 197–8, 234
Abu Simbel 166
Abusir 197
Abydos 16, 112, 168
acromegaly 218–19, 295–6
Ahhotep 16, 83, 273
Ahmose-Nefertari 16, 83, 217, 219, 273
akh, concept of 97–9, 184
Akhenaten 3–4, 15, 40, 45–6, 50–56, 81–2, 86–90, 159, 168–78, 185–210, 220
    accession of 281–6
    and Nefertiti 145–6, 237–45, 249, 268
    appearance of 216–18
    building by 232–6; *see also* Tell elAmarna
    death of 50, 253
    homosexuality of 138, 142–3
    marriages of 268, 273, 288–9
    medical condition of 218–19
    names of 48, 257–8, 261, 286
Akhetaten 87, 258, 288; *see also* Tell elAmarna
Akhmim 158
Akkadian language 50, 257
alchemy 94
Aldred, Cyril 43, 159, 169, 175, 224, 288

Alexander the Great 77
Amarna style of art 50–51, 201, 220–25, 267, 284
Amen 84–9, 105, 113, 134–5, 139, 165, 170, 177, 185, 189–91, 202, 209, 235–6
Amenemhet I 25
Amenemope, text of 205
Amenhotep I 83
Amenhotep II Aakheprure 85, 152, 172, 207, 218, 264, 295
Amenhotep III Nebmaatre 26–31, 54, 82–6, 134, 139, 142, 147–57, 161–76, 186, 191, 208–9, 214–18, 223, 232, 237–43, 249, 257, 261, 264, 269, 273, 278–87
Amenhotep IV Neferkheprure Waenre 48, 52, 86–7, 113, 169–75, 186–92, 199–200, 210, 216, 220, 232, 235, 242–3, 257–8, 281–6; *see also* Akhenaten
Amenhotep son of Hapu 163, 279
Amenia 250
Amenophis 26
Amen-Re 152, 208
Amosis 16, 83

Amun 15, 55, 87, 91, 139, 152, 163, 199–200, 209, 279, 281, 294

Anen 160–61, 223, 278

Ani, text of 138

Ankh(et)kheprure 113, 118–19, 269–70, 273, 291–2

Ankhesenamun 89, 104–5, 111, 117, 134–7, 294–300, 309–10; *see also* Anhesenpaaten

Ankhesenpaaten 52, 88–9, 134–8, 142, 222, 230, 250, 253, 259, 261, 266, 286, 290, 294; *see also* Ankhesenamun

Ankhkheprure Djeserkheprure 230; *see also* Smenkhkare

Antiquities Organisation 35–8, 42, 58, 72, 121

Anubis 102

Arab settlers in Egypt 94

archaeology 33–5, 50, 62, 78–82, 90–93, 140, 180, 205, 212–14
   romance of 78, 92, 117, 136, 271
   see also excavation reports

army, ancient Egyptian 28–9, 215–16, 235, 239

Artatama 167

Ashmunein 50, 52, 231, 238

Aswan 279

Aswan High Dam 187

atef crown 105

Aten, the 48, 55, 87–91, 105, 113–14, 121, 135, 139, 165, 171–2, 185–210, 222, 224, 229, 233–6, 245, 260–61, 265, 281–6, 294
   as a metaphor for god the creator 198, 200, 206
   as the disc of the sun 193, 196, 206
   see also Great Hymn to the Aten

Atum 188, 196

Avaris 83

Ay 29, 40, 89, 124, 141, 144, 161, 163, 178, 228, 243–5, 249, 260–61, 265, 278, 282–4, 291–4, 298–9, 305–11

Ayrton, Edward 39, 43, 45, 262

ba, concept of 96–7, 113

beds in Tutankhamen's tomb 106–7, 115, 135–6

Bek 284

Beketaten 174, 238

Beni Hasan 52

birth names of kings 25–6, 258

Blackman, Aylward 187, 265

Blue Crown 246

Blue Cup 39–40, 42, 47

Boghaz-koi 299

Bolton Museum 1, 5–7, 271–2

Borchardt, Ludwig 264

Bourriant, Urbain 50

Breasted, J.H. 61

Brier, Bob 124, 144, 299–300

British Museum 68, 146, 153, 163, 175, 204, 206, 267

Brogrove, Sir Edward 72

Brooklyn Museum 144

Burton, Harry 67

Butler, George 255

Byblos 249

Cache Tomb 42–3, 45, 49

Cairo Museum 16, 34–6, 54, 113, 121–2, 138, 198, 222, 290

calendars, Egyptian 148–50

Cambridge Ancient History 157

cannibalism 15

canon of proportion 220

carbon dating 148

Carnarvon, 5th Earl of 41–2, 46, 56–71, 101, 129–30

Carnarvon, Lady 72, 75

Carter, Howard 36–42, 46–7, 51, 56–77, 81–2, 91, 101, 104, 113–19, 129–30, 136, 144
chairs in Tutankhamen's tomb 103–6
Champollion, Jean-François and Jacques-Joseph 254
Cheops 197
Chephren 25, 198
Chicago Institute 151
Christianity 205, 260; see also Jesus Christ
Clayton, Peter 151
coffins 116–18, 308–9
Colossi of Memnon 153, 162
Connolly, Charles 44, 124
Continental Hotel, Cairo 71
Coptos 163, 278, 280
Corelli, Mario 129–30
coronations 25; see also Tutankhamen, coronation of
cosmologies 183, 197
Costa, Pedro 295
Cottrell, Leonard 213
Crete 31, 166
'crook and flail' emblems 112
cuneiform letters 257
'curse' of Tutankhamen 130–32
Cyprus 31, 166

Darwin, Charles 33, 205
Davies, Theodore M. 36–49, 56, 62, 172, 262–4, 303
Davies, W.H. 245–6
de Garis Davies, Nina and Norman 259
Deir el Bahri 34, 36, 95, 209
Deir el Ballas 158–9, 240, 278
Deir el Bersheh 52
Deir el Medina 20, 137
Dendera 153
Derry, Douglas 116, 121
Desroches-Noblecourt, Madame 103

Djarukha 167, 240
Djedefre 198
Djeserkheprure 259, 261
DNA analysis 153, 296
Doyle, Sir Arthur Conan 129–30
Dream Stela 206–8, 210, 323–5
Duff-Gordon, Lady Lucie 202

Eaton-Kraus, Marianne 306
Ecclesiastical Throne 103
Edwin Smith Papyrus 301–2
Egypt Exploration Society 203, 250, 265, 271
Eighteenth Dynasty 4, 8, 15, 17, 26–31, 40, 48, 54, 83–4, 86, 100, 132, 183, 198, 261–2, 273
El Ahram 71
El Amrah 49
Eleventh Dynasty 197
Engelbach, Rex 169
enkheperre 162
Et Till 49
Euphrates, river 30
excavation reports 5–6, 38, 43, 50, 79–80, 166, 190, 262–5, 270–72
Exodus, the 192

Fairman, H.W. 187
fans 110
Fayum, the 154–6
Fifth Dynasty 198
First Occasion 12, 14–15
Fitzwilliam Museum 23
folk religion 181
food and drink in Tutankhamen's tomb 114–15
foster-parenting 154–5
Fourth Dynasty 198
Frankfort, Henri 94
Fröhlich's syndrome 218; see also acromegaly
funeral rites 22–3, 97, 136–7

games 110
Gardiner, Sir Alan 17, 151, 217, 267
Geb 188
Gebel Silsileh 235
Gempaaten, the 232, 234–5, 245, 290, 292
Giludkhipa 167, 240, 281
Giza 197, 206, 208, 210, 277
gloves 107–8
God's Wife (of Amen), title of 17–18, 105, 153, 245
Golden Throne 104–6, 134–5, 294
Grand Tour 205
Great Harris papyrus 161
Great Hymn to the Aten 260, 326–9
Great Pyramid 197
Great Royal Wife, title of 18–19, 86, 156–7, 173–5, 240–41, 284
Greek forms of Egyptian names 26–7
Green, F.W. 158, 187
Griffiths, J.G. 187
Gurob 155

Harris, John 268–9
Harrison, R.G. 116, 122–3, 144, 254, 298, 300
Hathor 152, 190
Hatnub 279
Hatshepsut 25, 36, 57–8, 84, 95, 154, 160, 162, 172, 209, 270, 273, 290
Hawateh 49
Hayes, W.C. 151, 169
headrests 106–7
Hearst Foundation 158
Hekhernekhekh 154–7
Heliopolis 86, 168, 183, 199, 203, 225, 234, 281, 285
Herbert, Lady Evelyn 59–61, 63–6, 71–2, 101, 130
heresy 203–5, 210, 214, 260
Herihor 174

Hermopolis 144, 291
Herodotus 179, 181, 184–5
hierarchical nature of Egyptian society 13
hieratic script 29, 46
hieroglyphs 213, 254–5, 258
Highclere Castle 56, 61, 63, 68, 70, 130
Hildesheim Museum 156
Hittites, the 30–31, 88–9, 142, 177, 216, 286, 297–300, 309–10
homosexuality 54, 88, 138–45, 176
Hor 284
Horemheb 4, 29, 40, 52, 54, 89–90, 141, 178, 203–4, 214, 231–9, 260–62, 285–300, 306–11
  identity of 250–51
horses, use of 29
Horus 22, 112, 117, 184, 190, 196, 245
L'Hote, Nestor 256, 259
household gods 181
Hoving, Thomas 68, 119
human sacrifice 94
Huy 279; *see also* Amenhotep son of Hapu
Huya 31, 193, 227–8
Hyksos, the 40, 82–3, 159, 215

iconoclasm 201–3
inbreeding 218
incest 176, 214, 218, 239
Ineni 20
insibya names 257
intellectual stagnation 179
Isfet 14–15, 24, 183
Isimehtet 115
Isis 22, 184
Islam 73, 180–81

Janssen, Jac and Rosalind 289
Jesus Christ 97, 260
jewellery 111–13, 136

Jones, Harold 44, 262
Joseph (of the multicoloured
    coat) 81, 158, 205
Josephus 151

ka, concept of 95–9, 114, 182–3
Kamose 83, 285
Karnak temple 12, 25, 34, 55–6,
    84–9, 134, 161–2, 165, 170,
    191, 194, 198–203, 209,
    279–84, 294
  Akhenaten's buildings within
    232–6, 239, 245, 310
Keme 94
Kha 137
Khaemhet 168
Khedive of Egypt 35
khepresh crown 246
Kheruef 168–9, 174
Khnum 95
Khons 55
Khut-benben 234
Khutwaret 83
Khyan 83
kilts 107–11, 221
king-lists 39–40, 261
kings
  burial of 19–24
  coronation of 25
  dating of reigns 150–52
  marriage with sisters 19, 157
  mothers of 25
  naming of 25–7, 256–7
  numbering of 26
  queens and wives of 17–19,
    24–5
  seen as living gods 14, 198
kingship
  nature and duties of 14–16,
    183–4, 210
  succession to 24–5, 39
Kiya 267–8, 272–3, 288–9, 295–6,
    307–8
KV54 42

language, Egyptian 287; *see also*
    Akkadian language;
    pronuciation
Lebanon 30
Leek, Frank 122
Leiden Museum 203, 250
Lepsius, Karl Richard 50, 114,
    186, 203, 256
Libya 31
life after death 93, 95, 193
literacy 29
Liverpool City Museum 111
Liverpool University 187, 297
local gods 181–3, 190
Louvre Museum 217, 267
Luxor 11–12, 20, 27–8, 33–9, 49,
    55, 63–4, 71, 83, 86–9, 105,
    125, 135, 139, 162, 164, 183,
    186, 189, 191, 202, 285, 288,
    294
  Museum 233–4
  temple 34, 134, 166, 203, 279–80
  see also Karnak temple; Malkata
Lythgoe, Alfred 39, 158

Maat 12–15, 18, 90, 132, 176,
    183–4, 188, 203, 210, 239, 281,
    284
Mahu 228
Malkata 151, 168–9, 173, 175, 191,
    209, 214, 232, 239, 280, 295
Manetho 151, 256, 269
Mariette, Auguste 16, 35
Martin, Geoffrey 248
Maruaten, the 6, 265–7, 270,
    272
Maspero, Gaston 36, 42
May 228, 285
Maya 21, 114, 125, 295, 297, 305,
    311–12
Medamud 183, 197, 232
Medjai, the 21, 227
Mehetweret 115
Meidum 170

Meketaten 52, 54, 88, 107, 222, 234, 245–9, 259, 285–91

Memphis 25, 27, 35, 86, 159, 162, 183, 202–3, 216, 225, 239, 278, 288, 293–4

Men 284

Menes 39

Menkaure 198

Mentuhotep Nebhepetre 158, 197

Merenptah 27

Meretseger 20–21

Meritaten 52, 88, 107, 111, 113, 140, 142, 145, 222, 232, 245–7, 250, 253–4, 259, 265–6, 270–73, 284, 288–92, 308

Meryre I 228

Meryre II 222, 228, 259, 267, 270

Meryt 137, 154–5

Metropolitan Museum of Art (New York) 39, 46, 67–8, 75, 158, 163, 168, 204, 267

Middle Kingdom 15–16

military campaigns 84–5

military rule 89, 178, 236

Min 158, 163, 278, 280

Minnakht 113

Minoan civilisation 31, 165–6

Mit Rahina 27

Mitanni 30–31, 167, 241, 281, 289

monotheism 178, 185, 189, 259–61

Mont 162, 183, 232

Moses 81, 158, 192, 205, 208, 213, 269

Mother of the God 153

mummies 22, 34, 41, 45–6, 118–19, 125, 135, 152–3, 174
  of infant girls 115–16, 137–8, 307
  see also Tutankhamen, mummification of

murder, suspicions of 25, 124–5, 215, 253–4, 298, 300–301

Murnane, W.J. 170

Mursilis 299–300

musical instruments 110–11

Mut 55, 163, 209, 279, 281

Mutemweia 152–4, 159, 208, 278

Mutnodjmet 89, 178, 244, 247, 250–51, 282, 290, 292

Naharin 30–31

Nakhtmin 113, 118, 125, 290–91, 305

Napoleon 34, 50

Naville, Edouard 205

Nebkheprure 39, 42–3, 54, 63, 101, 113, 118, 177, 257, 262; see also Tutankhaten

Neferkheprure Waenre 52, 86, 113; see also Amenhotep IV

Nefernefruaten, name of 306

Nefernefruaten Mery Waenre 52, 87, 113, 200, 258, 269–70, 286, 290, 307; see also Nefertiti

Nefernefruaten Tasherit 52, 230, 249–50, 259

Nefernefrure 52, 142, 230, 249, 259, 307

Nefertiti 48, 52–3, 81, 86–8, 113, 138, 141–3, 146, 171, 174, 192, 198, 200, 219–24, 238–48, 265–6, 270–73, 282–4, 288–92
  dynastic ambitions of 249, 290
  see also Nefernefruaten Mery Waenre

Nefrure 154

Neith 198, 223

Nekhpaaten 228

Nephthys 117

netjeru 99

New Kingdom 34, 40, 148, 215

New York Times 129

Newberry, Percy 51, 299

News of the World 131

news scarabs 156, 279

Nile, river 149–50

Nineteenth Dynasty 4, 29, 40, 90, 178

Nubia 31, 165–6, 186, 189, 214, 243, 283
Nubian wig 268

Old Kingdom 14, 16
Omm Seti 181
Opening of the Mouth 22, 97–8, 136, 184, 308
Opet, the 163
Opet festival 55, 134, 139, 261, 294
Orion 196
Orus 151
Osiris 22–3, 87, 97, 184–5, 188
Osman, Ahmed 158
out-of-body experience 95

Paatenemheb 228, 250, 287
Paser Stela 267–9
Pathé News 69
pectorals 111–12
Pendlebury, John 169
Penthu 114, 228
Per-Nefret, the 22
Per-Wabet, the 22
Perrennefer 228
Petrie, Flinders 36, 50–51
philosophy of life, ancient Egyptian 12–14, 98
Pinnedjem 174
Plutarch 22
Pramesse 4, 90; *see also* Ramesses I
'Princess', title of 17
Prisse-D'Avennes, Achille 256, 259
pronunciation of ancient Egyptian language 26, 257
Psalm 104 192
Ptah 112, 162, 183, 246
Ptahmay 251
Ptolemy I 151
Pyramid Texts 195–6, 245

pyramids 19–21

queens and wives of kings 17–19, 24–5

Radjedef 25
Ramesses I 4, 29, 40, 90, 310–11
Ramesses II Usermaatre Setepenre 19, 24, 40, 90, 131–2, 137, 166, 236, 257
Ramesses III 23, 25, 111
Ramesses VI 58–60
Ramose 168, 171–2, 228
Re, cult of 183, 199; *see also* sun religion
Redford, Donald 232, 234
Redjedef 198
Reeves, Nicholas 38, 100, 105, 107, 113, 117, 307
Re-Horakhte 188–9, 196, 210, 283
Re-Horemakhet 206–8, 277
reincarnation, belief in 97
Reisner, G.A. 158
Rekhmire 13
relations, ancient Egyptian references to 145
religion, ancient Egyptian 92–4, 178–95; *see also* sun worship
Restoration Stela 54, 125, 134, 139, 141, 144, 203, 216, 260–61, 274, 292–3, 317–19
Ridley, Michael 123
Robins, Gay 183, 220–21, 293
Rosetta Stone 255
de Rothschild, Baron 41
royal family of Egypt 15–19
Rwdmenu, the 234

Samson, Julia 268–70
Saqqara 35, 38, 100, 114, 201, 225, 289
sarcophagi 23, 116, 132, 306–7
sashes 111–12

Sayce, A.H. 51
scarabs 156
  of Amenhotep III 320–22
sceptre, royal 135, 202
sed festivals 168–9, 174, 188–9,
    232, 234
Sedeinga 166, 186, 283
Sekhmet 112, 209, 280
Selkis 117
'Senior Royal Wife', title of 19
Senmut 154
Sennefer 106
Seqenenre Tao 83
Seqenenre Tao II 16
'sequins' 113
Sesebi 186–7, 192, 220, 239, 243,
    283
Setepenre 52, 142, 230, 248–9, 259,
    307
Seth 117, 166
Sethe, Kurt 261
Seti I Menmaatre 40, 90, 112, 187,
    202
Seti II 67
shabtis 100, 113, 118
Sheikh Abd el Qurna 42
shendyt kilts 109
Shu 188–9, 210
Shuttarna 167, 174
Sinatra, Frank 98–9
Sirius (star) 149, 196
Sitamun 167, 173–6, 214, 238, 241,
    248, 284, 287
Smenkhkare 40, 49, 53, 64, 82,
    88–9, 124–5, 132–47, 175–8,
    214, 219, 230, 237–8, 246–254,
    259–62
  identity of 264–73
Smith, Elliot 46, 263
Sobek 154
society in ancient Egypt 27–32
Soleb 166, 168, 186, 283
spelling of names, alternatives for
    26

Sphinx, the 206–8, 277
statues 109, 117
Steindorff, George 169
Stela K 222
sticks in Tutankhamen's tomb
    108–10
sun temples 197–8
sun worship 188, 195–200, 277,
    280–81
'Surgical Papyrus' 301
Suti 284
syncretisms between pairs of
    gods 199

Tadukhipa 242–3, 287–9
talatat blocks 229–35, 238–9,
    245–6, 270, 291–2
Tanis 99, 132
Taweret 180–81, 190
Tell el Amarna 3–6, 48–53, 82,
    87–90, 106, 125, 134, 138, 142,
    146, 169, 173–4, 185, 190–201,
    210, 220–50, 258–66, 288–94
  abandonment of 230–31, 294
  building of 229–30
  discovery of 255–6
  dismantling of 310
  first excavation of 264
  material sent to Bolton 6,
    271–2
  Northern Palace 53, 88, 227,
    249, 266
  Southern Palace 265; *see also*
    Maruaten, the
Tell el Daba 83
Tenimenu, the 232, 234
Tetisheri 16, 83, 273
Teye 244, 282, 299
Thomas, Angela 155, 228
Thoth 197
throne names 39, 42, 52, 258
Thuya 41–2, 137, 139, 156–63, 172,
    241, 278–9
The Times 67, 70, 74, 129

Tiye 43, 45, 86, 111, 113, 139, 156–68, 172–6, 192, 209, 227, 240–44, 249, 260–65, 279–87, 290–91

tomb robberies 5, 20, 57, 66, 80, 99

tomb paintings 98

'Tomb 55' at Thebes 43–9, 63, 170, 172, 262, 280, 307–8
  body in 121–4, 144–5, 270, 273–4, 295–6

tombs
  building of 20–22
  contents of 23, 96; see also Tutankhamen
  of nobles 223, 225–7, 244, 259
  of royal officials 100, 228
  visitors to 96

tourists 33–4, 58, 69

transsexuals 95

Tuna el Gebel 50, 195

Tura 279

Turin Museum 251, 287

Tushratta 167, 173, 241–2

Tutankhamen
  accession of 49, 136, 237, 266
  birth of 3, 175–6, 214, 289
  blood group of 124, 296
  body of 119–23
  burial of 305–10
  childhood of 88–9, 144–6, 291, 294
  contents of tomb 99–124
  coronation of 12, 105, 111–12, 237, 292–3
  death of 12, 122, 124–5, 197, 298, 303
  family and parentage of 139, 141, 144–5, 147, 175–6, 214, 273, 289, 316
  marriage of 253
  mask of 118–19, 308–9
  mummification of 303–8
  'official' story of 82–91

  problems with 'official' history 132–44
  shaving of head 301–3
  skull of 122, 125, 221, 254, 305
  teeth of 122
  throne name of 39, 42

Tutankhamen exhibition 130–31

Tutankhaten (Nebkheprure) 49, 88–9, 103, 112, 134–5, 177, 230, 260–61, 292; see also Tutankhamen

Tuthmosis I 20, 83–4, 293

Tuthmosis II 84, 218

Tuthmosis III Menkheperre 25, 28, 30–31, 64, 84–5, 209, 218

Tuthmosis IV Menkheprure 31, 85, 142, 151–5, 160, 167, 206–10, 218, 277–9, 311

Tuthmosis (elder brother of Akhenaten) 86, 110, 167–8, 175, 199, 240, 281, 296

Tuthmosis (assistant overseer of tombs) 114, 125

Tuthmosis (sculptor at Tell el Amarna) 53, 264

Twelfth Dynasty 183, 197

Tyldesley, Joyce 181

Ulu Burun 166

Userhet 285–6

Userkaf 198, 223–4

Valley of the Kings 12, 20–23, 34–43, 56–8, 67–9, 76, 96, 114, 172–4, 207, 249–52, 262, 267, 287, 303

Valley of the Queens 21, 137

van Borchardt, Ludwig 51

viceroys 141

Vile Kush 165–6

Wadjet 152–3

'War Helmet' 246

weapons 108
Webensennu 207
Weigall, Arthur 35–8, 43–6, 49, 71, 263
Wenamun 166
Westcar papyrus 197
Wilde, Oscar 54
Wilkinson, Sir John Gardner 40, 255–6
wine jars in Tutankhamen's tomb 114–15, 133
Winfield Smith, Ray 234
Winlock, H.E. 43, 46, 67
Winter Palace Hotel, Luxor 71
wisdom texts 13, 95, 138, 205

women, status of 16–18, 24, 84, 154, 282

X-ray analysis 121–3, 152, 296, 298, 300, 305

Yey 158–61
Young, Thomas 255
Yuya 29, 41–2, 81, 137, 139, 156–63, 172, 241, 278–9

Zannanzash 89, 300
Zivie, Alain 289

Photographic Credits

———

BILLIONS AND BILLIONS

CARL SAGAN

Astronomer Carl Sagan, the world's most celebrated science writer, Pulitzer Prize winner, and bestselling author, here brings together his last inspirational and provocative collection of essays.

Ranging in subject matter from the invention of the game of chess to the question of life on Mars, from global warming to the abortion debate, *Billions and Billions* is Carl Sagan at his enlightening, entertaining and eclectic best. Applying what we know about science, mathematics and space to everyday life, he also addresses some of today's most controversial issues, helping us to make sense of the world around us as it prepares for the challenges of the coming millennium. In addition, we are given a rare glimpse of Sagan himself in the final essay, written as he approached his own death.

'My candidate for planetary ambassador can be none other than Carl Sagan himself. He is wise, humane, polymathic, witty, well read, and incapable of composing a dull sentence.' Richard Dawkins, *The Times*

'No other scientist of our century has matched the great breadth of imagination, erudition and prolific accessibility of Professor Carl Sagan . . . Humanity has lost one of its most important and articulate guides . . . Through his books, his great clarity of mind and amazing energy, he touched and enlarged all of us.' *Guardian*

'Inspiring millions with his writings and broadcasts was just one of his many talents . . . If we do manage to find our way, it will be thanks to the efforts of Carl Sagan. The inhabitants of the pale blue dot mourn his departure.' *Independent*

NON-FICTION / POPULAR SCIENCE 0 7472 5792 2

More sport from Headline

PLAYFAIR FOOTBALL ANNUAL 1999–2000

GLENDA ROLLIN AND JACK ROLLIN

Playfair Football Annual has the greatest range of
up-to-date facts and figures, including:

- English and Scottish League club directories

- Statistical information on players with the
92 English League clubs

- Comprehensive coverage of results in the qualifying
stages of Euro 2000

- All the scores from the three major European
cup competitions

- At-a-glance English League positions for 25 years

- League and international fixtures for the
1999–2000 season

NON-FICTION / SPORT 0 7472 5975 5

If you enjoyed this book here is a selection of other bestselling non-fiction titles from Headline